VALUES AND MORALS

Essays in Honor of William Frankena,
Charles Stevenson, and Richard Brandt

Edited by

ALVIN I. GOLDMAN and JAEGWON KIM
The University of Michigan

D. REIDEL PUBLISHING COMPANY

DORDRECHT : HOLLAND / BOSTON : U.S.A.

LONDON : ENGLAND

Library of Congress Cataloging in Publication Data

Main entry under title:

Values and morals.
  (Philosophical studies series in philosophy; v. 13)
  Bibliography: p.
  Includes index.
    1. Ethics – Addresses, essays, lectures. 2. Frankena, William K. –
Addresses, essays, lectures. 3. Stevenson, Charles Leslie, 1908-   –
Addresses, essays, lectures. 4. Brandt, Richard B. – Addresses, essays,
lectures. I. Frankena, William K. II. Stevenson, Charles Leslie, 1908-
III. Brandt, Richard B. IV. Goldman, Alvin I., 1938-   V. Kim,
Jaegwon.
BJ1012.V34   170   78-16409
ISBN 90-277-0914-9.

Published by D. Reidel Publishing Company,
P.O. Box 17, Dordrecht, Holland

Sold and distributed in the U.S.A., Canada, and Mexico
by D. Reidel Publishing Company, Inc.
Lincoln Building, 160 Old Derby Street, Hingham,
Mass. 02043, U.S.A.

Printed in The Netherlands

TABLE OF CONTENTS

WILLIAM FRANKENA

CHARLES STEVENSON

RICHARD BRANDT

PREFACE

This Festschrift seeks to honor three highly distinguished scholars in the Department of Philosophy, University of Michigan: William K. Frankena, Charles L. Stevenson, and Richard B. Brandt. Each has made significant contributions to the philosophic literature, particularly in the field of ethics.

Michigan has been fortunate in having three such original and productive moral philosophers serving oh its faculty simultaneously. Yet they stand in a long tradition of excellence, both within the Department and in the University. Let us trace that tradition briefly.

The University of Michigan opened in 1841. Its Department of Literature, Science, and the Arts at first resembled a typical American college of that period, with religious and ethical indoctrination playing a central role in course offerings. But when Henry Tappan, a Presbyterian clergyman and Professor of philosophy, became President in 1852, he succeeded in shifting the emphasis from indoctrination to inquiry and scholarship.

Though he was dismissed for his policies in 1863, Tappan's efforts to establish a broad and liberal curriculum prevailed. Michigan was to take its place among the leading educational institutions in this country, and to achieve an international reputation as a research center.

Several past philosophers are worthy of mention here. George Sylvester Morris, an absolute idealist, joined the Department in 1881, having served from 1870 as Chairman of the Department of Modern Languages and Literature. He assumed the Chairmanship of Philosophy in 1884.

Morris had taught the fall terms at Johns Hopkins from 1881 until 1884, and there one of his students was John Dewey, who was strongly influenced by Morris' Hegelianism. When Dewey completed his doctorate in 1884, Morris brought him to Michigan, where he taught psychology before becoming interested in ethics, social philosophy, and education.

John Dewey became Chairman in 1889 and hired James H. Tufts and George Herbert Mead, both of whom, like Dewey, were to become pragmatists. By 1894, all three had been attracted to the newly established University of Chicago.

Upon Dewey's departure, Robert Mark Wenley, an absolute idealist trained under Edward Caird at Glasgow University, was made Chairman. He added two young philosophers to the staff, both of whom were destined to distinguish themselves: Roy Wood Sellars, in 1905, and DeWitt H. Parker, in 1908.

Sellars, a particularly prolific writer, was a critical realist and evolutionary naturalist. Parker was a panpsychist and voluntarist in meta-physics; in particular, he applied voluntarism to both ethics and aesthetics.

DeWitt Parker became Chairman in 1929, after Wenley's death, and served until 1947. Interestingly, Parker chose C. H. Langford, coauthor of the pioneering *Symbolic Logic* with C. I. Lewis (1932), to replace Wenley. Thus the Department's last absolute idealist was replaced by a mathematical logician.

Of the three philosophers honored in this volume, William Frankena was first to join the Department, in 1937, having taken his Ph.D. at Harvard. Earlier, DeWitt Parker, Roy Wood Sellars, and C. H. Langford had all taught him as a graduate student at Michigan.

Frankena was especially interested in Parker's naturalistic ethics, in which the good was defined as that which satisfies desire. Parker worked out the implications of this definition in *Human Values* (1931). Much later, Frankena was to edit Parker's *The Philosophy of Value* for posthumous publication (1957).

William Frankena was Chairman of the Department of Philosophy from 1947 until 1961, years that saw an already distinguished department of six grow to an even more widely recognized department of twelve.

In 1946, Charles Stevenson was welcomed to Michigan, having earned his Ph.D. at Harvard in 1935 and having taught both there and at Yale, his undergraduate alma mater.

Richard Brandt succeeded Frankena as Chairman in 1964. He had received his Ph.D. from Yale in 1936, and had taught at Swarthmore College for twenty-seven years, during nineteen of which he had held the departmental chairmanship. The administrative skills he brought to his new post served the University and the Department well for thirteen years.

*

The biographies of William Frankena, Charles Stevenson, and Richard Brandt have much in common, including their entry into the world at roughly the same time. Frankena and Stevenson were born only six days apart, on June 21 and June 27, respectively, in 1908; Brandt was born on October 17, 1910.

All three graduated from college in 1930, studied at Cambridge University for varying lengths of time before completing their doctorates in this country, and commenced their teaching careers in the mid-thirties. The Michigan Department of Philosophy is also losing their services at about the same time: Stevenson retired in 1977; Frankena in 1978; and Brandt will retire in 1981. Needless to say, all three are still actively engaged in philosophic research at this writing.

Each in his own style has excelled in teaching, at both the graduate and the undergraduate levels, bringing remarkable freshness and ingenuity to the classroom. Together, they have contributed in many and varied fashions to the intellectual, cultural, administrative, and social life of the institutions where they have taught.

Frankena, Stevenson, and Brandt have also been similarly recognized for their professional accomplishments. All received Guggenheim Fellowships, were Fellows at the Center for Advanced Study in the Behavioral Sciences, received the Distinguished Achievement Award from The University of Michigan, and were elected to the Presidency of the American Philosophical Association, Western Division.

Let us turn now to a more detailed sketch of each of these men, in order of age as well as of joining the faculty of The University of Michigan.

With the reader's indulgence, I shall refer to them henceforth, on occasion, as Bill, Steve, and Dick, as they are affectionately known to their colleagues and their many friends outside the Department.

* *

William Klaas Frankena was born in 1908 in Montana, of parents who had emigrated from the Netherlands. Soon thereafter, the family settled in Zeeland, Michigan. Bill graduated from Calvin College in 1930, majoring in English literature and philosophy. He entered the Graduate School of The University of Michigan that same year, and in 1933 passed the preliminary examinations.

At this juncture, he decided to transfer his doctoral studies to Harvard: the depression was in its depths, openings in philosophy were extremely scarce, and he saw an opportunity to broaden his intellectual base.

Charles Stevenson also enrolled at Harvard in 1933, and a close friendship soon developed between the two couples, Bill and Sadie Frankena and Charles and Louise Stevenson.

Frankena studied at Harvard with C. I. Lewis, R. B. Perry, and A. N. Whitehead. He spent the year 1935–36 at Cambridge University, where he studied with G. E. Moore and C. D. Broad. He wrote his thesis on intuitionism in ethics, receiving his Ph.D. from Harvard in 1937. From that thesis came his highly regarded article, 'The Naturalistic Fallacy,' published in *Mind* in 1939, in which he refuted Moore's claim that every naturalistic definition of good is fallacious.

Bill returned to Michigan as an Instructor in 1937, coincidentally with the arrival of another outstanding expositor, Paul Henle. Paul and Bill were to become close colleagues, as well as fast personal friends. Together they undertook to improve and expand the curriculum. In particular, their new introductory course, Phil. 34, not only achieved fame on campus, but set a pattern that was followed for years to come. It was organized around a core of selected readings from Plato, Lucretius, Descartes, Berkeley, and James; whereas beginning philosophy at Michigan at that time was taught as a survey of problems, utilizing a single textbook.

Frankena and Henle were perfect complements for a joint offering of a large lecture course: the one, tall, lean, quiet, studious, determined; the other, smaller, aggressive, quick, ready to take any side of a question for the sheer pleasure of debate. They worked their students hard, but the students responded readily to the original materials and to the enthusiasm and skill of the lecturers.

It was a special treat to attend one of the Frankena–Henle sessions in which they took opposite sides of some basic philosophic issues. Paul relished assuming an extreme position and defending it to the hilt, with clever and prickly argumentative twists; while Bill systematically and decisively exposed its defects, to the pleasure and enlightenment of everyone.

During his long career, William Frankena has published many articles in theoretical ethics, applied ethics, and the philosophy of education. The most important of those in ethics have been collected in *Perspectives on Morality– Essays by William K. Frankena*, 1976, edited by his former graduate student, Kenneth E. Goodpastor.

Frankena's *Ethics* appeared in 1963. In just one hundred pages, he presented a rigorous, balanced, and critical review of the central issues of the whole subject. A second edition appeared in 1973. It has been translated into Chinese, Dutch, German, Japanese, Spanish, and Swedish.

Bill's influence on philosophy students at Michigan has been enormous. For many years he taught a course in the history of ethics, taken by most graduate students. They invariably acclaimed this course for the assiduousness and fair-mindness with which the positions and contributions of each thinker were formulated and expounded. Even as his retirement commences, Bill is busy writing a history of ethics that is certain to become the definitive work in the field.

Frankena's interest in the philosophy of education is of long standing, and he has frequently offered courses in it. His *Three Historical Philosophies of Education: Aristotle, Kant, Dewey* appeared in 1965; in that same year, Frankena was elected to the National Academy of Education.

William Frankena has been a visiting professor at Columbia, Harvard, Princeton, and the University of Tokyo. In 1974, he was designated Carus Lecturer of the American Philosophical Association, and was also named to the Roy Wood Sellars Chair in Philosophy at Michigan.

When he retired in 1978, he had served the Department for forty-one years. While on retirement furlough, he was appointed Distinguished Faculty Lecturer in the College of Literature, Science and the Arts at The University of Michigan; the first to be singled out for this newly-established honorary lectureship.

No tribute to William Frankena would be complete without special mention of the contribution he and Sadie made, over those forty-one years, to the University community through their gracious hospitality. At recent retirement functions for them, it came out repeatedly that the first people newcomers to the Department had met were the Frankenas; or that it was at the Frankenas' that members of the Department had met certain others from outside the Department; or that the Frankenas had consistently welcomed the office staff, graduate students, and visiting faculty into their home and helped them and their families to find their way in unfamiliar surroundings. Together, they made countless lives easier, and happier.

* * *

Charles Leslie Stevenson was born in Cincinnati, Ohio, in 1908. He studied at Yale, where he majored in English literature, completing his B.A. in 1930. He then went to Cambridge University to continue his study of literature, only to be attracted to philosophy by G. E. Moore and Ludwig Wittgenstein. He earned a Cambridge B.A. in philosophy in 1933, and a Harvard Ph.D. in 1935.

At Cambridge, Steve had attended most of Wittgenstein's courses and discussion seminars, and he and Louise had entertained Wittgenstein socially on several occasions. I once asked Steve if he had experienced any difficulty over Wittgenstein's well-known sensitivity concerning the publication, by his students or associates, of ideas he felt had originated with him. Steve replied that he had not, and that his ethics had actually been influenced by Wittgenstein only in a very general way. "Indeed," he added with characteristic airiness and pungency, "one reason I chose to write on ethics was precisely because I did not know what Wittgenstein thought about the subject."

After finishing at Harvard, Stevenson stayed on for a few years and taught. In that period, three essays on his emotive theory appeared in *Mind*: 'The Emotive Meaning of Ethical Terms' (1937), 'Ethical Judgments and Avoidability' (1938), and 'Persuasive Definitions' (1938).

Charles Stevenson joined the faculty of Yale as an Assistant Professor in 1939. He remained there for seven years, after which he was let go, largely owing to his philosophic views.

Steve had published *Ethics and Language*, the definitive statement of his emotive theory of ethics, in 1944. At that time, positivism was unpopular among most traditional American philosophers, including some of Steve's senior colleagues at Yale. Positivism in ethics was especially unpalatable to the traditionalists. Some even felt that Steve's ethics could corrupt morality by removing its objective basis. One declared that Stevenson had "committed positivism"!

All of this occurred despite the fact that Stevenson's emotive theory was a meta-ethics, not a normative ethics. Moreover, he was always at pains to point out that his theory had no direct implications for ethical norms. On the final page of *Ethics and Language* he wrote, "The most significant moral issues, then, begin at the point where our study must end."

It is regrettable that Steve's positivistic ethical position led to his discharge at Yale. The Michigan Department of Philosophy, on the other hand, was delighted to learn that Stevenson was available. No one shared Yale's view that any moral implications of a philosopher's meta-ethics, however radical, should constitute a reason for not hiring him.

Thus, he joined the Michigan faculty in 1946, as an Associate Professor, and stayed for thirty-one years, teaching and writing with equal vigor and success. The University and the Department were most fortunate. Charles Stevenson's articles and books have been widely read, both in this country and abroad, especially in England. Overall, they have had an immense impact on the philosophic world. *Ethics and Language* went through many printings and was ultimately translated into Italian, Spanish, and Japanese. Discussions of and rejoinders to emotive ethics still appear in the literature.

In 1963, Steve published *Facts and Values*, a collection of nearly all his papers in ethics. In one of these, he explains his indebtedness to John Dewey, a predecessor of his at Michigan. The volume concludes with a new essay entitled, 'Retrospective Comments.'

Charles Stevenson is clearly one of the most important and influential moral philosophers of the century. His *Ethics and Language* is perhaps the most original work in meta-ethics since G. E. Moore's *Principia Ethica*.

In recent years, Steve had continued to refine his emotive ethics, has developed a parallel theory of aesthetic evaluation, and has delved into such diverse disciplines as the logic of subjunctives and the relation of poetry to music.

It seems fitting here to remark upon Charles Stevenson's profound and abiding interest in music; indeed, upon his entire family's devotion to music and the world of musicians. The piano and the cello have constituted an essential element of his daily life. I recall the afternoon, years ago, when my wife and I dropped in on him and Louise and found parts of one of their two grand pianos systematically distributed over the floor. Steve was experimenting with tuning and repair! He and his wife Nora, whom he married after Louise's death, have continued to reach out to the musical community and have been active participants in a number of ensembles, as well as informal, often spontaneous, musical gatherings.

Let us conclude with a story Steve used to tell his undergraduate classes. It is typical of the pedagogical techniques that gave his lectures their clarity and appeal.

Imagine a neurosurgeon whose expertise on the human brain and whose knowledge of daily events are such that he can, with probes, dictate a subject's experiences. After he has implanted electrodes in the brain of a certain male volunteer, the surgeon causes him to experience the removal of the probes, although they are still in place; then to experience going home through the rain, spending the night with his wife, receiving a call from the surgeon in the morning asking him to return to the laboratory, and returning − all this while he is, in fact, still on the operating table.

The next day, the surgeon does actually remove the electrodes and sends the subject home, whereupon his wife inquires indignantly, "Where were you last night?" "Right here with you," the man replies. "Oh, no, you weren't," she rejoins, "and I can prove it. I had the whole neighborhood out searching for you."

Then the enlightened husband smiles and says, "Ah, now I see. That surgeon fooled me. He made me *think* I came home. But I was on the operating table the whole time."

His smile quickly fades, however, never to return, because from that point forward the poor fellow can never be certain he is not still on the operating table.

Steve would close a lecture with this story. In the next session, he would introduce the concept of Cartesian skepticism.

* * * *

Richard Booker Brandt was born in Wilmington, Ohio, in 1910. He graduated from Denison University in 1930, with majors in both philosophy and classical studies, after which he entered Cambridge University. There he completed a second B.A. in 1933, in the philosophy of religion, and then stayed on for an additional year of study.

At Cambridge, he worked with F. R. Tennant, theologian and philosopher of religion, and began the research on Schleiermacher that was to form the substance of his doctoral dissertation and his first major publication, *The Philosophy of Friedrich Schleiermacher*, which appeared in 1941. That work remains the best study in English of Protestantism's great nineteenth-century systematic theologian.

Dick spent the year 1934–35 at the University of Tübingen, after which he returned to this country and Yale, where he received his Ph.D. in 1936. Given the scarcity of jobs at that time, he remained at Yale for another year, on fellowship, devoting himself primarily to the study of logical positivism; his first article, criticizing positivism, was published in 1938.

In 1937, Richard Brandt began his long association with Swarthmore College, which proved an ideal milieu for further expansion of his philosophic interests; indeed, for expansion into several outside disciplines and interdisciplinary pursuits.

Swarthmore was a small and wealthy college of such high academic standing that it not only attracted superior scholars to its staff, but enjoyed a steady stream of prominent visitors. Moreover, in an undergraduate college, one was inevitably drawn into the teaching of a wide variety of courses, as well as into close intellectual contact with colleagues in other departments. A third factor that affected Dick was the disruption in academia caused by World War II.

Thus, in his first year at Swarthmore, he was called upon to teach both philosophy of religion and philosophy of science, in the latter of which he developed an interest that persisted through the war years, when he found himself immersed in mathematics and physics. His interest in epistemology, on which he has written a number of influential papers, also arose from a teaching assignment, in 1946.

It was during those early years at Swarthmore, too, that ethics came to be the focus of Brandt's research; henceforth, his concern over the good and the right was to be central to his philosophic thought.

The two main areas outside philosophy that appealed to him were psychology and anthropology. Psychology at Swarthmore was extremely strong, particularly in the area of perception. The psychological theories of attitudes and of motivation, as they relate to values, have played a large role in the long-range development of Brandt's ethical position.

Wolfgang Köhler was one of many psychologists who influenced Brandt. Köhler, whose own interests embraced several disciplines, taught at Swarthmore from 1935 until 1957; he and Brandt exchanged ideas frequently, and together they offered a seminar on the mind-body problem.

Anthropology similarly intrigued Brandt, and, again, he was concerned with the place of ethical values. He devoted his Guggenheim fellowship in 1945–46 to an exploration of that problem; later, his *Hopi Ethics: A Theoretical Analysis* (1954), based upon actual research among the Hopis of Arizona, combined his empirical and ethical views. It has been a landmark in the use of anthropological data to examine fundamental philosophic issues.

I would like at this point to inject a personal note, since I first came to know Dick Brandt during the war, when I lived in Philadelphia.

Those were unusual times, of course, and untypical for philosophy in many ways. Yet, philosophers in the Swarthmore-Bryn Mawr-Haverford-Penn region kept in touch, through monthly meetings of the Fullerton Club and through informal social events. No one was warmer and more solicitous than Dick and Betty Brandt in that stressful period.

Brandt's *Ethical Theory* was published in 1959. It is a comprehensive and systematic treatise covering both normative ethics and meta-ethics. His own position as set forth in this volume, a form of rule-utilitarianism, has been the object of considerable debate. *Ethical Theory* has been reprinted several times, having become a primary source in moral philosophy.

Overall, Brandt has produced not only several noteworthy books, but many sound articles. Since coming to Michigan in 1964, he has published a number of normative discussions of current topics, including war, suicide, and abortion.

His crowning achievement in ethics, a work entitled *A Theory of the Good and the Right*, is in press at this writing. In this book, Brandt addresses two traditional ethical questions: What is worth wanting? What is morally right? To analyze and answer these questions, he employs certain untraditional types of evidence and modes of reasoning. He draws important implications,

xvi   ARTHUR W. BURKS

not only for personal decision-making, but for the moral appraisal of individual and societal actions.

In addition to his research accomplishments, Brandt has been a superb teacher: at Swarthmore and at Michigan, he has trained many students who are now recognized philosophers. Needless to say, he has been an excellent administrator, as well, serving the two institutions most ably for a combined total of some thirty years!

Among other honors, Richard Brandt was chosen to give the John Locke lectures at Oxford in 1974; and he has served as President of the American Society for Political and Legal Philosophy.

His has been and continues to be a distinguished career, marked by breadth of philosophic outlook. Moreover, the very qualities that stimulated his broad outlook have also constituted his basic approach, whether to administration, to teaching, to writing, or to the arena of scholars. That is to say, thorough acquaintance with the field – his knowledge of philosophers, past and present, is extraordinary – coupled with careful nurturing of that acquaintance. Steadfastness and thoroughness are indeed his hallmark.

* * * * *

William K. Frankena, Charles L. Stevenson, and Richard Brandt have contributed beyond measure to the intellectual life of The University of Michigan. Each of them has shouldered more than one professor's share of responsibility for the growth and quality of the Department of Philosophy and for representing both the Department and the University throughout the world.

Each has ungrudgingly joined in the search for likely candidates to fill vacancies, has offered stimulating papers at departmental colloquia, and, perhaps most valuably of all, has given freely of his time to colleagues and students in quest of new solutions and new approaches to philosophic problems. In addition, each has made important contributions in areas outside philosophy proper.

Together, these three have made the Michigan philosophy department exciting, congenial, and conducive to hard, but rewarding, work.

Lastly, they and their wives have generously opened their homes to all, in a manner that was not the pattern in an earlier era and that has become all but impossible in today's complex academic environment.

We at Michigan and scholars everywhere are in their debt. It is in a spirit of gratitude and esteem, then, that the editors and authors of this Festschrift tender these essays.

The University of Michigan   A R T H U R W. B U R K S

DAVID LYONS

MILL'S THEORY OF JUSTICE[1]

DAVID LYONS

It is time we reconsidered the relations between justice and utilitarianism. Thanks to a convergence of political and philosophical developments, interest in political philosophy and the problem of justice is greater than it has been for many years. Significant contributions have recently been made to the field.[2] But our understanding of the political face of utilitarianism is, by contrast, rather crude. By re-examining Mill's theory, I shall try in this paper to help us gain a better grasp upon the utilitarian view of justice.

I

Mill begins the chapter of his *Utilitarianism* 'On the Connection Between Justice and Utility' by acknowledging that "one of the strongest obstacles to the reception of the doctrine that utility or happiness is the criterion of right and wrong has been drawn from the idea of justice" (1)[3]. That obstacle remains: most critics of utilitarianism see justice as its Achilles' heel. Indeed, we tend to think of utilitarians as having no appreciable account of social justice, and thus as neglecting a most important aspect of morality. This is understandable. Mill aside, the classical utilitarians pay little attention to the concept and problems of justice — and what little they say often seems wrong. Bentham hardly mentions justice in his philosophical works (though he has much to say, of course, about the justification of punishment). Austin and Sidgwick appear to have an impoverished conception of justice as mere regularity or conformity to rule. Few recent writers have done much better on this score. More important, this general neglect of justice does not seem accidental. The principle of utility worries about such things as 'pleasure' and 'pain,' happiness, or welfare; it says nothing about justice. It has been understood to require that one always 'maximize utility,' regarding any other way of acting as wrong, while ignoring what may be *due* a person and what one may have *a right* to or to do. Considerations of justice could not carry any independent weight in such a theory, so its neglect by utilitarian writers seems perfectly natural.

1

A. I. Goldman and J. Kim (eds.), Values and Morals, 1–20. All Rights Reserved.
Copyright © 1978 by D. Reidel Publishing Company, Dordrecht, Holland.

Critics of utilitarianism have not let the matter rest there. Social justice is understood by many to concern the 'distribution' of benefits and burdens among persons, and critics have contended that utilitarianism suffers logical as well as moral flaws in this connection. A logical flaw is found in the utilitarian formula that requires us to serve 'the greatest happiness of the greatest number.' It is said that this directs us to pursue two distinct and incompatible ends. The 'greatest happiness' criterion tells us to promote satisfactions and prevent frustrations to the maximum degree possible, without regard to how they are distributed among individuals, while the 'greatest number' requirement says that we must spread benefits and burdens as uniformly as possible. But satisfying one criterion might conflict with satisfying the other. This shows (it may be said) that the formula is incoherent or, at best, that it has indeterminate implications.

It should be noted, however, that the 'greatest happiness of the greatest number' formula is associated with utilitarianism chiefly through works published under Bentham's name (not all of which were actually written by Bentham).[4] It is not used much, if at all, by Mill, for example, and even in Bentham's system its status is questionable. Bentham's idea appears to be that, when we try to promote happiness, we are not always able to serve the best interests of all those who are affected by our actions. The most important conflict of interests, according to Bentham, is that between those in power and those who are ruled — the ordinary people, 'the greatest number.' Bentham believes that, as a matter of fact, happiness will best be served when we aim at serving the interests of the latter group, and so he came to use the derivative, nonbasic formula, 'the greatest happiness of the greatest number.' Of course, his factual beliefs may be mistaken. But that does not show that the basic utilitarian commitment to serving happiness is itself incoherent.

A critic may reply that this way of answering objections to the 'greatest happiness of the greatest number' formula merely illustrates the utilitarian's neglect of 'distribution.' Faced with a choice between maximizing satisfactions and distributing them equitably, the utilitarian is theory-bound to choose the former. At best, he might strike a compromise with the idea of social equality by formulating his criterion in terms of maximizing the average per capita satisfaction level (rather than in terms of maximizing total satisfactions). But even this version of utilitarianism is thought vulnerable to objections. It is often claimed, for example, that utilitarianism is defective from a moral point of view because it condones unjust social arrangements. It is, after all, *logically possible* that enslaving some would sometimes serve the general welfare better than any of the available alternative arrangements. And, it is said, a principle with such implications must be rejected.

Utilitarians have not embraced such institutions. Some have appealed to the phenomenon of diminishing marginal utility, for example, in arguing for social equality. And utilitarians have believed that happiness will best be served in free societies. But contentions of this sort are often dismissed out of hand – not because they rely on false factual claims, but rather because they turn on facts at all. This sort of objection to utilitarianism assumes, in effect, that facts are totally irrelevant to certain moral judgments. A utilitarian who tried to answer the objection by citing the actual disutility of slavery or of inequality would be accused of missing its essential point.

The objection has some interesting features. In the first place, it takes for granted that slavery could not possibly be justified, no matter what the alternatives might be. On what basis does it make this sweeping moral judgment? If the judgment is accepted as a 'moral intuition,' it requires critical examination. A normally sound reaction may here be overextended. If the judgment is derived from an assumed independent principle, then the question is simply begged against utilitarianism.

In the second place, it is difficult to see how facts can be excluded from the argument. If moral principles are not regarded as 'self-evident,' then they are subject to criticism and need to be defended in some manner. The only plausible arguments that I know of – such as Rawls' – make extensive use of facts about the human condition. And most general principles can be applied to the varied circumstances of human life only with the help of considerable information. Since facts are assumed relevant to the defense and application of nonutilitarian principles, they must also be entertained when we scrutinize utilitarianism. Until we have established some principles of justice on nonutilitarian grounds and shown that utilitarian arguments for them are ineffective, we must consider what utilitarians have to say about such matters.

In the third place, the objection assumes that the logical possibility that slavery will maximize utility shows that utilitarians regard slavery as morally permissible, at least in some circumstances. But, if Mill is a utilitarian, then this is mistaken. On Mill's view, I shall argue, nothing is shown to be right by showing that it maximizes utility; nothing is wrong simply because it fails to maximize utility. For Mill distinguishes between evaluations of expediency and moral judgments: the former concern utility, the latter obligation. To show that something is not morally wrong, we must show that it does not breach a moral obligation, and this is not a matter of maximizing utility. Mill also holds that justice is the most important segment of morality, involving the weightiest obligations, which correlate with personal rights. To show that something is not unjust, we must show that it does not violate rights. This too is not a matter of maximizing utility.

Mill's theories of justice and morality are found in, or can be reconstructed from, the last and longest chapter of *Utilitarianism*, which discusses justice. I shall explain those theories further by noting and interpreting the most relevant parts of Mill's discussion.

II

Mill begins his discussion of justice by observing that the feelings associated with justice are stronger than and different from those connected with mere expediency. This leads some writers invalidly to infer that considerations of justice are independent of utility. Mill proposes to dissect the sentiment of justice, these feelings, in order to undermine entirely this fallaciously developed theory (1–3). Mill accordingly embarks upon a study of the idea or concept, as opposed to the sentiment, of justice, in order to identify the beliefs that are fundamental to judgments about justice and the circumstances in which the feelings associated with justice arise. We are primarily concerned here with Mill's attempt to analyze the concept of justice.

Mill begins this attempt by surveying the central uses of the terms 'just' and 'unjust.' His survey finds justice connected with rights, desert, voluntary undertakings, impartiality, and equality (4–10). But the survey yields no unifying hypothesis about the concept of justice. Mill turns to etymology for illumination. This leads him to discuss the idea of law and that of 'punishment,' which brings him back to the realm of moral notions (11–13). Mill then outlines a conception of morality in terms of obligations and of justice in terms of rights (14–15). After this, he is ready to return to the sentiment of justice (16–23). Following an important passage on the nature of rights (24–25), Mill thereafter concentrates on substantive standards of justice. He discusses some conflicting views about punishment, wages, and taxation (26–31) and then sketches very broadly the substantive principles of justice which, he claims, could be based upon considerations of utility (32–38).

Mill's discussion is complex, sometimes subtle, often confusing. His formulations are, characteristically, wavering and imprecise. But his analysis of justice, centered in paragraphs 14 and 15, is striking and suggestive. I proceed on the assumption that it is important to take Mill's official pronouncements seriously, and that is is more illuminating to see what sort of consistent utilitarian view might then be attributed to Mill, than to take the usual interpretations for granted and to decide that he is inconsistent or unreasonable.

Some general points emerge clearly from Mill's initial survey of 'just' and 'unjust' that should be noted at the outset. First, unlike many other writers in his tradition, from Hobbes to the present, Mill avoids endorsing an obviously impoverished conception of justice. He is, for example, no legalist: the 'ultimate criterion of justice' must be independent of positive law (6). Nor does he confuse justice with mere regularity or conformity to rule.

Secondly, Mill recognizes rights that are independent of both positive law and merely conventional morality. These are rights that we may fail to respect and enforce, the ascriptions of which can be justified by appeal to valid general principles. These rights, which are referred to in his analysis of justice, he thus calls 'moral rights.' In recognizing them, Mill parts company with Bentham, whose abhorrence of political hyperbole provoked him to deny their possibility.

Thirdly, Mill holds that the obligations of justice are (like other moral obligations) not 'absolute' but can be overridden. The corresponding moral rights are accordingly not in principle inviolable. Now, few, if any, writers on the subject would basically disagree with Mill here, at least concerning the particular rights Mill identifies. But the point is important because it may seem to threaten the very idea of a utilitarian account of justice. For (it may be said) suppose Mill does talk about 'moral rights' and 'obligations of justice.' Such talk is empty if his utilitarianism compels him to regard any right or obligation as overridden for the sake of a marginal increment in the general welfare level. This suspicion assumes that a utilitarian is morally committed to maximizing utility. I shall try to show that this is not a feature of Mill's utilitarianism. The principle of utility is a principle concerning ends. It is not, in Mill's view, a moral principle; that is, it does not directly concern moral rights or obligations. Such principles are gotten by applying values within the constraints imposed by the moral concepts. Mill's views about the central moral concepts are thus crucial for his moral and political theory.

Mill leads us to his theory of justice in the following way. He speculates that the original idea of justice amounted to the idea of conformity to law. But as defects in laws were recognized, the concept evolved into the idea of what *ought* to be (rather than what *is*) law. This still does not express the concept of justice that we have today, for the standards of justice are understood to apply in other contexts, even when there ought not to be any legal intervention. "But even here," Mill says, "the idea of what ought to be law still lingers in a modified shape" (13). Mill holds that "the essence of law" is "the idea of penal sanction," so he links the idea of what *ought* to be law with *justified* punishment. As he makes clear, however, 'punishment' is not limited to legal penalities; it covers the entire range of sanctions, external and internal, including public condemnation and the reproaches of one's own conscience. On this understanding, Mill observes that 'punishment' for injustice is thought fitting, gives us pleasure, is what we like to see — in brief, is thought warranted (13). Now we have arrived, Mill thinks, at a distinctively *moral* notion. This is the idea of *conduct for which guilt feelings are warranted*. At first it looks as if Mill is going to say that this is the root idea of injustice. But he quickly observes that this expresses instead the more general idea of immorality, wrong action, the breach of moral obligation (14).

Mill has not yet differentiated injustice from immorality in general. An act can be wrong without being unjust, and we need another notion to account for that difference. So far as conduct is concerned, morality is for Mill the realm of right and wrong, which are functions of moral duty or obligation. But justice goes beyond these notions. "Justice implies something which it is not only right to do, and wrong not to do, but which some individual can claim from us as his moral right" (15). Some moral obligations correlate with moral rights, others do not.

It seems to me that this feature in the case — a right in some person, correlative to the moral obligation — constitutes the specific difference between justice and generosity or beneficence. . . . No one has a moral right to our generosity or beneficence because we are not bound to practice those virtues toward any given individual. (15)

The obligations of justice are those that correlate with moral rights.

Some qualifications seem implicit in Mill's expressly stated views. Mill suggests, for example, that morally wrong action consists in the breach of a moral duty or obligation. But he also recognizes that obligations can conflict, that one can override another. He would presumably connect morally wrong action with the breach of a moral obligation somewhat as follows. Failure to meet a moral obligation is sometimes justified, that is, when the obligation is overridden by another. To act wrongly, then, is not simply to breach a moral obligation but to do so in the absence of an overriding obligation.

All of this applies to the obligations of justice, which correlate with moral rights. These obligations can be overridden and the rights are not in principle inviolable. Mill would presumably qualify his analysis of injustice, which is given in terms of the violation of a moral right, somewhat as follows. The infringement of a right is sometimes justified, that is, when it is overridden by another right or even (Mill seems to envisage) in some special circumstances by an obligation that does not correlate with rights. To act unjustly, then, is not simply to infringe a right but to do so in the absence of an overriding right or obligation.

So far, nothing has been said or implied about 'maximizing utility.' But Mill is usually taken to be an 'act utilitarian,' who holds that any failure to promote happiness in the most productive and efficient manner possible is morally wrong. If that were Mill's view, it would deprive his talk of moral rights and obligations of any practical significance. They would provide no special considerations relevant to the morality of conduct. But that is not Mill's view, as can be seen from his distinction between morality and 'expediency,' which parallels his distinction between justice and morality (14–15).

As justice is a sector of morality, so morality is a sector of the more general realm of act appraisals that Mill places under the heading of 'expediency.' The distinctions are best made, as Mill suggests, by reference to negative judgments. An act can be wrong without being unjust; this is because injustice involves the violation of a right and not merely the breach of a moral obligation. Similarly, to call an act wrong is to imply that it is not merely inexpedient, but that it (unjustifiably) breaches a moral obligation. On Mill's view, this is to imply that 'punishment' of the act (in the broad sense already noted) would be justified. Guilt feelings for it would be warranted; but guilt feelings are not necessarily warranted for other conduct that is negatively appraised.

Since, on Mill's view, moral right and wrong are a function of moral rights and obligations, we might say, alternatively, that they are governed by moral principles, principles of obligation (including principles of justice, which also confer rights). But what are we to say about expediency, or act appraisals in general? Mill presumably believes that they have some rational basis. Since they are the broadest class of act appraisals, the applicable standard should presumably be Mill's most comprehensive principle. That is the principle of utility. The principle of utility is thus not a moral principle; it does not itself determine which acts are right and which are wrong, which are just and which unjust. If it does so at all, it must do so indirectly.

How this might work is suggested by Mill's account of rights:

When we call anything a person's right, we mean that he has a valid claim on society to protect him in the possession of it, either by the force of law or by that of education and opinion. If he has what we consider a sufficient claim, on whatever account, to have something guaranteed him by society, we say that he has a right to it. If we desire to prove that anything does not belong to him by right, we think this is done as soon as it is admitted that society ought not to take measures for securing it to him, but should leave him to chance or to his own exertions. (25)

To support the judgment that one has a right is to justify a claim about sanctions which do not merely secure a certain pattern of behavior (as in the case of obligations without rights) but which serve in particular to protect or defend the individual in a certain way. Mill goes on to say that he would argue for such claims by appealing to 'general utility' (25). He thus sketches something like a 'rule utilitarian' account of moral rights.

Some passages in *Utilitarianism* do admittedly suggest a different moral theory. When Mill first expounds and defends utilitarianism against an array of objections and misunderstandings, he says that "actions are right in proportion as they tend to promote happiness; wrong as they tend to produce the reverse of happiness" (Chapter II, paragraph 2).[5] Even at the start of Chapter V, which we have been examining, Mill refers to his "doctrine that utility or happiness is the criterion of right and wrong" (1). These passages suggest that the principle of utility directly determines the morality of actions. They are a bit vague on just how that would work, but they might be cited as support for the usual reading of Mill as an act utilitarian.

If Mill were an act utilitarian, his explicit, deliberate discussion of morality, in Chapter V, would be, not just pointless, but positively misleading and inconsistent with that position. Mill's talk of rights and obligations would be empty, since ascriptions of them would have little or no significance for practice. We might of course be forced to this interpretation of Mill, but it is worth while seeing if he has something more interesting to tell us.

In Mill's most extensive discussion of the principle of utility itself, in Chapter IV, he treats it as a principle concerning ends, not actions. In arguing for his principle, he is trying to prove that "happiness is the sole end of human action" (Chapter IV, paragraph 8). It may be said that this commits Mill to a certain manner of appraising actions — instrumentally, relative to the promotion of happiness. But the idea that happiness is the sole end of human action (or in more recent jargon, that it is the sole thing of intrinsic value) does not logically commit Mill to an act utilitarian conception of morality. He may be committed to ranking acts relative to their promotion of happiness. But that does not commit him to regarding acts below the top levels in such rankings — acts that fail to maximize utility — as morally wrong.

Mill might of course erroneously believe that his principle of utility logically commits him to act utilitarianism, or he might have other reasons

for embracing it. But does he embrace it? Chapter V answers this question
by explicitly outlining a different conception: judgments of instrumental
value correspond to judgments of expediency, not to moral act appraisals.

In Chapter IV, Mill brings in the appraisal of conduct as follows:

> happiness is the sole end of human action and the promotion of it the test by which
> to judge of all human conduct; from whence it necessarily follows that it must be the
> criterion of morality, *since a part is included in the whole*. (paragraph 8, emphasis
> added)[6]

This is a puzzling formulation. It is clarified, however, by the account of
morality that Mill gives in Chapter V: *morality is a sector of expediency*.
Considerations of expediency (instrumental value) govern morality – but not
directly. That is because moral judgments, in Mill's view, concern the justification of sanctions. To judge an act wrong is to judge that sanctions against
it would be warranted. In the case of social or external sanctions, this clearly
involves conduct by people other than the agent whose conduct is being
appraised. For social sanctions are imposed by others. Something of this
sort applies to internal sanctions too, so far as their justification is an argument for internalizing values and thus for acts of moral education. And it is
a utilitarian platitude (presumably accepted by Mill) that sanctions, or the
acts providing or imposing them, have disutility, and thus require justification.
As Mill also understands, from the fact that an act is inexpedient (does not
maximize utility) it does not follow that those other acts (involving sanctions)
would be justified; it therefore does not follow (on Mill's view) that an act
that fails to maximize utility is wrong. Someone with Mill's idea that moral
wrongness is essentially connected with warranted sanctions – especially
someone who is also a utilitarian – would have clear reasons for distinguishing
morality and expediency, or in other words for avoiding act utilitarianism.
As we have observed, Mill's view that happiness is the ultimate end does not
logically commit him to an act utilitarian conception of morality. The passages
that I have cited are often taken as evidence that Mill identifies wrong action
with the failure to maximize utility. But Mill does not say this, and his
explicit account of morality conflicts with this interpretation. Consequently,
it would seem worse than uncharitable to saddle Mill with an act utilitarian
conception of morality.

Since Mill is no act utilitarian, there are no apparent grounds for regarding
his talk of moral obligations as devoid of practical significance. He would not
require that an obligation be breached or be regarded as overridden merely
in order to maximize utility. Given this, there is no reason to attribute to

Mill the notion that an act is obligatory if and only if it would maximize utility. Mill holds that obligations can be overridden by other obligations, and we have no reason to understand this in act utilitarian terms. Moral obligations are determined as well as overriden in Mill's system by some more complex utilitarian calculation.

Similar reasoning applies to moral rights. Mill maintains that moral rights correlate with a subclass of moral obligations, so he presumably holds that the conditions establishing and overriding rights are the same as for the corresponding obligations. Neither the claim that one has a right nor the claim that a right may justifiably be infringed can in Mill's view be established on act utilitarian grounds. Mill's explicit account of rights appears to confirm this.

I have suggested that Mill has something like a rule utilitarian account of moral rights, and that needs to be explained. Part of the explanation is, as we have seen, that Mill's moral theory involves the *indirect* application of the principle of utility to conduct; he is no act utilitarian. Beyond this, rules enter into Mill's theory as follows. Rights and obligations are, for Mill, *general* considerations governing conduct. Since rights correspond to a subclass of obligations, it will suffice for now to concentrate on the latter. Mill's talk about sanctions indicates that he is thinking of them operating prospectively as well as retrospectively — they deter and dissuade as well as reprove and rebuke. They can so act only if they apply to classes or kinds of actions, not just to particular acts taken singly. As I have argued elsewhere,[7] Mill appears to be working with a model based on ordinary social rules, except that the rules of obligation we are talking about here are 'ideal' in the sense that they concern justified sanctions. Such a rule exists when the corresponding value is internalized widely. In that case, the people who have internalized the value will be affected by the promptings of conscience (the internal sanction) before and after the occasions they have for adhering to the value; they will also be disposed to exert pressure on others (the social sanction) who deviate or threaten to deviate from the value. To justify the existence of such a rule is to justify the widespread internalization of the corresponding value. To argue for an obligation is to justify the establishment or maintenance of such an 'ideal' rule.

The *analysis* of obligation that I am attributing to Mill makes no reference to utility. In this it resembles his explicit account of rights — both are neutral with respect to utilitarianism and alternative value systems. Mill claims, as we have seen, that valid ascriptions of rights are the conclusions of arguments of a certain type. These argue for sanctions that defend or protect the individual in a certain way. This analysis makes no reference to utility.

To use such analyses — to justify such a rule and thereby show that an obligation exists and, in a special class of cases, that a correlative right exists too — one must appeal to substantive values. Mill's utilitarianism becomes engaged here. For a utilitarian like Mill, to show that such a rule would be justified is to show that the various costs attached to moral education, guilt feelings, and social pressures are more than outweighed by the benefits to be obtained from the resulting effects on behavior. Such costs are not negligible, so an obligation is not proved merely by showing that a failure to perform as the rule would require amounts to a failure on the part of the agents to maximize utility in those cases. The stakes must be higher.

This division within Mill's theory between analysis and justification is important for a proper contrast between his view and ordinary rule utilitarianism. The rule utilitarian begins by formulating his basic principle as a moral principle, linking the moral appraisal of conduct indirectly to the promotion of happiness or welfare. A rule utilitarian principle that might be confused with Mill's moral theory could be formulated as follows: an act is right if and only if it conforms to a set of social rules the widespread internalization of which would promote happiness.[8] That is not the way Mill's moral theory develops.

As his account of moral rights makes clear, Mill claims, in effect, that the moral concepts provide schemas for evaluating conduct *from a moral point of view*. If one wishes to determine whether an act is just, one finds out whether it violates a right. To find this out, one asks whether that person should be defended or protected in a certain way, or whether something should be guaranteed to him. This is a question about a certain kind of ideal social rule. So far, nothing utilitarian has been said. In order to answer such questions, however, one must invoke substantive values, utilitarian or other. On this view of the matter, evaluating conduct from a moral point of view *does not leave it optional* whether to take rights seriously. A utilitarian who failed to do so (an act utilitarian, for example) would have a theory that clashed with the moral concepts. Such a theory would neglect rights, and thus would neglect a certain class of obligations, and it is the breach of an obligation (in the absence of an overriding obligation) that makes an act morally wrong. To neglect rights and obligations as the act utilitarian does is to confuse moral with instrumental value, immorality with inexpediency. Mill does not reach this conclusion by advancing a rule utilitarian principle, however; he does so by considering the logic of the central moral concepts. His *basic* principle is thus a claim about ultimate ends or intrinsic value.

To get to *moral* judgments, he must appeal to nonmoral values in the way mapped out by the analysis of rights and obligations.

Mill's moral theory is important, then, because it provides a significant theoretical alternative to both act *and* rule utilitarianism. The particular analyses of moral concepts that are suggested by Mill may be defective. Nevertheless, it may well be that correct analyses would have comparable implications, that is, would indicate how one can argue from nonmoral values to moral conclusions.

It is not obvious that this approach is sound. Many would undoubtedly reject it (especially those who maintain the utter independence of moral values). But it is not obviously unsound, either. It seems to me to warrant very serious consideration.

III

Mill sees justice as the realm of morality that concerns rights as well as obligations. So far I have mainly tried to show that this notion is not rendered vacuous by Mill's utilitarianism and that it is in fact based on Mill's ideas about the relevant moral concepts. Now I shall discuss some problems and other noteworthy features of Mill's theory.

Mill's analysis of rights

To have a right, then, is, I conceive, to have something that society ought to defend me in the possession of. If the objector goes on to ask why it ought, I can give him no other reason than general utility. (25)

Mill claims, in effect, that valid ascriptions of rights are the conclusions of arguments of a certain type. The characterization of this sort of argument does not require commitment or even reference to utilitarianism. Of course, one cannot construct such an argument, cannot defend a moral right, without invoking substantive values. And Mill does not hesitate to say that he would ground such an argument upon utility. But the analysis itself does not identify or limit the values that might be used in arguing for such protections and thus, in Mill's view, for rights.

Some further brief comments are in order. First, since some of the things to which one may be said to have a right are things one may not actually possess, we should prefer, I think, one of Mill's various formulations to the others. It is not that one must have something (beside the right), possession of which is to be preserved, but rather that something (which one may not yet have) is to be 'guaranteed' to one.

Second, Mill says this is or should be done by 'society.' As in his account of obligation, Mill does not restrict the guarantees to those of the law; we might rely on 'education and opinion' without legal intervention. Given my interpretation of Mill's analysis of obligation, I suggest that 'society' is involved in the sense that an argument for a right is an argument for the establishment and maintenance of a point of shared social morality. The internal sanction is still central, but the value is to be shared widely within the community.

Third, it would be difficult to give either Mill's analysis or his application of it an act utilitarian interpretation. Rules play a decisive role in 'protecting,' 'defending,' and 'guaranteeing' things. They are conceived of, in part, as regulating behavior in advance, not just as authorizing sanctions retrospectively. Such rules may be broken only for the sake of superior rights or obligations, never just to maximize utility.

Fourth, it seems reasonable to ask what differences Mill sees between the case of a moral right and that of a moral obligation without a correlative right. He seems to provide three different answers. (a) When he first invokes the idea of a right, to explain the difference between justice and the rest of morality, Mill describes the differences (somewhat hesitantly, and rather crudely) from the standpoint of the person bound. He says that obligations with corresponding rights bind one, not merely to act in certain ways, as other obligations do, but to do so with respect to definite persons at prescribed times (15).

(b) When Mill discusses the sentiment of justice, he refers to the hurt or harm that may be done to an individual (18–23). And this might be taken as implying that respect for a right always serves the interests of the right holder, at least in the sense that others refrain from hurting or harming him. But the evidence for this inference is equivocal, because Mill is trying to account for the sentiment of justice on the basis of antecedently existing desires to defend oneself and to retaliate. In that context, he would quite naturally emphasize hurt or harm. It would not follow that Mill thinks hurt or harm is always the result of the infringement of a right, or of an injustice. When he discusses the idea of a right and of justice (as opposed to the sentiment of justice), he prefers to speak of a 'wrong' or 'injury,' which do not imply a hurt or harm.

(c) Mill's explicit analysis of rights does emphasize the position of the right holder, without implying that he is merely an intended beneficiary. He is someone with 'a valid claim on society' (24). This suggests that he is entitled to stand upon the right, to press it, to call for its observance by others, and so on.

Mill's analysis is vague, but it is not devoid of content. Of current views, it seems closest to the claim theory, which emphasizes the special position of the right holder. It is compatible with the narrower choice theory. And, as we have seen, Mill's discussion sometimes suggests a version of the interest or beneficiary theory.[9] It is not obvious that Mill is on the wrong track entirely. A fully adequate account of rights might well be used as Mill envisages – to determine the moral commitments of, say, a utilitarian.

The superiority of justice

Although the concept of a right may not make essential reference to an interest, it is not implausible to suppose that the rights we have involve interests. Mill indicates that the interests served by the principles of justice that could be defended on utilitarian grounds are by and large the most important.

Justice is a name for certain classes of moral rules which concern the essentials of human well-being more nearly, and are therefore of more absolute obligation, than any other rules for the guidance of life. (32)

Foremost among these are the rules "which forbid mankind to hurt one another (in which we must never forget to include wrongful interference with each others' freedom)." For these are "more vital to human well-being than any maxims, however important, which only point out the best mode of managing some department of human affairs" (33). The primary obligations of justice correlate, then, with what we may call rights to security of person and to freedom of action.

Mill believes that these obligations generally take precedence over all others because they serve our most vital interests. But Mill's precise reasoning is, to say the least, unclear. Since he is not an act utilitarian, we would not expect him to rank obligations case by case, considering the 'expediency' of individual acts when obligations conflict; and there is no clear evidence that Mill would adjudicate conflicts in that way. It would seem to follow that he must rank rules on some more general utilitarian reckoning, along the lines of recent rule utilitarian theories. But on this topic Mill himself is silent, and his thinking appears unsystematic.

The ranking that Mill perceives can to some degree be explained by differences between the two large classes of obligations. Obligations without corresponding rights can, he thinks, be met in various ways, in alternative situations. The obligation of charity, for example, is understood to require a general pattern of sharing, not specific transfers to determinate individuals.

Such an obligation leaves more room for choice on the part of the person bound than does a debt, say, to a particular person. For that reason alone, it can more readily be overridden. For there will be other opportunities to do what it requires. By contrast, Mill says, the obligations of justice require us to act in determinate ways towards determinate persons at determinate times. That is an exaggeration, but the point would seem to have some validity.

At any rate, it seems reasonable for Mill to hold that the obligations of justice concern interests that are by and large the most important. As we have seen, the stakes must be higher than merely securing some marginal increment of utility if we are to justify an ordinary moral obligation on Mill's utilitarian reckoning. For the risks and costs of sanctions must be outweighed by the benefits to be gotten from the rule. The stakes must be even higher to justify an obligation of justice, one that correlates with a moral right. For greater costs attach to these obligations than to those without corresponding rights. They leave the person boundless room for choice and they involve greater liability to both external and internal sanctions, as well as to demands by others on one's conduct. To justify a right is not simply to justify a requirement on others. It is to justify right holders to act in certain ways, to demand respect for their rights, to challenge those who threaten or infringe them, to be indignant and perhaps noisy and uncooperative when they are violated or threatened, and so on. Here, as before, considerations that have nothing especially to do with utilitarianism may be invoked to determine the utilitarian's moral commitments.

Fidelity and justice

Mill begins his discussion of justice with a survey of central cases. These, we have noted, concern rights, desert, voluntary undertakings, impartiality, and equality. Later Mill maintains that the idea of a right is most central. He would therefore seem committed to recasting all of the initial examples in terms of rights and corresponding obligations. He does not do this explicitly. I will consider two of Mill's central cases here, beginning with voluntary undertakings.

It is confessedly unjust to break faith with anyone: to violate an engagement, either express or implied, or disappoint expectations raised by our own conduct, at least if we have raised those expectations knowingly and voluntarily. (8)

There is a complication here that I wish to place on one side. It is doubtful that disappointed expectations can be assimilated to promises as Mill suggests.

I may knowingly and voluntarily raise others' expectations about my future conduct without intending to commit myself to the relevant performances, without expecting others to rely upon me in that way. In such a case it is doubtful that my conduct constitutes any kind of undertaking. But I waive this point. Mill clearly means to limit such cases, and perhaps that can be done more effectively.

More to the point, it is doubtful whether all binding undertakings can be cast in terms of rights and obligations. There is, of course, a standard philosopher's way of doing this: If the undertaking is morally valid and binding, we say that the one who makes it is 'under an obligation' that is 'owed to' the other party, who acquires 'a right' to the first party's performance. But it is unclear that every undertaking that has moral significance can be described in terms of rights.

Suppose I am invited to a large, informal social gathering. My presence is desired but will not be required. The host urges me to come. I say that I will, without meaning to mislead. At the last moment I decide to stay home — not because something morally more imperative has arisen, but simply because I believe I would not enjoy myself at such a party that evening. The original undertaking can be said to have some moral significance, because I said I would come. This is evidenced by the fact that I might later offer a simple, polite excuse for not coming after all. But it would be a strange obligation that could be overridden by my reason for staying home. Obligations aside, could it be said that the host *had a right* to my attendance? Did I violate or infringe a right by staying home? The host might be said to have a right to *expect* me at the party. But that is not a right to my attendance, nor is it the sort of right that I could be said to have violated or infringed by staying home.

Clearly, the terms we use to describe cases will depend upon the circumstances and the understanding of the parties about the stakes involved. As the stakes get higher and our image of the undertaking and its consequences becomes more solemn, it seems more fitting to ascribe a right to the host and an obligation to me. Let us change the example till we get a case in which the host might be said to have a right to my attendance. Let my presence be required. Once I give my word to come, the host acts in reliance on it. I cannot in good conscience deal with this undertaking as I dealt with the other. If I wish to stay at home, I should ask to be released from my commitment. If I fail to do that and fail to perform as promised, I am subject to some criticism. Perhaps it could be said that I would then have failed to meet my obligations; perhaps, too, it could be said that I have violated or infringed the host's right. But — and here is my main point — can we also say that I have done him *an injustice?* I find no plausibility at all in the suggestion. Fidelity and justice seem separate moral notions, the former not a special case of the latter.

This case is not peculiar. When we are not riding our favorite philosophical theories, we do not hesitate to speak of rights to life, to liberty, to security of person, and so on. Such rights can be violated or infringed — by killing, hindering and coercing, assaulting, stealing — but it does not seem to follow, nor does it seem to be true, that the victim is thereby done an injustice. He may be wronged, but not all wrongs against particular persons are injustices. Perhaps Mill is right in thinking that every unjust act is the violation of a right. It does not follow (nor does it seem to be true) that all violations of moral rights are injustices. If so, some principles that confer rights are not principles of justice.

This marks one respect in which Mill's analysis of morality seems too simple. But it does not necessarily represent a significant problem for his theory. If justice is simply a narrower category than rights, then if Mill can account for moral rights he would in the process account for justice. The rest would seem to be a matter of detail.

Desert and rights

Many philosophers would seem to share Mill's notion that questions of rights are all questions of justice. On that view, fidelity might seem a facet of justice. By contrast, most philosophers would expect Mill to have trouble accounting for desert. Part of the reason, of course, is that principles of desert are often assumed to be independent of utility. But another part has to do with the scope of desert. As Mill understands, one can deserve either good or evil.

Speaking in a general way, a person is understood to deserve good if he does right, evil if he does wrong; and in a more particular sense, to deserve good from those to whom he does or has done good, and evil from those to whom he does or has done evil. (7)

Mill later reiterates the point, in his discussion of equality:

If it is a duty to do to each according to his deserts, returning good for good, as well as repressing evil by evil, it necessarily follows that we should treat all equally well (when no higher duty forbids) who have deserved equally well of *us*, and that society should treat all equally well who have deserved equally well of *it*, that is, who have deserved equally well absolutely. This is the highest abstract standard of social and distributive justice, toward which all institutions and the efforts of all virtuous citizens should be made in the utmost possible degree to converge. (36)

There are two problems here. First, how can Mill recast this talk of desert in terms of rights? Second, how can Mill — as a utilitarian — endorse principles of desert? The two questions are connected. If he cannot construe questions of desert in terms of rights, then his theory fails or must substantially be revised. I shall concentrate on suggesting how Mill might recast claims about desert of the sort he endorses in terms of rights.

Mill endorses principles under which one can deserve bad treatment. These cannot be translated simply into principles about rights. For, whereas one can deserve either good or evil, the concept of a right seems more restrictive. It is paradoxical to suggest that someone has a right to bad treatment; and the apparent exceptions only reinforce the rule. Philosophers sometimes claim, for example, that people have 'a right to be punished.' The idea seems paradoxical until it emerges that the right primarily concerns *eligibility for* punishment, not punishment itself. Being regarded as eligible for punishment is made to seem desirable, a good, relative to the alternative, which is being regarded as something less than a full person, something that cannot be held responsible for its behavior, something to be adjusted or manipulated.

If there is this difference between desert and rights, it follows that one who wishes to account for desert claims in terms of rights will have to deal with some desert claims indirectly. Where what is deserved is a good (e.g., good treatment by others), one can, perhaps, translate the claim directly into a right (a right to the good treatment). I see no insuperable obstacles here. But where what is deserved is an evil (e.g., bad treatment by others), the account must be more complex.

Consider, then, the possibility of understanding judgments about deserved bad treatment in terms of rights. When one acts badly, one may deserve bad treatment, or at least worse treatment than one would have deserved from those whom one has treated badly. The relevant moral relations might be characterized in terms of rights by utilizing the idea of *forfeiting* one's rights.

It might be held, for example, that one deserves special services or consideration from those one has aided in the past. Mill appears to endorse this and to regard it as equivalent to the claim that one has a right to special services or consideration from those one has aided in the past. Suppose, then, that I have aided you in the past but have since treated you badly. Before treating you badly, I might have deserved special consideration from you; after treating you badly, however, I no longer deserve that special consideration (or deserve it less, or deserve less of it). Mill might describe the situation by saying that, before I treated you badly, I had a right to special consideration from you; by treating you badly, by wronging you, I forfeited that right. The translation is not hopelessly implausible.

We can apply this sort of translation to the case of 'punishment.' We must begin with Mill's assumption that each person has a right to freedom of action and to security of person. Such rights correlate with obligations upon other people — not to interfere, generally, with one's activities, not to assault one, and so on. Unwarranted violations of such rights constitute what Mill calls "the most marked cases of injustice, . . . acts of wrongful aggression or wrongful exercise of power over someone" (33). I say 'unwarranted' because no rights are regarded by Mill as 'absolute' — not even these, which are supposed to rank highest in the scale of moral values.

Mill would seem to recognize at least three ways in which such rights are not 'absolute,' that is, in which hindering or hurting someone might be warranted. In the first place, such rights would initially be understood as *limited* in ways that are essential to their very existence. My right to act unimpeded by others, for example, would not cover acts of mine that are intended to impede others' freedom. (If I have the right to do that, it would be for other reasons.) In the second place, Mill allows the possibility that other rights and obligations take precedence in special circumstances. My right to act unimpeded could be *overridden* by, say, others' rights to protect themselves from my clearly dangerous behavior, however innocent my intentions. In the third place, I can *forfeit* such a right, at least to some degree, by my own bad conduct. My rights to act unimpeded and to security of person can be regarded as a right to generally good treatment by others — the kind of treatment that is required for a minimally agreeable sort of social existence. But this right can be forfeited by sufficiently bad conduct on my part. If my conduct is sufficiently bad, then the stakes are high enough to justify external sanctions, including punishment. The use of such sanctions is, precisely, bad treatment of some people by others. But this bad treatment is nonstandard; it requires the special justification given by my bad conduct. In just such cases we may be willing to say, not only that I *deserve* such treatment because of my bad conduct, but also that I have *forfeited* part of my *right* to generally good treatment by others. These are the cases in which Mill would presumably say that one deserves bad treatment 'from society.'

Such an approach to at least a limited range of the principles of desert does not strike me as patently implausible or unpromising. Whether the argument can be substantiated in strictly utilitarian terms is a question I shall leave for another occasion.

Cornell University

DAVID LYONS

NOTES

¹ This paper is a sequel to 'Mills's Theory of Morality', *Nous* **10** (1976) 101–120. An earlier version was presented at the University of Texas; I am grateful for the comments I received on that occasion. I would also like to thank Stephen Massey and Robert Summers for their comments and suggestions. (Somewhat similar problems were explored, from a different point of view, in 'Human Rights and the General Welfare', *Philosophy and Public Affairs* **6** (1977) 113–129.) For a somewhat different reading of Mill, see Jonathan Harrison, 'The Expedient, the Right and the Just in Mill's *Utilitarianism*', *Canadian Journal of Philosophy,* Supplementary Volume **I**, Part 1 (1974) pp. 93–107, which I did not have an opportunity to study before completing this essay.

² See, for example, Joel Feinberg, 'Justice and Personal Desert', *Nomos VI: Justice,* ed. by Friedrich and Chapman (New York: Lieber-Atherton, 1974), pp. 69–97, and 'Noncomparative Justice', *Philosophical Review* **83** (1974) 297–338; John Rawls, *A Theory of Justice* (Cambridge, Mass.: Belknap Press, 1971); Robert Nozick, 'Distributive Justice', *Philisophy and Public Affairs* **3** (1973) 45–126.

³ All references in the text are to paragraphs of *Utilitarianism* – Chapter V, unless otherwise noted.

⁴ Bentham's views are discussed in my *In the Interest of the Governed* (Oxford: Clarendon Press, 1973).

⁵ Even here Mill distinguishes between the utilitarian theory of morality and 'the theory of life on which this theory of morality is grounded.' The theory of life is the principle of utility that Mill defends in Chapter IV; the theory of morality is the one under discussion, presented in Chapter V.

⁶ Mill's characterization of his 'doctrine' at the start of Chapter V, cited above, comes soon after this longer statement. I suggest the former be read as short for the latter.

⁷ 'Mill's Theory of Morality', *op. cit.,* Sec II.

⁸ A recent theory that somewhat resembles Mill's is to be found in R.B. Brandt, 'Some Merits of One Form of Rule-Utilitarianism', *University of Colorado Studies, Series in Philosophy* (1967), pp. 39–65; see pp. 57f for a brief discussion of Mill. This paper is complemented by 'A Utilitarian Theory of Excuses', *Philosophical Review* **68** (1969) 337–361.

Though I arrived at the interpretation of Mill that is being presented in this paper by considering Mill's remarks about sanctions and their relation to Bentham's theory of punishment, which Mill embraced, the development of my hypothesis has undoubtedly been stimulated by Brandt's significant work in this area.

⁹ For these three types of theory, see, respectively, Joel Feinberg, *Social Philosophy* (Englewood Cliffs, N.J.: Prentice-Hall, 1973), pp. 64–67; H.L.A. Hart, 'Bentham on Legal Rights', in *Oxford Essays in Jurisprudence, Second Series,* ed. by A.W.B. Simpson (Oxford: Clarendon Press, 1973), pp. 171–201; and my 'Rights, Claimants, and Beneficiaries', *American Philosophical Quarterly* **6** (1969) 173–185.

JOEL FEINBERG

THE INTEREST IN LIBERTY ON THE SCALES

There is one version of John Stuart Mill's famous 'harm principle' for determining the moral limits of state coercion that is virtually beyond controversy.
Few would deny that it is always a morally relevant reason in support of a
proposed criminal prohibition that it is reasonably necessary (that is, that
there are reasonable grounds for taking it to be necessary) to prevent harm
or the unreasonable risk of harm to parties other than the persons whose
conduct is to be constrained. Some might deny that the necessity to prevent harm to others is a *sufficient* reason for state coercion on the grounds
that prevention of minor harms may not be worth the social costs of state
intervention. Others might deny that the prevention of harm to others is
a *necessary* condition of justified interference on the grounds that there are
other reasons for coercion (e.g. the prevention of mere offense, or the enforcement of morality as such) that can apply even to harmless behavior.
But hardly anyone would deny that the need to prevent harm to others is
always *a* reason in support of state coercion even if it is not always a conclusive reason, and even if it is not the only kind of reason that can apply.

Whatever this weakened version of the harm principle gains in plausibility, however, it loses in practical utility as a guide to legislative decisions.
Legislators must not only decide *whether* to use the weakened harm principle, but also *how* to use it in cases of merely minor harms, moderately
probable harms, reasonable and unreasonable risks of harm, aggregative
harms, competitive harms, accumulative harms, and so on.[1] Solutions to
these problems cannot be provided by the harm principle in its simply stated
version, but absolutely require the help of supplementary principles, some of
which represent controversial moral decisions and maxims of justice. In this
paper, I shall consider some of those problems involved in the legislative
application of the harm principle that require that classes of personal interests
be compared and ranked in importance. The process of ranking interests in
order to determine how to minimize social 'harms' is invariably described in
terms of the metaphor of a scales: interests are 'balanced' in order to determine which has the greater 'weight.' Specifically, I shall be concerned to
characterize the balancing process when one of the interests to be weighed
is the generalized interest in liberty which the law presumes to be shared

21

A. I. Goldman and J. Kim (eds.), Values and Morals, 21–35. All Rights Reserved.
Copyright © 1978 by D. Reidel Publishing Company, Dordrecht, Holland.

(like the interests in health and economic sufficiency) equally by all citizens.

I

Typically the interests that must be compared and graded ('weighed and balanced') by a legislature do not include, or include only to a minor degree, the interest in liberty. I have in mind cases of the following kind: a certain kind of activity has a tendency to cause harm to the people who are affected by it, but effective prohibition of that activity would tend to cause harm to those who have an interest (that is, a stake) in engaging in it, and not merely in the often trivial respect in which *all* restrictions of liberty (even the liberty to murder) are *pro tanto* harmful to the persons whose alternatives are narrowed, but rather because other substantial interests of these persons are totally thwarted. In all such cases, to prevent A from harming B's interest in Y would be to harm A's interest in X (as well as his general interest in liberty, for whatever that is worth). The legislator therefore must decide whether B's interest in Y is more or less important — more or less worth protecting — in itself (questions of degree of risk aside) than A's interest in X. And the legislator must think not merely of some specific persons A and B, but of *all* persons of types A and B, that is, of standard A's and B's. The harm principle, without further specification, is a largely empty formula. It tells him that protecting B's interest from harm is a good and relevant reason for restraining A, but that is *all* it tells him. It doesn't tell him *how* good a reason it is compared with the obvious reason, itself derived from the need to minimize harms, for permitting A to pursue *his* interest untrammeled. If A has a genuine stake in the promotion or achievement of X, then any constraint to his pursuit of X will set back or thwart that interest, and thus in the relevant sense cause *him* 'harm.'

To be sure, we should protect an interest that is certain to be harmed in preference to one whose liability to harm is only conjectural, other things being equal, and we should deem it more important to prevent the total thwarting of one interest than the mere invasion to some small degree of a conflicting interest, other things being equal. Harm (in the relevant legal sense) is the invasion of an interest, and invasions do differ in degree, but when interests of quite different kinds — for example a motorcyclist's interest in speed, excitement, and economical transport, and the interests of the professional scholar residing in the suburbs in the peace and quiet of his neighborhood — are invaded to the same degree, where is the greater harm?

That depends, of course, on which of the two kinds of interest is the more important.

The 'importance' of interests other than the interest in liberty is normally measured by at least three different indices: their importance to their possessor, that is, their 'vitality' within his total system of personal interests; the degree to which they are reinforced by other interests, private and public; and perhaps (this is more controversial) their inherent moral quality. The standard of vitality is applied to a particular interest when we consider the extent to which the thwarting of that interest is likely to harm the whole economy of one's personal interests. The interests of a 'standard person' of a given type in X may be more important than his interests in Y in that harming his interest in X will do less harm on balance to his net personal interest (in the singular) than would harming his interest in Y, just as harm to one's heart or brain will do more damage to one's bodily health than an 'equal degree' of harm to less vital organs. Where a standard person's interest of high vitality in his system conflicts with another standard person's interest of relatively low vitality in *his* system, then, other things being equal, the former interest can be deemed more important than the latter.

The most vital interests in a personal system of interests are those I choose to call 'welfare interests' in the indispensable means to one's ulterior goals whatever the latter may be, or later come to be. In this category are the interests in one's own physical health and vigor, the integrity and normal functioning of one's body, the absence of distracting pain and suffering or grotesque disfigurement, minimal intellectual acuity, emotional stability, the absence of groundless anxieties and resentments, the capacity to engage normally in social intercourse, at least minimal wealth, income, and financial security, a tolerable social and physical environment, and a certain amount of freedom from interference and coercion. These standard interests are in conditions that are generalized means to a great variety of possible goals and whose joint realization, in the absence of very special circumstances, is necessary for the achievement of more ultimate goals. In one way, then, they are the very most important interests a person has, for without their fulfillment a person (the 'standard person' who is always before the eyes of the legislator) is lost.

In various other ways, however, welfare interests are likely to seem rather trivial goods, necessary but grossly insufficient for a good life. They are the 'basic requisites of a man's well-being'[2] but by no means the whole of that well-being itself. Moreover, as I shall understand them, welfare interests share the common character of bare minimality. One can achieve one's more ulterior goals and thus one's 'higher good' in most cases even if one is in poor health, or has little money, or lives in an unattractive environment, but one has no chance at all if one's health is totally broken, or one is totally and irretrievably destitute, or lives in a pestilential sink. One can threaten another person's welfare interests by weakening his health or diminishing his wealth, but one does not actually invade those interests until one brings them below a tolerable minimum.

Corresponding to many of the basic welfare interests are possible ulterior interests, which some of us do and some of us do not have, in achieving a much higher level of a particular element of welfare than is actually required. Thus the interest in becoming prosperous or affluent resembles the welfare interest in having enough money for a decent life in that both of them are economic interests, and would be so categorized in a different system of classification. But an interest in affluence, while differing from the welfare interest in financial sufficiency only in degree, is by no means itself a welfare interest. Similarly, the interest in putting oneself in vibrant, blooming health and the very best athletic condition is a kind of physical interest like the welfare interest in not being sick, but is not itself a welfare interest.

Any given welfare interest when considered entirely by itself may at first sight seem a trivial and obvious component of a wider and genuinely important structure of welfare interests, one whose singular violation could easily be compensated for by gains in other sectors of welfare. This impression ceases, however, when one notices that welfare interests, unlike more ulterior interests, are linked together so that they are no stronger than their weakest link. Nicholas Rescher traces the medical analogy: "Deficiencies in one place are generally not to be compensated for by superiority in another; there are few, if any trade-offs operative here — just as cardiovascular superiority does not make up for a deficient liver so added strengths in one sector of welfare cannot cancel our weaknesses in another."[3] All the money in the world won't help you if you have a fatal disease, and great physical strength will not compensate for destitution or imprisonment.

Despite these various respects in which any given welfare interest is likely to seem a trivial thing, there is no doubt that the welfare interests severally and collectively are the most vital and therefore in one clear sense, at least, the most important, in a person's interest-system. When they are blocked or damaged, a person is very seriously harmed indeed, for in that case his more ultimate aspirations are defeated too; whereas setbacks to a given higher goal do not necessarily inflict damage on the whole network of his interests. To be sure, one cannot live on bread alone, but without bread one cannot live at all.

While welfare interests are the most vital ones, non-welfare interests too can be ranked in terms of relative vitality, just as the hand can be deemed a more vital appendage than the little toe even though neither is an essential organ, and harm to one's hand can be deemed more serious than harm to the little toe. Determining which of two non-welfare interests is the more vital is no easy task, especially when we are restricted to a consideration of the interest systems of various types of 'standard men;' but even if we could settle this matter, there would remain difficult complexities. Interests tend to pile up and reinforce one another. My interest (as a professional scholar residing in the suburbs in peace and quiet) may be more vital in my system than the motorcyclist's interests in speed, excitement, and economy are in his, but there is also the interest of the cyclist's employer in having workers efficiently transported to his factory, and the economic interest of the community in general (including me) in the flourishing of the factory owner's business; the interest of the motorcycle manufacturers in their own profits; the interest of the police and others (perhaps including me) in providing a relatively harmless outlet for adolescent exuberance, and in not having a difficult rule to enforce. There may be nowhere near so great a buildup of reinforcing interests, personal and public, in the quietude of my neighborhood. For that reason, the motorcyclist's interest may be a more vital component of the system of *community interests* than mine, though when we also consider the effects of his noise on property values and on the attractiveness of the community to peace-loving outsiders who would otherwise be tempted to move into it and contribute their talents, the question can be seen in its full complexity as a close and difficult one.[4]

The final consideration that may complicate the delicate task of interest-balancing invokes the inherent moral worth of the compared interests themselves quite apart from their vitality or their relation to other interests. At most this factor is considered only in extreme cases, in respect to interests that are thought to be unworthy of any protection at all. If there are such things as 'sick,' 'morbid,' 'sadistic,' or 'depraved' *interests* (as opposed to mere desires) — and in the absence of an agreed-upon detailed analysis of the concept of an interest philosophers can be expected to disagree about this — then such interests could plausibly be found to be without 'weight' or importance, and thus easily counterbalanced by *any* legitimate conflicting interest.

II

Two intertwined questions can arise when interest-balancers turn their attention to the interest in liberty. Whenever a person's interest in X is thwarted, say by a legal prohibition against anyone's doing, pursuing, or possessing Xs, an interest in liberty is also impeded, namely, the interest in having a choice whether to do, possess, or pursue X or not. We can ask, then, how important generally speaking is the interest in being free to choose, and also in a given case of legal coercion, how great an invasion has been made of that general interest. The latter question presupposes that we can make sense of quantitative expressions about 'greater' and 'lesser' depletions of liberty.

If our personal liberties were totally destroyed by some ruthlessly efficient totalitarian state, most of us would be no more able to pursue the ultimate interests that constitute our good than if the sources of our economic income were destroyed or our health ruined. For that reason our interest in liberty is best understood as a basic welfare interest. When some specific kind of conduct is made illegal, every citizen's liberty is diminished in at least one respect: no one is at liberty to engage in the newly prohibited conduct. But it does not follow by any means that everyone's welfare interest in liberty has been thwarted by new legal prohibitions any more than a new tax, as such, is an invasion of the welfare interest in economic sufficiency. These welfare interests, as we have seen, are not violated until they are brought below a tolerable minimum level. There may also be a non-welfare, trans-minimal interest in liberty analogous to the interest some people have in possessing as much money as possible, though the image of the 'liberty-miser' is sufficiently blurred to weaken the analogy somewhat. Invasions of the interest in having as much money (or liberty) as possible, of course, are much less harmful than invasions of the interest in having *enough* money (or liberty) for a decent life, and possess correspondingly less weight on the interest balancing scales.

Everyone has a derivative interest, however, in possessing more money or liberty than he actually needs, as a 'cushion' against possible future invasions of his welfare interest in having enough to get along. Consequently, the closer are one's assets (in money, liberty, or health) to the minimum line, the more harmful are depletions of them above the minimum line. For all welfare interests there is some analogue of the principle of the diminishing marginal utility of money. The legislative interest-balancer then will ascribe some weight to all legitimate interests including all interests in liberty, but he will ascribe greater weight to the welfare interest in liberty than to the security interest in cushioning that welfare interest, and greater weight to the interest in securing minimal liberty than to the interest in accumulating extensive trans-minimal liberty or 'as much liberty as possible.'

III

There is a standing presumption against all proposals to criminalize conduct that is derived simply from the interest 'standard persons' are presumed to have in political liberty, but the strength of this presumption varies not only with the type of interest in liberty (welfare, security, or accumulative) but also with the degree to which that interest is actually invaded by the proposed legislation. Invasions of the interest in liberty are as much a matter of degree as invasions of the interest in money, though we lack clear-cut conventional units for measuring them, corresponding to dollars, pounds, and francs. The interest in liberty *as such* — as opposed to the various interests we have in doing the things we may be free or unfree to do — is an interest in having as many *open options* as possible with respect to various kinds of action, omission, and possession. I have an open option with respect to a given act X when I am permitted to do X and I am also permitted to do *not-X* (that is to omit doing X) so that it is up to me entirely whether I do X or not. If I am permitted to do X but not permitted to do *not-X*, I am not in any usual sense at liberty to do X, for if X is the only thing I am permitted to do, it follows that I am compelled to do X, and compulsion, of course, is the plain opposite of liberty. The possession of a liberty is simply the possession of alternative possibilities of action, and the more alternatives, the more liberty. Some criminal statutes reduce our alternatives more than others, though as Isaiah Berlin reminds us, "possibilities of action are not discrete entities like apples which can be exhaustively enumerated,"[5] nor like shillings and pence (we might add) which can be accurately counted. Counting and evaluating options, therefore, "can never be more than impressionistic,"[6] but there are better and worse ways of gathering one's impressions, and some persons' impressions may be more accurate than others', for all that.

We can think of life as a kind of maze of railroad tracks connected and disjoined, here and there, by switches. Wherever there is an unlocked switch which can be pulled one way or the other, there is an 'open option;' wherever the switch is locked in one position the option is 'closed.' As we chug along our various tracks in the maze, other persons are busily locking and unlocking, opening and closing switches, thereby enlarging and restricting our various possibilities of movement. Some of these switchmen are part of a team of legislators, policemen, and judges; they claim *authority* for their switch positionings. Other switchmen operate illicitly at night, often undoing what was authoritatively arranged in the daylight. This model, of course, is simpler than the real world where the 'tracks' and 'switches' are not so clearly marked; but it does give us a sense for how some closed options can be more restrictive of liberty than others. When a switchman closes and locks a switch, he forces us to continue straight on, or stop, or back up. What we cannot do is move on to a different track heading off in a different direction from the one we are on. Before the switch was locked we had the option of continuing on or else moving to the new track, but now that particular option is closed to us. If the track from which we are barred is only a short line leading to a siding, and coming to a dead end in a country village, then our liberty has not been *much* diminished. We are not at liberty to go to one precise destination, but the whole network of tracks with all its diverse possibilities may yet be open before us. If, on the other hand, the closed switch prevents us from turning on to a trunk line, which itself is connected at a large number of switching points with branch lines heading off in many directions, then our liberty has been severely diminished, since we are debarred not only from turning at this one point, but also from enjoying a vast number of (otherwise) open options at points along the trunk line and its branches. In this case, one locked switch effectively closes dozens of options further up the line. Options that lead to many further options can be called 'fecund;' those that are relatively unfecund can be called 'limited.' The closing of fecund options, then, is more restrictive of liberty, other things being equal, than the closing of limited options, and the more fecund the option closed, the more harm is done to the general interest in liberty.

The railroad model is inadequate in a number of respects. It is an approximate rendering of our idea of liberty of movement, but it is difficult to apply to liberty of expression and opinion, or to 'passive liberties' like the freedom to be let alone, and the like. Moreover, it needs many complications before it can adequately render the full complexity of choices designated by the single word 'options.' Free men are often faced with choices of the form 'to X or not to X': to vote or not to vote, to buy a car or not to buy a car, to travel or to stay at home. Even our more complicated decisions can be crammed into this logical form, but the form in which they present themselves to our minds is often many sided: to vote for candidate A or B or C or D? to buy a Ford or Chevrolet or a Datsun or a Volkswagen or a Renault? to travel to England or France or Holland or Sweden or Spain or Italy? to marry Tom or Dick or Harry or . . . ? Our options in these cases are shaped more like tuning forks than wedges, and a barrier at the base of the fork restricts our liberty more than one at the base of a single prong. Other options disjoin conjunctions of alternatives rather than single possibilities. When the highwayman sticks his gun in one's ribs and says "your money or your life," he allows one the option of giving or not giving one's money, and the option of staying or not staying alive, but he closes the option of keeping *both* one's money *and* one's life — a most fecund option indeed.

The 'open option' theory of liberty is to be preferred, I think, to its main rival, the theory of liberty as the absence of barriers to one's actual desires, whatever they should happen to be.[7] Suppose that Martin Chuzzlewit finds himself on a trunk line with all of its switches closed and locked, and with other 'trains' moving in the same direction on the same track at his rear, so that he has no choice at all but to continue moving straight ahead to destination D. On the 'open option' theory of liberty, this is the clearest example of a total lack of liberty: all of his options are closed, there are not alternative possibilities, he is forced to move to D. But now let us suppose that getting to D is Chuzzlewit's highest ambition in life and his most intensely felt desire. In that case, he is sure to get the thing in life he wants most. Does that affect the way the situation should be described in respect to liberty? According to the theory that one is at liberty to the extent that one can do what one wants, a theory held by the ancient Stoics and Epicureans and many modern writers too, Chuzzlewit enjoys perfect liberty in this situation because he can do what he wants, even though he can do nothing else. But since this theory blurs the distinction between liberty and compulsion, and in this one extreme hypothetical case actually identifies the two, it does not recommend itself to common sense.

Common sense may seem to pose difficulties for the 'open option' theory too. The problem for that analysis of liberty is to explain why we attach so great a value to liberty if it is understood to have no necessary connection to our actual desires. Suppose Tom Pinch's highest ambition in life (again speaking in the terms of the railroad metaphor) is to go to destination E, a small siding at a warehouse on a dead end line of a minor branch. Suppose further that the switch enabling trains to move on to that track is unalterably locked in the position barring entry, and is, furthermore, the only locked switch in the entire network of tracks. It may be a small consolation indeed to our frustrated traveler that he is perfectly free to go everywhere except to the one place he wants most to go. The problem for the open-options account is to explain why Chuzzlewit, who *can* do what he wants most to do, but nothing else, *lacks* something of value, and also why Pinch, who *cannot* do what he wants most to do but can do everything else, *possesses* something of value (his liberty).

There are two moves open to a theorist who accepts this challenge. The first is to compromise his open-option theory (as Berlin apparently does) by admitting other elements. Berlin, in a qualifying footnote, suggests that the total amount of liberty enjoyed by a given person at a given time is a function not only of the number and fecundity of his open options, but also "the value [that] not merely the agent, but the general sentiment of the society in which he lives, puts on the various possibilities."[8] If we accept Berlin's suggestion some strange consequences follow. Chuzzlewit, who in our example is compelled to go to D whatever he might wish, is not really unfree after all, provided D is considered a desirable destination both by Chuzzlewit and "the society in which he lives." I fail to see how the desirability of D affects one way or the other the question whether Chuzzlewit has any choice about going there. If Chuzzlewit is allowed no alternative to D, it follows that he is forced willy-nilly to go to D. His situation pleases him, no doubt, but that simply shows that persons can do quite willingly what they are compelled to do, that they can be contented in their unfreedom, a fact of experience that has been much observed and long known. As for our poor frustrated traveler Pinch, Berlin's suggestion can take away his last consolation. If his preferred destination is deemed a desirable place to be both by himself and by the 'general sentiment' of his society, then he is not very free after all, even though his options to move through the system of tracks are almost completely open. He may in fact be no freer, or even less free, than Chuzzlewit, although this is hard to determine since Berlin, who accepts both the number and the value of open possibilities as liberty-determining factors, gives us no clue as to their relative importance. If society at large does not agree with Pinch's eccentric estimate of the desirability of his destination (a fact that Pinch might be expected to find irrelevant to the question of how free he is) and thus finds the barriers to his desire not only singular and limited, but also of no great disvalue, it will tell him that he is 'truly free' no matter how frustrated he feels.

A more plausible way of accounting for the value of liberty will make firm but more modest claims on its behalf. As Berlin himself says many times in his main text, liberty is a thing of solid value, but not the only thing that is valuable. In particular, it is implausible to identify liberty with happiness or contentment, other states to which most persons attach high value. Chuzzlewit may be contented with his heart's desire in the absence of alternative possibilities; indeed he may even be better off, on balance, contented and unfree, than he would be free and uncontented. And Pinch might understandably be willing to trade a great amount of unneeded liberty for the one thing that is necessary to his contentment. But what these examples show is not that 'true freedom is contentment' or that compulsion and freedom are compatible (when one is contented with the compulsion), but rather that freedom is one thing and contentment another, that they are both valuable, but sometimes in conflict with one another so that one cannot have both.

IV

What then is the basis of our interest in liberty? Why should it matter that we have few 'open-options' if we have everything else we want and our other interests are flourishing? Our welfare interest in having a tolerable bare minimum of liberty is perhaps the easiest to account for of the various kind of interests persons have in liberty. If human beings had no alternative possibilities at all, if all their actions at all times were the *only* actions permitted them, they might yet be contented provided their desires for alternative possibilities were all thoroughly repressed or extinguished, and they might even achieve things of value, provided that they were wisely programmed to do so. But they could take no credit or blame for any of their achievements, and they could no more be responsible for their lives, in prospect or retrospect, than are robots, or the trains in our fertile metaphor that must run on 'predestined grooves.' They could have dignity neither in their own eyes nor in the eyes of their fellows, and both esteem for others and self-esteem would dwindle. They could not develop and pursue new interests, nor guide the pursuit of old interests into new and congenial channels, for their lack of key to life's important switches would make it impossible for them to maneuver out of their narrow grooves. Only a small number of kinds of ultimate interests would be consistent with what is permitted, and there would be no point in wanting to develop new ones more harmonious with one's temperament or natural propensities. There would be no point, in fact, in thinking of changing in any important way, in changing one's mind, one's purposes, one's ambitions, or one's desires, for without the flexibility that freedom confers, movements in new directions would be defeated by old barriers. The self-monitoring and self-critical capacities, so essential to human nature, might as well dry up and wither; they would no longer have any function. The contentment with which all of this might still be consistent would not be a recognizably human happiness.

Most of us have fallen into fairly settled grooves by middle life, so the enjoyment of a vast number of open options beyond the requirements of the welfare interest in liberty may not seem very urgent to us. There is no particular comfort in the thought that if I should happen to change my desires or ambitions there will be no externally imposed barrier to my pursuit of the new ones, when the probability of such change seems virtually nil. Still there is something very appealing in the realization that just in case there should be changes in me or my circumstances (contrary to my present expectation), the world will not frustrate and defeat me. The 'breathing space' conferred by alternative possibilities then is an important kind of security.

Another source of the interest in liberty is quite independent of security. Enjoyment of open options is valued by many persons for its own sake, in quite the same way as the enjoyment of a pleasing natural and social environment. There is a kind of symbolic value in possessing a library with more books than one will ever read, or having access to a museum with more exhibits than one can ever see, or eating in a restaurant which offers more dishes than that which one wants most to choose. It is good to have a choice to exercise even when one would be content anyway without it. Alternative options not only secure a person against the possibility of changes of preference, they also permit an appreciation of the richness and diversity of the world's possibilities, and form themselves an environment in which it is pleasant to live.

For young persons whose characters are not fully formed, however, and even for older persons who have not become fixed in their ways, the primary base of the interest in liberty is the necessity to experiment with modes and styles of life, and to search among as large as possible a stock of possible careers for the one that best fits the shape of one's ideals, aptitudes, and preferences. For such persons, open options may be more a vital need than a luxury. But for others, the accumulation of open-options well beyond necessity or security may be itself a kind of ulterior interest, one of those focal aims[9] whose joint advancement constitutes a person's well-being. For some persons an accumulative interest in liberty may have the same status and footing as the interests others may have in the beauty of their surroundings, or in blooming health beyond mere instrumental utility, or in vast wealth or power.

V

Two points about the interest in liberty should be re-emphasized before we conclude. The first is that the interest in liberty is not derived simply from the prior interests we have in things we may or may not be at liberty to do. The motorcyclist's interest in getting to his job quickly and inexpensively is not the same as his interest in having a choice among alternative ways to get to his job, and the suburban scholar's interest in the peace and quiet of his neighborhood is not the same as his interest in having various alternative places where he might study. When we come to 'weigh' and 'balance' the conflicting interests of the motorcyclist and the scholar, their interests in speed, economy, and quiet will go directly and entirely on the scales, but their respective interests in liberty are only fractionally involved. The person against whose interests the legislature or court decides will still have left a great deal of liberty in other respects even though one of his options, in the case at hand, will be authoritatively closed. The weight to be ascribed to the respective interests in liberty, then, will be only part of the total weight of interests each party puts on the scale, and whether it is greater or lesser than the rival's interest in liberty will depend on their respective degrees of fecundity.[10] Criminal proscriptions sometimes infringe our interest in doing the thing prohibited, though this is not frequently the case, since most of us have no interest in the prohibited conduct to begin with, but the interest in open options is something of quite independent value, and is *always* invaded to some degree by criminalization even when no other actual interest is. That fact has little moral bearing, however, except when the options closed by criminal statutes are relatively fecund, in which case it is a fact of high moral importance.

The second point about the interest in liberty derives from the fact that options can effectively be closed by illicit actions of private individuals as well as by the authoritative decrees of legislators as enforced by the police, the courts, and the prisons. Criminal laws are designed to protect interests, including the interest in having open options, from such private incursions. Contemplating criminal legislation, therefore, always involves appraisals of the 'trade-off' between diminished political liberty and enlarged *de facto* freedom. When the statute is clearly justified by the harm principle, most of us *usually* make a gain in *de facto* freedom that more than compensates us for any loss of liberty to engage in the proscribed conduct.

Since legislators normally have interests other than the interest in liberty in mind when they prohibit or discourage certain kinds of conduct, it is difficult to think of clear examples of criminal statutes that enlarge freedom on balance. The clearest cases, of course, are laws prohibiting false imprisonment, kidnapping, high-jacking, forcible detention, and other direct incursions of the liberty of victims to come and go as they wish. When a person is wrongfully locked in a room, for example, it is as if he were an engine on a siding when the only switch connecting to the main track-network is locked against his entry. The option thus closed is therefore an extremely fecund one. On the other side, no matter how circumstances may have brought the 'false imprisoner's' interest in his own liberty into the situation, that interest will surely not sit on the legislative scales with anywhere near so great a weight, since the option closed by the prohibition against false imprisonment, in all but the most exceptional cases,[11] will not be as fecund as the options protected.

Most criminal prohibitions, however, are designed primarily to protect interests in life and limb, health, property, privacy, and the like, and protect liberty only incidentally. Even these statutes often find some justification in their net enlargement of liberty, though they would be fully justified by the harm principle in any case because of their protection of other interests. The law forbidding rape, for example, while designed to prevent women from psychological trauma and physical harm, and fully justified on those grounds, also protects the interest in liberty to whatever minor extent that interest sits on the scales. That law closes one relatively unfecund option of most adult males while depriving females of no liberty whatever.[12] At the same time it not only protects the interest that all females have in the absence of harmful and offensive bodily contacts (an independent merit that looms much larger than liberty in the law's rationale), it protects various of their relatively fecund open options from forcible closure by private individuals. All females, therefore, gain protection of fecund open options with no sacrifice of any other liberty, while most males suffer the closure of one small limited option − a clear net gain for liberty. Criminal legislation, however, is not always and necessarily so good a trade from the point of view of liberty.[13] And in any case, it is the weights of affected interests other than liberty that are likely to be decisive when interests conflict.

University of Arizona

NOTES

[1] In a forthcoming book I discuss these problems in detail. The problem of *aggregative harms*, as I use the term, arises when specific instances of generally harmful activities (e.g. drinking alcoholic beverages, possessing firearms) are often, or even usually, socially harmless in themselves. Blanket permission leads to an increase of harm in the aggregate, but blanket prohibition would interfere with harmless and beneficial as well as harmful instances of the activity. The middle road, a system of licensure, often has severe difficulties of its own. *Competitive harms* are incurred by competitive interests, those aimed at achieving a certain position relative to others: priority, victory, or ascendance. The persons harmed are losers in structured competitions. The problem of *accumulative harms* is that which stems from the familiar phenomenon where single occurrences of

certain activities are harmless up to a threshold, but general performance of those activities would be harmful. Again, blanket prohibitions would necessarily ban harmless and beneficial, as well as harmful, actions.

2 Nicholas Rescher, *Welfare, The Social Issue in Philosophical Perspective* (Pittsburgh: The University of Pittsburgh Press), p. 6.

3 *Ibid.*, p. 5.

4 Much of the material in this paragraph is drawn from my essay, 'Limits to the Free Expression of Opinion', in J. Feinberg and H. Gross (eds.), *Philosophy of Law* (Encino, CA: Dickenson Publishing Co., 1975), pp. 141–42.

5 Isaiah Berlin, 'Two Concepts of Liberty'. in *Four Essays on Liberty* (London: Oxford University Press, 1969), p. 130 n.

6 *Loc. cit.*

7 I discuss these rival theories in a not altogether satisfactory fashion in 'The Idea of a Free Man', in James F. Doyle, ed., *Educational Judgments* (London: Routledge & Kegan Paul, 1973), pp. 149–151, and in *Social Philosophy* (Englewood Cliffs, N.J.: Prentice-Hall, 1973), pp. 5–7 and 18–19.

8 Berlin, *op. cit.*, p. 130. I think that this passage in a long footnote is an aberration from arguments in the main text with which I am largely in agreement.

9 This term is from C.L. Stevenson, *Ethics and Language* (New Haven: Yale University Press, 1944), p. 203. Stevenson's formal definition is as follows: "an end which is also such an exceptionally important means to so many divergent ends that if anything else is not, in its turn, a means to this, it will be without predominating value." Since a person may have more than one focal aim, the definition should be amended as follows: ". . . if anything else is not a means to this, *or to another focal aim*, it will be without predominating value."

10 Strictly speaking, the conflicting interests are: one party's interest in a specific open option and another party's interest in another specific open option. These are 'interests in liberty' only in the sense that they are interests in the 'liberty category,' as opposed, for example, to the 'life,' 'property,' or 'privacy' categories. Fecundity is a property, strictly speaking, of the options themselves, not of the interests.

11 In many of these 'most exceptional cases,' the party who is tempted to capture, detain, kidnap, or highjack, is driven to such desperate means by threats to his own fecund liberties that are ultimately of his own making, or the consequences of his own wrongdoing, e.g. his need to escape arrest and eventual incarceration for some earlier crime. In some other very exceptional cases, the detainer may have the justification of 'necessity' or forced choice of the lesser evil, as when one 'borrows' another's automobile in an emergency leaving the owner at least temporarily stranded and immobile. The 'lesser evil' in this case could be an infringement of a less fecund liberty.

12 Except insofar as a woman is legally capable of committing rape herself as an accomplice to the main perpetrator who must, legally speaking, be male. This is a trivial qualification of the point in the text, and deserves at most a footnote.

13 Consider, for example, mandatory curfew laws, ordinances forbidding minors from purchasing alcoholic beverages or from lingering in places where they are sold, statutes prohibiting the sale of obscene books or the showing, even to audiences of willing and eager adults, of pornographic films. If such laws are justified, it is because they protect interests other than the interest in liberty, for they open nowhere near as many or as fecund options as they close.

W.V. QUINE

ON THE NATURE OF MORAL VALUES

Imagine a dog idling in the foreground, a tree in the middle distance, and a turnip lying on the ground behind the tree. Either of two hypotheses, or a combination of them, may be advanced to explain the dog's inaction with respect to the turnip: perhaps he is not aware that it is there, and perhaps he does not want a turnip. Such is the bipartite nature of motivation: belief and valuation intertwined. It is the deep old duality of thought and feeling, of the head and the heart, the cortex and the thalamus, the words and the music.

The duality can be traced back to the simplest conditioning of responses. A response was rewarded when it followed stimulus a, and penalized when it followed b; and thereafter it tended to be elicited by just those stimulations that were more similar to a than to b according to the subject's inarticulate standards of similarity. Observe then the duality of belief and valuation: the similarity standards are the epistemic component of habit formation, in its primordial form, and the reward-penalty axis is the valuative component.

The term 'belief' of course ill fits this primitive level. Even the term 'similarity standard' requires a word of caution: such implicit standards of similarity are ascribed to the subject only on the behavioral basis of the experiments themselves, experiments in the reinforcement and extinction of his responses. The experiments afford at the same time a criterion for comparing the subject's implicit values, along the reward-penalty axis. His values are easier to plot, however, than his similarities. They are largely recognizable from innate reflexes, such as wincing, even without the recourse to experiments in reinforcement and extinction. Moreover, they stand in the simple dyadic relation of better and worse, whereas similarity is at least triadic: a is more similar to b than to c. The evaluations thus line up in a single dimension, while the similarities may be expected to require more dimensions.

Clearly all learning, all acquisition of dispositions to discriminatory behavior, requires in the subject this bipartite equipment: it requires a similarity space and it requires some ordering of episodes along the valuation axis, however crude. Some such equipment, then, must precede all learning; that is, it must be innate. There need be no question here of awareness, nor of ideas, innate or otherwise. It is a matter rather of physiological details of our complex and incontestably innate nervous system, which determine our

37

A. I. Goldman and J. Kim (eds.), Values and Morals, 37–45. All Rights Reserved.
Copyright © 1978 by D. Reidel Publishing Company, Dordrecht, Holland.

susceptibilities to the reinforcement and extinction of responses. Those details are perhaps not yet fully understood, but we need know little to be assured that what is required for all learning must not have been learned.

Our innate similarity space is our modest head start on the epistemic side, for it is the starting point for induction. Induction consists, primitively, in the expectation that similar episodes will have similar sequels; and the similarity concerned is similarity by our subjective lights. In our innate likes and dislikes we have our modest head start on the valuative side, and then induction is our guide to worthwhile acts. I find it instructive to dignify the lowly neural phenomenon of reinforcement and extinction in these subjectivist terms, for it represents that neural phenomenon as technology in the small: the use of inductive science for realizing values.

Our similarity space is progressively changed and elaborated as our learning proceeds. Similarity standards that led to bad predictions get readjusted by trial and error. Our inductions become increasingly explicit and deliberate, and in the fullness of time we even rise above induction, to the hypothetico-deductive method.

Likewise our ordering of sensory episodes along the valuation axis is progressively changed and elaborated. In some cases an epistemic factor contributes to the change. We learn by induction that one sort of event tends to lead to another that we prize, and then by a process of transfer we may come to prize the former not only as a means but for itself. We come to relish the sport of fishing as much as we relish the fresh trout to which it was a means. Values get shifted also in other ways — perhaps something to do with chemistry, in the case of the acquired taste for strong peppers or anchovies. Or in more baffling ways, if one moves on to Schönberg or Jackson Pollock.

The transmutation of means into ends, just now illustrated by fishing, is what underlies moral training. Many sorts of good behavior have a low initial rating on the valuation scale, and are indulged in at first only for their inductive links to higher ends: to pleasant consequences or the avoidance of unpleasant ones at the preceptor's hands. Good behavior, insofar, is technology. But by association of means with ends we come gradually to accord this behavior a higher intrinsic rating. We find satisfaction in engaging in it and we come to encourage it in others. Our moral training has succeeded. There are exceptions to this pattern of development, I regret to say, but happily not among my readers.

The penalties and rewards by which the good behavior was inculcated may have included slaps and sugar plums. However, mere show of approval and disapproval on the parent's part will go a long way. It seems that such bland manifestations can directly induce pleasure and discomfort already in the very young. Perhaps some original source of sensual satisfaction, such as a caress, comes to be associated very early with the other more subtle signs of parental approval, which then come to be prized in themselves.

The distinction between moral values and others is not an easy one. There are easy extremes: the value that one places on his neighbor's welfare is moral, and the value of peanut brittle is not. The value of decency in speech and dress is moral or ethical in the etymological sense, resting as it does on social custom; and similarly for observance of the Jewish dietary laws. On the other hand the eschewing of unrefrigerated oysters in the summer, though it is likewise a renunciation of immediate fleshly pleasure, is a case rather of prudence than morality. But presumably the Jewish taboos themselves began prudentially. Again a Christian fundamentalist who observes the proprieties and helps his neighbor only from fear of hell-fire is manifesting prudence rather than moral values.[1] Similarly for the man with felony in his heart who behaves himself for fear of the law. Similarly for the child who behaves himself in the course of moral training; his behavior counts as moral only after these means get transmuted into ends. On the other hand the value that the child attaches to the parent's approval is a moral value. It had been a mere harbinger of a sensually gratifying caress, if my recent suggestion is right, but has been transmuted into an end in itself.

It is hard to pick out a single distinguishing feature of moral values, beyond the vague matter of being somehow irreducibly social. We do better to recognize two largely overlapping classes of moral values. *Altruistic* values are values that one attaches to satisfactions of other persons, or to means to such satisfactions, without regard to ulterior satisfactions accruing to oneself. *Ceremonial* values, as we might say, are values that one attaches to practices of one's society or social group, again without regard to ulterior satisfactions accruing to oneself. Definitions appealing explicitly to behavioral dispositions rather than thus to hidden motivations would be desirable, but meanwhile a vague sketch such as this can be of some help if we do not overestimate it.

It is clear from the foregoing examples of prudential taboos, hell-fire, repressed felony, and child training, that two members of a society may value an act equally and yet the value may be moral for the one and prudential for the other. But we like to speak also of the moral values or moral code or morality of a society as a whole. In so doing we may perhaps be taken to mean those values that are implemented by social sanctions, plus any further values that are moral values for most of the members individually.

I follow Schlick in placing the moral values in among the sensual and aesthetic values on an equal footing.[2] Some non-moral values, for instance that of fishing, are subject to transmutation of means into ends, and some are innate, and some accrue in other ways. But so it is in particular with moral values: some accrue by transmutation of means into ends, through training, and some perhaps require no training.

Schlick, like Hume, set great store by sympathy: by the pleasure and sorrow that are induced by witnessing others' pleasure and sorrow. We have these susceptibilities, he believed, without training. If they are somehow gene-linked, it would be interesting to understand the mechanism. This would then account also for the previous point, the infant's early responsiveness to signs of parental approval and disapproval, as a special case.

Tinbergen in his study of herring gulls determined what simple configurations on paper served to rouse the chick to an expectant attitude, as if toward its mother, and what simple configurations would arouse a complementary attitude in the hen.[3] He noted a human analogue in the simple formula for 'cuteness': fat cheek, big eye, negligible nose. Disney knew how to induce audible female cooing in the movie theatre with a few strokes of the pen. The herring gull's response is instinctive; must ours, in this case, be otherwise? Again the rabbit that squeals from between the wolf's jaws is making an instinctive response that is altruistic in a functional sense; for the squeal does not deter the wolf, but it warns other rabbits. Hereditary altruism at its heroic extreme raises a genetic question, if the young martyr is not to live to transmit his altruistic genes; but biologists have proposed an answer. Altruism is mainly directed to close kin, and they transmit largely the same genes.

I represented our moral values as falling into two overlapping classes, the altruistic and the ceremonial. The classes overlap in two ways. Altruistic values are in part institutionalized and so may take on an added ceremonial appeal. Conversely, there is altruistic value in so behaving as not to offend against a neighbor's ceremonial values.

There is also a cross-classification, imposed by considerations of origin. Some values, in the altruistic category, perhaps issue freely from an innate faculty of sympathy, unless this class is empty and sympathy is an acquired taste. Some, in the ceremonial category, are embraced out of sentiments of solidarity; thus the dietary observances in some cases, and the old school tie. The basis here is perhaps sympathy still, in an attenuated way. Further, in any event, there are both altruistic and ceremonial values that are inculcated by precept, unsupported still by palpable reward or punishment. This is already a case of training in its mild way, a case of transmutation of means into ends; the good behavior is indulged in at first as a means to the non-moral though ethereal end of parental or social approval, and only afterward comes to be valued as an end in itself. Finally, there is moral training by recourse to palpable reward or punishment over and above parental or social attitude. Few of us are of such saintly docility as to need no training of this earthier kind. But in due course, here again, means get transmuted into ends, and conscience is further fortified.

I remarked that this account places the moral values in among the sensual and aesthetic ones. By the same token it represents each of us as pursuing exclusively his own private satisfactions. Thanks to the moral values that have been trained into us, however, plus any innate moral beginnings that there may have been, there is no clash of interests as we pursue our separate ways. Our scales of values blend in social harmony.

I am using the first-person plural rather narrowly here, to include my readers and myself but not as many further persons as I could wish. There are those — I mention no names — whose moral training has been neglected or has not proved feasible. Their ordering of values has remained in such a state that these persons stand to maximize their satisfactions by battening on our good behavior while cheating on their own. Society accommodates such misfits by introducing penalties to offset the imbalance in their values.

The moral values tend by virtue of their social character to be more uniform from person to person, within a culture, than many sensual and aesthetic values. Hence the tendency with regard to the latter to allow that *de gustibus non disputandum est*, while ascribing absoluteness and even divine origin to the moral law.

Hypotheses less extravagant than that of divine origin account well enough for such uniformity as obtains among moral values, even apart from possible innate components. It is merely that these values are passed down the generations, imposed by word of mouth, by birch rod and sugar plum, by acclaim and ostracism, fine, imprisonment. They are imposed by society because they matter to society, whereas aesthetic preferences may be left to go their way.

Language, like the moral law, was once thought to be God-given. The two have much in common. Both are institutions for the common good. They reflect, somewhat, the primitive duality of belief and valuation on which I remarked at the beginning. Language promotes the individual's inductions by giving him access to his neighbor's observations and even to his neighbor's finished inductions. It also helps him influence his neighbor's actions, but it does this mainly, still, by conveying factual information. On the other hand the moral law of a society, if successful, coordinates the actual scales of values of the individuals in such a way as to resolve incompatibilities and thus promote their overall satisfaction.

In language there is a premium on uniformity of usage, to facilitate communication. In morality there is a premium on uniformity of moral values, so that we may count on one another's actions and rise in a body against a transgressor. In language as in morality the uniformity is achieved by instruction, each generation teaching the next. In the case of language there is less recourse to birch rod and sugar plum, because the rewards of conformity are built in. In morals, private deviations such as theft can augment one's satisfactions unless one's values have been rearranged by moral training or offset by external sanctions; but in language, private deviation directly defeats one's own immediate purpose by obscuring one's message. There is, however, an exception: lying is a deviation in verbal behavior that can work to one's private advantage. The utility of language for each of us hinges on a predominance of truthfulness on the part of others, but any of us can enjoy that advantage and lie a little too, to his private profit. Thus it is that the liar invites the reproaches not of the orthoëpist but of the moralist. Moral values need to be instilled into him that will offset the values served by lying. Failing that, we may incapacitate his future lies by spreading warnings.

For the usefulness of a language it is required that most speakers associate the same expression with the same sort of object, but it does not matter how the expression sounds as long as all members of the society make it sound about alike. An expression to the same purpose in another language can therefore differ utterly and it will not matter, if the two societies do not seek to communicate. Language thus tends to extreme uniformity within isolated societies and chaotic diversity between them. We see linguistic gradation in the world, but only because of gradations in the intimacy of communication.

Moral values may be expected to vary less radically than language from one society to another, even when the societies are isolated. True, there are societies whose bans and licenses boggle our sheltered imaginations. But we can expect a common core, since the most basic problems of societies are bound to run to type. Morality touches the common lot of mankind as the particularities of sound and syntax do not. Where language touches the common lot is rather in the intelligence and influence that the sounds and syntax serve to convey. Thus any variation of morality from culture to culture invites comparison perhaps with the variation of world view or scientific outlook from culture to culture, but certainly not with the extravagant variation of language.

When we set about comparing moralities from culture to culture, assessing variations and seeking the common core, we may begin by considering how to separate the native's moral values from his other values. How much of what he does or refrains from doing is attributable to mistaken notions of causal efficacy on his part, and accountable therefore to misguided prudence rather than to moral scruples? He may believe in so full a complement of super-natural sanctions as to leave no scope for moral values as distinct from prudential ones. In this event we can do no better than recur to our derivative concept of the morality of a society, as distinct from that of an individual. The question then becomes that of determining what behavior is imple-mented by socially established rewards and penalties. This standard will fail us too, however, if the society is so successfully indoctrinated regard-ing supernatural sanctions that no social enforcement is called for. At this point the most we can do is compare the native's acts with ours in situations where ours qualify as moral acts by our own lights. We will observe whether he respects property, and, if he does not, whether he seems worried and furtive in taking it. We will observe whether he kills harmless creatures without meaning to eat them. We will try to observe whether he is promiscu-ous in his love life, and, if so, whether he is furtive about that. We can observe his behavior, when he lets us, and we can applaud or reprehend it in our way.

Moral contrasts are not, of course, so far to seek. Disagreements on moral matters can arise at home, and even within oneself. When they do, one regrets the methodological infirmity of ethics as compared with science. The empiri-cal foothold of scientific theory is in the predicted observable event; that of a moral code is in the observable moral act. But whereas we can test a pre-diction against the independent course of observable nature, we can judge the morality of an act only by our moral standards themselves. Science, thanks to its links with observation, retains some title to a correspondence theory of truth; but a coherence theory is evidently the lot of ethics.

Scientific theories on all sorts of useful and useless topics are sustained by empirical controls, partial and devious though they be. It is a bitter irony that so vital a matter as the difference between good and evil should have no comparable claim to objectivity. No wonder there have been efforts since earliest times to work a justification of moral values into the fabric of what might pass for factual science. For such, surely, were the myths of divine origins of moral law.

There is a legitimate mixture of ethics with science that somewhat mitigates the methodological predicament of ethics. Anyone who is involved in moral issues relies on causal connections. Ethical axioms can be minimized by reducing some values causally to others; that is, by showing that some of the valued acts would already count as valuable anyway as means to ulterior ends. Utilitarianism is a notable example of such systematization.

Causal reduction can serve not only in thus condensing the assumptions but also in sorting out conflicts. Thus take the question of white lies. If we once agree to regard truthfulness as good only as a means to higher moral ends, rather than as an ultimate end in itself, then the question becomes a question essentially of science, or engineering. On the one hand, the utility of language requires a preponderance of truthfulness; on the other hand the truth can cause pain. So one may try to puzzle out a strategy.

Causal reduction is often effective in resolving moral conflicts not only within the individual but between individuals. One individual disputes another's position on some point of morals. The other individual tries to justify his position instrumentally, hence by causal reduction to some ulterior end which they both value. The first individual is then either persuaded or proceeds to contest the causal reduction, in which case the issue has been gratefully transformed into a cognitive question of science. This way of resolving moral issues is successful to the extent that we can reduce moral values causally to other moral values that command agreement. There must remain some ultimate ends, unreduced and so unjustified. Happily these, once identified, would tend to be widely accepted. For we may expect a tendency to uniformity in the hereditary component of morality, whatever it may be, and also, since the basic problems of societies are much alike, we may expect considerable agreement in the socially imposed component when it is reduced to fundamentals.

Even in the extreme case where disagreement extends irreducibly to ultimate moral ends, the proper counsel is not one of pluralistic tolerance. One's disapproval of gratuitous torture, for example, easily withstands one's failure to make a causal reduction, and so be it. We can still call the good good and the bad bad, and hope with Stevenson that these epithets may work their emotive weal. In an extremity we can fight, if the threat to the ultimate value in question outweighs the disvalue of the fighting.

There remains the awkward matter of a conflict of ultimate values within the individual. It could have to do with the choice of a career, or mate, or vacation spot. The predicament in such a non-moral case will concern only the individual and a few associates. When the ultimate values concerned are moral ones, on the other hand, and more particularly altruistic ones, the case is different; for the individual in such a dilemma has all society on his conscience.

The basic difficulty is that the altruistic values that we acquire by social conditioning and perhaps by heredity are vague and open-ended. Primitively the premium is on kin, and primitively therefore the tribe in its isolation affords a bold boundary between the beneficiaries of one's altruism and the alien world. Nowadays the boundary has given way to gradations. Moreover, we are prone to extrapolate; extrapolation was always intrinsic to induction, that primitive propensity that is at the root of all science. Extrapolation in science, however, is under the welcome restraint of stubborn fact: failures of prediction. Extrapolation in morals has only our unsettled moral values themselves to answer to, and it is these that the extrapolation was meant to settle.

Today we unhesitatingly extrapolate our altruism beyond our close community. Most of us extend it to all mankind. But to what degree? One cannot reasonably be called upon to love even one's neighbor *quite* as oneself. Is love to diminish inversely as the square of the distance? Is it to extend, in some degree, to the interests of individuals belonging to other species than own? As regards capricious killing, one hopes so; but what of vivisection, and of the eating of red meat?

One thinks also of unborn generations. Insofar as our moral standards were shaped by evolution for fostering the survival of the race, a concern for the unborn was assured. One then proceeds, however, as one will, to systematize and minimize one's ethical axioms by reducing some causally to others. This effort at system-building leads to the formulation and scrutiny of principles, and one is then taken aback by the seeming absurdity of respecting the interests of non-existent people: of unactualized possibilities. This counter-revolutionary bit of moral rationalization is welcome as it touches population control, since the blind drive to mass procreation is now so counter-productive. But the gratification is short-lived, for the same rationalization would seem to condone a despoiling of the environment for the exclusive convenience of people now living.

It need not. A formulation is ready to hand which sustains the moral values that favor limiting the population while still safeguarding the environment. Namely, it is a matter of respecting the future interests of people now unborn, but only of future actual people. We recognize no present unactualized possibilities.

Thus we do what we can with our ultimate values, but we have to deplore the irreparable lack of the empirical check points that are the solace of the scientist. Loose ends are untidy at best, and disturbingly so when the ultimate good is at stake.

Harvard University

NOTES

[1] Bernard Williams, *Morality* (New York: Harper, 1972), pp. 75f, questions the disjointness of these alternatives. I am construing them disjointly.
[2] Moritz Schlick, *Fragen der Ethik,* (Vienna, 1930).
[3] Nikolaas Tinbergen, *The Herring Gull's World,* (London: Collins, 1953).

JOHN RAWLS

THE BASIC STRUCTURE AS SUBJECT*

I

An essential feature of the contractarian conception of justice is that the basic structure of society is the first subject of justice. The contract view begins by trying to work out a theory of justice for this special but plainly very important case; and the conception of justice that results has a certain regulative primacy with respect to the principles and standards appropriate for other cases. The basic structure is understood as the way in which the major social institutions fit together into one system, and how they assign fundamental rights and duties and shape the division of advantages that arises through social cooperation. Thus the political constitution, the legally recognized forms of property, and the organization of the economy, and the nature of the family, all belong to the basic structure. The initial objective of the theory is to find a conception, the first principles of which provide reasonable guidelines for the classical and familiar questions of social justice in connection with this complex of institutions. These questions define the data, so to speak, for which the theory seeks an account. There is no attempt to formulate first principles that apply equally to all subjects. Rather, on this view, a theory must develop principles for the relevant subjects step by step in some appropriate sequence.

In this essay I should like to discuss why the basic structure is taken as the first subject of justice. Of course, it is perfectly legitimate to restrict the initial inquiry to the basic structure. We must begin somewhere, and this starting point may turn out to be justified by how well the theory that results hangs together. But there should be a more illuminating answer than this; and moreover one that draws upon the special features of the basic structure in contrast with other social arrangements, and connects these features with the characteristic role and content of the principles of justice themselves. I hope to give an answer that does precisely this.[1]

Now a social contract is a hypothetical agreement (1) between all rather than some members of society, and it is (2) between them as members of society (as citizens) and not as individuals who hold some particular position or role within it. In the Kantian form of this doctrine, which I shall call

47

A. I. Goldman and J. Kim (eds.), Values and Morals, 47–71. All Rights Reserved.

justice as fairness, (3) the parties are thought of as free and equal moral persons; and (4) the content of the agreement is the first principles that are to regulate the basic structure. We take as given a short list of conceptions of justice found in the tradition of moral philosophy and then ask which of these conceptions the parties would agree to when the alternatives are thus restricted. Assuming that we have a clear enough idea of the circumstances necessary to insure that any agreement reached is fair, the content of justice for the basic structure can be ascertained, or at least approximated, by the principles that would be adopted. (Of course, this presupposes the reasonableness of the tradition of moral philosophy; but where else can we start?) Thus pure procedural justice is invoked at the highest level: the fairness of the circumstances transfers to fairness of the principles acknowledged.

I shall suggest the following: first, that once we think of the parties to a social contract as free and equal (and rational) moral persons, then there are strong reasons for taking the basic structure as the primary subject (Secs. IV–V). Second, that in view of the distinctive features of this structure, the initial agreement, and the conditions under which it is made, must be understood in a special way that distinguishes this agreement from all others (Secs. VI–VII); and third, doing this allows a Kantian view to take account of the profoundly social nature of human relationships. And finally, that while a large element of pure procedural justice transfers to the principles of justice, these principles must nevertheless embody an ideal form for the basic structure in the light of which ongoing institutional processes are to be constrained and the accumulated results of individual transactions continually adjusted (Sec. IX).

II

Before taking up these points, I should like to remark that starting with the basic structure and then developing other principles sequentially, gives justice as fairness a distinctive character.[2]

To illustrate this, consider first the contrast with utilitarianism: it is usually interpreted as a completely general theory. Certainly this is true of the classical doctrine as definitively formulated by Sidgwick.[3] The principle of utility applies equally to all social forms and to the actions of individuals; in addition, the assessment of character and dispositional traits, as well as the social practice of praising and blaming, are to be guided by it. To be sure, rule-utilitarianism recognizes that certain distinctions between subjects may raise special problems. But the distinction between rules and acts, besides being itself very general, is a categorial or metaphysical distinction, and not one within the class of social forms. It evokes the question of how the principle of utility is to be applied across category differences; and the general way in which this question is treated by rule-utilitarianism preserves the contrast with the contract view.

Of course, utilitarian theory recognizes the peculiarities of different kinds of cases, but these peculiarities are treated as springing from various kinds of effects and causal relationships that have to be allowed for. Thus it is agreed, let's suppose, that the basic structure is an important complex of institutions, given the deep and pervasive nature of its social and psychological effects. It might be agreed also that it is useful to distinguish this structure from particular associations within it, as well as from the larger surrounding international system. These distinctions may be helpful in a systematic application of the standard of utility. In no case, however, is there a change of first principle, although, of course, a variety of secondary norms and precepts, derivative from utility, may be justified in view of the characteristic features of different problems. Thus, for utilitarianism, neither the number of individuals concerned, nor the institutional forms by which their decisions and activities are organized, affect the universal scope of the principle of utility: number and structure are relevant only indirectly through their effects on how the greatest net balance of satisfaction (summed over all persons affected) is most effectively attained.

The first principles of justice as fairness are plainly not suitable for a general theory.[4] These principles require (as stated below, first par. of Sec. VI) that the basic structure establish certain equal basic liberties for all and make sure that social and economic inequalities work for the greatest benefit of the least advantaged against a background of fair opportunity. In many if not most cases these principles give unreasonable directives. To illustrate: for churches and universities different principles are plainly more suitable. Their members usually affirm certain shared aims and purposes as essential guidelines to the most appropriate form of organization. The most we can say is this: because churches and universities are associations within the basic structure, they must adjust to the requirements that this structure imposes in order to establish background justice. Thus, churches and universities may be restricted in various ways, for example, by what is necessary to maintain the basic equal liberties (including liberty of conscience) and fair equality of opportunity.

At first sight the contract doctrine may appear hopelessly unsystematic: for how are the principles that apply to different subjects to be tied together?

But there are other forms of theoretical unity than that defined by completely general first principles. It may be possible to find an appropriate sequence of kinds of subjects and to suppose that the parties to a social contract are to proceed through this sequence with the understanding that the principles of each later agreement are to be subordinate to those of all earlier agreements, or else adjusted to them by certain priority rules. The underlying unity is provided by the idea that free and equal moral persons are to construct reasonable and helpful guidelines for moral reflection in view of their need for such organizing principles and the role in social life that these principles and their corresponding subjects are presumed to have.

It should be noted here, to avoid misunderstanding, that in developing a conception of justice for the basic structure, or indeed for any subject, we do not assume that variation in numbers alone accounts for the appropriateness of different principles. Rather, it is differences in the structure and social role of institutions that is essential, although variations in number are sometimes a necessary condition, and encourage certain institutional forms. Thus a constitutional democracy is larger than a family: greater numbers are required to staff its component parts. But it is the distinct purposes and roles of the parts of the social structure, and how they fit together, that explains there being different principles for distinct kinds of subjects. Indeed, it seems natural to suppose that the distinctive character and autonomy of the various elements of society requires that, within some sphere, they act from their own principles designed to fit their peculiar nature.

III

A completely general theory like utilitarianism is not the only kind of view that rejects the idea that special first principles are required for the basic structure. Consider for example the libertarian theory, which holds that only a minimal state limited to the narrow functions of protection against force, theft, fraud, enforcement of contracts, and so on, is justified; and that any state with more comprehensive powers violates the rights of individuals. For our purposes here, perhaps the main features of this theory are these:[5]

The aim is to see how the minimal state could have arisen from a perfectly just situation by a series of steps each of which is morally permissible and violates no one's rights. If we can see how this could happen when everyone acts as they ought and why a no more extensive state could arise, then we shall have justified the minimal state, provided of course that the moral theory that identifies the initial situation as just, and defines the permissible departures from it, is correct. To this end, we assume that a state of nature once existed in which there was relative abundance and the actual configuration of people's holdings raised no moral questions. The existing configuration was just and all were adequately provided for. This state of nature is also characterized by the absence of any institution (such as the state) that enforces certain rules and thereby establishes an institutional basis for people's expectations as to how others will act.

Next, a libertarian theory defines certain basic principles of justice that govern the acquisition of holdings (the appropriation of previously unheld things) and the transfer of holdings from one person (or association) to another. Then a just configuration of holdings is defined recursively: a person is entitled to hold whatever is acquired in accordance with the principles of justice in acquisition and transfer, and no one is entitled to something except by repeated application of these principles. If one starts from a state of nature in which the existing array of holdings is just, and if everyone always acts subsequently in accordance with justice in acquisition and transfer, then all later configurations are likewise said to be just. It is maintained that the principles of just acquisition and transfer preserve the justice of holdings throughout the whole sequence of historical transactions, however extended in time. They only way injustice is thought to arise is from deliberate violations of these principles, or from error and ignorance of what they require and the like.

Finally, and most relevant for our purposes here, a great variety of associations and modes of cooperation may form depending upon what individuals actually do and what agreements are reached. No special theory is needed to cover these transactions and joint activities: the requisite theory is already provided by the principles of justice in acquisition and transfer, suitably interpreted in the light of certain provisos. All forms of legitimate social cooperation are, then, the handiwork of individuals who voluntarily consent to them; there are no powers or rights lawfully exercised by associations, including the state, that are not rights already possessed by each individual acting alone in the initial just state of nature.

One noteworthy feature of this doctrine is that the state is just like any other private association. The state comes about in the same way as other associations and its formation in the perfectly as-if just historical process is governed by the same principles.[6] Of course, the state serves certain characteristic purposes, but this is true of associations generally. Moreover, the relation of individuals to the state (the legitimate minimal state) is just like their relation with any private corporation with which they have made an agreement. Thus political allegiance is interpreted as a private contractual obligation with, so to speak, a large and successful monopolistic firm: namely, the locally dominant protection agency. There is in general no uniform public law that applies equally to all persons, but rather a net-work of private agreements; this net-work represents the procedures the dominant protection agency (the state) has agreed to use with its clients, as it were, and these procedures may differ from client to client depending on the bargain each was in a position to make with the dominant agency. No one can be compelled to enter into such an agreement and everyone always has the option of becoming an independent: we have the choice of being one of the state's clients, just as we do in the case of other associations. While the libertarian view makes important use of the notion of agreement, it is not a *social* contract theory at all; for a social contract theory envisages the original compact as establishing a system of common public law which defines and regulates political authority and applies to everyone as citizen. Both political authority and citizenship are to be understood through the conception of the social contract itself. By viewing the state as a private association the libertarian doctrine rejects the fundamental ideas of the contract theory, and so quite naturally it has no place for a special theory of justice for the basic structure.

By way of concluding these preliminary matters, the point of noting these differences with libertarian and utilitarian doctrines is to clarify by illustration and contrast the peculiar features of justice as fairness with its emphasis on the basic structure. Similar contrasts hold in regard to perfectionism and intuitionism and other familiar moral views. The problem here is to show why the basic structure has a special role and why it is reasonable to seek special principles to regulate it.

IV

I shall begin by noting several considerations that might lead us to regard the basic structure as the first subject of justice, at least when we proceed within the framework of a Kantian social contract theory.

The first consideration is this: suppose we begin with the initially attractive idea that social circumstances and people's relationships to one another should develop over time in accordance with free agreements fairly arrived at and fully honored. Straightaway we need an account of when agreements are free and the social circumstances under which they are reached are fair. In addition, while these conditions may be fair at an earlier time, the accumulated results of many separate and ostensibly fair agreements, together with social trends and historical contingencies, are likely in the course of time to alter citizens' relationships and opportunities so that the conditions for free and fair agreements no longer hold. The role of the institutions that belong to the basic structure is to secure just background conditions against which the actions of individuals and associations take place. Unless this structure is appropriately regulated and adjusted, an initially just social process will eventually cease to be just, however free and fair particular transactions may look when viewed by themselves.

We recognize this fact when we say, for example, that the distribution resulting from voluntary market transactions (even if all the ideal conditions for competitive efficiency obtain) is not, in general, fair unless the antecedent distribution of income and wealth, as well as the structure of the system of markets, is fair. The existing wealth must have been properly acquired and all must have had fair opportunities to earn income, to learn wanted skills, and so on. Again, the conditions necessary for background justice can be undermined, even though nobody acts unfairly or is aware of how the overall result of many separate exchanges affects the opportunities of others. There are no feasible rules that it is practicable to require economic agents to follow in their day-to-day transactions that can prevent these undesirable consequences. These consequences are often so far in the future, or so indirect, that the attempt to forestall them by restrictive rules that apply to individuals would be an excessive if not an impossible burden.

There are four points to emphasize in these familiar observations: First, we cannot tell by looking only at the conduct of individuals and associations in the immediate (or local) circumstances whether, from a social point of view, agreements reached are just or fair. For this assessment depends importantly on the features of the basic structure, on whether it succeeds in maintaining background justice. Thus whether wage agreements are fair rests, for example, on the nature of the labor market: excess market power must be prevented and fair bargaining power should obtain between employers and employees. But in addition, fairness depends on underlying social conditions, such as fair opportunity, extending backwards in time and well beyond any limited view.

Second, fair background conditions may exist at one time and be gradually undermined even though no one acts unfairly when their conduct is judged by the rules that apply to transactions within the appropriately circumscribed local situation. The fact that everyone with reason believes that they are acting fairly and scrupulously honoring the norms governing agreements is not sufficient to preserve background justice. This is an important though obvious point: when our social world is pervaded by duplicity and deceit we are tempted to think that law and government are necessary only because of the propensity of individuals to act unfairly. But, to the contrary, the tendency is rather for background justice to be eroded even when individuals act fairly: the overall result of separate and independent transactions is away from and not towards background justice. We might say: in this case the invisible hand guides things in the wrong direction and favors an oligopolistic configuration of accumulations that succeeds in maintaining unjustified equalities and restrictions on fair opportunity. Therefore, we require special institutions to preserve background justice, and a special conception of justice to define how these institutions are to be set up.

The preceding observation assumes, thirdly, that there are no feasible and practicable rules that it is sensible to impose on individuals that can prevent the erosion of background justice. This is because the rules governing agreements and individual transactions cannot be too complex, or require too much information to be correctly applied; nor should they enjoin individuals to engage in bargaining with many widely scattered third parties, since this would impose excessive transaction costs. The rules applying to agreements are, after all, practical and public directives, and not mathematical functions which may be as complicated as one can imagine. Thus any sensible scheme of rules will not exceed the capacity of individuals to grasp and follow them with sufficient ease, nor will it burden citizens with requirements of knowledge and foresight that they cannot normally meet. Individuals and associations cannot comprehend the ramifications of their particular actions viewed collectively, nor can they be expected to foresee future circumstances that shape and transform present tendencies. All of this is evident enough if we consider the cumulative effects of the purchase and sale of landed property and its transmission by bequest over generations. It is obviously not sensible to impose on parents (as heads of families) the duty to adjust their own bequests to what they estimate the effects of the totality of actual bequests will be on the next generation, much less beyond.

Thus, fourth and finally, we arrive at the idea of a division of labor between two kinds of social rules, and the different institutional forms in which these rules are realized. The basic structure comprises first the institutions that define the social background and includes as well those operations that continually adjust and compensate for the inevitable tendencies away from background fairness, for example, such operations as income and inheritance taxation designed to even out the ownership of property. This structure also enforces through the legal system another set of rules that govern the transactions and agreements between individuals and associations (the law of contract, and so on). The rules relating to fraud and duress, and the like, belong to these rules, and satisfy the requirements of simplicity and practicality. They are framed to leave individuals and associations free to act effectively in pursuit of their ends and without excessive constraints.

To conclude: we start with the basic structure and try to see how this structure itself should make the adjustments necessary to preserve background justice. What we look for, in effect, is an institutional division of labor between the basic structure and the rules applying directly to individuals and associations and to be followed by them in particular transactions. If this division of labor can be established, individuals and associations are then left free to advance their ends more effectively within the framework of the basic structure, secure in the knowledge that elsewhere in the social system the necessary corrections to preserve background justice are being made.

V

Further reflections also point to the special role of the basic structure. So far we have seen that certain background conditions are necessary if transactions between individuals are to be fair: these conditions characterize the objective situation of individuals vis-a-vis one another. But what about the character and interests of individuals themselves? These are not fixed or given. A theory of justice must take into account how the aims and aspirations of people are formed; and doing this belong to the wider framework of thought in the light of which a conception of justice is to be explained.

Now everyone recognizes that the institutional form of society affects its members and determines in large part the kind of persons they want to be as well as the kind of persons they are. The social structure also limits peoples' ambitions and hopes in different ways; for they will with reason view themselves in part according to their position in it and take account of the means and opportunities they can realistically expect. So an economic regime, say, is not only an institutional scheme for satisfying existing desires and aspirations but a way of fashioning desires and aspirations in the future. More generally, the basic structure shapes the way the social system produces and reproduces over time a certain form of culture shared by persons with certain conceptions of their good.

Again, we cannot view the talents and abilities of individuals as fixed natural gifts. To be sure, even as realized there is presumably a significant genetic component. However, these abilities and talents cannot come to fruition apart from social conditions, and as realized they always take but one of many possible forms. Developed natural capacities are always a selection, and a small selection at that, from the possibilities that might have been attained. In addition, an ability is not, for example, a computer in the head with a definite measurable capacity unaffected by social circumstances. Among the elements affecting the realization of natural capacities are social attitudes of encouragement and support and the institutions concerned with their training and use. Thus even a potential ability at any given time is not something unaffected by existing social forms and particular contingencies over the course of life up to that moment. So not only our final ends and hopes for ourselves but also our realized abilities and talents reflect, to a large degree, our personal history, opportunities, and social position. There is no way of knowing what we might have been had these things been different.

Finally, the preceding considerations must be viewed together with the fact that the basic structure most likely permits significant social and economic inequalities in the life-prospects of citizens depending on their social origins, their realized natural endowments, and the chance opportunities and accidents that have shaped their personal history. Such inequalities, we may assume, are inevitable, or else necessary or highly advantageous in maintaining effective social cooperation. Presumably there are various reasons for this, among which the need for incentives is but one.

The nature of inequalities in life-prospects can be clarified by contrasting them with other inequalities. Thus imagine a university in which there are three ranks of faculty and everyone stays in each rank the same length of time and receives the same salary. Then while there are inequalities of rank and salary at any given time, there is no inequality in life-prospects between faculty members. The same may be true when members of an association adopt a rotation scheme for filling certain more highly privileged or rewarded positions, perhaps because they involve taking greater responsibility. If the scheme is designed so that barring accidents, death and the like, all serve the same time in these positions, they are again no inequalities in life-prospects.

What the theory of justice must regulate is the inequalities in life-prospects between citizens that arise from social starting-positions, natural advantages and historical contingencies. Even if these inequalities are not in some cases very great, their effect may be great enough so that over time they have significant cumulative consequences. The Kantian form of the contract doctrine focuses on these inequalities in the basic structure in the conviction that these inequalities are the most fundamental ones: once suitable principles are found to govern them and the requisite institutions are established, the problem of how to regulate other inequalities can be much more easily resolved.

VI

In justice as fairness the institutions of the basic structure are just provided they satisfy the principles that free and equal moral persons, in a situation that is fair between them, would adopt for the purpose of regulating that structure. The main two principles read as follows: (1) Each person has an equal right to the most extensive scheme of equal basic liberties compatible with a similar scheme of liberties for all. (2) Social and economic inequalities are permissible provided that they are (a) to the greatest expected benefit of the least advantaged; and (b) attached to positions and offices open to all under conditions of fair equality of opportunity.[7]

Let us consider how the special role of the basic structure affects the conditions of the initial agreement and necessitates that this agreement be understood as hypothetical and non-historical. Now by assumption the basic structure is the all-inclusive social system that determines background justice. (Observe that I leave aside here the problem of justice between nations.[8]) Thus first of all, any fair situation between individuals conceived as free and equal moral persons must be one that suitably evens out the contingencies within this system. Actual agreements reached when people know their present place in an ongoing society are influenced by disparate social and natural contingencies. The principles adopted depend on the actual course of events that takes place within its institutional structure. We cannot by actual agreements get beyond happenstance nor specify a suitably independent standard.

It is also clear why, when we interpret the parties as free and equal moral persons, they are to reason as if they know very little about themselves (referring here to the restrictions of the veil of ignorance). For to proceed otherwise is still to allow the diverse and deep contingent effects to influence the principles that are to regulate their social relations as such persons. Thus we suppose that the parties do not know their place in society, their class position or social status, their good or ill fortune in the distribution of natural talents and abilities, all within the normal range.[9] Nor do the parties know their final aims and interests, or their particular psychological makeup.

Finally, in order to establish fairness between generations (for example, in the agreement on a principle of just savings), the parties, who are assumed

to be contemporaries, do not know the present state of society. They have
no information about the stock of natural resources or productive assets, or
the level of technology beyond what can be inferred from the assumption
that the circumstances of justice obtain. The relative good or ill fortune
of their generation is unknown. For when contemporaries are influenced by
a general description of the present state of society while agreeing how to
treat each other, and the generations that come after them, they have not
yet left out of account the results of historical accident and social contingency found within the basic structure. And so we arrive at a thicker rather
a thinner veil of ignorance: the parties are to be understood so far as possible
solely as moral persons and in abstraction from contingencies. To be fair,
the initial situation treats the parties symmetrically, for as moral persons
they are equal: the same relevant properties qualify everyone. Beginning with
a state of no information, we allow in just enough information to make the
agreement rational, though still suitably independent from historical, natural
and social happenstance. Considerably more information would be compatible
with impartiality but a Kantian view seeks more than this.[10]

Thus, it is evident why the social contract must be regarded as hypothetical
and non-historical. The explanation is that the agreement in the original
position represents the outcome of a rational process of deliberation under
ideal and non-historical conditions that express certain reasonable constraints.
There exists no practicable way actually to carry out this deliberative process
and to be sure that it conforms to the conditions imposed. Therefore, the
outcome cannot be ascertained by pure procedural justice as realized by
deliberations of the parties on some actual occasion. Instead the outcome
must be determined by reasoning analytically: that is, the original position
is to be characterized with sufficient exactness so that it is possible to work
out from the nature of the parties and the situation they confront which
conception of justice is favored by the balance of reasons. The content of
justice must be discovered by reason: that is, by solving the agreement
problem posed by the original position.

To preserve the present-time of entry interpretation, all questions of
justice are dealt with by constraints that apply to contemporaries. Consider
the case of just savings: Since society is a system of cooperation between
generations over time, a principle for savings is required. Rather than imagine
a (hypothetical and non-historical) direct agreement between all generations,
the parties can be required to agree to a savings principle subject to the
further condition that they must want all *previous* generations to have
followed it. Thus the correct principle is that which the members of any

generation (and so all generations) would adopt as the one their generation is to follow and as the principle they would want preceding generations to have followed (and later generations to follow), no matter how far back (or forward) in time.[11]

That the initial situation is hypothetical and non-historical poses no difficulty once its theoretical purpose is correctly understood. On the present-time of entry interpretation, we can, as it were, enter that situation at any moment simply by conducting our moral reasoning about first principles in accordance with the stipulated procedural constraints. We have considered judgments at many levels of generality, from the more particular to the most abstract. So if we affirm the judgments expressed by these constraints, and therefore the values embodied in the idea of fairness between equal moral persons when first principles for the basic structure are to be adopted, then we must accept the limitations on conceptions of justice that result. The initial situation is an attempt to represent and to unify the formal and general elements of our moral thought in a manageable and vivid construction in order to use these elements to determine which first principles of justice are the most reasonable.

I conclude by remarking that once we note the distinctive role of the basic structure and abstract from the various contingencies within it in order to find an appropriate conception of justice to regulate it, something like the notion of the original position seems inevitable. It is a natural extension of the idea of the social contract when the basic structure is taken as the primary subject of justice.

VII

At this point I consider why the initial agreement has features that distinguish it from any other agreement. Once again, the explanation lies in the distinctive role of the basic structure: we must distinguish between particular agreements made and associations formed within this structure, and the initial agreement and membership in society as a citizen. Consider first particular agreements: typically these are based on the parties' known (or probable) assets and abilities, opportunities and interests, as these have been realized within background institutions. We may assume that each party, whether an individual or an association, has various alternatives open to them, that they can compare the likely advantages and disadvantages of these alternatives, and act accordingly. Under certain conditions someone's contribution to a joint venture, or to an ongoing association, can be estimated: one simply notes how the venture or association would fare without that person's joining, and the difference measures their worth to the venture or association. The attractiveness of joining to the individuals is ascertained by a comparison with their opportunities. Thus particular agreements are reached in the context of existing and foreseeable configurations of relationships within the basic structure; and it is these configurations that provide a basis for contractual calculations.

The context of a social contract is strikingly different, and must allow for three facts, among others: namely, that membership in our society is given, that we cannot know what we would have been like had we not belonged to it (perhaps the thought itself lacks sense), and that society as a whole has no ends or ordering of ends in the way that associations and individuals do. The bearing of these facts is clear once we try to regard the social contract as an ordinary agreement and ask how deliberations leading up to it would proceed. Since membership in their society is given, there is no question of the parties comparing the attractions of other societies. Moreover, there is no way to identify someone's potential contribution to society who is not yet a member of it; for this potentiality cannot be known and is, in any case, irrelevant to their present situation. Not only this, but from the standpoint of society as a whole *vis-a-vis* any one member, there is no set of agreed ends by reference to which the potential social contributions of an individual could be assessed. Associations and individuals have such ends, but not a well-ordered society; although it has the aim of giving justice to all its citizens, this is not an aim that ranks their expected contributions and on that basis determines their social role or their worth from a social standpoint. The notion of an individual's contribution to society viewed as an association (so that society is entitled to offer terms for joining derived from the aims of those already members of the association) has no place in a Kantian view. It is necessary, therefore, to construe the social contract in a special way that distinguishes it from other agreements.

In justice as fairness this is done by constructing the notion of the original position. This construction must reflect the fundamental contrasts just noted and it must supply the missing elements in order that a rational agreement can be reached. Consider in turn the three facts in the preceding paragraph. In connection with the first, the parties in the original position suppose that their membership in their society is fixed. This presumption reflects the fact that we are born into our society and within its framework realize but one of many possible forms of our person; the question of our entering another society does not arise. The task of the parties, therefore, is to agree on principles for the basic structure of the society in which it is assumed that they will lead their life. While the principles adopted will no doubt allow for emigration (subject to suitable qualifications), they will not permit arrangements that would be just only if emigration were allowed. The attachments formed to persons and places, to associations and communities, as well as cultural ties, are normally too strong to be given up, and this fact is not to be deplored. Thus the right to emigrate does not affect what counts as a just basic structure, for this structure is to be viewed as a scheme into which people are born and are expected to lead a complete life.

Turning now to the second fact noted above, observe that the veil of ignorance not only establishes fairness between equal moral persons, but by excluding information about the parties' actual interests and abilities, it corresponds to the way in which, apart from our place and history in society, even our potential abilities cannot be known and our interests and character are still to be formed. Thus, the initial situation suitably recognizes that our nature as reasonable and responsible beings apart from society includes but a potential for a whole range of possibilities. Third and finally, there are no social ends except those established by the principles of justice themselves, or else authorized by them; but these principles have yet to be adopted.

Nevertheless, although the calculations that typically influence agreements within society have no place in the original position, other aspects of this initial situation provide the setting for rational deliberation. Thus the alternatives are not opportunities to join other societies, but instead a list of conceptions of justice to regulate the basic structure of one's own society. The parties' interests and preferences are given by their desire for primary goods.[12] Their particular final ends and aims indeed are already formed, although not known to them; and it is these already formed interests, as well as the conditions necessary to preserve moral personality, that they seek to protect by ranking conceptions on the basis of their preference (in the original position) for primary goods. Finally, the availability of general social theory gives a sufficient basis for estimating the feasibility and consequences of alternative conceptions of justice. In view of these aspects of the original position, the idea of the social contract as a rational undertaking can be maintained despite the unusual nature of this agreement.

VIII

Consider now three ways in which the social aspect of human relationships is reflected in the content of the principles of justice themselves. First, the difference principle (which governs economic and social inequalities) does not distinguish between what is acquired by individuals as members of society and what would have been acquired by them had they not been members.[13] Indeed, no sense can be made of the notion of that part of an individual's social benefits that exceed what would have been their situation in another society or in a state of nature. We can, if we like, in setting up the argument from the original position, introduce the state of nature in relation to the so-called non-agreement point. This point can be defined as general egoism and its consequences, and this can serve as the state of nature.[14] But these conditions do not identify a definite state. All that is known in the original position is that each of the conceptions of justice available to the parties have consequences superior to general egoism. There is no question of determining anyone's contribution to society, or how much better off each is than they would have been had they not belonged to it, and then adjusting the social benefits of citizens by reference to these estimates. Although we may draw this kind of distinction in the case of associations within society, the parallel calculations when adopting principles for the basic structure have no foundation. Neither our situation in other societies, nor in a state of nature, have any role in assessing conceptions of justice. And clearly these notions are not relevant in applying the two principles of justice.

Second, and related to the preceding, the two principles of justice regulate how entitlements are acquired in return for contributions to associations, or to other forms of cooperation, within the basic structure. As we have seen, these contributions are evaluated on the basis of the particular aims of individuals and associations; and what people have contributed is influenced partly by their efforts and achievements, and partly by social circumstances and happenstance. Contributions can only be defined as contributions to this or that association in this or that situation. Such contributions reflect an individual's marginal usefulness to some particular group. These contributions are not to be mistaken for contributions to society itself, or for the worth to society of its members as citizens. The sum of an individual's entitlements, or even of their uncompensated contributions to associations within society, is not to be regarded as a contribution to society. Within a Kantian view there is no place for the idea of an individual's contribution to society that parallels that of an individual's contribution to associations within society. Insofar as we compare the worth of citizens at all, their worth in a just and well-ordered society is always equal;[15] and this equality is reflected in the system of basic liberties and fair opportunities, and in the operations of the difference principle.[16]

Third, and last, recall that in a Kantian view the parties are regarded as free and equal moral persons. To say that they are moral persons is to say that they have a conception of the good (a system of final ends) and a capacity to understand a conception of justice and to follow it in their life (a sense of justice). Now the freedom of moral persons can be interpreted under two headings: first, as free persons, they regard themselves as having a highest-order interest in regulating all their other interests, even their fundamental ones, by reason, that is, by rational and reasonable principles that are express-ive of their autonomy. Moreover, free persons do not think of themselves as indissolubly tied to any particular final end, or family of such ends, but regard themselves as always capable of appraising and revising their aims in the light of reasonable considerations. Secondly, we assume that free persons are responsible for their interests and ends: they are able to control and revise their wants and desires, and as circumstance requires, they accept the responsibility for doing so.[17]

Now freedom as applied to social institutions means a certain pattern of rights and liberties; and equal freedom means that certain basic liberties and opportunities are equal and that social and economic inequalities are regulated by principles suitably adjusted to preserve the fair value of these liberties. From the preceding definitions of freedom as applied to moral persons and to social forms, it is plain that free and equal persons are not defined as those whose social relations answer to the very principles that would be agreed to in the original position. For to say this would undermine the argument for these principles that is grounded on their being the principles that would be adopted. But once the parties are described in terms that have an institutional expression, then, given the role of the basic structure, it is no accident that the first principles of justice apply directly to the basic structure. The free-dom and equality of moral persons require some public form, and the content of the two principles fulfills this expectation. And this stands in contrast, for example, to classical utilitarianism, which takes as basic the capacity for pleasure and pain, or for certain intrinsically valuable experiences, defined in such a way that no particular institutional expression is required, although of course certain social forms are superior to others as more effective means to achieve a greater net balance of happiness, or a greater sum of value.

IX

We now come to the fourth and last point (see end of Sec. I): namely, that although society may reasonably rely on a large element of pure procedural justice in determining distributive shares, a conception of justice must incorporate an ideal form for the basic structure in the light of which the accumulated results of on-going social processes are to be limited and adjusted.[18]

Now in view of the special role of the basic structure, it is natural to ask the following question: by what principle can free and equal moral persons accept the fact that social and economic inequalities are deeply influenced by social fortune, and natural and historical happenstance. Since the parties regard themselves as such persons, the obvious starting point is for them to suppose that all social primary goods, including income and wealth, should be equal: everyone should have an equal share. But they must take organizational requirements and economic efficiency into account. Thus it is unreasonable to stop at equal division. The basic structure should allow organizational and economic inequalities so long as these improve everyone's situation, including that of the least advantaged, provided these inequalities are consistent with equal liberty and fair equality of opportunity. Because they start from equal shares, those who benefit least (taking equal division as the benchmark) have, so to speak, a veto. And thus the parties arrive at the difference principle. Here equal division is accepted as the benchmark because it reflects how people are situated when they are represented as free and equal moral persons. Among such persons, those who have gained more than others are to do so on terms that improve the situation of those who have gained less. These intuitive considerations indicate why the difference principle is the appropriate criterion to govern social and economic inequalities.

To understand the difference principle several matters have to be kept in mind. First, the two principles of justice as they work in tandem incorporate an important element of pure procedural justice in the actual determination of distributive shares. They apply to the basic structure and its system for acquiring entitlements; within appropriate limits, whatever distributive shares result are just. A fair distribution can be arrived at only by the actual working of a fair social process over time in the course of which, in accordance with publicly announced rules, entitlements are earned and honored. These features define pure procedural justice. Therefore, if it is asked in the abstract whether one distribution of a given stock of things to definite individuals with known desires and preferences is more just than another, then there is simply no answer to the question.[19]

Thus the principles of justice, in particular the difference principle, apply to the main public principles and policies that regulate social and economic inequalities. They are used to adjust the system of entitlements and earnings and to balance the familiar everyday standards and precepts which this system employs. The difference principle holds, for example, for income and property taxation, for fiscal and economic policy. It applies to the announced system of public law and statutes and not to particular transactions or distributions, nor to the decisions of individuals and associations, but rather to the institutional background against which these transactions and decisions take place. There are no unannounced and unpredictable interferences with citizens' expectations and acquisitions. Entitlements are earned and honored as the public system of rules declares. Taxes and restrictions are all in principle foreseeable, and holdings are acquired on the known condition that certain transfers and redistributions will be made. The objection that the difference principle enjoins continuous corrections of particular distributions and capricious interference with private transactions is based on a misunderstanding.

Again, the two principles of justice do not insist that the actual distribution conform at any given time (or over time) to any observable pattern, say equality, or that the degree of inequality computed from the distribution fall within a certain range, say of values of the Gini coefficient.[20] What is enjoined is that (permissible) inequalities should make a certain functional contribution to the expectations of the least favored, where this functional contribution results from the working of the system of entitlements set up in public institutions. The aim, however, is not to eliminate contingencies from social life, for some contingencies are inevitable. Thus even if an equal distribution of natural assets seemed more in keeping with the equality of free persons, the question of redistributing these assets (were this conceivable) does not arise, since it is incompatible with the integrity of the person. Nor need we make any specific assumptions about how great natural variations are; we only suppose that, as realized in later life, they are influenced by many kinds of happenstance. Institutions must organize social cooperation so that they encourage constructive efforts. We have a right to our natural abilities and a right to whatever we become entitled to by taking part in a fair social process. The problem, of course, is how to characterize such a process. The two principles express the idea that no one should have less than they would receive in an equal division of primary goods, and that when the fruitfulness of social cooperation allows for a general improvement, then the existing inequalities are to work to the benefit of those whose position has improved the least, taking equal division as the benchmark.

The two principles also specify an ideal form for the basic structure in the light of which ongoing institutional and procedural processes are constrained and adjusted. Among these constraints are the limits on the accumulation of property (especially if private property in productive assets exists) that derive from the requirements of the fair value of political liberty and fair equality of opportunity, and the limits based on considerations of stability and excusable envy, both of which are connected to the essential primary good of self-respect.[21] We need such an ideal to guide the adjustments necessary to preserve background justice. As we have seen (in Sec. IV) even if everyone acts fairly as defined by the rules that it is both reasonable and practicable to impose on individuals, the upshot of many separate transactions will eventually undermine background justice. This is obvious once we view society, as we must, as involving cooperation over generations. Thus even in a well-ordered society, adjustments in the basic structure are always necessary. And so an institutional division of labor must be established between the basic structure and the rules applying directly to particular transactions. Individuals and associations are left free to advance their ends within the framework of background institutions which carry out the operations required to maintain a just basic structure.

The need for a structural ideal to specify constraints and to guide adjustments does not depend upon injustice. Even with strict compliance with all reasonable and practical rules, such adjustments are continually required. The fact that actual political and social life is often pervaded by much injustice merely underlines this necessity. A purely procedural theory that contained no structural principles for a just social order would be of no use in our world, where the political goal is to eliminate injustice and to guide change towards a fair basic structure. A conception of justice must specify the requisite structural principles and point to the overall direction of political action. In the absence of such an ideal form for background institutions, there is no rational basis for continually adjusting the social process so as to preserve background justice, nor for eliminating existing injustice. Thus ideal theory, which defines a perfectly just basic structure, is a necessary complement to non-ideal theory without which the desire for change lacks an aim.

X

This completes my discussion of the four points stated at the end of Sec I. One result of what has been said is a reply to idealism. The problem is this: in order to work out a Kantian conception of justice it seems desirable to detach the structure of Kant's doctrine from its background in transcendental idealism and to give it a procedural interpretation by means of the construction of the original position. (This detachment is important if for no other reason than that it should enable us to see how far a procedural interpretation of Kant's view within a reasonable empiricist framework is possible.) But to achieve this aim we have to show that the original position construction, which uses the idea of the social contract, is not open to the cogent objections that idealists raised to the contract tradition of their day.

Thus Hegel thought that this doctrine confused society and the state with an assocation of private persons; that it permitted the general form and content of public law to be determined too much by the contingent and specific private interests and personal concerns of individuals; and that it could make no sense of the fact that it is not up to us whether we are born into and belong to our society. For Hegel the doctrine of social contract was an illegitimate and uncritical extension of ideas at home in and limited to (what he called) civil society. A further objection was that the doctrine failed to recognize the social nature of human beings and depended on attributing to them certain fixed natural abilities and specific desires independent from, and for theoretical purposes prior to, society.[22]

I have attempted to reply to these criticisms first by maintaining that the primary subject of justice is the basic structure of society, which has the fundamental task of establishing background justice (Secs IV–V). And while this contention may offhand appear to be a concession, it nevertheless is not: the original position can still be characterized so that it establishes a fair agreement situation between free and equal moral persons and one in which they can reach a rational agreement. This characterization depends upon conceiving of free and equal moral persons in a certain way and interpreting their wants and needs (for purposes of the argument in the original position) in terms of an account of primary goods. To be sure, we must distinguish the agreement on a conception of justice from all other agreements, but this requirement is not surprising: we should expect the agreement that settles principles for the basic structure to have features that mark it off from all agreements made within that structure (Secs VI–VII). Finally, I have indicated how justice as fairness can accommodate the social nature of human beings (Sec VIII). At the same time, since it proceeds from a suitably individualistic basis (the original position is conceived as fair between free and equal moral persons), it is a moral conception that provides an appropriate place for social values without sacrificing the freedom and integrity of the person.

It may be that other contract views cannot answer the idealist critique. Historical process doctrines such as those of Hobbes and Locke, or the libertarian view, although importantly very different from one another, all seem open to objection. First, since the social contract is made by people in a state of nature (in the case of Hobbes and Locke), or individuals agree to become a client of the dominant protection agency (on the libertarian scheme), it appears inevitable that the terms of these agreements, or the circumstances that they ratify, are bound to be substantially affected by contingencies and accidents of the as-if just historical process which has no tendency to preserve or to move towards background justice. This difficulty is strikingly illustrated by Locke's doctrine. He assumes that not all members of society following the social compact have equal political rights: citizens have the right to vote in virtue of owning property so that the propertyless have no vote and no right to exercise political authority.[23] Presumably the diverse accumulations of the as-if just historical process over generations has left many without property through no fault of their own; and although the social contract and the subsequent entrusteeship of political authority is perfectly rational from their standpoint, and does not contradict their duty to God, it does not secure for them these basic political rights. From a Kantian viewpoint, Locke's doctrine improperly subjects the social relationships of moral persons to historical and social contingencies that are external to, and eventually undermine, their freedom and equality. The constraints that Locke imposes on the as-if historical process are not strong enough to characterize a conception of background justice acceptable to free and equal moral persons. This can be brought out by supposing that the social compact is to be made immediately following the creation of human beings as free and equal persons in the state of nature. Assuming that their situation with respect to one another suitably represents their freedom and equality, and also that (as Locke holds) God has not conferred on anyone the right to exercise political authority, they will presumably acknowledge principles that assure equal basic (including political) rights for all throughout the later historical process. This reading of Locke's view makes it an as-if nonhistorical doctrine when we suppose that during the relevant period of time people were too widely scattered for any agreement to be reached. That Locke seems not to have considered this alternative possibility brings out the historical aspect of his theory.[24]

I have also suggested that any contract theory must recognize that a division of labor is necessary between the operations of the basic structure in maintaining background justice and the definition and enforcement by the legal system of the rules that apply directly to individuals and associations, and govern their particular transactions. Finally, there is no use in a Kantian contract theory for the contrast between the situation of individuals in the state of nature and their situation in society. This kind of comparison belongs solely to agreements struck within the framework of background institutions and has no role in determining basic rights of the members of society. Moreover, any benchmark of comparison between the relative advantages of citizens must be founded on their present relationships and the way in which social institutions work now, and not on how the actual (or some as-if just) historical sequence of transactions extending backwards over generations has improved (or would improve) everyone's circumstances in comparison with the initial (or some hypothetical) state of nature.

My aim here is not to criticize other contract theories. To do that would require a separate discussion. Rather, I have tried to explain why justice as fairness takes the basic structure as the first subject of justice and attempts to develop a special theory for this case. Given the unique features and role of this structure, the idea of an agreement must be appropriately transformed if the intent of the Kantian form of the contract doctrine is to be realized. I have sought to show how the necessary transformations can be made.

Harvard University

NOTES

* This essay is a considerable revision of a paper with the same title presented at the meetings of the American Philosphical Association (Pacific Division) at Portland, Oregon in March 1977 and reprinted in the *American Philosophical Quarterly,* 14 (April 1977). Sections II and III are new. I am indebted to Joshua Cohen, Joshua Rabinowitz, T.M. Scanlon, and Quentin Skinner for valuable discussions on the topic of this paper. To Burton Dreben I am grateful for many improvements; and to Thomas Hill and Hugo Bedau for their instructive comments.
[1] In *A Theory of Justice* (Cambridge, Mass., Harvard University Press, 1971) the basic structure was regarded as the primary subject and discussion focused on this case. See pp. 7ff. But the reasons for this choice of subject and its consequences were not sufficiently explained. Here I want to make good this lack.
[2] I am grateful to Hugo Bedau for pointing out to me the need to emphasize this. In his comments on the earlier version of this paper he noted that the last paragraph of § 2 of *A Theory of Justice* is particularly misleading in this respect.
[3] See *Methods of Ethics,* 7th ed. (London, 1907).
[4] This fact is regarded as an objection to these principles by J. C. Harsanyi, 'Can the Maximin Principle Serve as a Basis for Morality,' *American Political Science Review,* 69 (June, 1975), 594–606. I cannot reply adequately to Harsanyi's forceful objections here, but I note the following: the maximin principle was never proposed as a basis for morality; in the form of the difference principle it is one principle constrained by others that applies to the basic structure; and when this principle is seen in this limited role as

a criterion of background justice, its implications in normal cases (see footnote 9 below) are not, I believe, implausible. Finally, confining the application of the principles of justice to the basic structure does not imply, contrary to Harsanyi's suggestion (see p. 605), that only the number of persons involved determines which principles hold for a given case. On this, see the last paragraph in this Section.

[5] I follow the account in Robert Nozick, *Anarchy, State, and Utopia* (New York, Basic Books, 1974).

[6] I distinguish here and elsewhere below between an as-if historical and an as-if non-historical process (or procedure). In both cases the process is hypothetical in the sense that the process has not actually occurred, or may not have occurred. But as-if historical processes can occur: they are not thought to be excluded by fundamental social laws or natural facts. Thus on the libertarian view, if everyone were to follow the principles of justice in acquisition and transfer, and they can follow them, then the as-if historical process leading to the formation of the state would be realized. By contrast, an as-if non-historical process, for example, the procedure leading up to the agreement in the original position, cannot take place. See below Section VI, p. 58.

[7] These principles are discussed in *A Theory of Justice* §§ 11–13, and elsewhere. A summary statement, including the principle of just savings and priority rules, is given on pp. 302f.

[8] The reason for doing this is that, as a first approximation, the problem of social justice concerns the basic structure as a closed background system. To start with the society of nations would seem merely to push one step further back the task of finding a theory of background justice. At some level there must exist a closed background system, and it is this subject for which we want a theory. We are better prepared to take up this problem for a society (illustrated by nations) conceived as a more or less self-sufficient scheme of social cooperation and as possessing a more or less complete culture. If we are successful in the case of a society, we can try to extent and to adjust our initial theory as further inquiry requires.

[9] The normal range is specified as follows: since the fundamental problem of justice concerns the relations among those who are full and active participants in society, and directly or indirectly associated together over the course of a whole life, it is reasonable to assume that every one has physical needs and psychological capacities within some normal range. Thus the problem of special health care and how to treat the mentally defective are laid aside. If we can work out a viable theory for the normal range, we can attempt to handle these other cases later.

[10] For this way of putting the distinction between a thicker and a thinner veil of ignorance I am indebted to Joshua Rabinowitz.

[11] This formulation of the conditions for the agreement on a just savings principle differs from that in *A Theory of Justice*, pp. 128f and 291f. There it is not required that the parties must want the previous generations to have followed the principle they adopt as contemporaries. Therefore, assuming that generations are mutually disinterested, nothing constrains them from refusing to make any savings at all. To cope with this difficulty it was stipulated that the parties care for their descendants. While this is a reasonable stipulation, the requirement above has the virtue that it removes the difficulty without changing the motivation assumption. It also preserves the present time of entry interpretation of the original position and coheres with the strict compliance condition and ideal theory generally. I am indebted to Thomas Nagel and Derek Parfit for this

revision; it is also proposed by Jane English who notes the connection with ideal theory. See her 'Justice Between Generations', *Philosophical Studies*, **31** (1977), 98.

¹² These goods are defined as things that, from the standpoint of the original position, it is rational for the parties to want whatever their final ends (which are unknown to them). They serve as generalized means, so to speak, for realizing all, or most all, rational systems of aims. See *A Theory of Justice*, pp. 92–95, 396f, 433f.

¹³ One aim of Sections VII–VIII is to indicate a reply to David Gauthier's illuminating critique of the difference principle, 'Justice and Natural Endowment', *Social Theory and Practice*, **3** (1974), 3–26. I refer to his discussion here because his argument depends on being able to distinguish between what is acquired by individuals as members of society and what would have been acquired by them in a state of nature. If this distinction has no useful meaning, then I believe that the way is cleared to meeting Gauthier's objection. Of course, much more needs to be said. In any case, I fully agree with his remarks on pp. 25f and much of my discussion is designed to show how a Kantian contract view can be stated to accord with them.

¹⁴ See *A Theory of Justice*, pp. 136, 147; cf 80.

¹⁵ The worth of citizens in a well ordered society is always equal because in such a society everyone is assumed to comply with just institutions and to fulfill their duties and obligations moved, when appropriate, by a sufficiently strong sense of justice. Inequalities do not arise from unequal moral worth; their explanation lies elsewhere.

¹⁶ See below, the second paragraph of Section IX.

¹⁷ These remarks are stated a bit more fully in 'Reply to Alexander and Musgrave', *Quarterly Journal of Economics*, **88** (November, 1974), 639–643.

¹⁸ On pure procedural justice, see *A Theory of Justice*, pp. 84–89, 310–315; and also pp. 64, 66, 72ff, 79, 274–280, 305–310.

¹⁹ Ibid., p. 88.

²⁰ For this and other measures of inequality, see A. K. Sen, *On Economic Inequality* (New York, W. W. Norton, 1973). Chapter 2.

²¹ See *A Theory of Justice*, pp. 224–227, 277f, 534–537, 543–546.

²² See *The Philosophy of Right*, trans T. M. Knox (Oxford, at the Clarendon Press, 1942), pp. 58f, 70f, 156f, 186.

²³ See *Second Treatise of Government*, reading together § § 140 and 158.

²⁴ For this way of seeing the historical aspect of Locke's theory I am indebted to Quentin Skinner.

RELEVANCE

My reason for contributing this, rather than some other, paper to this volume is that its central idea came to my mind in the course of a discussion with Richard Brandt when he was in Oxford in 1974 to give the John Locke Lectures — one out of many fruitful and enjoyable discussions which I have had with all three of the honorands. Since it bears in different ways on the interests of them all, I hope that they may find it an acceptable offering, although it does not mention their work directly and their names do not appear in the notes. Certainly no one could write anything informed about moral philosophy without taking into account the writings of this extraordinary constellation of talent.

In the mouths of many radicals, a piece of philosophical or other academic work is said to be relevant if it lends support to the speaker's own political opinions. I shall not be using the word in that sense; nor even in the sense in which I used it in the title of my inaugural lecture 'The Practical Relevance of Philosophy'[1], although I do think that what I am going to say has that kind of relevance, because it helps to sort out some practical issues of great importance. The problem I have in mind to discuss is the following: How, when we are confronted with a situation or an action, do we decide what features of it are relevant to its moral appraisal?

The claim that certain features are morally irrelevant can play a crucial part in moral argument. To give two examples: if I am being blamed for missing an appointment, the fact that there was a flight at such and such a time which would have enabled me to keep the appointment if I had caught it is irrelevant, if I could not have caught it; and it is generally held that it is irrelevant to moral appraisals of my actions that it was I, that individual, who did them (it is said that morally relevant features of situations or actions have to be specifiable without using individual constants, and that, instead, universally quantified individual variables have to be used in stating the moral principle which gives a feature its relevance). The use made of this thesis in moral argument, though it has given rise to controversy about the details, is too well known to need exposition.

Some have sought to extend this imputation of irrelevance to descriptions in universal terms which include features of situations that *in fact* serve to

A. I. Goldman and J. Kim (eds.), Values and Morals, 73–90. All Rights Reserved.
Copyright © 1978 R.M. Hare

pick out particular individuals, although formally speaking the descriptions are universal. Thus Professor John Rawls, in the section of his book called 'The Formal Constraints of the Concept of Right', says of his principles that 'it must be possible to formulate them without the use of what would be intuitively recognized as proper names, *or rigged definite descriptions*' (my italics);[2] and Marcus Singer attempts a somewhat similar manoeuvre in his book *Generalization in Ethics*.[3] The essence of the manoeuvre is to adapt an argumentative move, which is legitimate in the case of individual references, to cover features which are, formally speaking, described in universal terms, but look as if they were selected to pick out just one favoured individual. Some people want to go even further, and claim that the same kind of manoeuvre can be used to rule out, as morally relevant features of, e.g., people, their black skin or even their sex.

Others again have wanted to say that there are quite narrow *material* restrictions on what features can be morally relevant. For example, that a man clasps and unclasps his hands cannot be relevant;[4] and the production of benefits and harms to human beings is paradigmatically relevant.[5] I have already in many places said what is wrong with this view: it confuses our extreme surprise that anybody should *hold* a certain view with an inability to understand what he is saying.[6] If a man said that another man was a good man because he clasped and unclasped his hands, I should *understand* what he was saying, and might even, if he said 'morally good man' understand that it was a moral judgment; indeed, if I did not understand it in this way, there might be no occasion for my surprise. The surprise is occasioned by an inability to understand, not what the view is, but why anybody should think that. As well as being based on this confusion, the position in question is practically futile as a way of achieving what seems to be the aim of its propounders; if they tried to use this kind of argument to constrain somebody to accept or reject some moral opinion, he would be likely to reply 'If that is how you interpret the expression 'morally good', I am just not interested in being morally good'.[7] This is always the result of trying to write material stipulations into our explanations of the meanings of moral words or of the world 'moral'.

All these extensions of the restriction are illegitimate; there are indeed reasons for thinking the features in question irrelevant to moral appraisal, but the philosophers I am attacking have taken much too short a way with them.[8] A very much deeper understanding of the whole question is needed before we can see why they are irrelevant, in cases in which they are. What we seem to require, as a basis for this understanding, is a general account of what makes features of situations, etc., morally relevant. This paper is intended as a prolegomenon to such an account, though I shall also be trying to shed light on some vexing subsidiary problems.

The first thing that must be said is that the decision to treat certain features of a situation as morally relevant is not independent of the decision to apply certain moral principles to it, i.e. to make certain moral judgments about it. It is a great mistake to think that there can be a morally or evaluatively neutral process of picking out the relevant features of a situation, which can then be followed by the job of appraising or evaluating the situation morally. We can indeed *describe* a situation without committing ourselves to any moral judgments about it (that this is not so has become a dogma in some circles, but I know of no good reasons for accepting the dogma); nevertheless, when we decide what features of the description are morally relevant, we are already in the moral business. There are certain exceptions to this rule; some features of situations can be ruled out as irrelevant on purely formal grounds, as we have seen. But in the main to call a feature morally relevant is already to imply that it is a reason for or against making some moral judgment; and to say this is already to invoke a moral principle. That the act resulted in the death of a patient is relevant because of the principle that one ought not, in these circumstances, to cause the death of a patient; abandon the principle, and *that* reason for thinking the feature relevant goes by the board, though others may survive.

The question, therefore, of what features can be relevant to moral appraisal is the same question as that of what features can figure in moral principles. Even the formal restrictions that I mentioned just now are covered by this general statement of the position. The reason why the fact that it was that individual who did the act cannot be relevant is that individual references are formally excluded from moral principles. The reason why it could not be relevant that there was a flight at that time if the man could not have caught the flight is that, for formal reasons connected with the prescriptivity of moral judgments, there cannot be a moral principle which bids us catch flights that we cannot catch.[9]

The question of what features of a situation are morally relevant thus collapses into the question of what moral principles apply to the situation; any feature which figures in one of these principles is relevant. And the question of what features *can* be morally relevant collapses into the question of what restrictions there are on the form or the content of moral principles. I have given some examples of such restrictions and suggested restrictions already.

I will now try to explain why we do not treat skin-colour as a morally relevant feature of people, except in unusual cases (for example, when I have a duty to take a faithful photograph of somebody's face and therefore must get the exposure right). I shall assume without argument that merely individual references cannot figure uneliminably in moral principles; and also that the proposed extension of this restriction to 'rigged definite descriptions' cannot stand unsupported.

Two other illegitimate extensions, not yet mentioned, may be taken in on the way. It is sometimes thought that, besides individual references, all references are ruled out which logically must be unique. For example, it is thought that this is why the expression 'the only man with fifteen toes' could not figure in a moral principle, because there logically cannot be more than one 'only man with' a certain feature. There are intuitively obvious counter-examples to this thesis: e.g. 'The first man past the post ought to be given the prize'; it is logically impossible for more than one runner to be 'the first man past the post', but nevertheless most of us accept this moral principle. The intuition which acquits this principle of deviance is a linguistic one, and therefore not subject to the strictures which I would make against substantial moral intuitions as a basis of argument; but we do not need in any case to rely on it, because it is not hard to spell out what has gone wrong. A term does not stop being a universal term just because it logically can apply only to one thing. The thesis of universalizability, therefore, rules out only individual references, not all unique (even logically unique) references. Put more informally, that it was I who did it could not be a reason for a moral judgment about an act; but any universal property of the act could be a reason, even though his possession of it rules out anybody else's possession of it.

The second illegitimate extension of this restriction that I must mention here is one which I have dealt with elsewhere[10] but which keeps on cropping up. It is thought that if there is some individual who is related to me by a relation which logically can tie an individual to one other individual and one only, the relation in question cannot figure in a moral principle. For example, it is thought that I cannot have duties to my mother as such, because it is logically impossible for a man to have more than one mother, and because of the occurrence of the individual reference 'my' in the expression 'my mother'. These are actually two separate reasons, both of them bad ones. The first (uniqueness) falls to the same objection as was raised in the preceding paragraph against an essentially similar mistake: uniqueness in a universal term (this time a relation) is not the same thing as individual reference. The second reason is ambiguous. It is true that I cannot have duties to my mother just because she is *my* mother (duties which other people in similar circumstances do not have to *their* mothers). The thesis of universalizability establishes that much. But it is not true that I cannot have duties to my mother just because she is my *mother* (duties which *any* son has to *his* mother in circumstances just like mine). If anybody stands in just this relation to any woman, then he ought to treat her in such and such a way. Sentences of this form:

$$(x)(y)(R_1x, y \rightarrow OR_2x, y)$$

(where 'O' is the obligation-sign of deontic logic) are properly universal and contain no individual references. Another even more obvious example, intuitively, is the duty to fulfil *one's own* promises, but not other people's.

Having got these two false moves out of the way, let us ask why we do not treat skin-colour as morally relevant. It is a properly universal property which any individual man might have. It has been alleged that if I, a white man, became just like some black man, I should stop being me (the person that I now am). This is a difficult question into which I shall not enter in this paper; the point is effectively answered in a paper by Professor Zeno Vendler,[11] as are similar points arising from Professor Kripke's views about proper names. Briefly, I can well conceive of *my* being in precisely the situation of that black man, black skin and all, even though I could not conceive of Richard Hare being in that precise situation, because then it would not be Richard Hare (at least not *this* Richard Hare; there might be a totally dissimilar black of the same name). But we do not need to go into this, because the question is whether skin colour by itself could be morally relevant; and it is certainly the case that my skin might turn black without my ceasing to be me *or* Richard Hare.

So why do we not treat skin colour as morally relevant? For great periods of history people did. The reason is that we have been through a process of moral reasoning (briefly described in my book *Freedom and Reason*, pp. 108 f.) which, though indeed based on universalizability, is more complex than the simple move so far considered. And the move involves more than universalizability alone; it involves prescriptivity; i.e. it involves asking whether we are prepared to *prescribe* universally that, e.g., black people should be at a legal disadvantage compared with white people. We could without formal or logical offence prescribe this, but are we prepared to? The reason why we are not is that, since black skin is a universal property, it is logically possible that we might ourselves have it. If, therefore, we are asked what we are prepared to prescribe for all logically possible situations (in other words what we want to happen in them all), we have to prescribe that in situations in which we have a black skin we should be treated in one way or another. And we are unlikely to prescribe that in that situation we should be disadvantaged in the way proposed. So we cannot prescribe universally that this should be done, and therefore, because of universalizability, cannot prescribe that we ought to do it now.

So far, so good; but there are grave difficulties in this golden-rule argument which I shall be trying to overcome in the rest of this paper. First of all, it might be alleged that the racist could easily defeat the argument by the following manoeuvre. He is confident that he and his white friends are not in fact ever going to have black skins. So why should he not happily prescribe that those with black skins should be disadvantaged? Or consider the man with fifteen toes or with a spot on his face in just that position: he knows that he will never lose his distinguishing mark, so why should he not adopt and subscribe to a prescriptive principle which says that people with this distinguishing mark should be privileged in some way? The essence of this objection is that we have not justified our claim that we have, in adopting moral principles, to be prescribing for all logically possible situations. There are two variant interpretations of this, but they come in practice to the same: either it is being objected that a man could prescribe happily that he be himself disadvantaged in some logically possible situation, knowing that in fact he would never be in that situation; or it is being objected that in adopting moral principles we do not have to be prescribing for all logically possible situations, but only for all situations which will actually occur.

Let us take these two interpretations of the objection in turn. On the first interpretation the answer to the objection hinges on a requirement of sincerity. If a person is sincerely prescribing something, he *wants* it to happen.[12] Now there is no restriction on the concept of wanting which prevents our wanting something to happen in a hypothetical situation — a situation which is not in fact going ever to obtain. This is clear at any rate in cases where we do not know whether the situation is going to obtain or not. I can want to have money to rebuild my house if it burns down (that is why I insure it against fire); the fact that it never does burn down does not entail that I never really had the desire. More difficult are cases where I know that a situation is not going to obtain: can I then want something to happen in that situation?

When reading novels or watching plays, we certainly want the hero to succeed in his enterprises, although we know that neither he nor his enterprises exist in real life. We want this because we *imagine* him existing. And we can also imagine a situation existing even though nobody is acting the situation for us in a play or describing it in a book; we can be our own play-wrights. Nor can anything hang on how much a particular person can imagine; for the reach of people's imaginations is variable. The fact that I cannot imagine what it is like to be submitted to a certain torture does not entail that I could not, logically or even in fact, be submitted to it. And if I am contemplating inflicting that torture on somebody else, I cannot defend myself against golden-rule arguments on the ground that, since I cannot imagine the torture being inflicted on me, I cannot want it not to be in-flicted on me. If a person has previously been unable to imagine himself in the situation of some victim of his, but then, through an increase in sensi-tivity, becomes able to do so, this fortunate change may indeed make him more *receptive* to golden-rule arguments, but can hardly make them into better arguments than they were before. His previous insensitivity was a defect in his moral thinking (for reasons which we shall be exploring), and even before the change we could have legitimately asked him to try to over-come it, with the object of making himself better able to do his moral think-ing with a full appreciation of the facts of the situation, including facts about the experiences of his victim. Until he can imagine what those experiences are, he does not in the required sense know what they are.

Let us now put together these two points: first the point that we can want things to happen in situations which we imagine (including situations in which we ourselves would be the victims); and secondly the point that if we are to do our moral thinking in knowledge of the facts, we have to be able to imagine what it is like to be our victim, and therefore what it would be like for us if we were subjected to the same treatment. It then becomes easy to see that it is both possible (provided that we have the necessary sensitivity) and a requirement of moral thinking, that we should, in doing it, imagine ourselves, not only in situations which are actually going to happen, but in ones which logically might obtain, and in particular in the situation of our proposed victim, even though we are never actually going to be in it, and know this. We then have to ask whether the man who says that he wants to be tortured (i.e. desires that he should be tortured) if he should ever be in that situation, but says this only because he knows that he will never be in it, is doing anything that is logically at fault, or in other ways ruled out from moral thinking.

We can, as we have already seen, require of such a man that he should imagine himself being in the situation of his victim (with, of course, the victim's desires and other experiences). Can he then fail to desire that he should not be treated in that way (i.e. in a way which, he now knows, the victim very much dislikes)? Certainly he can have *other* desires and, in general, motives which outweigh the desire in question; for example, he may desire things for himself or for other affected parties which, taken in sum, outweigh the suffering of the victim. But that would introduce complications which are irrelevant to the present argument; so let us assume that it is a simple bilateral situation in which the agent has a desire of strength m to torture his victim, and the victim has a desire of strength n not to be tortured, and that n greatly exceeds m; and that these are all the desires that we need take into account. The agent then says that, in spite of n being greater than m, he desires and prescribes that he should torture his victim, and is prepared to universalize this prescription to apply to all logically possible similar cases, including that in which the roles are reversed; and he is able to say this because he knows that they will not be reversed, so that he will never have actually to suffer the effects of the carrying out of his universal prescription.

Such a man is guilty of insincerity. He cannot really think what he says he thinks and want what he says he wants. Suppose that he were watching a play and were imagining vividly (as moral thought requires) the experiences of the characters. And suppose that he were doing this, as the impartiality of moral thinking demands, equally for all the characters. Suppose, further, that the situation in the play is just the same as that of himself and his proposed victim in real life. Can he, having imagined vividly the experiences of all the characters equally, sincerely say that he wants the person in the play who corresponds to himself to torture the person who corresponds to his victim, although the victim's desire not to be tortured greatly exceeds the desire of the other person to torture him? I do not think so. And if not, then neither can a person sincerely prescribe this who has been through the same thought-processes in the actual situation.

The objection may be made that it is possible to imagine vividly the sufferings of another real or fictional person without wanting him not to have to suffer them. This is true; no doubt any talented torturer can do as much. But can he do this if he is wanting universally (i.e. accepting a universal prescription) that something should happen whoever is at the receiving end? The manoeuvre which he is attempting is to want the victim to be tortured, though he is imagining himself in the victim's place with the victim's desires, relying on the fact that he knows that he is not actually ever going to be in that situation.

The answer to this objection is that, if he is not treating the victim, in his thought, as if he himself were the victim, he is not really imagining what it would be like to be the victim. If we are to make an informed moral judgment, we have to make it in full knowledge and awareness of the available facts; and the agent does not have this full knowledge and awareness of one of the available facts, namely the sufferings of his victim, unless he is aware of what it is like to be that person; and this he cannot be aware of unless he puts himself in thought in that person's position. But if he does this, he will be having the same desires as that person has. If he does not have them, he lacks the necessary awareness, because the desires are what he has to be aware of, and one can be aware of desires, in the required sense, only by having them. The objection rests on the supposition that we can be fully aware of the desires and feelings of others without imaginatively sharing them; but this is not so. Complete sympathy, not mere empathy, is a requirement of moral thought.

If the objection be now made that it is possible to know the *intensity* of another's desire, though not its precise experiential quality, by ascertaining that it has the same intensity as some past or present desire of our own, though having a different object (e.g. that he wants not to be tortured as much as we want not to be bankrupted), the answer is that the argument can be quickly reconstructed even if this objection be a sound one. For in order to know that the desires have the same intensity, it would be necessary to know the intensity of the other's desire; so we are back where we were before.

We must now turn to consider the other possible interpretation of the objection mooted on p. 78. The first interpretation said that a man might happily prescribe that he himself be disadvantaged in some logically possible situation, knowing that in fact he would never be in that situation; we have answered that form of the objection by claiming that such a man would be guilty either of insincerity, because he did not really want what he was prescribing, or of lack of knowledge of a material fact, namely what it was like for his victim to desire not to be treated in a certain way. The second interpretation was in form different. It said that it is not a requirement of moral thought that we should prescribe for all logically possible situations, but only for those which are going to be actual.

To this second form of the objection we have to reply by showing that moral thought does require us to prescribe, not perhaps for *all* logically possible situations, but at any rate for all logically possible situations which differ from actual ones only in that different individuals are playing the several roles in them. But here we have to be very careful. In other places I have urged that we should distinguish two different levels of moral thinking: one of them, which I have called level 1, for practical use in most situations, in which we simply apply to the situations sound general *prima facie* or intuitive principles; and the other, called level 2, which we employ when we have to select these general principles, or adjudicate between them in cases of conflict, or even override them when in a most unusual case we judge them to be inapposite.[13] This suggestion is not in the least original; it goes back in origin to Plato's distinction between the level of thought required in his auxiliaries and that required in his rulers, which was refined by Aristotle when he distinguished the roles of the moral and intellectual virtues in practical thinking. It has reappeared in the controversies between the utilitarians and their opponents; but it has never to my knowledge been formulated with sufficient clarity, and so we must go on trying. I now think that the terms I chose in earlier writings for designating the two levels were unhappy, because nobody can remember which level is which (i.e. which order the numbers come in). I therefore propose now to substitute for 'level-1' the term 'intuitive' or, as applied to principles, the term *'prima facie'* (which is of course familiar from the writings of the intuitionist Sir David Ross); and for 'level-2' I shall substitute the term 'critical', which conveys plainly enough that at this level we are engaged in criticizing (judging, appraising or assessing) our intuitive or *prima facie* principles.

It will be evident already from what I have said that critical moral thinking, which is what we have been considering, is in practice an unrealizable ideal to which we can only try to approximate. We could not consider all logically possible cases; and there are other hazards which I have described elsewhere.[14] In most of our actual moral thinking we are compelled to estimate what the results of critical thinking would be if we were able to pursue it; and we base on these estimates a set of fairly simple general principles and motivational dispositions (our *prima facie* principles and the intuitions and character-traits that go with them) which we try, so far as we can, to inculcate into ourselves and others. A reflective and articulate person will, however, never take his *prima facie* principles for granted; when he is free from stress and from temptations to special pleading, he will examine them by engaging in critical thinking so far as he is able. It is this critical thinking to which nearly all that I have been saying so far applies.

When we are using critical thinking in order to scrutinize our *prima facie* principles, and select the best ones, I have said that we ought to give weight to the cases we consider in proportion to the probability of their occurring.[15] People who know that I have said this are likely to hold it against me in the present argument unless I make some careful distinctions. Critical thinking proceeds in two stages. It first considers cases (and can in principle consider *any* logically possible cases) and comes to a decision about what ideally ought to be done in them, after ascertaining or positing all the detailed facts about the situations which might be claimed to be relevant. This is the stage with which we are concerned in the present argument. In the second stage it estimates the probability of these cases occurring, and on the basis of this estimate selects the best *prima facie* principles in the way just mentioned. This second stage we can ignore in the present argument, because all that I am now trying to establish is that at the first stage the manoeuvre attempted by our objector is illegitimate. Once our moral thought has finished with the first stage, it then has to make estimates of probability and concentrate on the cases which are likely to be actual when selecting the *prima facie* principles. But we have to ask, for the present, only whether the manoeuvre is legitimate at the first stage. Could an objector claim that even at the first stage only cases likely to occur need be considered?

He could not, because what are being subscribed to at the first stage are properly universal principles not containing individual references. The cases are put up for consideration in universal terms, and must be so put up because of the logical character of the moral words. At this stage, the moral thinker has to judge that such and such should be done in a case *of a certain kind*. He is therefore forbidden to rule out the consideration of a certain case (that in which he himself will suffer from the application of a principle) merely because that case is not going to be actual. At this point we are in danger of getting engulfed in the complexities of possible-world modal logic; but I will resist the temptation to explore more of that jungle (which indeed I am hardly competent to do) than is required for the present argument. Let us simply suppose (*pace* Leibniz) that there are two possible world-histories which are identical in all their universal properties and differ solely in the roles occupied in them by different individuals. It is clear that one of these world-histories can be distinguished from the other only by referring to those individuals and saying that in one of the world-histories the individuals occupy one set of roles, in the other another. If, then, one of these possible world-histories is the history of the *actual* world in which our agent occupies a certain role and his victim another, it can be distinguished from a possible world-history in which the roles are reversed only by referring to those individuals and saying that in the first of them individual *a* tortures individual *b*, whereas in the second it is the other way round. It follows, if we accept the universalizability of moral judgments, that no moral distinction can be drawn between the two world-histories, and that therefore our objector cannot, if he is prescribing morally and universally, prescribe differently for them. It is therefore not possible for him to prescribe morally solely for the actual world in which he is safely ensconced in his privileged position; for any universal prescription which he accepts for this actual world will automatically apply to the other hypothetical world in which he occupies the less comfortable seat. So at this stage and level the objection cannot get a grip.

Can it then get a grip at the next stage, at which we are selecting the best *prima facie* principles for use at the intuitive level? I do not think so. For what we are then selecting are still universal principles, having at that second stage the added feature of greater generality;[16] and we are selecting them on the basis of the answers given in all cases reviewed at stage 1. The new feature of stage 2 is that cases are to be excluded if they are unlikely to occur. But that is of no use to the objector if the cases (*all* the cases) that were reviewed at stage 1 were specifiable without individual references. But we have seen that this is so; for individual references make no difference at stage 1, and are necessarily ignored; the two qualitatively identical world-histories considered in the last paragraph will come on to stage 2 as one case, not two. If special pleading cannot get in at the first stage, it cannot get in at all. All the cases to be considered at stage 2, and to be weighted for probability of occurrence, will be stated in the form 'a case in which a person of a certain kind does a thing of a certain kind in circumstances of a certain kind to another person of a certain kind'. Granted, at stage 2 the moral thinker has then to assign probabilities to the occurrence of cases of this kind. But since he is not mentioned, *qua* that individual, in the description of the cases, the probability of a case of this kind occurring will be the same whichever role in it he as an individual plays. Probability is relative to evidence, and evidence as to the role which he as an individual plays is denied him. He has, in assigning probabilities, to lump together all cases of this kind; he has no way of distinguishing those in which *he* plays a certain role.

It might be objected that although the individual is not mentioned as such in the specification of the cases at stage 1, our moral thinker might make a private mental note that such and such were cases in which he would occupy the role of victim in the actual world, and so select his *prima facie* principles in such a way as to favour his own interest. But if he did this, he would be selecting between the candidate principles on grounds other than the probability of the universally specified cases considered at stage 1 actually occurring. And this would be to frustrate the purpose of the entire procedure. It must be remembered that it is critical thinking which is ultimate, in the sense that if we were able to pursue it with the omniscience and the freedom from self-deception and special pleading of the Archangel Gabriel, the highly specific principles which it arrived at for all logically possible cases would be the ones which we ought to follow. It is only because of our human limitations that we have to have recourse to simple general *prima facie* principles. They help us approximate to the answers which we should give were we to apply critical thinking to every case. Although the expression 'mere rules of thumb', which is sometimes used of these *prima facie* principles, is highly misleading, for reasons which I have given elsewhere,[17] they are not ultimate. The manoeuvre which is now being suggested by our objector will obviously frustrate the whole purpose of having these *prima facie* principles; they will no longer help us approximate to the results of critical moral thinking, but at best to those of self-interested prudential thinking.

Rejecting, therefore, this manoeuvre, let us suppose that, as in our example, the cases whose probability we have to assess are qualitatively identical ones in which somebody tortures somebody else in an identical manner in all the cases. The moral thinker is not able to rule out from consideration cases in which he occupies a certain role, in favour of cases in which *he* occupies some other role. The reason for this is that the cases do not come to him from stage 1 distinguished in this way. (We may notice that this is why we are able to distinguish moral from prudential thinking; I am not relying on an argument of the form 'It would not be *moral* thinking if we proceeded in a certain manner', since nothing hangs on the word 'moral'; I mention the point only because of its interest.)

I hope I have now shown that special pleading cannot enter in at stage 1, and therefore cannot at stage 2 either. It follows that the principles which get selected for use at the intuitive level will be, not merely universal in form, but impartially selected. We may notice that by this means we have achieved one of the purposes for which, I surmise, Professor Rawls' 'veil of ignorance' was introduced, but without employing that questionable device. Our moral thinker does not have to be ignorant of his own role in the situation for which he is legislating; the logical nature of the thinking in which he is engaging prevents him from making use of this knowledge even if he has it.

If it be objected that the clever man we are considering might observe all these logical restrictions with his tongue in his cheek (i.e. with the intention all the time of getting at the end *prima facie* principles which suited him in his actual situation) he will be open to the charge of insincerity as already levelled against his colleague. For he is claiming to subscribe to prescriptive principles (i.e. to want things) to which he cannot really be subscribing. The above argument has put him into a position in which he has to prescribe for logically possible qualitatively identical cases, and not merely for actual ones;

we are back to the first interpretation, and the argument against that form of the objection suffices.

It will next be asked whether all these requirements of moral thought that I have mentioned are *logical* requirements, as I have claimed, in the sense that they can be seen to be requirements by looking at the logical properties of the moral concepts. I should like to maintain that this is indeed so. Let us take the requirements one by one. First, the moral thinker has to know what someone would be doing (himself for example) if he did the act under discussion. This knowledge of the facts includes, as we have just seen, an awareness of its impact on the persons affected, which cannot be had without sharing, in imagination, the desires of those persons. This is a logical requirement, not in the sense that to break it would be self-contradictory, but in the sense in which it is a logical requirement that we should ascertain that the cat *is* on the mat before we state that the cat is on the mat. Statements, in the proper sense of that word, are by definition truth-claims; and therefore the person who makes one is obliged by this logical property of the statement-making form of speech to satisfy himself that what he is saying is true. This *logical* requirement is to be distinguished from the *moral* duty to tell the truth, and cannot be used as the sole ground of that moral duty; there may be cases where there is a moral duty to make a false statement, but even in those cases the person who makes it is committing a logical (semantical, dialectical, conversational) fault.

Moral judgments share with factual statements the feature called universalizability,[18] and this brings with it an analogue of the requirement, when making statements, to speak the truth. Moral judgments are *about* situations, acts, people, etc.; they have subjects, just as factual statements have, and attach predicates to them, but the predicates are in this case moral ones.[19] However, because moral predicates are governed by this requirement of universalizability, they have what has been called descriptive meaning. The effect of this is that if I apply a moral predicate to something (an act, for example), I am committed to applying the same predicate to any precisely similar thing, if I am to be consistent, just as, when in a factual statement I apply a predicate to a thing, I am committed to applying the same predicate to any precisely similar thing. This has the consequence that when I am considering *what* predicates to apply to things, I have to consider, in both cases, what universal properties the things possess. For if I did not do this, I should be committing myself logically to I knew not what; in other words, I should not know what I was saying in either case.

This obscure point can also be put (at the cost of a certain undue rigidity) in terms of rules for the use of words. In using either descriptive or moral words we have to follow rules (i.e. we have to be consistent). And these rules have to be rules which prescribe the application of certain predicates to certain *kinds* of subjects and not others. In the case of factual statements, or of purely descriptive predicates, the rules are merely semantical ones; in the case of moral statements and predicates, they are moral rules. But in both cases we cannot observe such a rule without ascertaining what universal properties a subject possesses; if we could make statements without doing this, we could state without knowing what we were stating; for what we are stating is determined by the rules we are following in our use of expressions. Even in the moral case, we must know what the moral rule is, in the sense of knowing what it is about the subject that makes it appropriate to apply the moral predicate to it.[20]

In the factual case, when I say 'That thing is red', I am stating what I am stating only because 'red' has a certain meaning, i.e. is governed by a rule confining its use to the description of a certain kind of thing. If it were not for this rule, nobody would know (not even myself) what I was stating. In the moral case, the restriction is not so severe; moral predicates are not (*pace* the naturalists) restricted as to the universal descriptive properties which things have to have before the moral predicates are applied to them. But even from this less severe restriction it follows that, unless I am consistent in my moral judgments, applying moral predicates consistently to similar things, nobody will know (not even myself) what *moral* principles I am using in my judgments. And so the main function of moral judgments, to teach moral principles by instantiation, will be unfulfilled. The person who makes moral judgments without ascertaining the relevant facts about the subjects of them cannot have any principle in mind according to which he is making the judgments. The requirement to ascertain the facts is therefore a logical one. And, as we have seen, this extends to facts about the desires, etc., of those affected, which can only be ascertained by somebody who puts himself imaginatively in their places.

Next, let us consider the requirement of impartiality. It is impossible for a person without logical offence to make different moral judgments about cases which, after observing the requirement just mentioned of knowledge of the facts, he knows to be exactly similar. So much, at least, follows from the logical requirements of universalizability. Moreover, we can always adduce a case (a hypothetical one) which *is* exactly similar (in its universal properties) to the actual case in which, say, a person is contemplating torturing somebody. In this hypothetical case the universal properties will remain the same, but the individuals will change places. The agent in question has to be prepared to prescribe (as the prescriptivity of evaluative judgments, another of their logical features, requires) that the same thing be done in both cases. If he has satisfied the requirement of the preceding paragraph, he knows what it is like to be that person, and in order to have that knowledge must, as we have seen, also have the desires that his prospective victim has (for if he did not have them he would not really know what they were). So these two applications of universalizability, coupled with prescriptivity, compel him to give weight to the desires of the parties (himself and his victim) solely in proportion to their intensity, not giving his own desires in his actual situation extra weight. Thus impartiality also is shown to be a logical requirement.

Applying all this to the case of skin colour, we can perhaps, by illustrating the requirements involved, make them less obscure. Let us imagine, as before, a simple bilateral situation in which a white man is trying to justify some discriminatory act against a black man solely on the ground of his skin colour. The act will have effects to which the black man has an aversion greater than the desire of the white man to do the act. The white man proposes the principle that whites ought to do this sort of thing to blacks but not vice versa, relying on his knowledge that his own skin will never be black, and that therefore he will never suffer the effects of the application of his proposed principle. The principle is formally universal, and therefore, so far, logically unobjectionable. But can he *embrace* this prescriptive principle? To do so, he has, because it is prescriptive, to desire that it be observed; and, because it is universal, that it be observed universally in all cases to which it applies, including the hypothetical case in which he occupies the position of his proposed victim.

He says that he does desire this; but he says it only because he knows that he will never in fact occupy that position. We then ask him whether he really knows what the position is. In order to know this, he has to put himself in the position imaginatively, and in his imagination experience the desires which a person has in that situation, which entails himself (in imagination) having them. When he is doing this, we ask him whether he still wants the act to be done to him in that situation. He cannot answer, as he was previously disposed to answer, 'Yes', because if he did he would be being insincere; he would be claiming not to have a desire which he actually has: the desire not to be treated in that way if he were in that situation. If he did not have that desire, he would, as we have seen, not have full knowledge of the situation, which is a logical requirement for moral thinking, and itself requires the thinker to have, in imagination, the desires which are an integral part of the situation. Having this desire, which *ex hypothesi* is greater than his original desire to do the act, he cannot, if he is to make the same judgment about the actual situation as about this hypothetical similar one (another logical requirement), give greater weight to his own original desire than to his victim's; for to do so would be to give greater weight to the lesser desire among desires *which he himself has* (one of them originally, and one of them latterly in his imagination). That is why he cannot really and sincerely assent to the principle on which he claims to be relying, that whites ought to do this to blacks in such a situation.

In order to see why skin colour is not morally relevant in such a case, we have had to go very deep into the requirements for moral thought. A superficial application of the universalizability-requirement such as is made by some writers will not do the trick, because the principles to which racists might appeal could be strictly universal ones. We have to ask whether they can go on appealing to them when they have understood (1) that moral principles are prescriptive; (2) that their universalizability requires knowledge of all the relevant facts; and (3) that these facts include one, namely the desire of their victim, whose full intensity cannot be known to them unless they have in imagination shared it. The answer is that, if the relative strengths of the desires is as we have supposed, they cannot then go on appealing to these racist principles, because they cannot desire, and therefore cannot sincerely prescribe, that greater present desires of theirs should be subordinate to lesser.

This does not dispose of by any means all the difficulties and objections which can be raised against golden-rule arguments. There is, for example, the objection that our opponent might claim, not that whites *ought to* treat blacks in the way proposed, but only that it is *all right* for them to do it.[21] To answer this objection would require another very deep examination of the requirements of moral thinking, and in particular of the logical properties of permissions (of which there are several diverse kinds, not always carefully enough distinguished), and also of the escape-route from moral thinking known as amoralism. The too brief remarks about this in my *Freedom and Reason*[22] would have to be expanded to at least the same length as in this paper I have expanded another paragraph in that book, in order fully to answer that objection.

Oxford University

NOTES

[1] Printed in my *Essays on Philosophical Method* (London, Macmillan, 1971; Berkeley, University of California Press, 1972).
[2] *A Theory of Justice* (Cambridge, Mass., Harvard University Press, 1971), p. 131.
[3] See my review, *Ph. Q.* 12 (1962), p. 353.

[4] Cf. P.R. Foot, 'Moral Beliefs', *Proc. of Arist. Soc.* 59 (1958/9).

[5] Cf. G.J. Warnock, *Contemporary Moral Philosophy* (London, Macmillan, 1967), p. 67.

[6] See my 'Descriptivism', *Proc. of Br. Acad.* 49 (1963), reproduced in my *Essays on the Moral Concepts* (London, Macmillan and Berkeley, University of California Press, 1972), sec. 7.

[7] See my review of G.J. Warnock, *Contemporary Moral Philosophy, Mind* 77 (1968).

[8] See my 'Wrongness and Harm', in my *Essays on the Moral Concepts*.

[9] See my *Freedom and Reason* (Oxford, Oxford University Press, 1963), ch. 4 and my 'Prediction and Moral Appraisal', *Midwest Studies in Philosophy,* 3 (1978).

[10] 'Universalisability', *Proc. of Arist. Soc.* 55 (1954/5).

[11] 'A Note to the Paralogisms', in G. Ryle (ed.), *Contemporary Aspects of Philosophy* (Oxford, Oriel Press, 1976).

[12] For the relation between wanting and sincerely prescribing see my *Freedom and Reason,* p. 111; 'Wanting: Some Pitfalls', in R. Binkley et al. (eds.) *Agent, Action and Reason* (Toronto, Toronto U.P. and Oxford, Blackwell, 1971), repr. in my *Practical Inferences* (London, Macmillan, 1971; Berkeley, University of California Press, 1972).

[13] See my 'Principles', *Proc. of Arist. Soc.* 73 (1972/3) and 'Ethical Theory and Utilitarianism', in H.D. Lewis (ed.), *Contemporary British Philosophy* 4 (London, Allen and Unwin, 1976).

[14] See 'Ethical Theory and Utilitarianism', cited above.

[15] Ibid., p. 125.

[16] For the distinction between universality and generality see my 'Principles', cited above.

[17] See my 'Ethical Theory and Utilitarianism', cited above, pp. 123 f.

[18] See my *Freedom and Reason,* ch. 2.

[19] It would be tedious to complicate this remark in order to cover moral and other statements which are not of subject-predicate form; but it could be done.

[20] This is explained more fully and accurately in my *Freedom and Reason,* ch. 2.

[21] Cf. D.P. Gauthier, 'Hare's Debtors', *Mind* 77 (1968).

[22] pp. 100 ff.

ALLAN GIBBARD

ACT-UTILITARIAN AGREEMENTS*

1. INTRODUCTION

Would rational act-utilitarians keep their agreements? Suppose two highly rational act-utilitarians agree to meet for a walk in the park. The best outcome they can achieve is to meet as agreed, and the next best is for both to stay home and read. Because each would find it distressing to come and not find the other, the worst outcome they can achieve is for one to come to the park and the other to stay at home. Suppose everything above is *common knowledge* between them, in the sense that each knows it, each knows the other knows it, each knows the other knows that he knows it, and so on *ad infinitem*. Under these circumstances, either person would keep the agreement if he knew the other would, for he could then conclude that his coming as agreed would yield the best outcome, that they meet, whereas his staying at home would yield the worst outcome, that one comes and the other stays home. On the other hand, either would break the agreement if he knew that the other would break it, for in that case he could reason that if he came as agreed, he would achieve the worst outcome, that one comes and the other stays at home, whereas if he stayed home, he would achieve the intermediate outcome that both stay home. All this will be common knowledge between the two. Does any of it, though, give either of them grounds for keeping the agreement?

According to D. H. Hodgson (1967, pp. 38–50), neither would have any more reason for keeping the agreement than he would have for coming to the park without an agreement — than he would have if meeting at the park had only been mentioned as a possibility. Precisely because both are highly rational, knowledgeable act-utilitarians, he argues, agreements between them are pointless: agreeing to an arrangement will have no effect on what they actually do. Even if the consequences of meeting would be splendid, they will have no way of bringing these consequences about.

The lesson of this case applies to whole societies. According to Hodgson, if by common knowledge a society consisted of highly rational act-utilitarians, that society would fall apart, because its members would be unable to

91

A. I. Goldman and J. Kim (eds.), Values and Morals, 91–119. All Rights Reserved.
Copyright © 1978 by D. Reidel Publishing Company, Dordrecht, Holland.

coordinate their actions by agreement. Such act-utilitarians would produce few good consequences indeed.

David Lewis (1969, Chs. I–III; 1972) argues that nothing so surprising is the case. He concludes, in effect, that if the society of the two who agreed to meet for a walk in the park had a history of agreement-keeping, their agreement to meet would give them each good reason to come to the meeting-place as agreed. I shall discuss the arguments both of Hodgson and of Lewis in the next section. It is Lewis's argument that provides the starting point for the work in this paper.

The question I want to ask is whether, in the circumstances Hodgson considers, the inability of act-utilitarians to make agreements binding would cause any loss of good results. Suppose a society consists of highly rational act-utilitarians, and this fact is common knowledge among them. Call a society of this kind *openly act-utilitarian*. Now imagine that members of the society could somehow bring it about — perhaps by magic — that any agreement they made would be kept. There are many agreements they would then avoid. They would make no agreement they could improve: they would reject an agreement if the consequences of making it binding would not be as good as the consequences of making some alternative agreement binding. Call the agreements they might indeed make in these circumstances *optimal*. An optimal agreement, then, is an agreement act-utilitarians might make if they could somehow make binding any agreement they chose. This term defined, my question now concerns an openly act-utilitarian society of a less astonishing kind, where there is no magical way of making agreements binding. Are there, I shall ask, optimal agreements that, if made in such an openly act-utilitarian society, would be broken no matter how extensive the history of agreement-keeping in that society might be?

The answer may be crucial to the appeal of act-utilitarianism. Act-utilitarianism presumably appeals to those who think that morality is grounded in the production of good consequences. Now suppose that an openly act-utilitarian society would attain less good than would that same society if it had a morality that made optimal agreements binding independently of consequences. That may give someone who thinks morality a matter of doing good a reason for preferring a morality which makes optimal agreements binding. This line of attack on act-utilitarianism fails if it is indeed the case that, in an openly act-utilitarian society, any optimal agreement can be made as good as binding by a suitable history of agreement-keeping.

In this paper, the answers I give to my question are preliminary. I shall state conditions for a practice to be, in a sense, self-perpetuating in an openly act-utiliarian society; such practices I shall call *AU-conventions*. I shall characterize a kind of agreement that there could be an AU-convention of keeping. Such agreements will be said to be in *foreseeable U-equilibrium*. Finally, I shall shall give a set of conditions sufficient for all optimal agreements to be in foreseeable *U*-equilibrium.

Three of these conditions are of prime importance: first, that the parties be highly rational, second, that when they make an agreement, they can share their information so that all agree on the nature of the situation they face, and third, that the good and bad consequences of making an agreement binding would stem entirely from its being carried out, rather than from anticipation or dread of its being carried out. These are conditions which we might expect to hold frequently, but certainly not invariably. What I claim to establish then, is limited. Perhaps, as Hodgson says, act-utilitarians would lose opportunities to bring about good consequences because they could not bind themselves to reasonable agreements. If that is so, however, then the argument that shows it will have to appeal to circumstances in which at least one of the conditions I state is violated.

2. HODGSON'S ARGUMENT AND LEWIS'S ANSWER

Return to the pair who agree to meet for a walk in the park. John and Harriet, let us suppose, are highly rational act-utilitarians, and they agree to meet at the park at noon. The best outcome is for them to meet, the worst is for one to come and not find the other. Each, we have already seen, will keep the agreement if he expects the other to keep it and break the agreement if he expects the other to break it. Indeed for each there is presumably a probability that is *critical*, in the sense that he will come if the probability he ascribes to the other's coming exceeds it and stay home if the probability he ascribes to the other's coming is less than it.

Now according to Hodgson, neither person has any more reason to go to the park at noon than he would have if they had not agreed, but simply mentioned the possibility. I shall give in free form the part of his argument I think correct, and then try to give the part I think wrong.

From the common knowledge that each will come if and only if he thinks it sufficiently likely that the other will, each could reason about the other's coming in an endless, increasingly involved spiral. Take Harriet's reasoning on whether John will come. She knows that he will come iff he thinks it sufficiently likely that she will come. Thus the agreement gives her reason for expecting him to come iff it gives her reason for expecting him to think it sufficiently likely that she will come. Does it? She can carry the reasoning further: she knows that he knows that she will come iff she considers it sufficiently likely that he will come. Thus the agreement gives her reason for expecting him to come iff it gives her reason for expecting him to think it sufficiently likely that she will think it sufficiently likely that he will come. This spiral can be extended indefinitely, without giving her any more reason for expecting him to come than she would have in the absence of an agreement, and hence without giving her any more reason for coming to the park than she would have in the absence of an agreement.

Indeed, no reasoning from the stated facts of the case could show that she had more reason for coming with an agreement than without. For it is consistent with the facts stated so far that, by common knowledge between the two, each be completely sceptical of the other's agreements — sceptical in the sense that neither would ever take the other's agreeing to something either as evidence that he would do it or as evidence that he would not. Now if that were so, then each would have various grounds for being completely sceptical of the other's agreement. One sound line of reasoning Harriet might use is this: "John is completely sceptical of my agreements. Thus in light of our agreement, he will think me sufficiently likely to come if and only if he would think me sufficiently likely to come without an agreement. Therefore he will come if and only if he would come without an agreement; thus the agreement will not affect his behavior." On this line of reasoning, then, it is rational for her to be completely sceptical of his agreement.

What this shows is that in at least one possible situation which fits all the original specifications of the park example, agreeing to meet gives neither person a reason for coming to the park. Hence the original specifications do not entail that agreeing to meet gives either person a reason for coming. Hodgson, though, wants to claim something much stronger: he apparently holds that in every possible situation that fits the original specifications, agreeing to meet would give neither person a reason for coming. Let S be the original specifications of the park example, and let ϕ be the conclusion that agreeing to meet would give John and Harriet a reason for coming at the agreed time. The argument I have given shows that S does not entail ϕ; Hodgson claims, on the basis of such an argument, that S entails $\sim \phi$.

If from the description of the case it follows neither that an agreement would affect behavior nor that it would have no effect on behavior, then the effect of an agreement on behavior may depend on aspects of the situation not included in the description. I claim it indeed does. It depends on the parties' common knowledge of whether they, or people in their society, have generally kept agreements in the past. If it is common knowledge that they have, they will rationally keep this agreement. If it is common knowledge that in the past they have given no heed to agreements, then they will rationally give no heed to this agreement. The effect of an agreement depends on whether past history has established what we might call a 'convention.'

I shall not stress the argument for this conclusion, since it is given by David Lewis. Here, though, is an argument that in some possible situations which fit the specifications of the park example, an agreement would make it rational for John and Harriet to come to the park as agreed. Suppose it is common knowledge between them that they have consistently kept their agreements in the past. This gives Harriet a good inductive reason for thinking John likely to come, and hence gives her a rational ground for coming. Moreover, similar reasoning gives him a rational ground for coming. She knows this, and that gives her a second reason for expecting him to come. Hence she has a second rational ground for coming. The process can be carried as far as the two can trust each other to reason. Similar reasoning gives John a second rational ground for coming, and since Harriet knows this, she has a third reason for expecting him — and so on. Suppose further that it is common knowledge that the two have never in the past come to the park without agreeing in advance. Then in the absence of an agreement, Harriet would have a series of good reasons not to come to the park. First, she would have inductive grounds for not expecting John. Second, knowing that John has inductive grounds for not expecting her, and that he would come only if he thought her sufficiently likely to come, she would have a second reason for not expecting him. Again the reasoning can be extended, and each step gives her an additional reason for not expecting him, and hence an additional reason for staying at home herself.

In short, given these two pieces of common knowledge — that in the past, John and Harriet have kept their agreements, and that they have never come to the park without an agreement — they have a good utilitarian reason for coming to the park if and only if they have agreed to. Contrary to what Hodgson says, an agreement can make a difference in an openly act-utilitarian society.

3. RATIONAL ACT-UTILITARIANS

Hodgson asks us to consider a society in which everyone attempts to act in accordance with the 'act-utilitarian principle' (1967, p. 38), which, as Hodgson uses the term, is a principle for what is *objectively right* — right in light of all facts, regardless of what the agent can know. His 'act-utilitarian principle' refers to actual consequences of acts, not to their probable or reasonably forseeable consequences (p. 13). Now theories of what is objectively right have no direct bearing on the problem Hodgson raises. Hodgson's thesis concerns the behavior of rational act-utilitarians who do not know what to expect from each other: they know they lack relevant information. In order to know what they will do, we need to know how they base their decisions on information they know is incomplete.

It will not do simply to say that these people 'attempt' to do what, according to act-utilitarianism, is objectively right. If that makes sense at all, it means that each of them always performs the act he thinks most likely to have the best actual consequences. That, however, would sometimes be preposterous: it would sometimes mean taking grave risks for the sake of a slight good — like the man who drives through a blind intersection in light traffic without slowing down because doing so is slightly more likely to save time than to cause an accident. Such a policy would indeed bring frequent disaster, but no one would need Hodgson's arguments to tell him so.

A theory of rationally attempting to act in accordance with act-utilitarianism must be a theory of how to behave in light of what one knows and believes, and of the probabilities one ascribes to things uncertain. Such a theory is an act-utilitarian theory of what is *subjectively right*, by which I mean right in the light both of what it is rational for the agent to believe about relevant non-moral states of affairs and of the probabilities it is rational for him to ascribe to them.[1] Thus by *act-utilitarianism* as a theory of subjective rightness, I shall mean the theory that an act is subjectively right iff the expected value of its consequences, as reckoned from the information available to the agent, is at least as great as that of any alternative. Such an act I shall call *AU-right*. A perfectly rational act-utilitarian of the kind relevant to Hodgson's problem is, I shall suppose, a person who performs only acts that are *AU-right*.

I shall develop act-utilitarianism for subjective rightness abstractly, for not all features of the theory need to be specified in order for the issues in this paper to be explored. I start with a simple non-moral framework for expressing expected value maximization. Let a finite number of *acts* be open to an agent on an occasion. The *actual outcome* of an act is the totality of its value-laden consequences; *an outcome* of an act is something which may, for all the agent knows, be the actual outcome of the act. The *outcome-probability* of an outcome on an act is the probability the agent rationally ascribes to its being the actual outcome of the act.[2] The assignment of outcome probabilities to the outcomes of an act will be called the *prospect* of the act. More generally, we can treat the prospect of an act as relative to certain information. The prospect of an act *given* information K is what the prospect of that act would be if K were the total information of the agent.

To this non-moral framework of outcomes and prospects, a utilitarian adds a theory of intrinsic value. If he wants only a theory of objective rightness, then a theory of intrinsic value will be adequate for his purposes if it gives a weak ordering of outcomes alone – if it tells when one outcome is *intrinsically better* than another. (A *weak* ordering is a complete ordering that allows ties.) For a utilitarian theory of subjective rightness, more is needed: to be adequate for that purpose, a theory of intrinsic value must give a weak ordering not only of outcomes but of prospects. We might speak of one prospect as being *more favorable* than another in terms of the intrinsic values it portends. I shall suppose, then, that we have a weak ordering of prospects by how *favorable* they are. According to act-utilitarianism, an act is subjectively right iff its prospect given what the agent knows is at least as favorable as that of any other act open to the agent on that occasion. An *AU-right* act will be an act that is subjectively right by this standard, and a *rational act-utilittarian* will be a person who performs only AU-right acts.

On this weak order of prospects, we shall need to impose a condition of coherence. A weak ordering of prospects might be incoherent in various ways; here is an example. Let prospect r differ from prospect s only in that r makes outcome O_1 more likely, at the expense of outcome O_2. It would seem incoherent to say both that (i) the prospect of O_1 as a sure thing is more favorable than the prospect of O_2 as a sure thing, and that (ii) s is more favorable than r. In the later, more technical part of this paper, a coherence condition will be imposed on the weak ordering of prospects that rules out situations like this one.

4. AU-CONVENTIONS

A history of keeping agreements in situations like that of the park example would lead to what we might call a convention. A convention in this sense can be defined as follows. An *occasion* is an agent at a time; a *situation* is a set of agents at a time. A *coordination plan* is given by a set of prescriptions telling how to act on certain occasions on the basis of one's non-moral beliefs. Let $\mathcal{C}$ be a set of people and $\mathcal{S}$ a set of situations involving only people in $\mathcal{C}$. A coordination plan P is an *AU proto-convention* (or simply *proto-convention*) iff at the time of each situation S in $\mathcal{S}$, it is common knowledge among

the agents in S that for each of them, given (i) what he knows, (ii) that all the
others follow P in S, and (iii) that all expect P to be followed in S, it is
AU-right to follow P on that occasion. A proto-convention P is an *AU-con-*
vention at t^* iff, at t^*, it is common knowledge among $\mathcal{C}$ that P has been
extensively followed by them in the past. Such common knowledge will be
called a *supporting history* for P; hence an AU convention is an AU proto-
convention with a supporting history.

An AU-convention is very much like a convention in the sense that David
Lewis (1969) explicates. At two points my analysis differs from Lewis's, but
this is only to suit my analysis directly to what Hodgson says. Lewis uses a
more realistic notion of common knowledge than Hodgson or I do. Hodgson
calls something common knowledge if "everyone knows of it, and everyone
knows that everyone knows, and so on." (p. 39) I have taken the "and so on"
to mean "and so on *ad infinitum*" — that no matter how many times 'everyone knows' is iterated, the assertion still holds. Lewis assumes that reasoning
can only be carried to a finite length. Lewis also has a more relaxed condition
of identical preferences than we need in discussing a society of perfectly
rational act-utilitarians. Hence I differ intentionally from Lewis on what a
convention is, but only because to answer Hodgson I do not need as sophisticated a notion as Lewis develops. Convention as defined by Lewis would
work as well for my purposes as what I have said.

At first glance, an appeal to AU-conventions might seem to subvert my
argument against Hodgson. Hodgson stipulates that in the society we are to
consider, there are no "conventional moral rules." If this rules out AU-
conventions, then in showing that members of an openly act-utilitarian
society would keep promises if they had an appropriate AU-convention, I
shall not be refuting Hodgson.

Hodgson, however, defines "conventional moral rules" much more narrowly than I am defining AU-conventions. Something is a conventional moral
rule in Hodgson's sense only if deviations from it "are generally regarded as
lapses or faults open to criticism." AU-conventions do not need to be sustained by criticism. They are sustained by common knowledge that each
person chooses the most favorable prospect when he acts, and that he reasons
inductively. Hence there can be an openly act-utilitarian society which satisfies Hodgson's stipulation that there be no conventional moral rules, and
which still has AU-conventions.

An AU-convention is self-perpetuating in the following sense. (1) Among
the agents involved, it is common knowledge that each has inductive grounds
for expecting it to be followed. (2) From the premises that their society is

openly act-utilitarian and that by common knowledge among them, each expects the AU-convention to be followed in that situation, each can reason in many ways that it is AU-right for each to follow it, and in no way can he reason that it is not AU-right for any of them to follow it. In this sense, the inductively grounded belief that an AU-convention will be followed is self-reinforcing.

There is an important point to note here. We have not specified the mores of a society when we say that by common knowledge among its members, everyone in it is a rational act utilitarian. We need to say what AU-conventions prevail. In a society with no convention of queuing, for instance, everyone might agree that queuing was superior to a free-for-all, and yet it might be rational for each person to join the conventional free-for-all, so that everyone will get roughly his share.

5. STARTING AN AU-CONVENTION

In an openly act-utilitarian society, any AU-convention would in a sense be self-perpetuating. A proto-convention, though, forms an AU-convention only if it has a supporting history. That leaves open the question of whether, in an openly act-utilitarian society, a proto-convention could ever acquire a supporting history — whether it would ever be followed in the first place. Either, it would seem, before there had been a history of its being followed, no rational act-utilitarian would start to follow it, or a supporting history would be superfluous: rational act-utilitarians would follow the proto-convention even without a supporting history.

Why would anyone follow a proto-convention before it had a supporting history? The answer, I think, lies in teaching. A rational act-utilitarian would follow certain proto-conventions simply to teach others to expect them to be followed. In a society where everyone had just openly converted to act-utilitarianism, there would be occasions on which the act with the best consequences would be to teach others what to expect. For from all we have said, it is evident that the utility of each knowing what to expect from others in such a society is enormous.

Take the case of agreements. How would an act-utilitarian go about teaching others to expect agreements to be kept? With no past history of keeping agreements among avowed act-utilitarians, people would have to choose carefully the agreements to which they subscribed. If they made an agreement it would not be rational to keep, the agreement would be broken, and this would teach people to expect agreements not to be kept. On the other hand, agreements to do things it would be rational to do even without an agreement do not serve as precedents for agreements that are needed to coordinate actions. For keeping such an agreement does not show people in the future that agreements have affected what people do. Thus the teacher needs to make agreements to do things it would not be rational for him to do without an agreement, but which he can rationally do given the agreement. In the absence of any supporting history for a proto-convention of keeping agreements, how is this possible?

The answer lies precisely in the good which would result if people could be made to expect agreements to be kept. This consideration changes the expected consequences of keeping or breaking an agreement. Keeping the agreement produces not only the results which would come from acting the same way without an agreement, but evidence that agreements will be kept, whereas breaking an agreement produces evidence that agreements will be broken. The teacher should agree to do things everyone knows would not be rational without an agreement, but which are made rational by the utility of teaching people to expect agreement-keeping.

Hodgson entertains the idea of a teaching effect, and concludes that in an openly act-utilitarian society there would be none.

> The one act of promise-keeping in such a case could arouse expectations of further such acts only if it was taken to indicate that such acts can have best consequences. It would be known that *this* act would have best consequences only if it aroused expectations of further such acts, and so there would be reason for such expectations only if the further acts would also arouse such expectations. And so on *ad infinitum*, or at least until there is doubt as to the rationality of future generations. Thus, even an act of promise-keeping, which would not have had best consequences apart from the promise, would not arouse expectations unless this infinite regress could be halted, and if it did not arouse expectations, it would not have best consequences. If universal rationality (and knowledge of this) is assumed, then the performance of a promise could be a ground for belief in future performances of future promises only if the first performance is taken as a sign of *commitment* to the rule that promises ought to be kept: and this is excluded if the person performing the promise is known to be an act-utilitarian. (p. 47)

Note the first sentence here. We have seen that sometimes keeping a promise will have best consequences because promise-keeping is expected. In such cases, the good consequences stem from coordination, not simply from promoting further expectations. Hence the 'infinite' regress Hodgson proclaims need not go beyond the second step, when some inductive ground has been established for expecting promises to be kept.

Perhaps Hodgson is saying it is irrational to rely on induction from past acts of promise-keeping. I can see no reason, though, why it should be irrational to do so. True, since everyone knows the same facts, it is rational to expect a promise to be kept only if it is rational to keep it. This does not mean, however, the the rationality of keeping it is the only possible rational ground for expecting it to be kept. The fact that it is possible to reason in a circle does not mean it is impossible to reason any other way.

It might be claimed not that reliance on induction is irrational, but that in an openly act-utilitarian society in the situations we are considering, induction is unnecessary.[3] The rule each party uses in making decisions is common knowledge, and enough else is common knowledge in these cases that the parties can predict each others' actions without regard to what has been done in like situations in the past.

So to argue, though, would be to ignore the most striking point about the situations we have been considering: that from the premise that both the immediate situation and the parties' act-utilitarian rationality are common knowledge, one cannot conclude deductively what it is AU-right for the parties to do. The parties, then, need not find further premises superfluous.

Let me turn back to the objection that began this section. If it is rational to follow a proto-convention only when it has a supporting history, then, it must have been irrational for anyone to follow it in the first place, and so in a society of rational agents, a supporting history could never arise. No history that can come into being, then, will ever give an agent in such a society reason to follow that proto-convention.

In order to answer this objection, let me first distinguish two kinds of proto-conventions. A *specific* proto-convention is one that applies to situations that are exactly alike in all respects relevant to decision except for their history. A *generic* proto-convention is one that is not specific.

Take first the case of a specific proto-convention in an openly act-utilitarian society. I agree that if it is rational to follow the proto-convention only when it has a supporting history, then a supporting history could never arise in the first place. It may, however, have been rational to follow the proto-convention before it had a supporting history precisely because a history of its being followed could later make it rational to follow it and a history of its not being followed − an 'undermining history', I shall say − could later make it irrational to follow it.

The status of a specific proto-convention might well be this. (1) Premises about the parties' decision rules and knowledge about the current situation, together with the premise that there will be no teaching effect, do not support the prediction that it will be followed. (2) These premises, plus the premise of a supporting history for the proto-convention, do support the prediction that it will be followed. (3) The premises in (1) plus the premise of an undermining history support the prediction that the proto-convention will not be followed. (4) In the first situation to which the proto-convention applies, where it has neither a supporting nor an undermining history, parties' knowledge of (1), (2), and (3) gives them reason for following the proto-convention, because establishing the beginnings of a supporting history has good expected consequences and establishing the beginnings of an under-mining history has bad expected consequences.

Thus before there is either a supporting or an undermining history for a specific proto-convention, it may be rational to follow it, not because history is irrelevant, but precisely because, teaching effect aside, it would be rational to follow it given a supporting history and irrational to follow it given an undermining history. Thus because of the teaching effect, people would follow the specific proto-convention even without a supporting history, but that is because they know that in the absence of a teaching effect, the follow-ing of that proto-convention in the future would depend on a supporting history.

In the case of a generic proto-convention, further considerations enter. By following the proto-convention in cases of little import, a person may teach others to expect the proto-convention to be followed when it is crucial that they expect it to be. Take agreements again: The agreements that matter are ones like that made by John and Harriet: agreements such that, teaching effect aside, it is a good thing if everyone keeps them, but a bad thing if some parties keep them and others do not. Now in some cases, the direct consequences of partial compliance to an agreement may be only mildly bad, whereas in other cases, those direct consequences may be disastrous. A teacher should start with agreements partial compliance to which has only mildly bad direct consequences, and by keeping those agreements, teach people to expect him to keep agreements of a wider kind. For through induction, experience gives evidence not only about future cases that are exactly like the experienced cases, but about future cases that are roughly similar to the experienced cases but not exactly like them.

Thus, in the case of a generic proto-convention, it may be rational to follow the proto-convention once there is a supporting history in cases in which it would be irrational, all things considered, to follow it without a supporting history, and yet a supporting history may arise through the proto-convention's being followed in cases of a different kind — in cases where the effects of partial compliance are only mildly bad.

6. OPTIMAL AGREEMENTS

Act-utilitarians who could make agreements binding at will would be careful about which agreements they chose to make binding. An agreement will be said to be *optimal* for a party to it iff the prospect of making it binding, given what the party knows at the time he makes the agreement, is at least as favorable as the prospect of making any alternative binding. Here by an *alternative* to an agreement, I mean another possible agreement by the same parties, to be carried out at the same time. An act-utilitarian who could make binding any agreement he chose would confine himself to optimal agreements. For suppose agreement P is not optimal. Then there is some alternative Q such that the prospect of making Q binding is more favorable than the prospect of making P binding. But since the party can make binding any agreement he chooses, among the acts open to him at the time he makes P binding is the act of making Q binding. Hence the prospect of making P binding is less favorable than the prospect of some other act open to him at the time, and making P binding is not AU-right.

For it to be AU-right to make agreement P binding, it is not sufficient that it be optimal. The prospect of some act other than making an alternative binding may be more desirable than the prospect of making P binding. This does not keep P from being optimal, but it does keep it from being AU-right to make P binding. When an agent can make binding any agreement he chooses, optimality is a necessary but not a sufficient condition for it to be AU-right to make a given agreement binding.

If we set conditions on our openly act-utilitarian society, we can say more about optimal agreements. If at the time they make an agreement, the parties can pool their knowledge and agree on the risks involved, then an agreement optimal for one of the parties will be optimal for all. If in addition, all the utility in making an agreement binding stems from carrying it out, then an agreement is optimal iff the prospect of carrying it out is at least as favorable as the prospect of carrying out any alternative, given what the parties know at the time the agreement is made. These conditions will be exploited later in the argument.

An optimal agreement may well not be an agreement categorically to perform a certain act at a certain time. At the time the agreement is to be carried out, some of the parties may have information they did not have when the agreement was made. An agreement may give each party a contingency plan, which tells him what to do for each state of knowledge he may be in when he is to act. If all pertinent calculations can be performed at no cost in utility, the agreement can be as complicated as need be to make it offer a most favorable prospect.

Consider the park example with new complications: As seen when the agreement is made, there is a one-in-ten chance that John will have visitors and a one-in-five chance that Harriet will. No telephone communicates between their houses, and hence neither will be able to tell the other if visitors have arrived. When the time comes to meet, then, each will know whether he has visitors but not whether the other does. Each, then, could agree to any of four possible contingency plans. (1) Stay at home no matter what. (2) Stay at home if visitors come; go to the park if not. (3) Go to the park if visitors come; stay home if not. (4) Go to the park no matter what. An agreement would assign one such contingency plan to each of the two parties.

The term 'contingency plan' can be characterized as follows. Let t_0 be the time the agreement is made; t_1, the time it is to be carried out. A contingency plan assigns an act to each state of new relevant information the agent may be in at t_1. Information is *new* iff the agent has it at t_1 but did not have it at t_0. It is *relevant* iff it alters the relative favorability of the prospects of the various acts open to him at t_1 (for only then it can affect his choice). A's state of new relevant information consists of all the new relevant information A has at t_1. A *may* be in state K at t_1 iff the probability the parties assign at t_0 to A's being in state K at t_1 is non-zero. A *contingency* for A is a state of new relevant knowledge A may be in at t_1. It *holds* or *obtains* iff A is in that state at t_1. A *contingency plan* for A is an assignment of an act to each contingency K for A, where the act assigned to K is one which will be open to A if K holds. An *agreement* assigns a contingency plan to each party.

7. BINDING AGREEMENTS AND ACT-UTILITARIANS

Hodgson argues that members of an openly act-utilitarian society would lose utility because they would be unable to bind agreements with promises. An agreement is *somewhat binding* in a given morality iff the morality gives some weight to keeping the agreement independently of whether the prospect of keeping it is most desirable; it is *binding* in that morality iff the morality requires it to be kept whatever opposing considerations there may be. Since act-utilitarians decide what to do entirely by the favorability of the prospects involved, act-utilitarians cannot make agreements binding, or even somewhat binding. If there were some way act-utilitarians could invoke automatic sanctions when they made agreements, though, these sanctions would have

the same effect among them as would making the agreement somewhat binding among non-act-utilitarians. Suppose, for example, the invocation "If I
break this agreement, may I be struck by lightning" actually led to violators
being struck by lightning. An act-utilitarian who knew this would keep almost
any agreement he so sealed with the invocation. Indeed, so stringent a sanction would have the effect of making the agreement almost fully binding. In
what I say here, I will not distinguish making an agreement binding in the
strict sense and invoking strong automatic sanctions — nor will I need to.

The question I want to answer, then, is this: could an openly act-utilitarian
society have an AU-convention of agreement-keeping that made the binding
of agreements superfluous, in the sense that even if it were possible to invoke
strong automatic sanctions for agreement-keeping, there would be no utility
in doing so?

8. U-EQUILIBRIUM

The question I am asking in this paper is whether an openly act-utilitarian
society could have an AU-convention of agreement-keeping that made the
binding of agreements superfluous. In this section, I shall define a broad
class of agreements there could be an AU-convention of keeping; I shall
call them agreements in 'U-equilibrium.' Later I shall state conditions under
which all optimal agreements are in U-equilibrium.

Let an agreement P be made at t_0 to be carried out at t_1. Let A_i be a party
to the agreement who can perform act x at t_1; the *prospect under trust* in P
of act x for A_i is the prospect of x with respect to the following information:
what A_i knows at t_1, that all parties other than A_i keep the agreement, and
that all parties expect the agreement to be kept. An agreement P is *utilitarian
given trust* iff for each party, the prospect under trust in P of keeping P is at
least as favorable as the prospect under trust in P of any other act open to
him at t_1. P is in *U-equilibrium* iff it is common knowledge among the parties
at t_1 that P is utilitarian given trust, and P is in *foreseeable U-equilibrium* iff
it is common knowledge at t_0 that P will be in U-equilibrium. (Here in the
definition of 'common knowledge,' I shall count a person as knowing something if he rationally ascribes it a probability of one.)

In the rest of this paper, I plan to show that (1) there could be an AU-
convention of keeping all agreements in U-equilibrium, and that (2) under
certain conditions which I shall state, all optimal agreements are in foreseeable U-equilibrium. Hence under the conditions I shall state, there could be
an AU-convention which included the keeping of all optimal agreements.

In most cases if the parties are to know when an agreement is made that it will be in U-equilibrium, it cannot be simply an agreement categorically to perform a certain act at a certain time. In this respect, foreseeable U-equilibrium is like optimality. Between the time t_0 when the agreement is made and the time t_1 when it is to be carried out, some agents will have learned new things. This new knowledge will affect the probabilities they assign, on the assumption that others keep the agreement, to the outcomes the acts open to them may have. Hence new knowledge may change the prospects under trust in the agreement of the various acts open to the parties. If an agreement P is to be in foreseeable U-equilibrium, keeping P must offer the best prospect under trust in P for each party in all contingencies. For this to hold, P may well need to prescribe different acts in different contingencies.

Suppose the parties to an agreement can pool their relevant knowledge at t_0, when the agreement is made, and hence agree on all probabilities and on all prospects under trust in an agreement. Suppose also that it is common knowledge at all times that at t_1, when the agreement is to be carried out, everyone remembers what he knew at t_0. Then we can characterize an agreement in foreseeable U-equilibrium which assigns a contingency plan to each agent. It will be an agreement such that for each agent, whatever contingency holds for him, the prospect under trust in that agreement of carrying it out is most favorable. At t_0 the parties can calculate what the prospect under trust in the agreement will be for each agent and contingency that may hold for him. By the supposition of perfect memory, they can remember these calculations at t_1. Hence at t_1 it is common knowledge that whatever contingency holds for each agent, the agreement is utilitarian given trust, and at t_0 the parties knew it would be common knowledge at t_1.

Suppose that by common knowledge in a society $\mathfrak{A}$, a practice of keeping all agreements in U-equilibrium has been extensively followed in the past. Then that practice is an AU-convention in society $\mathfrak{A}$. For let S be the class of all situations $\langle \mathfrak{B}, t \rangle$, where $\mathfrak{B} \subseteq \mathfrak{A}$ and t is a time, such that there is an agreement among the members of $\mathfrak{B}$ which is to be carried out at t and which is in U-equilibrium at t. The practice of keeping all U-equilibrium agreements is, by definition, an AU-convention governing S in $\mathfrak{A}$ if the following condition holds: at the time of each situation S in S, it is common knowledge among the agents in S that for each of them, given what he knows, that all the others follow the practice in S, and that all expect the practice to be followed in S, it is AU-right to follow the practice in S. By the way the practice and S were characterized, this condition is equivalent to saying that at the time each U-equilibrium agreement is to be carried out, the following holds: it is common knowledge among the parties to the agreement that for each of them, given what he knows, that all the others keep the agreement, and that all expect the agreement to be kept, it is AU-right to keep the agreement. Now this holds for any U-equilibrium agreement simply by the definition of U-equilibrium. Thus we have shown that if, in a society, a practice of keeping all agreements in U-equilibrium has been extensively followed in the past, that practice is an AU-convention in that society.

9. THE CONDITIONS

Any optimal agreement, it will be shown, is in foreseeable U-equilibrium if it is common knowledge that the following conditions are met. (1) *Full communication at t_0*. At the time the agreement is made, the parties share their relevant experience. Hence at t_0, they agree on all probabilities relevant to the effects of making the agreement binding and carrying it out. (This does not mean they will agree on these probabilities at t_1, when the agreement is to be carried out. At t_1 some of the parties may have new information which they cannot communicate to the others.) (2) *Full memory at t_1*. At the time the agreement is to be carried out, the parties know everything they knew at t_0, when the agreement was made. Hence if an agent A has new information K, the probability he assigns at t_1 to any condition ϕ is just the conditional probability $p(\phi/K)$ which he assigns at t_0 to ϕ given K. (3) *Utility from coordination only*. The utility of making the agreement stems entirely from the way it affects actions at the time t_1 the agreement is to be carried out. If no agreement were made, but everyone did the same thing at t_1 as they do given the agreement, then the resulting utility would be the same as it is given the agreement. Specifically, we have (a) *Irrelevance of anticipation*. Expectations affect utility only by affecting actions. Anticipation, dread, surprise, and disappointment which result from expecting the agreement to be kept are not of utility or disutility. (b) *No teaching effect*. Keeping or breaking the agreement does not affect anyone's confidence in future agreements. (c) *No calculating costs*. All rational calculations needed can be performed at no cost in utility. (4) *Finitude*. A finite number of choices is open to an agent at a time. Each act open to an agent has a finite number of possible outcomes.

These conditions, along with a coherence condition on the favorability ordering of prospects, entail that any optimal agreement is in foreseeable U-equilibrium. This theorem is given a precise formulation in Section 11 and is proved in Section 12. The idea of the proof is this. Suppose an agreement F is not in foreseeable U-equilibrium. Then for some agent A_i in some contingency K, **F** prescribes act x, but on the assumption that everyone else keeps **F**, act y has a more favorable prospect than does x. (By Condition 3, we can ignore whether everyone expects **F** to be kept.) Hence rather than make **F** binding, the parties would find a more favorable prospect in binding an agreement **F'** which is just like **F** except that it prescribes act y for A_i in contingency K. The argument for this is as follows. Since by Condition (3), the value-laden effects of making an agreement binding are just those of carrying it out, the two agreements have the same effect if contingency K does not arise. If K does arise, then by Conditions (1) and (2), the probabilities seen by A_i at t_i are just the conditional probabilities, given K, seen by everyone at t_0. The situation, then, is this: y offers a more favorable prospect to A_i in K than does x, given that everyone else carries out **F**; the utility of making an agreement binding stems only from the actions that carry it out; and **F'** and **F** differ only in prescribing y and x respectively for A_i in contingency K. Therefore, as seen by everyone at t_0, the prospect given K of making **F'** binding is more favorable than the prospect given K of making **F** binding. Since, as we have seen, the prospects given any other contingency of making the two agreements binding are the same, it follows from the coherence of a utilitarian's ordering of prospects that the prospect of making **F'** binding is more favorable than that of making **F** binding. Therefore **F** is not optimal. Given Conditions (1)–(4), this shows, an agreement not in foreseeable U-equilibrium is not optimal.

What happens if one of these Conditions (1)–(4) is violated? Some of the Conditions do not much matter. Suppose, for instance (3b) is violated: keeping optimal agreements produces good by teaching people to expect such agreements to be kept, which enables them to coordinate their actions in the future by non-binding agreements. That can only reinforce the U-equilibrium of optimal agreements. If calculation costs matter, so that (3c) is violated, the optimal explicit agreement might well not provide for all eventualities. The solution to this problem is to provide explicitly for the more likely eventualities, and agree implicitly that the agreement as stated should be broken if something unforeseen comes up which would make keeping the agreement harmful. That will give an agreement which is close to what the optimal agreement would be if there were no calculating costs — an agreement which will almost always be in U-equilibrium. Such a procedure is close to what we do in our actual society.

Condition (4) also should be of no great importance. If the set of acts or outcomes is infinite, it should be possible, by making less fine distinctions, to approximate the situation with one in which a finite number of acts are open and a finite number of outcomes possible.

A final condition whose violation would not greatly matter is Condition (2), the condition of perfect memory. Suppose memory is imperfect, but it is common knowledge that (a) each agent at least remembers that the agreement was optimal, and (b) each agent knows that any optimal agreement would be in U-equilibrium if memory were perfect. Each would then realize that if he remembered what made the agreement optimal in the first place, the prospect under trust in keeping it would be most favorable. That a prospect would be most favorable with fuller information seems a rational ground for choosing it. Hence it could be common knowledge that each would have grounds for keeping the agreement if he expected others to. If there were an extensive history of keeping optimal agreements, then the parties could each construct a chain of reasons for expecting the others to keep the agreement like the one in Section 2.

Dropping Conditions (1) or (3b), on the other hand, would have serious consequences. If (1) is violated, so that the parties ascribe different probabilities at t_0, then it is as if they worked from different utility scales altogether. Even if they agree on their ultimate ends, they may disagree on what more immediate ends would foster those ultimate ends. The study of what happens when rational agents cannot make binding agreements and pursue ends which may conflict is standard non-cooperative game theory. In those circumstances, different people may find different agreements optimal. There may be cases, such as that of the prisoners' dilemma, in which all parties would find the outcome of making an agreement binding better than the outcome of rational actions in the absence of an agreement. Dropping Condition (1), then, would change the conclusions of this paper radically.

Dropping Condition (3a) could destroy the U-equilibrium of optimal agreements in two ways. In the first place, making an agreement binding may produce happy or unhappy anticipation of its being carried out. An agreement may be optimal partly because making it binding would produce a good kind of anticipation. This anticipation cannot be a result of the actions which carry out the agreement, and hence the anticipation has no bearing on whether that agreement is in U-equilibrium. A stock example of this[4] is a promise I make to a dying woman to take care of her child. Making this promise binding might have best consequences even if some other child is slightly more needy and I cannot take care of both. For the good of setting the woman's mind at rest, plus the good of taking care of her child,

may in total be greater than the good of taking care of the slightly more
needy child. In that case, the agreement to take care of the child of the dying
woman is optimal. It is not in U-equilibrium, for when the time comes to
carry out the agreement, I can produce more good by taking on the more
needy child.

A second way in which dropping Condition (3a) may destroy the
U-equilibrium of optimal agreements stems from surprise or disappointment.
Take a birthday party: a person may produce more happiness by giving it if
the party is a surprise. Suppose that where α is the probability the birthday
child ascribes to the party, the good produced by the party is $15 - 10\alpha$. The
expected utility of binding an agreement with the birthday child to have the
party with probability α, then, is $\alpha(15 - 10\alpha)$. This is maximal at $\alpha = \frac{3}{4}$, and
so the optimal agreement is to have the party with probability $\frac{3}{4}$. That agreement, though, is not in U-equilibrium: if the birthday child expects the party
with probability $\frac{3}{4}$, the good of having the party is $7\frac{1}{2}$ and the good of not
having it is zero, so that it is AU-right to have the party and not AU-right
not to have it.

The rough conclusion to be drawn is this: Members of an openly act-
utilitarian society could lose utility through their inability to bind promises
for three sorts of reasons. In the first place, they may lack an AU-convention
of keeping agreements in foreseeable U-equilibrium. In the second place, they
may be unable to agree on the non-ethical facts of their situation even at the
time an agreement is made. In the third place, the making of an agreement
may have value-laden consequences which are not simply the result of everyone's doing what the agreement tells him to do. Making an agreement may
arouse hope, provoke dread, and alter the degree of happy or unhappy
surprise which the acts the agreement prescribes would produce.

The next three sections are technical. They establish formally the conclusions which I have been giving informally.

10. COHERENCE CONDITIONS

Let $\mathcal{C}$ be a set of outcomes (as defined in Section 3). A *prospect* over $\mathcal{C}$ is an
assignment of probabilities to the outcomes in $\mathcal{C}$; these probabilities are non-
negative real numbers that add up to one. Variables p, q, r, and s will take as
values prospects over $\mathcal{C}$. Let R be a two-place relation between prospects
over $\mathcal{C}$, to be interpreted as 'is at least as favorable as'. We shall assume that
R is a *weak ordering* of the prospects over $\mathcal{C}$; that is, R satisfies these two
conditions.

$(\forall p,q)[pRq \vee qRp]$ (*full connectivity*)

$(\forall p,q,r)[pRq \, \& \, qRs) \rightarrow pRs]$ (*transivity*)

A prospect p, we have said, assigns a probability $p(C)$ to each outcome $C \in \mathcal{C}$. Where α is a probability, the *compound prospect* $[\alpha p + (1 - \alpha)q]$ is the prospect that assigns a probability $\alpha p(C) + (1 - \alpha)q(C)$ to each outcome C. Thus the compound prospect amounts to risking prospect p with probability α and prospect q with probability $1 - \alpha$. Here are two standard coherence conditions on R; only the first will be needed in what ensues.

Compounding Condition: For any prospects p, q, and s over $\mathcal{C}$ and any α such that $0 < \alpha \leqslant 1$,

$$[\alpha p + (1 - \alpha)s] \, R \, [\alpha q + (1 - \alpha)s] \text{ iff } pRq.$$

This says that if each of two prospects p and q is risked with the same probability, the alternative being r, the more favorable such compound prospect is the one formed from the more favorable of the original prospects p and q.

The statement of the second condition requires more notation: Let $R^>$ be the relation 'is more favorable than' and $R^=$ be the relation 'is equally favorable as'. Thus $pR^>q$ means $pRq \, \& \sim qRp$, and $pR^=q$ means $pRq \, \& \, qRp$. *Archimedean Condition*: For any prospects p, q, and s such that $pR^>q$ and $qR^>s$, there is a real number α with $0 < \alpha < 1$ such that

$$[\alpha p + (1 - \alpha)s] \, R^= q.$$

A weak ordering R of the prospects over a set of outcomes $\mathcal{C}$ is *coherent* iff it satisfies the compounding and Archimedean conditions.[5]

If and only if R is coherent, then for some real-numbered scale of value, R weakly orders the prospects over $\mathcal{C}$ by their expected value on that scale. That is to say, real numbers $V(C_i)$ can be assigned to the outcomes $C_i \in \mathcal{C}$ in such a way that for any two prospects p and q over C,

$$pRq \text{ iff } \sum_i p(C_i)V(C_i) \geqslant \sum_i q(C_i)V(C_i).$$

Of the two conditions, the Archimedean seems the more open to question. There are orderings of prospects which violate the Archimedean condition and do not seem completely wild.[6] The compounding condition, on the other hand, I find compelling: any set of preferences among prospects that violated it would strike me as plainly irrational. For what I have to say in this paper, only the compounding condition will be needed.

11. REFORMULATION OF CONDITIONS (1)–(4)

A framework for discussing expected utility maximization was given in Section 3. In this section, that framework will first be extended and applied to agreements of the kind discussed in this paper; then Conditions (1)–(4) will be restated as conditions on the formal structure that is developed. The theorem that under Conditions (1)–(4) and the Compounding Condition, all optimal agreements are in foreseeable U-equilibrium will then have a precise formulation; at that point the proof of the theorem is straightforward.

At time t_1, each act open to an agent has an actual outcome. This actual outcome depends on what others do at t_1, and on aspects of the world that are independent of what any of the parties do at t_1.

Among these act-independent factors may be the expectations of people affected. For expectations, as I have remarked, may affect the value-laden consequences of an act: an act may produce happy surprise or disappointment. Here a *pattern of expectations* will be taken as a primitive notion. One should think of the actual pattern of expectations as assigning to each person involved in a situation all the beliefs he has about what various people would do at t_1 in each state consistent with what he knows. A pattern of expectations is something which might be the actual pattern of expectations.

An *act-configuration* is an assignment of an act to each party; an *environment* for a party A_i is an assignment of an act to each party other than A_i. An act-configuration or environment is *consistent* with information K iff K is consistent with the supposition that each party to whom the act-configuration or environment assigns an act performs the act assigned him. A *state* S is a specification of aspects of the world that are independent[7] both of what the parties do at t, and of what people expect to happen, which meets the following requirements. (i) S determines which acts are open to each party at t_1. (ii) For each act-configuration x consistent with S, and pattern of expectations, S determines the actual outcome of each party's doing the act which x assigns him. (iii) For all the parties know at t_0, S may obtain. (iv) For each party, S determines all his knowledge at t_1 that is relevant to what the actual outcome of any act-configuration would be.

The knowledge of the parties at t_1 can be treated as follows. We can identify any set of states with the *proposition* that the actual state is in that set. A *contingency* for A_i is a proposition which, for all A_i knows at t_0, may express A_i's total knowledge at t_1. Requirement (iv) on the set of states, then, says that for each party A_i, each state S determines a contingency that would express A_i's total knowledge at t_1 (except for knowledge of what people will do and what they expect to be done) if S obtained. Suppose further that acts are described in such a way that, whatever contingency obtains for a party, he knows at t_1 what acts he can perform. Thus what acts an agent can perform depends on the contingency that obtains for him.

Formally put, then, what we are assuming is the following structure Γ. (i) A set of *n parties* A_i, a set of *acts* for each party at t_1, a set of *states*, a set of *patterns of expectations*, and a set of *outcomes*. (ii) A function K_i for each party A_i, which assigns to each state S a set of states $K_i(S)$, with $S \in K_i(S)$. A set of states which is $K_i(S)$ for some state S is called a *contingency* for A_i. (iii) A function M_i for each party A_i, which assigns to each contingency K for A_i a set of acts for A_i. $M_i(K)$ is the set of acts *open* to A_i *in* contingency K for A_i. $M_i(K_i(S))$, which will be written $M_i \circ K_i(S)$, is the set of acts open to A_i in state S. (The notation $\circ$ will be used to compound other functions as well.)

An act-configuration $\mathbf{x}$ is *consistent* with state S iff it assigns to each agent A_j an act in his set $M_j \circ K_j(S)$. Likewise, an environment $\mathbf{x}_{-i}$ for A_i is *consistent* with state S iff it assigns each agent A_j other than A_i an act in the set $M_j \circ K_j(S)$. We assume (iv) a function C which assigns to each state S, each act-configuration $\mathbf{x}$ consistent with S, and each pattern of expectations E, an outcome $C[\mathbf{x}, S, E]$, the *outcome* of act-configuration $\mathbf{x}$ in state S with expectations E. $\mathcal{O}$ is a *possible outcome* iff for some state S, act-configuration $\mathbf{x}$ consistent with S, and pattern of expectations E, we have $\mathcal{O} = C[\mathbf{x}, S, E]$.

A *contingency plan* F_i for party A_i is an assignment to each contingency K for A_i of an act $F_i(K)$ open to A_i in contingency K. An *agreement* $\mathbf{F}$ is an assignment of a contingency plan F_i to each agent A_i. We assume (v) a function e from agreements to expectation configurations. $e(\mathbf{F})$ should be thought of as the expectation-configuration in which everyone expects agreement $\mathbf{F}$ to be carried out. We want also to be able to speak of the outcome of making an agreement binding. Thus we assume (vi) a function C^* which assigns an outcome $C^*[\mathbf{F}, S]$ to any agreement $\mathbf{F}$ and state S; $C^*[\mathbf{F}, S]$ is called the *outcome of making $\mathbf{F}$ binding* in state S.

Assume further that (vii) for each party A_i there is a probability function P_i^0 over the states, A_i's probabilities at t_0. Moreover, for each state S and party A_i, there is a probability function P_i^S which gives what A_i's probabilities would be at t_1 if state S obtained. Here a *probability function P* is an assignment of a non-negative real number $P(T)$ to each state T, with $\Sigma_T P(T) = 1$. Where J is a set of states, $P(J)$ will be the sum $\Sigma_{T \in J} P(T)$. An open sentence with free variable T will be taken to denote the set of states which satisfy it, so that, for instance, the open sentence $T \epsilon J$ denotes the set J, and $P(T \epsilon J) = P(J)$.

That completes the characterization of structure Γ. The structure consists of a set of n parties, times t_0 and t_1, sets of acts, states, outcomes, and patterns of expectations, functions K_i, M_i, and P_i^0 for each party A_i, a function P_i^S for each party A_i and state S, and functions C, e, and C^*. A structure defined as Γ has been will be called an *agreement-structure*.

The *outcome-probability for A_i at t_0 of outcome $\mathbb{O}$ for making F binding* is P_i^0 ($\mathbb{O} = C^*[F, T]$). This will be written $prob_i^*$ ($\mathbb{O}$, F). The *prospect* for A_i at t_0 of making F binding is a function $pros_i^*$ (F) which assigns to each outcome $\mathbb{O}$ the value $prob_i^*$ ($\mathbb{O}$, F). Where R is a weak ordering of all prospects over possible outcomes, agreement F is *optimal* for A_i with respect to R iff for every agreement G, $pros_i^*$ (F) R $pros_i^*$ (G).

The act-configuration that assigns an act x_i to each party A_i will be written $\mathbf{x}$, and the environment that assigns an act x_j to each party A_j other than A_i will be written $\mathbf{x}_{-i}$. Where $\mathbf{K} = \langle K_1, \ldots, K_n \rangle$ assigns contingency K_j to each party A_j, we define $\mathbf{F}(\mathbf{K}) = \langle F_1(K_1), \ldots, F_n(K_n) \rangle$, and $\mathbf{F}_{-i}(\mathbf{K})$ is the environment for A_i that assigns each party A_j other than A_i the act $F_j(K_j)$. We define $\mathbf{K}(T) = \langle K_1(T), \ldots, K_n(T) \rangle$. The *environment of compliance* to F for A_i in state T is $\mathbf{F}_{-i} \circ \mathbf{K}(T)$. The *outcome* of act x for A_i in environment $\mathbf{y}_{-i}$ and state T for expectations E is the outcome in state T for E of the act-configuration $\mathbf{z}$ which assigns act x to A_i and the act y_j to each A_j other than A_i — that is, $C[\mathbf{z}, T, E]$. This will be written $C_i[x, \mathbf{y}_{-i}, T, E]$.

The *outcome-probability of $\mathbb{O}$ under trust in F of act x for A_i in state S* is P_i^S ($\mathbb{O} = C_i[x, \mathbf{F}_{-i} \circ \mathbf{K}(T), T, e(\mathbf{F})]$). In other words, it is the probability, as seen by A_i at t_1 in state S, that $\mathbb{O}$ is the outcome of A_i's doing x in an environment of compliance to F, given that everyone expects F to be carried out. This will be written $prob_i^S$ ($\mathbb{O}, x, \mathbf{F}$), and the corresponding prospect, which assigns to each outcome $\mathbb{O}$ the value $prob_i^S$ ($\mathbb{O}, x, \mathbf{F}$), will be written $pros_i^S$ ($x, \mathbf{F}$). This will be called the *prospect under trust in F* of act x for A_i in state S. Where R is a weak ordering of all prospects over possible outcomes, S is a *state of U-equilibrium* for F with respect to R iff for each party A_i, and each act $x \in M_i \circ K_i(S)$,

$$pros_i^S (F_i \circ K_i(S), \mathbf{F}) R \, pros_i^S (x, \mathbf{F}).$$

In other words, in state S, for each party, the prospect under trust in F of keeping the agreement will be at least as favorable as the prospect under trust in F of doing anything else he can do. F is in *foreseeable U-equilibrium* iff every state thought possible by someone at t_0 — that is, every state S such that for some A_i, $P_i^0(S) \neq 0$ — is a state of U-equilibrium for S.

We can now state Conditions (1)–(4) as formal conditions on the model.

Condition (1), Full Communication at t_0, says that all the parties have the same beliefs and probability ascriptions at t_0. In other words, we have:

Condition (1*). $P_1^0 = P_2^0 = \ldots = P_n^0$.

Condition (2), Full Memory at t_1, as applied to a perfectly rational party A_i, means that he forms his probability ascriptions P_i^S at t_1 by conditionalization: he conditionalizes his probability ascriptions P_i at t_0 on what he has learned since, which is $K_i(S)$.

Condition (2*): For any party A_i and states S and T,

$$P_i^S(T) = P_i^0(T/K_i(S)).$$

Condition (3), Utility from Coordination Only, has two parts. The first says that the expectations of the people involved make no value-laden difference to what happens, except as they affect what people do. This rules out surprise and disappointment.

Condition (3a*). For any act-configuration x, state T, and two patterns of expectation E and E^*,

$$C[x, T, E^*] = C[x, T, E].$$

The second part says that the results of making an agreement binding are just the results of its being carried out when everyone expects it to be carried out. This rules out anticipation, dread, and the effects of teaching people to expect agreements to be carried out.[8]

Condition (3b*). For any agreement F and state T,

$$C^*[F, T] = C[F \circ K(T), T, e(F)].$$

Condition (4) is Finitude.

Condition (4*). The set of states is finite, and in each state, the set of acts open at t_1 to each party is finite.

12. THEOREM AND PROOF

THEOREM. *Let an agreement-structure Γ satisfy Conditions* (1*), (2*), (3a*), (3b*), *and* (4*). *Let R be a weak ordering of all prospects over possible outcomes, and let R satisfy the Compounding Condition. Then any agreement which is optimal with respect to R for some party is in foreseeable U-equilibrium with respect to R.*

Proof. Suppose agreement **F** is not in foreseeable U-equilibrium with respect to R. Then for some state S and party A_j, $P_j^0(S) > 0$ and S is not a state of U-equilibrium for **F** with respect to R. Thus for some party A_i and some acts x and y, $x = F_i \circ K_i(S), y \in M_i \circ K_i(S)$, and

$$(1) \qquad pros_i^S (y, \mathbf{F}) R^> pros_i^S (x, \mathbf{F}).$$

Let **F'** be the agreement which assigns act y to A_i in contingency $K_i(S)$, and otherwise is exactly like **F**. We show that the prospect of making **F** binding is less favorable than the prospect of making **F'** binding, so that agreement **F** is not optimal.

We want to show, then, that $pros_j^* (\mathbf{F'}) R^> pros_j^* (\mathbf{F})$ for every A_j. Since $pros_j^* (\mathbf{F})$ assigns P_j^0 ($\mathcal{O} = C^*(\mathbf{F}, T)]$ to each $\mathcal{O}$, and by Cond (1*), $P_i^0 = P_j^0$ for all A_j, we have $pros_j^* (\mathbf{F}) = pros_i^* (\mathbf{F})$ for each A_j, and likewise for **F'**. Thus what we need to show is that

$$(2) \qquad pros_i^* (\mathbf{F'}) R^> pros_i^* (\mathbf{F}).$$

We shall show that for some prospect q and probability $\alpha > 0$,

$$(3) \qquad pros_i^* (\mathbf{F}) = \alpha \, pros_i^S (x, \mathbf{F}) + (1 - \alpha) q;$$

$$(4) \qquad pros_i^* (\mathbf{F'}) = \alpha \, pros_i^S (y, \mathbf{F}) + (1 - \alpha) q.$$

Thus from (1) and the Compounding Condition, (2) follows, and the Theorem will be proved.

Note that by the definitions of x and the functions C_i, we have

$$(5) \qquad C_i[x, \mathbf{F}_{-i} \circ \mathbf{K}(T), T, e(\mathbf{F})] = C[\mathbf{F} \circ \mathbf{K}(T), T, e(\mathbf{F})],$$

and by the way **F'** was defined,

$$(6) \qquad C_i[y, \mathbf{F}_{-i} \circ \mathbf{K}(T), T, e(\mathbf{F})] = C[\mathbf{F'} \circ \mathbf{K}(T), T, e(\mathbf{F})].$$

Now the definition of $prob_i^* (\mathcal{O}, \mathbf{F})$ is that

$$(7) \qquad prob_i^* (\mathcal{O}, \mathbf{F}) = P_i^0 (\mathcal{O} = C^*[\mathbf{F}, T]).$$

Let $\hat{K} = K_i(S)$, let $\sim \hat{K}$ consist of all and only states not in $\hat{K}$, and let $\alpha = P_i^0 (\hat{K})$. Then by (7) and standard probability calculus,

$$prob_i^* (\mathcal{O}, \mathbf{F}) = \alpha P_i^0 (\mathcal{O} = C^*[\mathbf{F}, T]/\hat{K})$$
$$(8) \qquad + (1 - \alpha) P_i^0 (\mathcal{O} = C^*[\mathbf{F}, T]/\sim \hat{K}),$$

$$prob_i^* (\mathcal{O}, \mathbf{F'}) = \alpha P_i^0 (\mathcal{O} = C^*(\mathbf{F'}, T)/\hat{K})$$
$$(9) \qquad + (1 - \alpha) P_i^0 (\mathcal{O} = C^*[\mathbf{F'}, F]/\sim \hat{K}).$$

Here $\alpha > 0$. For S is a state such that $P_j^0 (S) > 0$ for some A_j. Hence by Condition (1*), $P_i^0 (S) > 0$, and thus since $S \in \hat{K}, \alpha = P_i^0 (\hat{K}) > 0$.

Now by Condition (3b*), part of Utility from Coordination Only,

(10) $\mathcal{O} = C^*[\mathbf{F}, T]$ iff $\mathcal{O} = C[\mathbf{F} \circ \mathbf{K}(T), T, e(\mathbf{F})]$,

and by Conditions (3a*) and (3b*) combined,

(11) $\mathcal{O} = C^*[\mathbf{F}', T]$ iff $\mathcal{O} = C[\mathbf{F}' \circ \mathbf{K}(T), T, e(\mathbf{F})]$.

By the way $\mathbf{F}'$ was defined, for all states $T \notin K$, $\mathbf{F}' \circ \mathbf{K}(T) = \mathbf{F} \circ \mathbf{K}(T)$. Hence by (10) and (11),

For all $T \notin \hat{K}$, $\mathcal{O} = C^*(\mathbf{F}', T)$ iff $\mathcal{O} = C^*(\mathbf{F}, T)$.

Therefore $P_i^0 \, (\mathcal{O} = C^*[\mathbf{F}', T]/\sim \hat{K})$

$= P_i^0 \, (\mathcal{O} = C^*[\mathbf{F}, T]/\sim \hat{K})$.

Call this value $q(\mathcal{O})$; then

(12) $prob_i^* \, (\mathcal{O}, \mathbf{F}) = \alpha P_i^0 \, (\mathcal{O} = C^*[\mathbf{F}, T]/\hat{K}) + (1 - \alpha) q(\mathcal{O})$

(13) $prob_i^* \, (\mathcal{O}, \mathbf{F}') = \alpha P_i^0 \, (\mathcal{O} = C^*[\mathbf{F}', T]/\hat{K}) + (1 - \alpha) q(\mathcal{O})$

It follows from Condition (2*), Full Memory at t_1, that for any proposition ϕ,

(14) $P_i^S(\phi) = P_i^0 \, (\phi/K_i(S)) = P_i^0 \, (\phi/\hat{K})$.

From what has been said, we can now reason as follows:

$P_i^0 \, (\mathcal{O} = C^*[\mathbf{F}, T]/\hat{K})$

$= P_i^0 \, (\mathcal{O} = C[\mathbf{F} \circ \mathbf{K}(T), T, e(\mathbf{F})]/\hat{K})$ by (10)

$= P_i^S \, (\mathcal{O} = C[\mathbf{F} \circ \mathbf{K}(T), T, e(\mathbf{F})])$ by (14)

$= P_i^S \, (\mathcal{O} = C_i[x, \mathbf{F}_{-i} \circ \mathbf{K}(T), T, e(\mathbf{F})])$ by (5)

$= prob_i^S \, (\mathcal{O}, x, \mathbf{F})$,

this last by the definition of $prob_i^S$. Hence by (12),

(15) $prob_i^* \, (\mathcal{O}, \mathbf{F}) = \alpha \, prob_i^S \, (\mathcal{O}, x, \mathbf{F}) + (1 - \alpha) q(\mathcal{O})$.

Similarly,

$P_i^0 \, (\mathcal{O} = C^*[\mathbf{F}', T]/\hat{K})$

$= P_i^0 \, (\mathcal{O} = C[\mathbf{F}' \circ \mathbf{K}(T), T, e(\mathbf{F})]/\hat{K})$ by (11)

$= P_i^S \, (\mathcal{O} = C[\mathbf{F}' \circ \mathbf{K}(T), T, e(\mathbf{F})])$ by (14)

$$= P_i^S (\mathcal{O} = C_i[y, \mathbf{F}_{-i} \circ \mathbf{K}(T), T, e(\mathbf{F})]) \quad \text{by (6)}$$
$$= prob_i^S (\mathcal{O}, y, \mathbf{F}).$$

Hence by (13),

(16) $prob_i^* (\mathcal{O}, \mathbf{F}') = \alpha\, prob_i^S (\mathcal{O}, y, \mathbf{F}) + (1 - \alpha)\, q(\mathcal{O}).$

(15) and (16) are equivalent to (3) and (4) respectively, and so the Theorem is proved.

University of Michigan

NOTES

* Work on this paper was supported by a grant from the National Endowment for the Humanities.
[1] As I am using the term, 'subjectively right', then, an agent may be mistaken in thinking an act subjectively right. He may hold an incorrect moral theory; he may have irrational non-moral beliefs and probability ascriptions; or he may misapply a correct moral theory to rational non-moral beliefs and probability ascriptions. For discussions of this subjective sense, see Brandt (1959, pp. 360–67).
[2] In Gibbard and Harper (1978), we argue that this probability should be the probability of a subjunctive conditional 'If I were to do act A, outcome O would obtain.' Another view, which we argue against, is that the relevant probability is the conditional probability of outcome O on my doing A. We owe the distinction to David Lewis, and our interpretation of it to Robert Stalnaker. For the purposes of this paper, it does not matter which of these two views the reader takes.
[3] This argument is given in Sobel (1976). See especially footnotes 6 and 7.
[4] Cf. Ross (1930, p. 39) and Brandt (1959, pp. 387–8).
[5] These conditions are equivalent, in the present Framework, to the axioms given by von Neumann and Morgenstern (1947, p. 26).
[6] The lexical maximin ordering of Rawls (1971, p. 83), applied to prospects, violates the Archimedean condition but satisfies the Compounding Condition. The rule would be this: Of two prospects, prefer the one with the better worst outcome. In case of ties by this criterion, prefer the one whose worst outcome has the lower probability. In case of ties by this criterion, remove the worst outcomes and start over.
[7] In Gibbard and Harper (1978), we argue that these states should be causally independent of the acts in question. An alternative view, which we argue against, is that the states should be stochastically independent of the acts.
[8] In Section 9, the example of a surprise birthday party showed a violation of (3a*), and the example of a promise to a dying woman to take care of her child showed a violation of (3b*).

REFERENCES

Brandt, Richard B., *Ethical Theory*, Englewood Cliffs, N.J.: Prentice Hall, 1959.

Gibbard, Allan and Harper, William L., 'Counterfactuals and Two Kinds of Expected Utility', in C. A. Hooker, J. J. Leach, and E. F. McClennen (eds.), *Foundations and Applications of Decision Theory, I,* (Dordrecht, Holland: Reidel), 1978, pp. 125–162.

Hodgson, D. H., *Consequences of Utilitarianism: A Study in Normative Ethics and Legal Theory*, Oxford: Clarendon Press, 1967.

Lewis, David K., *Convention: A Philosophical Study*, Cambridge, Mass.: Harvard University Press, 1969.

Lewis, D. K., 'Utilitarianism and Truthfulness', *Australiasian Journal of Philosophy* **50**, 17–19 (1972).

Rawls, John, *A Theory of Justice*, Cambridge, Mass.: Harvard University Press, 1971.

Ross, W. D., *The Right and the Good*, Oxford: Clarendon Press, 1930.

Sobel, Jordan Howard, 'Utility Maximizers in Iterated Prisoner's Dilemmas', *Dialogue*, **15**, 38–53 (1976).

Von Neumann, J. and O. Morgenstern, *Theory of Games and Economic Behavior* (Princeton: Princeton University Press), 1947.

RODERICK M. CHISHOLM

INTRINSIC VALUE[1]

1. INTRODUCTION

It was obvious to Plato and Aristotle and, in more recent times, to Brentano
and Moore, that there is a distinction between 'intrinsic' and 'nonintrinsic'
value. These philosophers took it for granted that, if there is anything that
is good, then there is something that is intrinsically good or good in itself,
and that if there is anything that is bad, then there is something that is
intrinsically bad or bad in itself. But at the present time this distinction is
often called into question and even ridiculed. In this paper I will defend
the distinction.

2. THE PROBLEM OF DEFINING INTRINSIC VALUE

Our problem concerns, not the nature of value or of good and evil generally,
but the nature of *intrinsic* value and of *intrinsic* goodness and *intrinsic* evil. We
are concerned with the qualification 'intrinsic'. And so we might put our question this way: given the generic concept of *value*, can we define *intrinsic* value?

In raising this question, I am assuming, then, that we are given a generic
sense of such value expressions as 'good,' 'bad,' 'neutral,' and 'better.' (But
in setting forth the answer, I will take 'better' as the only undefined value
expression.) And I also assume that states of affairs (or propositions) are
bearers of value and that possible worlds are states of affairs and hence also
bearers of value.

Perhaps it may be agreed, preanalytically, that that state of affairs which
is *someone experiencing pleasure* is good and that, on a certain occasion, that
state of affairs which is *someone undergoing discomfort* is also good. But
the former state of affairs and not the latter is intrinsically good. Speaking
somewhat imprecisely, we might put this point by saying that the two states
of affairs differ in the following respect: the former, unlike the latter, *would*
be good no matter what else happened. The goodness of the latter is 'extrinsic'
in that it is dependent, somehow, upon the occurrence of something else.
Aristotle and Moore both suggest that the intrinsic value of a state of affairs
is the value that that state of affairs 'would have in isolation.'

121

A. I. Goldman and J. Kim (eds.), Values and Morals, 121–130. All Rights Reserved.
Copyright © 1978, by D. Reidel Publishing Company, Dordrecht, Holland.

But how are we to understand the 'would have' and in what sense can a state of affairs be 'isolated'?

We may be tempted to say this: a state of affairs is *intrinsically* good provided only it is good in every possible world in which it obtains, and analogously for intrinsic neutrality and intrinsic evil.[2] But this appeal to modal concepts is not sufficient to enable us to make the distinction we are looking for.

Consider, for example, a world in which some intrinsic good – say, someone's innocent pleasure – leads to an enormous amount of subsequent evil. Using 'good' in its generic sense, can we say that in such a world the pleasurable experience is good? It would hardly seem so. Hence we cannot say that an intrinsically good state of affairs is one which is good in every possible world in which it obtains. Similar considerations hold of intrinsic evil.

And it follows, of course, that we cannot use this method to characterize the relation of being *intrinsically better*. That is to say, it will not do to define 'p is intrinsically better than q' by saying 'p is better than q in every world in which they both obtain.' Thus we may wish to say that *Jones feeling pleasure* (p) is intrinsically better than *Jones undergoing discomfort* (q). But we cannot say, in the more generic sense of 'better,' that p is better than q in every possible world in which both p and q occur; for we may want to say, of those worlds in which q is productive of enormous amounts of good and p of enormous amounts of evil, that in those worlds q is better than p. Hence we cannot define intrinsic value merely by reference to what is valuable in every possible world.

Yet the point of saying that *Jones undergoing discomfort* is only 'extrinsically' good would seem to be: it wouldn't be good unless some *other* good state of affairs obtains which doesn't include it and isn't included in it. And the point of saying that *Jones feeling pleasure* is 'intrinsically' good would seem to be: its goodness doesn't require that there obtain some *other* good state of affairs which neither includes it nor is included within it; *Jones feeling pleasure* would be good even if, of all the states of affairs that obtain, it is included in every one that is good. And analogously for 'extrinsically' and 'intrinsically' bad.

Can we put the distinction more precisely?

3. INTRINSIC VALUE STATES

We first introduce the following intentional sense of entailment:

p entails $q = Df\, p$ is necessarily such that (i) if it obtains then q obtains and (ii) whoever accepts it accepts q.

Now we may say: a state of affairs p is 'part' of a state of affairs q, if and only if, q entails p.

I believe that the intrinsic value concepts that we are looking for may be found if we consider what it is for one state of affairs to 'reflect all the good and evil' that there is in another state of affairs. I suggest that this concept may be explicated as follows, in terms of the generic concepts that we are presupposing:

p reflects all the good and evil that there is in $q = Df\, q$ entails p; and every part of q that entails p has the same value as p.

If p thus reflects all the good and evil that there is in q, then, since every state of affairs is a 'part' of itself, p will have the same value as q. And therefore, if there is another state of affairs r, such that p also reflects all the good and evil that there is in r, then q will have the same value as r. More generally, if p reflects all the good and evil that there is in q, then p and q will enter into the same preferability relations: therefore, whatever is the same in value as the one is the same in value as the other; whatever is better than the one is better than the other; and whatever is worse than the one is worse than the other.

What would be a case of a p and a q such that p reflects all the good and evil that there is in q? In order to have an illustration let us assume, for simplicity, that hedonism is true. Now we may consider that state of affairs which is *Jones feeling pleasure*. But following the suggestions of Aristotle and Moore, let us attempt to consider this state 'in isolation.'

We are viewing possible worlds as being themselves states of affairs. Hence one relevant way of considering *Jones feeling pleasure* 'in isolation' is to conceive a possible world in which Jones feels pleasure and in which there is no other pleasure or displeasure. Then, if hedonism is true, *Jones feeling pleasure* will reflect all the good and evil there is in that world; so, too, for any wider state of affairs in that world that entails *Jones feeling pleasure*. And, given the assumption of hedonism, we may say that any such world is good.[3] Analogously, we may conceive a possible world which is such that *Jones feeling displeasure* reflects all the good and evil that there is in that world. And if hedonism is true, every such world is bad.

Let us use the expression 'intrinsic value state' to refer to states of affairs such as those we have just illustrated — states of affairs which are such that, for some possible world, they reflect all the good and evil that there is in that world.

> p is an intrinsic value state $= Df$ There is a possible world W such that: p reflects all the good and evil that there is in W; and if p is not neutral, then every thing that reflects all the good and evil that there is in W either entails or is entailed by p.

Why the second clause? How could it possibly be the case that (a) p reflects all the good and evil that there is in W and yet *not* be the case that (b) everything that reflects all this good and evil entails or is entailed by p? It should be kept in mind that we are presupposing only a generic value concept and that we are not yet in a position to distinguish intrinsic values from instrumental values. Using this more generic value concept, we may want to say that, on occasion, the means to a valuable result may have the same generic value as the result. For example, if the patient being well is generically good, then so, too, is the treatment that brought that state of affairs about. If these two things are thought of as being the same in generic value, then the treatment as well as the patient being well would satisfy the first condition of our definiens: in a world in which they obtained together, they could *both* reflect all the good and evil that there is in that world.[4] But the treatment is such that, in order to have this property, it must be followed by a good result. That is to say, the world must be such that, in addition to the treatment, there is still *another* state of affairs – in this case, the patient feeling well – which may be said to contain all the good and evil there is in that world. But, on the other hand, that intrinsic good which is the patient feeling well *could* be one that either entails or is entailed by everything that reflects all the good and evil that there is in that world. Intrinsic value states, then, are states of affairs that may be good or bad 'in isolation.' For our definition tells us, in effect, that an intrinsic value state is capable of containing all the good and evil that there is in a world.

Many states of affairs, we should note, are not thus intrinsic value states. For example:

> Jones is pleased or Smith is displeased
> Robinson is pleased and either Jones is pleased or Smith is displeased.

The first of these states of affairs is incapable of reflecting all the good and evil that there is in any possible world; for any possible world in which this disjunctive state of affairs occurs will be a world *also* containing the good and evil that is in one or the other or both of the two disjuncts. And analogously for the second state of affairs.[5]

Now let us distinguish two different types of intrinsic value states.

First, there are those states of affairs *p* which are such that both *p* and its negation are intrinsic value states. An example would be: Jones being pleased to degree 10.

And secondly, there are those states of affairs *p* which are such that *p* is an intrinsic value state and its negation is *not* an intrinsic value state. An example would be:

> It being false that Jones is pleased to degree 10 and it also being false that Jones is displeased to degree 10.

The negation of this state of affairs is incapable of containing all the good and evil there is in any possible world. For this negation is equivalent to the following disjunction:

> Either Jones being pleased to degree 10 or Jones being displeased to degree 10.

Every world in which this disjunction obtains will include, *in addition*, either the good that is Jones being pleased or the evil that is Jones being displeased.

Let us now restrict the *bearers of intrinsic value* to those intrinsic value states of the second sort — those which are such that they have intrinsic value states as their negations:

> *p* is a bearer of intrinsic value = *Df p* is an intrinsic value state and not-*p* is an intrinsic value state.

Now we are in a position to characterize intrinsic value.

4. DEFINITION OF INTRINSIC VALUE CONCEPTS

By making use of the undefined generic value concept expressed by '*p* is better than *q*' and the concepts we have just defined in terms of it, we may define the concept of *intrinsic preferability* — the concept of one state of affairs being *intrinsically better* than another. Then by reference to intrinsic preferability, we may define *intrinsic goodness, intrinsic badness* and *intrinsic neutrality*

The concept of intrinsic preferability, then, may be defined as follows:

p is intrinsically better than $q = Df\ p$ and q are bearers of intrinsic value; and any world $W1$, such that p reflects all the good and evil there is in $W1$, is better than any world $W2$ such that q reflects all good and evil there is in $W2$.

The second clause of the definiendum tells us the sense in which the result of considering p and q 'in isolation' enables us to say that p is intrinsically better than q.

The only states of affairs that are terms of the intrinsic preferability relation will be intrinsic value states.[6] Thus the mixed disjunction, *there are three happy Canadians or there are three happy non-Canadians* (p), is not intrinsically better than *there are stones* (q); for p is not an intrinsic value state (it cannot contain *all* the good and, evil that there is in any possible world), and hence it is not itself a bearer of intrinsic value.

Given this concept of intrinsic preferability, we may now explicate the various intrinsic value concepts and exhibit the relations among them. To illustrate one way of doing this, I will adapt certain features of the system of intrinsic value that has been set forth by Ernest Sosa and me.[7]

Abbreviating 'p is intrinsically preferable to q' as 'pPq', let us say:

p has the same intrinsic value as q $(pSq) = Df\ p$ and q are bearers of intrinsic value; and $\neg(pPq)$ and $\neg(qPp)$

p is intrinsically indifferent $(Ip) = Df\ pS\neg p$

p is intrinsically neutral $(Np) = Df\ (Eq)(Iq$ and $pSq)$

p is intrinsically good $(Gp) = Df\ (Eq)(Iq$ and $pPq)$

p is intrisically bad $(Bp) = Df\ (Eq)(Iq$ and $qPp)$

These definitions may be put informally as follows (provided the qualification 'intrinsically' is understood throughout): one state of affairs has the *same intrinsic value* as another if and only if both are bearers of intrinsic value and neither one is intrinsically better than the other; the *indifferent* is that which has the same value as its negation; the *neutral* is that which has the same intrinsic value as the indifferent; the *good* is that which is intrinsically better than the indifferent; and the *bad* is that which is such that the indifferent is intrinsically better than it.

I add this further definition to facilitate exposition:

p is at least as good intrinsically as q $(pAq) = Df\ p$ and q are bearers of intrinsic value; and $\neg(qPp)$

In other words, if p and q are bearers of intrinsic value, and if q is not intrinsically better than p, then p is *at least as good* intrinsically as q.

The axioms of the system may now be abbreviated as follows:

A1 $(p)(q)(pPq \rightarrow \neg(qPp))$
A2 $(p)(q)(r)[(qAp \text{ and } rAq) \rightarrow rAp]$
A3 $(p)(q)[(Ip \text{ and } Iq) \rightarrow pSq]$
A4 $(p)(Gp \vee B\neg p) \rightarrow pP\neg p$

In other words: (1) if p is better than q, then q is not better than p; (2) if q is at least as good as p, and if r is at least as good as q, then r is at least as good as p; (3) if p is indifferent and q is indifferent, then p as the same value as q; and (4) if p is good or if not-p is bad, then p is better than not-p.

It is important to note the distinction between intrinsic indifference (Ip) and intrinsic neutrality (Np). The class of the neutral is wider than that of the indifferent. A neutral state of affairs (e.g., *there being no pleasure*) may have a good negation. And a neutral state of affairs (e.g., *there being no displeasure*) may have a bad negation. But an indifferent state of affairs (e.g., *there being stones*) is a neutral state of affairs that has a neutral negation.

According to some theories of intrinsic value, but not according to the present theory, the negation of a state of affairs that is intrinsically good is intrinsically bad, and the negation of a state of affairs that is intrinsically bad is intrinsically good. Our intuition, however, may be more nearly in accord with that of Aristotle: "Positive goodness and badness are more important than the mere absence of goodness and badness: for positive goodness and badness are ends, which the mere absence of them cannot be."[8] Thus, if we are hedonists, we will say that *someone experiencing pleasure* is intrinsically good. But we will not say that its negation — *no one experiencing pleasure* — is intrinsically bad. For the negation may obtain in worlds in which nothing is good and nothing is bad. Thus it may obtain in worlds in which there are no living things and in which, therefore, there is neither pleasure nor displeasure. Analogous points may be made with respect to other things that have been said to be intrinsically bad or intrinsically good.

The present conception of the relation between good and evil was put in the following way by Oskar Kraus: "The nonexistence of a good is not an evil, and the nonexistence of an evil is not a good; one can say only that the existence of a good is preferable to its nonexistence, and conversely in the case of evil."[9]

5. THE INTRINSIC VALUE IN COMPOUND STATES OF AFFAIRS

Sosa and I did not set forth any axioms pertaining to the intrinsic value to be found in disjunctive states of affairs. The present approach to intrinsic value may now be seen to justify this omission.[10] Let us consider, then, the general question of the intrinsic value to be found in compound states of affairs.

In order to make certain theoretical points, I will suppose once again that hedonism is the correct theory of value. In other words, I will suppose that the only things that are intrinsically good are states of affairs implying that there is pleasure and that the only things that are intrinsically bad are states of affairs implying that there is displeasure. I will also suppose that pleasures and displeasures can be ordinally ranked, that the more pleasure the better and the less displeasure the better, and that equal amounts of pleasure and displeasure balance each other off. (But these hedonistic assumptions are not at all essential to the general conception of value that is here defended. They are made only for the purpose of simplifying examples.)

Let us now consider the following states of affairs, all being, according to our present account, bearers of value:

(p) Jones experiencing 1 unit of pleasure
(q) Smith experiencing 1 unit of displeasure
(r) There being stones
(s) Brown experiencing 2 units of pleasure
(t) Black experiencing 2 units of displeasure.

Given our hedonistic assumptions, there is, of course, no problem in assessing the intrinsic value of these five states of affairs and in ranking them. Thus p and s are good, q and t are bad, r is neutral, s is the best of the lot, and t is the worst.

There is no theoretical problem involved in evaluating the various possible *conjunctions* of the above states of affairs. Thus p and q is neutral; p and r is good; p and s is good; and p and t is bad and has the same value as q . . . And the conjunction of all five is neutral.

What of the *negations* of these states of affairs?

According to many theories of value, as we have noted, the negation of a bad state of affairs is good, and the negation of a good state of affairs is bad. According to our present criteria, however, the negation of each of these states of affairs is neutral. For each negation may obtain in worlds in which there is no pleasure and no displeasure, and hence in worlds in which (according to our hedonistic assumptions) there is nothing that is intrinsically good and nothing that is intrinsically bad. Any world which is such that all the good and evil that there is in that world may be found in the negations of any of the above states of affairs will be a world that is intrinsically neutral.

And now what of the *disjunctions* of these states of affairs? No disjunction, having any two of the above states of affairs as its disjuncts, is a bearer of intrinsic value. For none is capable of reflecting all the good and evil that there is in any possible world. Consider, for example, *pvq*. Any world in which *pvq* obtains will have, *in addition* to whatever generic value there might be in *pvq, also* either the positive intrinsic value that is in *p* or the negative intrinsic value that is in *q* or both. And analogously for the other disjunctions that may be formed from the above. None of them is a bearer of intrinsic value and hence none of them need be considered in assessing the value of any world in which it obtains.

Castaneda has noted that three quite different procedures have been used in evaluating disjunctions. These may be characterized by the following three rules: (a) the value of the disjunction is the same as that of the higher valued disjunct; (b) the value of the disjunction is the same as the value of the disjuncts if these are the same in value, and otherwise it lies between the disjuncts in value; and (c) the value of the disjunction is the same as the value of its lower valued disjunct.[11] These three procedures would have very different results in application to the disjunctions we have been considering. Consider only *pvq*. According to (a) it would be good; according to (b) it would be neutral; and according to (c) it would be bad. Hence these procedures would seem to be fundamentally different. And so we may feel that we should select just one of them. But how are we to make the choice?

The reasonable thing is to assume that they are *all* wrong.

Different as the three procedures may be in application to restricted states of affairs, they do not differ at all in application to possible worlds. That is to say, when we come to evaluate worlds, it will not matter in the least which method we choose, for the results will be the same in each of the three cases. If we know the value of the disjuncts of any given disjunction, and if we know which of the disjuncts obtains, then there is no point in trying to calculate the value of the disjunction. Any dispute, then, about the intrinsic value of the disjunctions of our five states of affairs above would seem to be entirely idle. Hence the finding that they have no intrinsic value at all should be one that is entirely welcome. And this finding is one of the consequences of the present explication of intrinsic value.

Brown University

NOTES

[1]   I wish to express my indebtedness to Fred Feldman and Lars Bergstrom.
[2]   I suggested this definition in 'Objectives and Intrinsic Value,' in Rudolf Haller, ed., *Jenseits von Sein und Nichtsein* (Graz: Akademisches Druck- und Verlagsanstalt, 1972), 261–9: see p. 262.
[3]   Suppose that, for any amount of pleasure that one may experience, it is also possible to experience a lesser but still positive amount of pleasure. Then *Jones feeling pleasure* would not itself be an intrinsic value state, since any world containing it would also contain the good that is in some wider state of affairs (e.g., *Jones feeling pleasure to degree 10*). In such a case the latter state of affairs, but not the former, will be an intrinsic value state. This possibility was pointed out to me by W. Rabinowicz.
[4]   This was pointed out to me by Eva Bodansky. Were it not for this possibility, we could replace '*p* reflects all the good and evil that there is in *q*' by '*p* contains all the good and evil that there is in *q*.'
[5]   We could now say that intrinsic value states are the 'source' of the good and evil that is to be found in any possible world. The 'ultimate source' of such good and evil could then be said to be certain *basic* intrinsic value states – those intrinsic value states which are either good or bad and which have no intrinsic value states as proper parts. It should be noted that 'proper part' is here understood in terms of a strict sense of entailment – a sense of entailment which does *not* enable us to say that for any state of affairs, *p* and *q*, *p* entails the disjunction, *p* or *q*. Compare the undefined concept of 'evaluatively basic proposition,' introduced in Warren S. Quinn, 'Theories of Intrinsic Value,' *American Philosophical Quarterly*, XI (1974), 123–132; see pp. 128ff.
[6]   An alternative to the present procedure would be to characterize the intrinsic value of a state of affairs *p* as being a function of the value of those intrinsic value states that reflect all the good and evil that there is in *p*. Then all states of affairs, and not just the ones I have called 'bearers of value,' would fall within the field of the intrinsic preferability relation. But the present procedure, as we shall see, enables us to solve the problem of the intrinsic value in disjunctive states of affairs. And the alternative does not have this advantage.
[7]   Roderick M. Chisholm and Ernest Sosa, 'On the Logic of 'Intrinsically Better'', *American Philosophical Quarterly*, III (1966), 244–9. In this system we made use of rules corresponding to *modus ponens* and to a principle of substitution for logically equivalent states of affairs. The latter principle enabled us to say that all logically equivalent states of affairs are the same in value. But that system, unlike the one presented here, did not restrict the intrinsic preferability relation to those states of affairs that are here called the bearers of intrinsic value.
[8]   *Rhetoric*, Book I, Ch. 7, 1364a.
[9]   Oscar Kraus, *Die Werttheorien: Geschichte und Kritik* (Brunn: Verlag Rudolf M. Rohrer 1937) 227. Compare Georg Katkov, *Untersuchungen zur Werttheorie und Theodizee* (Brunn: Verlag Rudolf M. Rohrer 1937), 67ff.
[10]   Concerning the intrinsic value of disjunctions, compare Lennart Aqvist, 'Chisholm-Sosa Logics of Intrinsic Betterness and Value,' *Nous*, II (1968), 253–70; and Roderick M. Chisholm, 'The Intrinsic Value in Disjunctive States of Affairs,' *Nous*, IX (1975), 295–308. The present approach would render superfluous the axioms about disjunction that were defended in the last-named paper.
[11]   See Hector-Neri Castaneda, 'Ought, Value, and Utilitarianism,' *American Philosophical Quarterly*, VI (1969), 257–275.

J. O. URMSON

THE GOALS OF ACTION

This paper contains a critical survey of some of the theories of Plato, Aristotle and Joseph Butler about the goals of action. Since my intention is philosophical, thought the matter is historical, I have avoided detailed argument on points of scholarship, elaborate documentation and copious bibliography, even when my interpretations are contentious, as they sometimes are. The primary sources with which I deal are all well-known and readily available, and in any case I want to consider the merits of certain possible views rather than to quarrel over their attribution.

In the *Protagoras*, especially from page 345 to page 354, and in the *Gorgias*, in the argument with Polus, Socrates puts forward a set of theses all of which are sometimes said to be paradoxical, and some of which clearly are so. Though Plato himself does not do so, I shall present these theses as a deductive argument starting from two premisses which Socrates undoubtedly thought were self-evident. The first of these premisses is one with which he explicitly says that all wise men would agree. It is often said that this claim is jesting or ironical, and that the premiss is an obvious paradox. But I think that the claim is serious and that no wise man who understands it will disagree with it, as Socrates claims. In transliterated Greek it reads *oudeis hekon hamartanei*. This has been variously translated; I have seen the translation 'no man sins willingly', which no doubt is paradoxical. But the translation I offer, and which I have no doubts about is:

1. Nobody makes mistakes intentionally;

if anyone prefers Dodd's translation 'no one commits an error if he can help it', that also is acceptable.

Whatever the verb *hamartanein* may mean in later literature, including the *New Testament*, in classical Greek its basic meaning is not 'to do wrong' but 'to go wrong', in the sense of missing the target or making a mistake, and it has no necessary moral implications, though moral error is not excluded. Further, the question raised in Socrates' thesis is not whether one makes mistakes willingly on the one hand or reluctantly and unwillingly on the other, but whether one does so intentionally or contrary to one's intention.

It would be possible to read the claim that no one makes a mistake

A. I. Goldman and J. Kim (eds.), Values and Morals, 131–141. All Rights Reserved.
Copyright © 1978 by D. Reidel Publishing Company, Dordrecht, Holland.

intentionally to imply that, whatever one does, if in the outcome it turns out to have been a mistake it must, under every description, have been contrary to one's intention. On this interpretation it is not merely a paradox, it is silly. If, however, we interpret it to mean that nobody intentionally does what at the time of action he regards as a mistake, it is surely true and, indeed, a conceptual truth. No doubt it is possible to speak of people making mistakes deliberately or on purpose, but this involves giving a secondary meaning to the word 'mistake'. Thus one may deliberately make a mistake in counting to see if a child will spot it. Something is a mistake in the secondary sense if it would have been a mistake in the primary sense, granted certain natural presumptions about the agent's intentions (in our illustration, that he intended to count correctly).

The second Socratic thesis that I shall treat as a premiss is that everyone aims at the good. This should not be interpreted to mean that everyone aims at what is, or what he takes to be, morally best. It means that everyone aims at what he conceives to be in his best interests. It can be argued whether the thesis is that we aim at our greatest good or at what we conceive to be our greatest good. No doubt Socrates holds that they in fact pursue what they conceive to be their greatest good, but that what they want to achieve is not what satisfies the description 'what I believe to be my greatest good' but what satisfies the description 'my greatest good', so that, if they came to realize that what they had sought was not in fact their greatest good, they would acknowledge that they had made a mistake. In this paper I shall use such expressions as 'their greatest good' and rely on the reader being aware of this complexity. Nothing important for our present purposes depends on marking the distinction carefully.

In the *Protagoras* and in many other of the earlier dialogues it is clear from the whole tenor of the argument that Socrates accepts without question that all men aim always at their greatest good. In the *Protagoras*, indeed, he allows that there is an apparent exception when people are 'overcome by pleasure'. But he argues that this exception is only apparent. Those who are said to be overcome by pleasure, he claims, are really aiming at the good but mistakenly choosing a short-term good, being blind to its long-term evil consequences. It is not within human nature, he holds, to act knowingly to one's detriment.

So we may state Socrates' second premiss as being:

2. Everybody aims at what is best for him.

I do not assert, or believe, that this is a truth, let alone a self-evident truth.

But it has certainly seemed self-evident to philosophers at all periods of history. Even Aristotle, who, as we shall see, knows better, begins his *Nicomachean Ethics* with the statement that every action of every kind seems to aim at some good.

From the two numbered premisses an evident deduction follows that nobody intentionally aims at what is not best for him nor, a fortiori, at what is bad for him. So we have the third step in the argument:

> 3. Therefore anybody who acts against his best interests is making a mistake.

There is a further inevitable deduction to be made, one which, indeed, follows from premiss 2 on its own. If everybody always aims at his greatest good there cannot ever be any interior conflict of aims. There may, certainly, be indecision. I may debate whether to spend my evening at the motion pictures or working, for example. But if my goal is, inevitably, my greatest good, this cannot be a conflict between goals but must be uncertainty about which course of action will yield my greatest good. I cannot, given the premisses of the Socratic argument, even be tempted to overlook the arguments in favour of working; to ignore this point is to forget Socrates' denial of the reality of being 'overcome by pleasure'. Pleasure is merely the nearer good, and the error we make in choosing it is a purely intellectual one; the nearer good may by illusion seem greater much as the nearer object of sight can seem greater to the uncritical eye. We misjudge; we are never misled. So we may add:

> 4. There can be no internal conflict between goals.

From these considerations it again clearly follows that there can be no such thing as weakness of will or *akrasia*, construed as intentionally doing what is known or believed to be against one's greatest good. For in order so to act one would have to be capable of aiming at something other than one's greatest good. But this has been declared to be impossible. So we have:

> 5. Akrasia, or weakness of will, is impossible.

All action whose goal turns out not have been one's greatest good will be mistaken, error, and the result of ignorance. At this stage the Socratic doctrine does indeed seem paradoxical; but how could we avoid it if we accept the premisses?

There are two further theses which are part of the position of Socrates with which we are at present concerned. One of these is:

6. To behave contrary to *arete* (moral excellence) is contrary to one's greatest good.

This is not thought by Socrates to be self-evident and he knows that most people deny it. He argues for it shortly in the *Gorgias* and at great length in the *Republic*. The tenor of the argument is that action contrary to *arete* is a way of damaging one's soul and is therefore a worse calamity for the agent than suffering injustice, which may harm the body but not the soul. I do not discuss the merits of this argument but note that by adding proposition 6 to our premisses 1 and 2 we can reach the conclusion that:

7. Anyone who acts contrary to *arete* is making a mistake.

I suspect that it is through a confusion of this proposition with the first premiss that people have been tempted to construe that premiss as having the content of proposition 7. Perhaps they have also been misled by misunderstanding the gloss of Socrates on premiss 1 which is typically translated by 'nobody voluntarily does evil (*kaka*) and base (*aischra*) actions', thinking that this commits him to the view that nobody intentionally acts immorally. Certainly Socrates held that nobody intentionally does what he takes to be evil and base; but people may certainly do immoral acts intentionally, mistakenly believing that so to act is in their best interest while morality is foolish weakness. Thus in Book I of the *Republic*, Thrasymachus, when asked by Socrates whether he thinks that wrongdoers are good, sensible men, answers that 'if they can win political power over states and peoples and their wrongdoings have full scope' they are.

Again, in the *Gorgias* Polus is revolted by the suggestion that it is preferable to be unjustly treated than to act unjustly. It is only when it is proved to him that it is more evil and base to act unjustly that he reluctantly admits the point. Acting against one's greatest good, knowingly, is what is said to be against human nature. To murder, to act unjustly, to do wrong are all well within human nature unless they can be seen to be contrary to one's greatest good. Socrates always realises that thesis 7 is highly controversial, requiring elaborate argument, and he never confuses it with the self-evident, or allegedly self-evident, premisses 1 and 2.

It is clear that the Socratic denial of *akrasia*, as it is here elucidated, does not require acceptance of such ambitious claims as those made in propositions 6 and 7, but only of the first two premisses. If we have but one aim, our greatest good, there can be no conflict and so no possibility of weakness in conflict. Those who think that in equating pleasure and the good in the

Protagoras Socrates is merely conceding for temporary purposes what is popularly believed fail to see that the equation is central to his argument (and even in the *Laws* the Athenian tells us that 'no one would consent, if he could help it, to a course of action that did not bring him more pleasure than distress'). Further the doctrine of the unity of the virtues in the *Protagoras* is a necessary corollary of the Socratic position; for nobody can excel anyone else save in wisdom and there is no goal other than the good, which wisdom alone can find.

Thus the doctrines of the *Protagoras* and the *Gorgias* form a consistent and tight-knit whole. But this view of the psychology of action, limiting man to the sole aim of achieving his greatest good and reducing all processes of deliberation to the mere calculation, on the basis of one's knowledge, which specific course of action will achieve this goal, is not the only one that we can find attributed by Plato to Socrates. In the *Republic* and in the *Phaedrus* we hear a very different story. Thus in the *Republic*, from page 435 to page 444, a much more complicated account of the goals of action is given. Here we are told that there are three elements in the soul: there is the 'rational' element, characterized as aiming at the good, the 'spirited' element, characterized as aiming at honour, and the 'appetitive' element, characterized as aiming at bodily pleasure. So now there is clearly the possibility of conflict of goals within the soul and therefore the possibility of *akrasia*, whether conceived of as action contrary to the goal of the good or, minimally, as acting contrary to one of one's goals. Now, indeed, so far from including a denial of the possibility of *akrasia*, the whole argument is based on the fact of its occurrence. The philosophic and good man is he in whom the rational element dominates, in whom the desire for the good always wins; the 'timocratic' man is he in whom the goal of honour is at least normally dominant; 'oligarchic', 'democratic' and 'tyrannical' men are those in whom, in different ways, appetite is normally dominant. It has been argued, without support from the text, that only the philosophic man has all three elements in his soul, or that only in him is the rational element active. But the whole argument for the tripartite division of the soul is based on the propositions that since there is conflict, and since conflict is a way of being contrarily affected, and since nothing can at the same time and in the same respect be contrarily affected, there must be different elements in the soul to be affected in the various ways. Leontius, at least, when he looks at the executed corpses, is represented as bitterly chiding himself for his weakness: 'For a time he struggled with himself and covered his eyes, but at last his appetite got the better of him and he ran up to the corpses, opening his eyes wide and saying

to them "There you are, curse you — a lovely sight." ' So the *Republic*
acknowledges that there can be conflict, and that when there is conflict
the 'higher' element is not always victorious; the story of Leontius is a
paradigm case of *akrasia*, though not the only case offered in the *Republic*.

We find an essentially similar account of these matters in the *Phaedrus*,
especially in the speech made by Socrates which begins on page 244. Essentially the same tripartite division of the soul as in the *Republic* is described
in the myth of the charioteer and the horses, though the mythical version
is naturally less precise. 'In the beginning of the tale', Socrates says, 'I divided
each soul into three parts, two of which had the form of horses, the third
that of a charioteer.' Though Plato gives no cross-reference (he never does), it
is natural to equate the charioteer with the rational element of the *Republic*,
the element which desires the good. One horse is a 'lover of honour joined
with temperance and modesty', and appears to represent the spirited element
in the soul; the other is 'the companion of insolence and pride' and apparently
represents the element of bodily appetite. There follows a graphic description
of the efforts of the charioteer to control the horses, and particularly of
the difficulties of contending with the gross bodily appetites of the second
horse. 'If now the better elements of the soul . . . prevail, they live a life
of happiness.' But the possibility of the unruly horse prevailing is clearly
envisaged.

Thus we can find two very different views in the Platonic dialogues. In
some earlier ones he portrays Socrates as holding that man has only one goal
of action, which is his greatest good. The apparent possibility of conflict
between desire for the good and appetite for the pleasant is explained away.
That the supposed conflict 'is ridiculous will be evident if only we give up
the use of various names, such as 'pleasant' and 'unpleasant', and 'good' and
'evil'.' Thus all failure to aim at and achieve the good can be explained only
as the result of ignorance and miscalculation. But in the rather later *Republic*
and *Phaedrus* the doctrine of the good as the sole goal of action is very
clearly abandoned, and thus the whole basis of the Socratic argument against
the possibility of *akrasia* is gone. Now the possibility of *akrasia* is freely
admitted, though its explanation in terms of three elements of the soul,
each with its own unitary goal, warring against each other, may not seem a
final answer to many of us.

The interpretation of the opening chapters of Book VII of the *Nicomachean
Ethics* is agreed to be already sufficiently problematic. But, if this interpretation of Plato is correct, a further problem of understanding Aristotle now
emerges.

That Aristotle's treatment of *akrasia* derives from a study of the *Republic* is beyond doubt. Certainly he knew this dialogue, as well as the others here mentioned. As the *Republic* recognizes three elements in the soul, the rational the spirited and bodily appetite, so Aristotle recognized three types of *orexis* (appetition) — *boulesis* (rational wish) for the good, *thumos* (spirit) for honour and *epithumia* (appetite) for the pleasant. So, as in the *Republic*, there are two types of *akrasia*; in the more disreputable case appetite prevails, in the less disreputable case spirit prevails against reason. The vocabulary also echoes Plato's in detailed ways; thus each speaks of reason as restraining, or trying to restrain the bodily appetite (*koluein*), and each uses the verb 'lead' (*agein*) in portraying a personified appetite as leading a man on to the acratic action.

Now Aristotle sees clearly that the possibility of *akrasia* requires that there be competing goals. In the second chapter of Book III of the *Nicomachean Ethics* he distinguishes rational choice (*prohairesis*) of a course of action aiming at the good from appetite and says explicitly: 'Appetite opposes rational choice, but appetite does not oppose appetite.' Appetite is, by definition, for the pleasant, rational choice of the good. There can be indecision between courses of action both directed either to the pleasant or to the good, but for opposition there must be different goals. Desire for the pleasant can oppose desire for the good, but it cannot oppose itself.

But in Book VII Aristotle seems to attribute to Socrates, and to partially endorse, a position which is neither that of the *Protagoras* nor that of the *Republic* nor discoverable in any other dialogue. On this view *akrasia* does not occur except because of failure of knowledge; 'we seem to be led to the conclusion which Socrates sought to establish. *Akrasia* does not occur in the presence of knowledge in the strict sense, and it is sensory knowledge, not science, which is dragged about by emotion.' But in the *Protagoras akrasia* does not and cannot occur; there are only intellectual errors and failures of knowledge, while in the *Republic* it is appetite, not lack of scientific knowledge that leads to the downfall of Leontius.

A more accurate account of Socrates' position is given when Aristotle represents it as being that 'it would be strange if, when a man possesses knowledge, something else should overpower it (the soul) and drag it about like a slave.' This is a direct echo of *Protagoras*, page 352. But in the *Republic*, where Socrates admits that we can have competing goals of action, he roundly asserts that appetite can, against the resistence of reason, 'drag it (the soul) like a wild beast to drink.' On the whole Aristotle incorrectly represents the position of Socrates, offering an unstable compromise between the *Protagoras* and the *Republic* in which desire for the good always wins over alternative goals provided knowledge is present. This is to have the worst of all possible worlds.

However this may be, we can at least say that the Socrates of the *Republic* and Aristotle recognize three general goals – the good, the pleasant and the honorable. But beyond these both Plato and Aristotle clearly recognize that we have also much more specific goals of action. Plato clearly thinks that we may desire knowledge, for example, while Aristotle distinguishes *energeiai* (activities) from *kineseis* (processes) by the criterion that the former are ends in themselves and the latter have quite specific products as their ends (bridles are the goal of bridle-making). In neither case is the end said to be one of the three general goals so far discussed.

It might be said that the acknowledgement of these less general goals was incompatible with the claim that we always aim at the good, the honorable or the pleasant. But I do not think that this is so, for reasons that were, I believe, reasonably clear to Plato; but since Aristotle is much more explicit and systematic on this point I shall here offer an account of his views. For Aristotle, as for Plato, the good and the pleasant are not merely very general goals of action, they are higher-order goals. Eudaemonia (that is, the good for man), says Aristotle, is 'a composite of many goods, for it is nothing beyond these, but these'. Thus to aim at one's overall good is not to aim at something separate, but to aim at those lower-order goals the achievement of which counts as achievement of the higher-order goal. Similarly Aristotle does not think of pleasure as something separate; I must also be aiming at some lower-order goal when I aim at the pleasant. Thus I may aim at eating sweet things or at contemplating the relation between the side and the diagonal of the square and in so doing may be aiming at the pleasant.

An analogy may be of help. A student may aim at writing a grade A term-paper. This will be a higher-order goal. To aim at this he must have some view of what makes a paper worthy of an A. If he considers this to be a combination of clarity, relevance, accuracy and originality, then he must be aiming at these. To say that only 'A-ness' is a true goal and that clarity and relevance are of no value would be absurd. To parody Aristotle: A-ness is a compound of certain merits (such as clarity and relevance) and is nothing beyond these but these.

Thus Aristotle recognized that higher-order goals presuppose lower-order goals and that the good and the pleasant are higher-order goals. Plato also, I believe, saw this point, though I shall not now try to substantiate this claim. But the point is nowhere made so clearly as in the works of Joseph Butler,

Bishop of Durham. In paragraph 31 of the preface to the *Sermons* (Gladstone's edition) which is headed 'Particular affections necessary to interest and happiness', he states the matter so clearly that anything but quotation would be pointless. 'Besides', he says, 'the very idea of an interested pursuit necessarily presupposes particular passions or appetites; since the very idea of interest or happiness consists in this, that an appetite or affection enjoys its object. It is not because we love ourselves that we find delight in such and such objects, but because we have particular affections towards them. Take away these affections, and you leave self-love absolutely nothing to employ itself about; no end or object to pursue except only of avoiding pain'. To this we may add that unless one had an aversion to pain it is unclear why one would avoid it out of self-love or self-interest.

So far, I think, Butler is saying what was already recognized by Plato and Aristotle, though not as clearly and consistently as by Butler. But now Butler parts company from them. For it certainly seems to be their doctrine that, while one cannot aim for the good, the pleasant or the honorable without also aiming at some lower-order goal, the converse is also true. It seems that for Aristotle always and for Plato sometimes every action will necessarily aim at one of the higher-order goals, while for the Plato of the *Protagoras* every action necessarily aims at the good; nothing presents itself to us as a lower-order goal which is not also a higher-order goal of one of these three types.

Butler, on the other hand, speaks in paragraph 29 of the preface to the *Sermons* as follows:

> There is a strange affectation in many people of explaining away all particular affections, and representing the whole of life as nothing but one continued exercise of self-love. Hence arises the surprising confusion and perplexity in the Epicureans of old, Hobbes, the author of *Reflexions, Sentences et Maximes Morales*, and this whole set of writers; the confusion of calling actions interested which are done in contradiction to the most manifest known interest, merely for the gratification of a present passion.

If Butler had spoken of the good and the pleasant instead of self-interest and self-love this could be an attack on Plato and Aristotle, with the expression 'the most manifest known interest' having the force of nullifying an explanation in terms of ignorance. Butler did not agree that all first-order goals were cases of some higher-order goal.

It is possible to understand the position of those who consider that pleasure is some particular type of feeling, of which pain is the opposite, and who claim that our only motivation is towards pleasure, construed as a first-order goal. Such a position is readily intelligible, though it may be hard to understand how anyone can be so simple-minded as to accept it.

It is also possible to understand, and to share, the position of those who, like Plato and Aristotle, recognize that in addition to such higher-order goals as the good and the pleasant there must be lower-order goals constitutive of those of higher-order. Butler himself apparently recognized three orders, conscience being the source of third-order aims, below which is the second-order self-love, below which are the first-order goals which he called particular affections or appetites (whether benevolence was for Butler a first-order or second-order goal I shall discuss briefly later). While we may not agree with any of them in their identification and classification of the higher-order aims, we may well agree that there are such.

What is hard to understand is how Plato and Aristotle, recognizing that there must be first-order aims, can apparently hold without argument that we never have first-order aims which are not also cases of some higher-order aim, and, *a fortiori*, that there can never be a conflict between a first-order and a higher-order aim, though a first-order aim may be a case of a higher-order aim which conflicts with another higher-order aim, and, still *a fortiori*, that there is no case of conflict between first-order aims that is not also a case of conflict between higher-order aims.

I say that this is hard to understand since, when Butler tell us that ambition is as disinterested as benevolence, the truth of his statement seems evident even in his deliberately provoking example. Certainly Butler realizes that, to quote his own words, 'self-love and any particular passion may be joined together'; ambition is not necessarily divorced from self-love. But it is surely true that someone may aim at, say, some high position without even raising the question whether it will be better for him, or more pleasant for him if he attains it. He may even persist in such an ambition when it conflicts with his 'manifest known interest'. That it may be, perhaps must be, irrational to persist in an ambition in the face of one's interest may be true; we may rhetorically ask how anybody could so act, with an air of incomprehension, if we are protesting against the irrationality of the action, but it is hard to deny that people do so act on occasion.

A well-known move may now be made. If, in Butler's sarcastic words, 'the words selfish and interested cannot be parted with', it may be said that if such choices are made it *must* be thought by the agent to be in his interest so to act. But the 'natural way of speaking plainly' is preferable; each man must indeed act 'from a desire or choice or preference of his own', but that is not a reason for calling the action interested. I shall not spend more time on this point, so clear to some, so impossible to others. The muddled comments of Gladstone himself and Whewell, in a footnote to the tenth paragraph of the eleventh sermon in Gladstone's edition, should warn us that any exposition of the matter, however clear and decisive, can still be misunderstood and perverted.

My aims, however, are not those of Butler. He was ridiculing the enlightened eighteenth-century cynics by telling them that their fault was not that of being too much but of being too little governed by self-interest. Mine has been to illuminate some of the problems of the psychology of action by presenting a thumbnail sketch of some episodes in the history of its discussion. The positions I have sketched have been in ancient rather than in modern dress; but I believe that they are still commonly held today.

My main design has been to bring out the distinction between higher- and lower-order goals, to support Butler's contention that such motives as self-interest and self-love, such goals as the good and the pleasant, are essentially of higher-order and presuppose aims and goals of lower order and, again following Butler, to reject the view, shared by Plato and Aristotle and many since, that nobody aims at lower-order goals without aiming at some such higher-order goal. But I do not wish to assert that any given goal can, as a conceptual truth, be assigned to some given order. Whether anything like a clear hierarchy of goals can be discovered seems very doubtful; but there is much room for further work on this topic.

I end with what is of the nature of a footnote. It is notoriously difficult to determine whether in Butler's theory benevolence is to be thought of as a particular affection or as a higher-order motivation on a level with self-love. I am not sure that he was consistent on this point, but offer an argument to suggest that he ought, however great its moral importance, to regard benevolence as a particular affection; at least it is not essentially higher-level like self-interest. For it seems that one's own interest is necessarily of higher order than the interest of another. Thus conceivably my only interest in life might be to achieve what is in your best interest. For reasons given, you could have no self-interest if you had not what were, for you, goals of a lower order. But I could aim at bringing about your achievement of these lower-level goals purely in order to serve your interest, having myself no desire for you to achieve these goals as such. Again, if I thought that you were mistaken about your interests or neglecting your interests, I could aim to bring about those things which I believed would be constitutive of your interest purely to promote your interest. This contrasts with one's own interest which, it has been argued, is necessarily a goal of a higher order.

Oxford University

GILBERT HARMAN

WHAT IS MORAL RELATIVISM?

Of the various views that have been called 'moral relativism,' there are three plausible versions, which I will label 'normative moral relativism,' 'moral judgment relativism,' and 'meta-ethical relativism.' The first of these views is a thesis about moral agents; the second, a thesis about the form of meaning of moral judgments; the third, a thesis about the truth conditions or justification of moral judgments. *Normative moral relativism* is the view roughly that different people, as agents, can be subject to different ultimate moral demands. *Moral judgment relativism* holds that moral judgments make implicit reference to the speaker or some other person or to some group or to one or another set of moral standards, etc. *Meta-ethical relativism* says that conflicting moral judgments about a particular case can both be right.

1. NORMATIVE MORAL RELATIVISM

According to our rough statement of normative moral relativism, different people, as agents, can be subject to different ultimate moral demands. Only ultimate differences are supposed to be relevant, since even the nonrelativist will agree that different agents are subject to some different moral demands because of differences in situation. Jack is morally obligated to pay George ten dollars, Mary is not. That is not yet normative moral relativism. Maybe Jack has borrowed ten dollars from George and Mary has not. In that case Mary and Jack might still be subject to the same ultimate moral demands, including for example that one should pay one's debts.

Differences in situation can include differences in custom. In England (in 1977) Jack ought to drive on the left side of the road. In France, Mary ought to drive on the right. This is again not yet normative moral relativism, since Jack and Mary may still be subject to the same overriding principle – e.g. one ought to drive on the side of the road designated by law and custom. Similarly, other differences between what Jack and Mary ought to do may reflect differences in custom concerning politeness and etiquette, family responsibility, property, and so forth, rather than any difference in ultimate principle.

A. I. Goldman and J. Kim (eds.), Values and Morals, 143–161. All Rights Reserved.
Copyright © 1978, by D. Reidel Publishing Company, Dordrecht, Holland.

What is an *ultimate* moral demand? A given demand D is an ultimate moral demand on an agent A if and only if there is no further moral demand D' on A which, given A's situation, accounts for A's being subject to D.

Actually, quite apart from the issue of relativism, it seems to be a possible view that there are no ultimate moral demands on a person in this sense – that whenever D applies to A there is always a more fundamental D' which explains, given A's situation, why D applies. But according to our initial formulation of normative moral relativism, someone who denies that there are ultimate moral principles could not be a normative moral relativist. That seems wrong. We need a better formulation.

Could we take normative moral relativism to be the view that there are no moral demands to which everyone is subject? No, because a nonrelativist might believe that there are people subject to no moral demands at all, for example infants and idiots. Could we take moral relativism to say that there are no moral demands that apply to everyone who is subject to at least some moral demands? That would be a very strong form of normative moral relativism. We also want to allow for a weaker version that is compatible with the existence of some universal moral demands.

This weaker version must claim there can be two people subject to different moral demands and not subject to some more basic demand that accounts for this, given differences in their situation. More formally, it says that there can be two people A and B and a moral demand D such that

(1) A is subject to D
(2) B is not subject to D
(3) B is subject to some moral demands
(4)   There is no demand D' to which A and B are both subject which accounts for (1) and (2) given the differences in situation between A and B.

This formulation allows for some moral universality and is compatible with the claim that there are no ultimate moral demands. This is basically the same view that Frankena calls 'normative relativism.'[1] He formulates the view as follows: "what is right or good for one individual or society is not right or good for another, even if the situations involved are similar." This is inexact, however, since any two situations are similar in some respects and different in others. We need to say that the situations are similar in the sense that there are no morally significant differences in the two situations. If we suppose that a difference is morally significant only if it is counted significant by some moral principle or demand, we are led to something like the formulations I have offered for 'normative moral relativism.'

Brandt uses the term 'normative relativism' differently, for any view which 'asserts that something is wrong or blameworthy if some person — or group — thinks it is wrong or blameworthy.' He gives two examples of such a view.

(a) "If someone thinks it is right (or wrong) to do A, then it *is* right (wrong) for him to do A." (b) "If the moral principles recognised in the society of which X is a member imply that it is wrong to do A in circumstances C, then it *is* wrong for X to do A in C."[2]

But this does not seem to be a very plausible view. Nor is it even clearly a version of relativism, since it appears to be advocating a moral principle that might be taken to have universal applications. In any event, it is certainly a different view from what I am calling normative moral relativism, which says that two people can be subject to different moral demands and not subject to some more basic demand that accounts for this, given their situation.

This ends my preliminary discussion of normative moral relativism, which makes a claim about moral agents. I turn now to a relativistic thesis about the meaning or form of moral judgments.

2. MORAL JUDGMENT RELATIVISM

According to moral judgment relativism, moral judgments contain an implicit reference to the speaker or some other person or some group or certain moral standards, etc. One version holds that moral judgments are always implicitly egocentric in the sense that they are always equivalent to judgments containing egocentric terms essentially. Egocentric terms in English include *I*, *me*, *this*, and *now*. So one example of this sort of moral judgment relativism would be Brandt's suggestion in *Hopi Ethics*: "It would be wrong to do X" means the same as "If I were normal, impartial, and fully informed, I should feel obligated not to perform X."[3] (Brandt later abandons this suggestion in *Ethical Theory*.)

Notice that this form of moral judgment relativism says that egocentric terms are *essential* to the equivalent paraphrase. Anyone can agree that 'Stealing is wrong' is equivalent to 'My stealing is wrong and so is everyone else's.' But that does not guarantee the truth of this form of moral judgment relativism. Notice also that this form of moral judgment relativism holds that *all* moral judgments are egocentric in this sense. It is obvious that some are, for example 'I should not steal' is, but, again, that is not enough to establish the truth of this form of moral judgment relativism.

Another version of moral judgment relativism takes moral judgments to be implicitly relative to one or another morality in something like the way in which a judgment that someone is tall is implicitly relative to one or another comparison class. To say that George is tall is to say that George is tall in relation to some implicitly indicated reference class. George can be tall in relation to one such class and not tall in relation to another. For example, George might be tall for a man but not tall for a basketball player. Note that it makes no sense to ask whether George is tall, period, apart from one comparison class or another.

Similarly, this form of moral judgment relativism holds that moral judgments make sense only in relation to one or another set of moral demands. Something can be right in relation to one morality and not right in relation to another. 'As a Christian, you ought to turn the other cheek: I, however, propose to strike back.' The judgment that X is wrong is always incomplete — just as the judgment that P is tall is incomplete. Just as we must always understand the latter judgment as the judgment that P is tall for a person, or for a basketball player, etc., so too we must understand the former judgment as saying that X is wrong *for* a Christian, *for* a Moslem, *for* someone who accepts such and such demands, etc.

Stevenson uses the term 'relativism' to indicate something like this second form of moral judgment relativism.[4] On the other hand, Firth counts an analysis as 'relativistic' if it is a version of the first form of moral judgment relativism in its essential use of egocentric terms.[5] Notice that an analysis that is relativistic in Firth's sense will not necessarily count as a form of relativism in Stevenson's sense. Nevertheless, both views see a hidden implicit relativity in the logical form or meaning of moral judgments, so both count as forms of moral judgment relativism in my sense. I turn now to a third form of relativism which sees a different sort of relativity in moral judgments — a relativity in the correctness of moral judgments.

3. META-ETHICAL RELATIVISM

According to meta-ethical relativism, there can be conflicting moral judgments about a particular case that are both fully correct. The idea is that two people with different moralities might reach conflicting moral judgments concerning a particular case — for example; one saying the agent was morally right, the other saying the agent was wrong — where both opinions are correct.

The two judgments must really conflict and therefore must be judgments about the same particular case. It is not enough to contrast a judgment about one act in society with a judgment about the 'same act' in another society.

Furthermore, it is not enough for meta-ethical relativism that there should be such conflicting judgments. Both judgments must be correct. In particular, neither judgment can rest on mistakes about the facts of the case, a failure fully to appreciate these facts, incorrect reasoning, or anything else that might distort someone's judgment.

Finally both judgments must be fully correct. Borderline cases are not enough — cases in which one might be equally justified in saying one thing or the opposite. According to meta-ethical relativism the one judgment is fully correct for the one speaker, the conflicting judgment is fully correct for the other speaker and not *vice versa*. It would not be correct for either speaker to make the other judgment.

Both Brandt and Frankena use the term 'meta-ethical relativism' in roughly this sense. According to Brandt, the meta-ethical relativist "denies that there is always one correct moral evaluation" of a given issue.[6] In his book *Ethical Theory*, he calls the same view 'ethical relativism,' which he there defines as the thesis that "there are conflicting ethical opinions that are equally valid."[7] However, Brandt would allow certain merely apparently conflicting opinions to count as conflicting, if moral judgment relativism should be true. So certain moral judgment relativists will count as meta-ethical relativists as Brandt uses this term but not as we are using it.[8]

As Frankena explains meta-ethical relativism, "It holds that, in the case of basic ethical judgments, there is no objectively valid, rational way of justifying one against the other; consequently two conflicting basic judgments may be equally valid."[9] Presumably he refers to 'basic ethical judgments' to allow for the possibility that less basic judgments might be justified on the basis of more basic judgments, the question then being how the most basic judgments are to be justified. But this part of his definition is best omitted, since we want to allow both relativists and nonrelativists to be able to deny that there are basic ethical judgments in this sense. This leaves us with the claim that two conflicting ethical judgments may be equally valid, which is essentially the way in which we have defined meta-ethical relativism.[10]

Brandt uses the term 'methodological relativism' to refer to what he takes to be a particular version of what we are calling meta-ethical relativism, a version which holds that 'there is no unique rational method in ethics' for assessing moral judgments.[11] Stevenson uses the term 'methodological relativism' slightly differently for the claim that statements about the reasons and justification of moral judgments are themselves implicitly relational, in something like the way in which moral judgments are held to be implicitly relational according to moral judgment relativism.[12] Brandt's but not Stevenson's definition counts as a 'methodological relativist' the sceptic who denies that moral judgments are ever correct or justified in any sense. Such a sceptic clearly does not count as a meta-ethical relativist in our sense, since a meta-ethical relativist holds that conflicting moral judgment can both be correct whereas such a sceptic denies that any moral judgment is ever correct.

4. THE THREE VERSIONS OF MORAL RELATIVISM BRIEFLY COMPARED

We have distinguished three versions of moral relativism: (1) normative moral relativism, which holds that two people can be subject to different moral demands and not subject to some more basic demand that accounts for this given their different situations; (2) moral judgment relativism, which says that moral judgments implicitly refer to one or another person, group, or set of moral demands; and (3) meta-ethical relativism, which holds that conflicting moral judgments about a particular case can both be right. It is clearly possible to accept one of these versions without accepting the others.

For example, an emotivist might accept meta-ethical relativism on the ground that people can differ in their moral attitudes without having relevantly different beliefs, without having reasoned incorrectly or failed to appreciate certain things, without being prejudiced or biased, etc. But, as Stevenson points out, the emotivist need not (and probably will not) accept moral judgment relativism.[13] And the emotivist can also deny normative moral relativism, since he can (and no doubt will) suppose that the principles he accepts apply to everyone.

Moreover, an existentialist might accept normative moral relativism on the grounds that each person is subject only to the principles that person accepts. This does not imply moral judgment relativism or meta-ethical relativism, since the existentialist can suppose that conflicting moral judgments about a particular agent cannot both be correct. Given the moral principles that agent accepts, at most one of the judgments will be right.

Finally, a relativistic ideal observer theorist with the sort of view Brandt puts forward in *Hopi Ethics* can accept moral judgment relativism without accepting meta-ethical relativism, since he can suppose that two really (as opposed to merely apparently) conflicting moral judgments cannot both be right. And such a theorist can reject normative moral relativism too, e.g. on the grounds that if he were an ideal observer he would apply the same basic principles to everyone.

So, it is possible to accept any one of these versions of moral relativism without being committed to the others. It is also possible, consistently, to accept more than one of these versions. Indeed, I am inclined to accept all three.

But someone might say that none of these is *really* a possible view — for each is subject to serious objections which we must now consider.

5. AN OBJECTION TO NORMATIVE MORAL RELATIVISM

According to normative moral relativism there can be two people A and B and a moral demand D such that

(1) A is subject to D
(2) B is not subject to D
(3) B is subject to some moral demands
(4)   There is no moral demand D' to which A and B are both subject which accounts for (1) and (2) given the difference in situation between A and B.

The obvious objection to this is that, if (1), (2), and (3) are true, there must be some reason why A but not B is subject to D, for surely this cannot be an arbitrary fact. *Something* must be true of A but not true of B which accounts for why A but not B is subject to D. It follows that there must be some sort of general principle which implies that people with certain characteristics F are subject to D and others are not. So there must be a general principle P more basic than that expressing the demand D which accounts for (1) and (2) given the difference in situation between A and B, i.e. given that A is F and B is not. But then it can seem that (4) must be false. For won't P express just the moral demand D' whose existence (4) denies?

Consider, for example, the existentialist who advocates normative moral relativism on the grounds that each person is subject only to moral principles that person accepts. Then A is subject to D but B is not because A accepts a principle expressing the demand D and B does not. But then it can seem that the existentialist is committed to supposing that there is after all a moral demand D' that applies both to A and to B and explains why A but not B is subject to D, namely the demand of non-hypocrisy, the demand that one should act in accordance with those principles one accepts. And it can seem that the same point will apply to any attempt to defend normative moral relativism, leading to the conclusion that this is not after all a coherent form of moral relativism.

I suspect indeed that reflections along these lines lead Brandt to use the term 'normative relativism' not for what we are calling normative moral relativism but for the view that something is wrong or blameworthy if some person — or group — thinks it is wrong or blameworthy. For it can seem that the existentialist is more plausibly taken to be advocating normative relativism in Brandt's sense than normative moral relativism in our sense, even though normative relativism in Brandt's sense is quite implausible on its face; for it can seem that normative moral relativism in our sense is quite incoherent.

I believe that this is wrong and that normative moral relativism is not only coherent but even true. But before saying why, let me go on to objections to the two other forms of moral relativism.

6. AN OBJECTION TO MORAL JUDGMENT RELATIVISM

Moral judgment relativism holds that moral judgments make implicit reference to the speaker, some other person or persons, or some set of moral demands. It follows from this that apparently conflicting moral judgments do not actually conflict if made by different speakers or made in relation to different people or moralities. But, as Stevenson has persuasively argued,[14] this seems to imply that certain genuine moral disagreements are mere pseudo-issues.

Recall Brandt's suggestions in *Hopi Ethics* that "It would be wrong to do X" means "If I were normal, impartial, and fully informed, I should feel obligated not to perform X." Now suppose that A and B are discussing whether abortion is wrong. A maintains that abortion is wrong; B maintains that it is not wrong. A and B imagine that they are disagreeing; they mean to be disagreeing with each other. But, Brandt's analysis implies that they are not really disagreeing. A is saying that if she, A, were normal, impartial, and fully informed, she would feel obligated not to have an abortion in certain circumstances; B is saying that if she, B, were normal, impartial, and fully informed, she would not feel obligated not to have an abortion in those circumstances. And both of these claims could be true. It is possible that under these conditions A would feel obligated not to have an abortion and B would not feel obligated. But this is implausible. For it seems that if A and B are using words normally they do genuinely disagree. In Stevenson's view, they may not disagree in belief but they certainly disagree in their attitude toward abortion. He takes this to be evidence for his view that moral judgments express favorable or unfavorable attitudes rather than beliefs.

7. AN OBJECTION TO META-ETHICAL RELATIVISM

Metal-ethical relativism holds that actually conflicting moral judgments about a particular case can both be right and not just in 'borderline' cases. The obvious objection here is that it is not clear what this could mean. It would seem that to say that a judgment is right is for oneself to endorse that judgment — to agree with it. The meta-ethical relativist therefore seems to be committing himself to agreeing with each of two judgments which, also according to him, genuinely conflict. This seems to involve an inconsistency. What can the meta-ethical relativist have in mind? We are supposing that the people making the judgments genuinely and not merely apparently disagree. So it seems that the meta-ethical relativist, in agreeing with both, must be disagreeing with himself!

In saying that both judgments are right, the meta-ethical relativist might mean either that both are true or that both are justified, given the facts and all other relevant considerations. In either case the objection seems to apply. Reverting to our earlier example, let us suppose again that A maintains that abortion is wrong and that B maintains that abortion is not wrong and let us agree that this is a genuine disagreement — that these judgments really and not just apparently conflict. Then what could it mean to say that both judgments are true. Presumably, it is true that abortion is wrong only if abortion is wrong, and it is true that abortion is not wrong only if abortion is not wrong. If the meta-ethical relativist says both judgments are true, he seems to commit himself to the contradictory conclusion that abortion is both wrong and not wrong.

On the other hand, suppose that the meta-ethical relativist says that, given all the facts and all other relevant considerations, the judgment that abortion is wrong is *justified* and so is the judgment that abortion is not wrong. What could he mean by this? He might mean that this is a borderline case — like deciding whether a certain person is bald — perhaps given all the facts, etc. the judgment that he is bald is justified and so is the judgment that he is not bald. But to say that there are borderline moral issues of this sort is not to say anything interesting — of course there are. We are supposing that the meta-ethical relativist is saying something more than that — that in a case like this both judgments might be justified although this is not a borderline case. But what can that mean?

Stevenson's suggestion might seem to help here. Perhaps the meta-ethical relativist is a methodological relativist in Stevenson's sense, holding that the term 'justified' is a relative term here, having application only to one or another person. Neither judgment is justified *period*; rather the one judgment is justified for A but not B and the other judgment is justified for B but not A. However, as Stevenson observes,[15] this sort of methodological relativism is faced with the same sort of objections raised against moral judgment relativism. For A and B will disagree not only about whether abortion is wrong but also about whether the judgment that abortion is wrong is justified, A maintaining that it is, B denying this. The second disagreement, like the first, seems to be a real disagreement and not the pseudo issue it is taken to be by this sort of normative relativism.

There are, then, serious objections to each of the versions of moral relativism we have distinguished. Against normative moral relativism, it can be said that if A is subject to a moral demand that B is not, there must be some reason for this, a reason that invokes a demand on both A and B, contrary to what is claimed in normative moral relativism. The objection to moral judgment relativism is that it wrongly treats certain real disagreements as verbal pseudo-issues. Finally, it can be objected that the meta-ethical relativist either must contradict himself by agreeing with each of two conflicting judgments or, in supposing that 'justified' is a relative term, must fall subject to the objection raised against moral judgment relativism; namely that it misrepresents certain real disagreements as merely apparent disagreements.

But all these objections can be met. I will now describe a highly plausible view which, in one way or another, involves all three versions of moral relativism and shows how the objections to each version can be met.

8. AN ARGUMENT FOR NORMATIVE MORAL RELATIVISM

Normative moral relativism might be derived from two assumptions. The first is this.

ASSUMPTION 1. A moral demand D applies to a person only if that person either accepts D (i.e. intends to act in accordance with D) or fails to accept D only because of ignorance of relevant (nonmoral) facts, a failure to reason something through, or some sort of (nonmoral) mental defect like irrationality, stupidity, confusion, or mental illness.

This assumption might be defended by an appeal to the sorts of considerations sometimes offered in support of 'internalist' accounts of moral obligation.[16] It might be said, for example, that the assumption captures what distinguishes moral demands from demands of other sorts, such as legal demands. Moral demands have to be acceptable to those to whom they apply in the way that legal demands do not.

The point might be made in terms of the notion of a reason to do something, since, if a moral demand applies to someone, that person has a compelling reason to act in accordance with that demand. This is not true of legal demands. A legal demand applies to anyone in a given area who satisfies certain conditions, whether or not he or she has a compelling reason to act in accordance with that demand. Now, reasons depend on reasoning. To say that a person has a conclusive reason to do something is to say that there is warranted practical reasoning that he could do, if he knew all the relevant facts, were smart enough, rational enough, etc., reasoning that would culminate in a decision to do the act in question.

Frankena observes that the 'externalist' can escape this sort of argument by claiming that it rests on an ambiguity in the term 'reason,' which might mean either 'justifying reason,' i.e. reason to think one ought to do something, or 'motivating reason.' The externalist can say that the analysis of 'conclusive reason to do something' in terms of practical reasoning culminating in a decision to do it is, perhaps, an analysis of 'motivating reason to do something.' But this, the externalist can say, is irrelevant to the point that, if a moral demand applies to someone, that person has a compelling reason to act in accordance with that demand. For here the relevant type of reason is a justifying reason: If a moral demand applies to someone, that person has a compelling reason to think he or she ought to do that thing.[17]

The internalist will reply that this is an ad hoc maneuver, since no evidence has been offered for the alleged ambiguity. (Frankena gives examples which show that reasons for doing something might be either moral or nonmoral, e.g. self-interested.[18] But that seems irrelevant to the claim of ambiguity.) Furthermore, the notion of a 'justifying reason,' as a reason to think one ought, leads to difficulties for externalism, since to think one ought to do something is to think one has reasons to do it, and these reasons must not in turn be taken to be justifying reasons, for then thinking one ought to do something would be explained as thinking one has reason to think one ought to do that thing.

This point is obscured if talk involving 'ought' is not clearly distinguished from talk of obligation. It can happen that, according to the law, one is supposed to do a certain thing, although there is not the slightest reason actually to do it — perhaps there is no penalty for not doing it and one has no moral reasons to observe this particular law. Here we might speak of legal obligation but we would not say, e.g., that legally one *ought* to do the act in question (even though there is a legal 'justification' only for doing that) — for the word 'ought' is used to speak of reasons in a way that 'obligation' is not.

Of course, if according to morality, one is supposed to do a certain thing then one ought to do it — one does have a reason in that case.

So, even if there is no way of proving the relativist's first assumption, a strong case can be made for it and it is at the very least a possible view to take.

The second assumption can be made stronger or weaker, depending on how strong a form of normative moral relativism is to be defended. The strongest assumption is this.

ASSUMPTION 2S. For any moral demand D, there is someone subject to some moral demands who does not accept D as a legitimate demand on him or herself, where this nonacceptance is not the result of any relevant (nonmoral) ignorance on that person's part or any failure to reason something through or any sort of (nonmoral) mental defect such as irrationality, stupidity, confusion, or mental illness.

Assumptions 1 and 2S logically imply that there are no universal moral demands which apply to everyone who is subject to some moral demands. We are interested here in a weaker normative moral relativism which can be based on a weaker second assumption.

ASSUMPTION 2W. There are two people A and B and a moral demand D such that

(1) A is subject to D

(2) B does not accept D as a legitimate moral demand on him or herself, where this nonacceptance is not the result of any relevant (nonmoral) ignorance on B's part or any failure to reason something through or any sort of (nonmoral) mental defect such as irrationality, stupidity, confusion, or mental illness.

(3) B is subject to some moral demands

(4)   Neither A nor B accepts a demand D' which would account for A but not B being subject to D given the difference in situation between A and B, and in neither case is this failure to accept such a D' the result of any relevant (nonmoral) ignorance or any failure to reason something through or any sort of (nonmoral) mental defect such as irrationality, stupidity, confusion, or mental illness.

Assumptions 1 and 2W together logically imply normative moral relativism as we have defined it.

What can be said on behalf of assumption 2W? Let us consider a couple of possible examples. Consider first the issue of cruelty to animals as it appears to typical middle class American citizens and as it appears to the Hopi Indians. It seems plausible to suppose that a moral demand applies to the typical middle class American citizen forbidding the infliction of needless suffering on animals. On the other hand, from Brandt's description of Hopi morality, it seems that a typical Hopi Indian does not accept such a strong demand as a legitimate moral demand, where this nonacceptance is not the result of ignorance, irrationality, stupidity, etc.[19] Furthermore, neither the typical middle class American citizen nor the typical Hopi Indian accepts any more basic demand that would account for why this should apply to middle class American citizens but not Hopi Indians given differences in their situations. And it would seem that in neither case is this failure to accept such a basic principle the result of ignorance, irrationality, stupidity, etc. So this seems to be an example establishing the truth of assumption 2W.

I am myself inclined to think there are many examples of this sort even within American Society. Consider the moral demand which seems to apply to most people that one should not kill other people. I am inclined to suppose that there are professional criminals who do not accept this demand who have no qualms about killing other people if there is something to be gained from doing so — where this is not because they are unaware of certain facts or have reasoned incorrectly or have failed to follow out certain reasoning, nor is it because of any stupidity, irrationality, confusion or mental illness on their part. And this is not because there is some more basic moral demand which accounts, given differences in situation, for why most people but not these criminals are subject to the prohibition against the killing of other people.

After thinking over these and similar examples, some people (like me) will suppose that assumption 2W is obviously true. Others will not. Some philosophers have argued — unconvincingly — that a rejection of moral demands of this sort must involve ignorance, irrationality, or some other (nonmoral) mental defect.[20] Others might hope that psychology would resolve the issue. "Unfortunately," as Brandt remarks about a related issue, "psychological theories do not provide a uniform answer to our question."[21] Gestalt theory and Piagetian theory point in one way, Hullean learning theory and psycho-analytic theory point in the other way.[22] In any event, I believe it is safe to say that neither philosophy nor psychology has produced a strong case against assumption 2W.

Assumption 1 says, roughly, that a moral demand applies to someone only if it is rational for that person to accept that demand. Assumption 2W says, roughly, that it can be rational for different people to accept different moral demands 'all the way down.' Together these assumptions logically imply, roughly, that different people can be subject to different moral demands 'all the way down.'

How can it be rational for different people to accept different moral demands 'all the way down'? This might be because what it is rational to accept depends on how one's mind works and that different people's minds work in different ways. A less radical suggestion is that what demands it is rational to accept depends on what demands one already accepts and that different people accept sufficiently different demands to begin with that it is rational for them to accept different demands. This is not to say that if one accepts a demand it is automatically rational for one to do so. Nor is it to say that the only thing relevant to the question whether it is rational to accept a given demand is what demands one accepts. Presumably one's desires, other intentions, and beliefs are important too. To accept a moral demand, in the relevant sense, is to intend to adhere to it. Whether it is rational to do this is a question of practical reasoning which in my opinion is to be resolved (roughly) by minimally modifying antecedent intentions, beliefs, desires, etc. in the interest of a certain sort of coherence.[23] But the details are not important here.

We must now see how our earlier objection to normative moral relativism can be met. The objection was that, if A is subject to D and B is not, then something must be true of A but not B which accounts for this; so there must be some sort of general principle which implies that people who are F are subject to D and those who are not F are not subject to D. This general principle will repress a moral demand D' which accounts for why A but not B is subject to D. But normative moral relativism denies that there is always such a demand D'.

The answer to this objection is that the principle in question does not always express a moral demand. A but not B is subject to D because it is rational for A to accept D but not rational for B to do so, and this is sometimes not the result of some more basic moral principle applying to both A and B but rather due simply to the fact that A and B actually accept sufficiently different moral demands in the first place.

Perhaps even in the key case for the relativist there is a demand which applies both to A and B which, given the differences in their situations accounts for why A but not B is subject to D, but this demand is not a *moral* demand — it is simply the demand that one should be rational.

9. RELATIVISM AND UNIVERSALIZABILITY

Frankena raises a somewhat different objection to normative moral relativism: "Such a normative principle seems to violate the requirements of consistency and universalization . . ."[24] Elsewhere he refers to the relevant principle as "The Principle of Universalizability: if one judges that X is right or good, then one is committed to judging that anything exactly like X, or like X in relevant respects, is right or good. Otherwise he has no business using these words."[25] Here Frankena seems to be suggesting that the use of moral terminology normally presupposes a Principle of Universalizability which is incompatible with normative moral relativism. This implies that normative moral relativism involves a misuse of language.

But that is too strong a conclusion. Perhaps many people do use moral terminology in a way that presupposes a Principle of Universalizability that is incompatible with normative moral relativism. Perhaps such a principle is even partly constituative of what these people mean by these terms. Nevertheless, other people — relativists, for example — do not use moral terminology in this way. It must be argued, not just assumed, that there is something wrong with this second usage.

Indeed, suppose that, although one initially uses moral terminology in the first way, one becomes convinced of assumptions 1 and 2W which logically imply normative moral relativism. Then one has become convinced of the falsity of a presupposition of one's use of moral terminology. What should one do? There are two options here. One might simply abandon moral terminology altogether, in the way that one abandons certain racist or sexist terminology after becoming aware of the false presuppositions of its usage. Or one might modify one's usage so that it no longer involves the presuppositions one takes to be false, in the way that Einstein modified the scientific usage of terms like 'simultaneous,' 'acceleration,' and 'mass,' after arguing that prior usage had involved a false presupposition. This second course, of modifying one's usage of moral terminology so as to eliminate the unwanted presupposition, seems clearly the preferable alternative.

How should one's usage be modified? Presumably along the lines suggested by moral judgment relativism. Judgments expressing moral demands can be treated as involving an implicit reference to a person or to a group of people who are presumed to accept certain demands or simply to certain demands themselves. But it is important to avoid or evade the objection raised against moral judgment relativism, namely that it represents certain real disagreements as mere pseudo-issues. If two people — even two relativists — disagree about whether it is morally wrong to cause pain and injury to animals, they really do disagree and are not just talking past each other — the one saying that causing pain and injury to animals is wrong in relation to our morality, the other saying it is not wrong in relation to Hopi morality.

Within a relativistic theory, the objection can be partially met as follows. When a relativist makes a simple moral judgment, expressing a moral demand, saying that a certain sort of act is morally wrong, for example, making no explicit reference to one or another morality, the speaker makes this judgment in relation to a morality he or she accepts, presupposing that this morality is also accepted by anyone to whom the judgment is addressed and by any agents referred to in the judgment (in the sense that what is at issue is whether it is wrong *of them* to do a certain thing). A relativist can make moral judgments in relation to moralities he or she (or the audience) does not accept, but it is a misuse of moral language — even when it has been relativized — to do this without making it clear that one is doing so. It is, furthermore, always a misuse of language to make a moral judgment about an agent in relation to a morality not accepted by the agent.

If two relativists disagree, one saying simply that it is morally wrong to cause pain and injury to animals, the other saying simply that this is not wrong, they do *mean to be* disagreeing with each other. They presuppose that they are making these judgments in relation to the same relevant moral demands. Of course, they may be mistaken about that, in which case they really are talking past each other despite their intentions. If they come to see that they are speaking in relation to relevantly different moralities, they will have to stop saying what they are saying or indeed be guilty of misuse of language.

A relativist can intelligibly disagree with an absolutist over whether something is wrong if the relativist makes his judgment in relation to a morality the absolutist accepts, in the same way that a relativity theory physicist can disagree with a Newtonian over what the mass of a certain object is, if the relativity theorist makes his judgment in relation to an appropriate inertial framework.

A relativistic judgment made in relation to a given morality concerning the moral demands applicable to a particular agent presupposes that the agent in question accepts that morality. So relativists with different moralities will, if they have their wits about them, tend not to make this sort of judgment about the same agents. And, at least as a first approximation, it will turn out that even superficially conflicting judgments cannot both be true of the same agent even if the judgments are made in relation to different moralities, since the judgments will involve conflicting presuppositions about the morality the agent accepts.

That is only a 'first approximation' because a particular agent will typically accept more than one morality — and those moralities can make conflicting demands concerning a particular case. In that case superficially conflicting moral judgments about that agent (e.g. Antigone) made in relation to different moralities can both be true if the agent accepts both moralities relative to which each of the judgments is made.

In any event, the relativist's usage does not permit unrestricted universalization. As a relativist, I cannot accept the principle that, if it would be wrong for me to do something, it would be wrong for anyone else in a similar situation to do that thing, since that is not true for those who do not accept the relevant aspects of my morality. But the following principle is acceptable: if it is wrong for someone else to do something, it would be wrong for me to do that in a similar situation; in other words, if it is okay for me to do something, it can't be wrong for anyone else in my situation.

10. ASSESSING META-ETHICAL RELATIVISM

Our second and third versions of moral relativism are theses about moral judgments. But whose judgments, the relativist's or the nonrelativist's? Well, moral judgment relativism is a thesis about the relativist's usage; it is not meant to apply to the nonrelativist's usage.

What about meta-ethical relativism? This is the claim that really conflicting moral judgments can both be right. Now superficially conflicting relativistic moral judgments can both be right if made in relation to different moralities, but these judgments do not really conflict. And it does not seem to make sense to suppose that really conflicting relativistic moral judgments can both be right. So meta-ethical relativism does not seem correct as a thesis about relativistic moral judgments.

Is it correct as a thesis about nonrelativistic moral judgments? One might suppose that normative moral relativism implies that no nonrelativistic moral judgments can be right, since all such judgments presuppose an unrestricted principle of universalizability. But that would be like denying that any Newtonian judgments concerning the mass of a particular object could be right, on the grounds that these judgments presuppose that mass is invariant from one inertial framework to another. In practice we would say that a Newtonian judgment of mass is right if the corresponding relativistic judgment is correct made in relation to an inertial framework that is not accelerated with respect to the person making the Newtonian judgment. Similarly we should count a nonrelativistic moral judgment right if the corresponding relativistic moral judgment is right made in relation to the morality accepted by the person making the nonrelativistic moral judgment. The relativist can intelligibly suppose that really conflicting nonrelativistic moral judgments are both right in this sense.

I conclude, then, that there is a reasonable form of moral relativism which involves normative moral relativism, moral judgment relativism as a thesis about relativistic but not nonrelativistic moral judgments, and meta-ethical relativism as a thesis about nonrelativistic but not relativistic moral judgments.

Princeton University

NOTES

[1] William Frankena, *Ethics*, Second edition (Englewood Cliffs, New Jersey: Prentice-Hall, 1973), p. 109.

[2] Richard B. Brandt, 'Ethical Relativism', in Paul Edwards (ed.), *The Encyclopedia of Philosophy*, Vol. III (New York: Macmillan and Free Press, 1967), p. 76.

[3] Actually he suggests this as an analysis of the Hopi term *Ka-anta* which he takes to be roughly equivalent to the English term *wrong*. R.B. Brandt, *Hopi Ethics* (Chicago: University of Chicago Press, 1954), p. 109.

[4] Charles L. Stevenson, 'Relativism and Nonrelativism in the Theory of Value', in Stevenson, *Facts and Values* (New Haven and London: Yale University Press, 1963), pp. 71–93.

[5] Roderick Firth, 'Ethical Absolutism and the Ideal Observer', *Philosophy and Phenomenological Research* **XII** (1952), 317–345.

[6] 'Ethical Relativism', p. 75.

[7] Richard B. Brandt, *Ethical Theory* (Englewood Cliffs, New Jersey: Prentice-Hall, 1959), p. 272.

[8] 'Ethical Relativism', p. 75; *Ethical Theory*, pp. 278–279.

[9] *Ethics*, p. 109.

[10] Cf. 'On Saying the Ethical Thing', in K.E. Goodpaster (ed.), *Perspectives on Morality: Essays by William Frankena* (Notre Dame: University of Notre Dame Press, 1976), p. 123, where Frankena calls this position simply 'relativism': "if two people hold conflicting normative judgments, . . . both judgments may be rational or justified."

[11] *Ethical Theory*, p. 275. Cf. 'Ethical Relativism', p. 76.

[12] 'Relativism and Nonrelativism in the Theory of Value', p. 86.

[13] Ibid.

[14] Ibid., p. 81. See also 'The Nature of Ethical Disagreements' in *Facts and Values*, pp. 1–9.

[15] Stevenson, 'Relativism and Nonrelativism in the Theory of Value', p. 86.

[16] Cf. Frankena's useful discussion of such considerations in 'Obligation and Motivation in Recent Moral Philosophy', in *Perspectives on Morality*, pp. 49–73.

[17] 'Obligation and Motivation in Recent Moral Philosophy', p. 52.

[18] Ibid., p. 51.

[19] Brandt, *Hopi Ethics*, pp. 213–215, 245–246. According to Brandt, the Hopi do recognise a weaker principle of concern for animals. More recently he has argued that basic psychological principles ensure that "our benevolence is and must be engaged by the suffering of animals – unless we wrongly believe they suffer little or not at all." 'The Psychology of Benevolence and Its Implications for Philosophy', *The Journal of Philosophy* **73** (1976), 450.

[20] I am thinking here of Plato, Kant, and more recently Thomas Nagel, *The Possibility of Altruism* (Oxford: Oxford University Press, 1970).

[21] *Ethical Theory*, p. 282.

[22] Cf. Brandt, *Ethical Theory*, Chapter Six, 'The Development of Ethical Values in the Individual', pp. 114–150. Also Martin L. Hoffman, 'Moral Development', in *Carmichael's Manual of Psychology*, ed. by Paul H. Mussen, 3rd ed. (New York: Wiley, 1970), vol. 2, pp. 264–332.

[23] See Gilbert Harman, 'Practical Reasoning', *Review of Metaphysics*, pp. 431–463.

[24] *Ethics*, p. 109.

[25] Ibid., p. 25. Brandt usefully discusses what might be said in favor of such a principle, which he calls "the requirement of generality," in *Ethical Theory*, pp. 19–24.

MONROE C. BEARDSLEY

INTENDING

The *goal* of this essay, to be arrived at in Section 4, is an answer to the question 'What is an action?' This answer will mark a distinction that accords as well as may be with common usage and is also of some philosophical significance. The *purpose* of the essay, especially of Sections 2 and 3, is to clarify the concept of intending, or rather the connected concepts of doing intentionally, intending to do, and having an intention. First, to build on, we need an account of doing and undergoing.

1. DOING

A bodily movement is a change in the position of a body, or of some part of a body, during a certain period of time. A bodily state is a continuation in position of a body, or of some part of a body, during a certain period of time. For convenience, I shall use the term 'bodily event' to cover both. Perhaps I am needlessly explicit here, but I want it to be clear from the start that, though for the most part my examples of bodily events will be movements (of arms, legs, etc.), I do not leave out of account such states as Z's standing still.

A bodily event may have as its *proximate* cause some behavior of a muscle in that body, i.e., its contraction or relaxation. When we report that Z reached out his arm or that he let it fall, we are saying what Z *did*; with apologies to the fastidious, I shall speak of these doings as *deeds*. The term 'proximate cause' need not give rise to serious distress in the present context; I do not mean, of course, to deny that the sequence

$$\text{muscle contraction} \rightarrow \text{arm movement}$$

can also be analyzed, on another level, as a more complex causal sequence, but only to affirm that, on the grosser level at which these terms apply, the muscle contraction immediately causes the arm movement. If, on the other hand, Z were to lift his left arm with his right, the right arm's muscle contraction would not be a proximate cause of the left arm's movement.

Z's bodily deeds, then, are those of Z's bodily events whose proximate causes are Z's muscular behavior. The class of Z's deeds in general will presently

163

A. I. Goldman and J. Kim (eds.), Values and Morals, 163–184. All Rights Reserved.
Copyright © 1978 by D. Reidel Publishing Company, Dordrecht, Holland.

be said to include other than his bodily deeds, but at the moment the task is to distinguish what Z does from what he undergoes, i.e, what merely happens to him. Having a heart attack, falling through a trap door, being pushed or struck by a falling leaf – these are not deeds. It is perhaps not necessary to provide a perfectly decisive distinction, i.e., one that will sort every example, since the focus of our concern is elsewhere. But the distinction is not worth much to us unless it takes care of most cases. In his careful analysis of doing and undergoing, Irving Thalberg has distinguished several sorts of happenings which he claims are neither doings nor undergoings.[1] This thesis itself does not contradict what I have been saying, since Thalberg equates deeds with actions, whereas I treat actions as a subclass of deeds. However, some of his examples might be thought to raise difficulties for the distinction I have proposed: bleeding, blushing, aging, digesting, perspiring. Are these something we do or something done to us? In such cases the proximate cause is subcutaneous, but not muscular, so by my definition these are not deeds. Since they will certainly not be actions by my later proposals, the only reason I can see for including them under deeds is that we can predicate their descriptions of persons: I perspire, you sweat, etc. It can be argued that predicability of persons ought to be regarded as a necessary condition for deed-descriptions: my heart beats; I don't beat my heart – though the contraction is caused by my muscles. I have no objection to saying that among the things I do, though without special attention, is keep my blood in circulation. In any case, predicability of persons is not a sufficient condition for deed-descriptions. We die, too, but that is not strictly something we do, even when we bring about our dying.

Thalberg argues that "a person may contribute causally to things that happen to him,"[2] and on this basis concludes that "causal notions are unserviceable to us when we analyse what it is to act and to have something happen to one."[3] I agree that action involves something quite different, but surely what happens to us is what we do not, at least, *immediately* bring about. My phrase 'proximate cause' excludes such cases as Thalberg's avalanche: though the skier 'touched off the avalanche' by his own actions, it was the sliding snow that swept him downhill, so that was an undergoing.[4] Thalberg's other example, being elected to office, may be more puzzling, partly because the causal process is more complex, and partly because there is some ambiguity about what is analytically involved in the concept of getting elected. Even if it consists in receiving more votes than other candidates, as Thalberg suggests, surely enough must intervene between the candidate's efforts on his own behalf and the official results of the ballot-counting so that we cannot call the former a proximate cause of the latter.

Z's bodily deeds, then, will include such things as knee-jerking, hiccupping, blinking, sneezing, shivering — none of which are to be considered, in the strict sense, Z's actions. But of course the range of Z's deeds extends far beyond what he does with his body. And to explain the nature of this extension I use (or abuse) a very fruitful concept introduced by Alvin Goldman — the concept of *act-generation*.[5] But I make two important adjustments to suit my own purposes, partly because I want to apply it initially to deeds, rather than actions, and partly because I differ with him about the individuation of actions or act-tokens.[6] Goldman distinguishes four kinds of act-generation, which I reduce to two: *causal generation* and *sortal generation*.

When a bodily deed causes the occurrence of another event (or the maintenance of a state of affairs — though I shall not always insert a reminder of this), it gives rise to a second, and distinct, deed, which is the bringing about of that other event.

(1) Z's hiccupping caused Z's wife to wake up.

Colloquially:

(2) Z's hiccupping waked Z's wife.

In technical terms:

(3) Z's hiccupping *causally generated* Z's waking his wife.

Similarly, when Z's hand moved in a certain way while it was holding a key and the key was in a lock, we can say that

(4) Z's moving his hand *causally generated* Z's turning the key,

and

(5) Z's turning the key *causally generated* Z's unlocking the door.

It may also happen that a bodily deed, because of the circumstances (very broadly considered) in which it is done, takes on a new character: it becomes a deed of another kind, while remaining a deed of the same kind as well. Suppose the door that Z unlocked was not his own; in the jurisdiction in which this deed occurred, Z's unlocking of the door violated a certain statute forbidding such deeds — in other words, it constituted a trespass. Then,

(6) Z's unlocking the door *sortally generated* Z's committing a trespass.

The trespass was not a distinct deed, but it was a deed (the same deed) of a different kind. Similarly, if Z's earlier deed was not only a hiccupping, but a loud hiccupping, we may say that

(7) Z's hiccupping *sortally generated* Z's hiccupping loudly.

The distinction between causal and sortal generation can also be expressed in terms of Goldman's prepositional suggestions. Speaking of deeds related by causal generation we can use the word 'by':

(8)   *By* turning the key, Z unlocked the door.

Speaking of deeds that are identical but differently characterized, we can use the word 'in':

(9)   *In* unlocking the door, Z committed a trespass.

(I don't claim, of course, that this distinction is constantly preserved in common speech — partly because in some contexts 'by' will suggest intentionality, so we get a character in a recent comic book exclaiming:

The dark gods must be laughing at this irony! For in slaying the serpent, we inadvertently slew Nar-Kal . . . *lost* the orb . . . and *doomed* Renya![7])

So: Z's deeds consist of all his bodily deeds and everything done in and/or by doing these deeds (where 'and/or' is supposed to allow for the logical products of these two relations). More technically,

(10) Z's deeds consist of the posterity of his bodily deeds with respect to the relation *generates*.

2. DOING INTENTIONALLY

We must next distinguish between intentional and nonintentional deeds. What I shall dub the 'know-and-want account' of intentional doing can be formulated thus:

(11) Z did D intentionally at t *iff*
        (a) Z did D at t,
        (b) Z knew-at-t that he was doing-at-t D, and
        (c) Z wanted-at-t to do-at-t D.

These awkward locutions, or some substitute for them, are needed to keep clearly distinct what might be called the 'presence-time' and the 'reference-time' of knowing and wanting. Though Z wants-on-Saturday to go-to-church-on-Sunday, he may feel different in the cold gray dawn; and though he knows-on-Sunday that he will stay-home-on-Sunday, he did not know-on-Saturday that he would stay-home-on-Sunday. The presence-time is the time at which the knowing or wanting occurs or obtains; the reference time is the time at which the deed known or wanted is thought of as occurring.

Since both 'know' and 'want' are often dispositional terms, but sometimes not, we will need to keep in mind the difference noted by Goldman between 'occurrent wants' and 'standing wants',[8] and between occurrent knowing and standing knowing. When I want to limit knowing to the occurrent kind, I shall take advantage of the term 'aware': to be aware of doing D is to know and be conscious of knowing that one is doing D. But I do not wish 'awareness' to imply that our knowledge of what we are now doing is solely of a 'non-inferential' or 'non-observational' sort — I am avoiding this often-debated question. For convenience, I appropriate (or perhaps mis-appropriate) the term 'yen' to mark the corresponding limitation for wanting: with a warning to free this term of its usual suggestion of a strong inclination, I shall say that when a want-to-do is actually felt, the wanter has a yen-to-do.

In my formulation of the know-and-want theory of intentional doing, I introduce this pair of restrictions. Unconscious knowing and wanting are not sufficient, so (11) becomes

(12) Z did D intentionally at t iff
    (a) Z did D at t,
    (b) Z was aware-at-t that he was doing-at-t D, and
    (c) Z had-at-t a yen to do-at-t D.

Occasional doubts have been expressed about wanting to do a deed while actually doing it (on this view, only prospective deeds can be wanted), but I see no philosophical difficulty about concurrent wants and deeds, or yens and deeds, and ordinary language certainly allows us to say such things as: "I am in Philadelphia and this is where I want to be" or "I am climbing Mt. Everest, and this is what I want to be doing." Perhaps such locutions go better with states and activities (which can also be regarded as states) than with more typical deeds, but if one is enjoying doing something, one must want to do it while doing it.

'Want' is here taken in a very broad sense — some will think, too broad. It includes wanting to do something 'for its own sake' as well as wanting to do something in order to do something else. If we restrict it to intrinsic wanting, then, as Goldman notes,[9] one can do intentionally what one does not want to do. But Goldman himself later accepts a broader use, bringing together intrinsic and extrinsic wants,[10] and I should think that, in this use, we can say that a person wants to go to the dentist, even though he also wants to avoid going. He has conflicting wants, but that will not affect my definition of 'doing intentionally' if we keep not-wanting distinct from wanting-not. I think the same thing should be said about conflicts of duty and inclination. Thus I disagree with Brandt and Kim, who say "that a person can be motivated, e.g., by considerations of duty, to do something we should not say he *wanted* to do."[11] What, after all, is it to be motivated? This person must care about doing his duty, must be drawn to doing the deed prescribed by duty, at the same time he is repelled by its unpleasantness or danger. Surely one can want to do one's duty.

On my view, a want always has a reference-time, which may be vague (wanting to see the pyramids some day) or very precise (wanting to turn on the TV at exactly 9:00 p.m.). A continuing want such as unslaked thirst refers always to the present: it is a want-to-do-now. In general, standing wants have longer (though not necessarily vaguer) stretches of reference-time than felt wants, or yens. Z's yen-on-Saturday to go-to-church-on-Sunday, for example, had as its more precise reference a travel-period ending a few minutes before the services would begin.

As far as I know, no very sustained or persevering defense of the know-and-want account has been presented, so there is little in the way of direct attack upon it. The brickbats ricochet from another account. Of the two sides exposed to possible attack, one does not seem to have excited unfavorable attention. No one seems disposed to argue that one can do D intentionally without being aware that one is doing D. Doubts have been occasionally felt about the want condition, as we have just noticed, but (I think) only when 'want' is taken with unwarranted narrowness. Note, once more: I do not in any way deny that one can do intentionally what he wants not to do; I only insist that he is not doing it intentionally unless he wants to do it (because it may save his teeth, or his life). There is a puzzle that may be drawn from deeds that take some time to complete. When Z intentionally administers the poison to Q, it may take hours to work, and during that time (but, let us say, too late to save Q) Z may not only repent, but even make a vain attempt to rescue his victim. We have to say, I think, that the intentionality of the killing did not outlast the yen to kill. If we ask whether this deed was initiated intentionally, the answer is Yes. But if we ask whether this deed (as a whole) was intentional, the answer is neither Yes nor No: it was intentional in its earlier (temporal) segment, but became nonintentional before it was completed. Thus odd as it may seem, we must supplement principle (12) with a qualification that occasionally applies to drawn-out deeds:

(13)   A deed is intentional through just that (temporal) segment of it
         in which the doer has the appropriate awareness and yen.

From the opposite direction, there has been some implied questioning
of the sufficiency of the conditions laid down in the definiens: it occurs in
the form of counterexamples against another account, which I shall call
'the causal know-and-want account of intentional doing'; since these objections allege the insufficiency of conditions in that account, they can be taken
as a fortiori arguments against the know-and-want account itself.

A fairly simple statement of the causal know-and-want account was
given by Brice Noel Fleming in his early and valuable essay; it has been much
elaborated and refined by Alvin Goldman. Fleming writes:

> To get at what it is to do something intentionally we might consider the following
> formula. To do x intentionally is to do x knowing you are doing it, wanting to do it,
> and doing it because you want to do it. The last clause seems necessary because, for
> example, a boy might bump into a girl and so bring about a meeting, knowing he was
> bumping into her, wanting to bump into her, but doing so because he stumbled or was
> pushed. Not that this formula, even if it is otherwise correct, throws much light on the
> matter. For one thing, wanting is too closely bound up with intending, and is itself
> something on which light needs to be thrown.[12]

The question of quantity of light can be set aside: whatever may still need to
be said in order adequately to clarify the concept of *wanting*, it is surely
possible to want to do something without doing it intentionally (or even
without intending to do it; a distinct matter to be considered later), so there
is no danger of circularity. But what about the main argument?

Fleming's reason for adding 'because you want to do it' to the know-and-
want conditions of intentional doing does not count against my version,
at least. For stumbling against someone and being pushed into someone are
not deeds at all, by my definition. What we would require as genuine and
telling counterexamples are deeds in which there is the appropriate awareness
and yen, yet the doing is not intentional.

Goldman proposes two cases.[13] In the first case, S wants to make Mary
blush, but cannot think of any way to do it. He tells a story to John, which
Mary overhears and at which she blushes. But if the doing in question is
making Mary blush, this is no counterexample to the know-and-want account,
for S is not even aware that he is making Mary blush when he does it. In the
second case, S is bent on offending his host at a dinner party and he knows
that he can do this by grimacing as he eats his soup. Someone slips foul-tasting
stuff into the soup, causing S to grimace as an "automatic reflex response to
the foul taste." S had a yen to grimace, he was aware that he was grimacing,

yet his grimacing, though a deed, was not intentional. Some pages later, Goldman notes that

the time of the grimacing does not correspond precisely to the time at which S planned to grimace. S wanted to grimace at time t_1, but S actually grimaced at an earlier time, t_0. Thus, this case could be guarded against by inserting relevant time references into the analysis of intentionality. Troublesome cases would still arise, however, since the time references included in our desires are usually rather vague.[14]

Goldman's resolution of the problem is right: the example is not one in which S has-at-t a yen to grimace-at-t. That disposes of this example; but how do we know that 'troublesome cases would still arise'? Goldman understandably does not feel the need to supply them, because he is concerned to develop his own interesting concepts of basic act-tokens and plans of action, which are designed to take care of all counterexamples to the causal know-and-want account. But the need for these concepts has not yet been shown.

Goldman also discusses a well-known counterexample originally proposed by Roderick Chisholm, to refute a Ducassean definition of 'purpose'.[15] The nephew wants to kill his uncle in order to inherit his fortune; his combined desire to inherit and belief that killing will lead to inheriting so agitate him that he drives recklessly, killing a pedestrian who turns out to be his uncle. But this example cannot be turned against the know-and-want account, for two reasons. First, the nephew is not even aware that he is killing his uncle, so the awareness condition is not satisfied. Second, the yen condition is not satisfied, either, for the nephew did not have a yen to kill-at-that-moment.

Chisholm's example can even be used to place the know-and-want account in a favorable light. Suppose at the last moment, just before the car struck, the nephew saw the pedestrian in the gleam of his headlights, and recognized him, so that when he killed his uncle he was aware that he was killing him. And suppose there was just time for him to feel elation at the prospect, so he had a yen to kill his uncle when he killed him. Then we must apply principle (13) again, but in a reverse direction from the poison case. Even though the killing was at that point unavoidable because of the nephew's previous driving, we should say that the deed became intentional when the appropriate yen and awareness appeared — assuming that the details of the incident were such that the killing really *was* a deed.

If the know-and-want account of intentional doing is to be refuted by severing the definiens from the definiendum, it looks as though this will have to be done at a fairly basic level. Let's say Z reaches out his finger to push an elevator button and just before the finger arrives at its destination, a sudden involuntary twitch causes it to make contact. It seems he does not push the buttom intentionally, yet he is aware that he is doing so and has a yen to do-so-at-that-moment. (Here the touching-at-t coincides exactly with the wanting to touch-at-t.) Must we add to our definiens, then, the condition that the touching is to be the result of (is caused by) the awareness-plus-yen? This would apparently do the trick, since the timing is too tight in this example to devise an ingenious Chisholm-type complication by which the yen, through some indirect causal chain, produces the finger-twitch, after all. Indeed, there may be a fatal dilemma here for all attempts to undermine the causal know-and-want account by counterexamples: if we introduce roundabout causal chains, as in the nephew-uncle case, we separate the presence-time of the yen from its reference-time. But if we bring these times into coincidence, we allow no possibility of an indirect causal chain that could make the definiens true though the definiendum is false.

But let us look at the elevator-button case from another angle. In the course of proposing his analyses of various concepts connected with intention, Chisholm remarks that his definition of 'intentionally brings it about that . . .' "allows for an element of luck that might be excluded by the ordinary use of the term."[16] Consider his two examples. A beginning golfer 'attempts a hole in one and by extraordinary good fortune succeeds. Did he do it intentionally?' Sure he did. He may not have shown much skill. But if we rule out this case as nonintentional, who knows how many other cases we will have to rule out because a putt is gently assisted by a small unseen irregularity of the green? If we were to modify the elevator-button case so as to assimilate it to Chisholm's, we might suppose that the man in the foyer is intoxicated, and when he reaches out his forefinger it is aimed slightly to the left of the button; but the involuntary twitch places it in proper position just before it touches. Luck helps him, too. But doesn't luck help in the original elevator-button case? Events outside the man's control intervene to complete the deed but his initiation of the deed made it possible for them to operate beneficently. His awareness and yen carried through, and his pushing the button is an intentional deed, even though he was helped by the twitch.

In Chisholm's second case, a man attempted to kill the King by shooting him; "The bullet hit a tree instead and caused a branch to fall and kill the King. Did he kill the King intentionally?" Now part of the difficulty in this case is that we may feel some uneasiness about stretching the causal generation so far. The man fired the gun, and did so intentionally; this deed causally generated his hitting the tree, which was not intentional; but when we add that his hitting the tree generated his killing the King, we may feel that the causal chain is a little stretched. And, of course, if the man did *not* kill the King, he did not do so intentionally. But suppose we waive this question, and allow that he did kill the King, though via a nonintentional deed: then I think we may say that he killed the King intentionally, even though he did not kill the King with a tree-branch intentionally. Again, the awareness and the yen carried through.

Doubts about the intentionality of the deeds just discussed may arise from an illegitimate inference. Any deed can be analyzed into parts according to various principles of decomposition, but given a particular property of a deed and a particular method of decomposing the deed, it does not follow logically that that property belongs to all the parts. Specifically, a deed can be intentional as a whole though some of its parts are not. Many complex and drawn-out intentional deeds, such as filming *Gone With the Wind*, number among their numerous constituent deeds quite a few that are nonintentional, yet not wholly lacking in serendipity.

3. INTENDING TO DO

The verb 'intend' takes five kinds of grammatical object, of which the most characteristic is the infinitive of a verb of doing:

(14) Z intends to pay his gas bill on the first of next month.

Infinitives of other verbs, which occur much less frequently, can be understood as elliptical versions of the first kind:

(15) Z intends to be a private detective

means

(16) Z intends to become a private detective.

In contrast, we have 'intend' followed by a 'that'-clause:

(17)   The Mayor had intended that the hospital be built with Federal aid.
(18)   When the framers of the Constitution drew up the Second Amendment, they did not intend that there should be no gun control laws.

Expressions of the form 'intend x to be y' are clearly paraphrasable by 'that'-clauses:

(19) Z intended his words to be taken ironically

is paraphrasable as

(20)   Z intended that his words be taken ironically.

And

(21)   Z intended his watch to go to his great-granddaughter

is paraphrasable as

(22)   Z intended that his watch go to his great-granddaughter.

Finally, nouns and noun-phrases following 'intend' can also be similarly paraphrased:

(23)   Evidently, Z intended that result

becomes

(24)   Evidently Z intended that that result occur.

And

(25)   The 'spontaneous demonstration' was obviously intended

becomes

(26)   Obviously it was intended that there would be this 'spontaneous demonstration.'

We have, then, two groups of idioms, most plainly represented by (1) infinitives of doing and (2) 'that'-clauses. But when we look more closely at (17) and (18), we note that, although these clauses refer to events or states of affairs, which are ostensibly said to be intended, those events or states of affairs are such as the intender could play some part in bringing about. They imply, or presuppose, a projected deed, though they have the legal and bureaucratic advantage of not committing anyone to specific deeds. We therefore cannot give confident precise paraphrases of them. (17) can be approximately paraphrased as

(27)   The Mayor had intended to obtain (or perhaps to get someone else to obtain) Federal aid in building the hospital.

And (18) can be approximately paraphrased as

(28)   When the framers of the Constitution drew up the Second Amendment they did not intend to prohibit gun control laws (or to make gun control laws unconstitutional).

When the boss says

(30)   I intend that there shall be no goofing off in my office

(another case with a bureaucratic ring), we take this as a warning that he will take steps. If we separate these events and states of affairs completely from any conceivable deed that could be done by the intender, we get non-sense:

(31)   If elected, I intend that there shall be no more earthquakes in America.

Strictly speaking, only deeds can be intended — more strictly, one can intend only one's own deeds.[17] A state of affairs can be wanted, even wished for though impossible, but not intended, save in so far as a deed intended consists in bringing about, or helping to bring about, that state of affairs. Must we now add a further restriction on what can be intended — that the deeds must be future ones? This turns out to be a rather difficult and delicate question, which involves the subtle relationship between *intending to do* and *doing intentionally*.

For, on one hand, such a restriction is wholly in accord with ordinary usage. There are apparently no clear-cut examples in which one is said to intend current deeds. We may ask someone, "Do you intend to stay here all day?", which refers to the person's future conduct, but hardly "Do you intend to be here (where you are) at this moment?" To put the matter more precisely, let us introduce special terms. If

$$Z \text{ intends-at-}t_1 \text{ to do-at-}t_2 \ D,$$

I shall speak of *prospective intending*. If

$$Z \text{ intends-at-}t_1 \text{ to do-at-}t_1 \ D,$$

I shall speak of *concurrent intending*. The question is whether all intending is prospective.

We can try to explain away the absence of references to concurrent intending in ordinary discourse. For example, since we already have another handy idiom, the person lying on the beach can certainly say that he is lying there *intentionally*; this idiom may have crowded out the other. Perhaps, as Fleming has suggested,[18] we tend to raise questions about what was intended when something has gone wrong, so we are generally thinking of the ante-cedents, rather than the concomitants, of the deed. But not everything worth saying is enshrined in ordinary language, and we must inquire what advantages are to be gained from introducing (if that's what we are doing) the concept of concurrent intending.

Consider first a principle that, in some sense, seems often to be invoked:

(31)   A deed is intentional if in doing it the doer does what he intended to do.

If we take the last clause broadly, as equivalent to 'what he *once* intended to do,' principle (31) is false; however the road to Hell is paved, it must be littered with abandoned intendings. To make (31) plausible, we must push up the intending at least to the very brink of the deed.

(32)   A deed is intentional if in doing it the doer does what he intended to do just before doing it.

This preserves the prospective character of intending, but has a certain artificiality. Must we suppose that the intending ceased as the deed began? Could the doer, especially if conscientious, fail to carry over his intending into the deed — or would he just no longer have any need to intend? If we leave open the possibility of a gap, however minute, between the cessation of intending and the inception of doing, even principle (32) may be falsified. And so we are led to substitute another principle:

(33) Z's doing-at-t D is intentional iff Z intends-at-t to do-at-t D.

If principle (33) is correct, it is the link between intentional doing and intending to do. According to it, one cannot do something intentionally without (concurrently) intending to do it, though one can do something intentionally without having prospectively intended to do it (this is acting on impulse). Of course, one can prospectively intend to do a deed without ever doing it — moreover, one can prospectively intend to do a deed, and do it, but not do it intentionally. If we are still troubled by this imposition on ordinary speech, we may note a fact about common ways of speaking that seems to tolerate principle (33). When someone in a rage knocks over a vase, we can ask:

> Did you break it intentionally?
> Did you intend to break it?

In so far as the uses of these distinct expressions tend to collapse into one (at least in this situation), we can take 'intend' as concurrent, rather than prospective.

In accepting principle (33) we lay down an important condition on any proposed analysis of 'intending to do.' For we have already proposed a definition of 'doing intentionally,' and we require a definition of 'intending to do' that will make principle (33) come out true. If the definition about to be proposed (taken with the previous definition of 'doing intentionally') has principle (33) as a logical consequence, that will be one reason for acceptng it. I give the schema for prospective intending, letting it be understood that the substitution of 't_1' for 't_2' and a shift in tense convert it into the schema for concurrent intending.

(34) Z intends-at-t_1 to do-at-t_2 D iff

    (a) Z wants-at-t_1 to do-at-t_2 D, and

    (b) Z believes-at-t_1 that he will do-at-t_2 D.

Before proceeding to a fuller explanation and a defense of this account, we may pause to note that it does satisfy principle (33). For if Z is doing D intentionally, then, by my earlier definition, he wants to do D and he knows (and therefore necessarily believes) that he is doing D. Therefore, by the concurrent-intending version of Definition (34), he intends to do D. This proves the 'only if' part of principle (33). Going in the other direction, if Z concurrently intends to do D, he believes he is doing D while doing it, so that he will have adequate evidence, from introspection and observation, to make his believing an awareness of doing D; and since he has doing D on his mind, his want to do D will be a yen. Consequently, if he concurrently intends to do D, he is doing D intentionally. That proves the 'if' part of principle (33).

But can the two elements of Definition (34) be defended against the inevitable doubts?

First, consider the want condition. Just as in doing intentionally, one can intend to do what one wants not to do, would rather not do, would willingly avoid doing if . . . , etc. But we cannot conceive of a prospective intending, carried through the deed itself, that does not give rise to some sense of achievement or accomplishment, however mild and short-lived, once the deed is done; certainly even the most timorous patient, as he leaves the dentist's chair, will feel not only relief and perhaps self-congratulation on his stoicism, but a sense that a want-to-do has been satisfied. Chisholm has said that 'A man may endeavour, or undertake, to bring about what he does not desire and what he does not even believe to be a means to anything that he desires,' and Bernard Berofsky has agreed with him.[19] Perhaps this can be true if 'endeavour' be given a technical sense. Berofsky's example is this: "Suppose I reach out to pick up a piece of dust. Does it *have* to be the case that I wanted to do that?" Since Berofsky doesn't distinguish, it's not clear which

thesis this is supposed to counter: that intentional doing requires wanting
or that concurrent intending requires wanting. But in either case, it seems
to fall short. If we ask him *why* – for what purpose – he picked up the
dust, he may reply that he had no purpose at all in mind; "I did it because
I wanted to." That's the *least* he can say without relegating his deed to a
reflex action or to total absent-mindedness.

One argument for weakening the want condition has been drawn by
Anthony Kenny from a case invented by Glanville Williams: an 'eccentric
and amoral surgeon' removes his patient's heart for experimental purposes,
not at all wanting him to die but foreseeing with much prescience that he
will. The death is an accepted, though not a wanted, consequence of the
heart removal. In this case, Kenny thinks, the layman, along with the lawyer,
will say that the surgeon 'intended the death of the patient whose heart he
removed'; and he recommends that we follow H. L. A. Hart in allowing as
intended any foreseen outcome that is "so immediately and invariably
connected with the action done that the suggestion that the action might not
have that outcome would by ordinary standards be regarded as absurd . . ."[20]
Now, there may be good reasons why the law should treat the bringing about
knowingly of such direct and certain consequences the same way it treats the
bringing about of wanted consequences; moreover, legal theory can stretch
its technical term 'intent' as it finds convenient. But if the supposititious
surgeon is indeed so callous as to be utterly indifferent to the death of the
patient, just as he is utterly indifferent, say, to the extinction of various
microorganisms also caused by his operation, then there can be no good
reason for regarding the former as intended if the latter is not.

Second, consider the belief condition. As I have formulated it, it may be
thought too weak or too strong. When, for example, Hampshire and Hart,
in their well-known essay, say that " 'I have decided to do this' entails 'I am
certain that I will do this, unless I am in some way prevented,' "[21] if we may
take 'deciding' as 'beginning to intend' and if we note that certainty, on their
view, seems to involve knowing,[22] they will be understood to be proposing that

(34)   If Z intends-at-t_1 to do-at-t_2 D, then Z knows-at-t_1 that he will
         do-at-t_2 D, unless prevented.

But this is certainly too strong, as even they implicity concede in remarking
that, after deciding-to-do, one can change his mind.[23] Every case of an
intending that is never carried out is a case in which the intender did not
know that he would do what he intended.

Perhaps, on the other hand, it is too much to require that Z believe he will do D if he intends to do D. At another point, Hampshire and Hart say that, in view of certain considerations, "the minimum force of 'I intend to do X' is 'I believe that I will try to do X.'"[24] In his book, Hampshire puts it that "intending to do something on some future occasion entails already knowing what one will do, or at least try to do, on that occasion."[25] I follow more recent discussions in attaching more weight to 'try' than these passages can bear (it does seem to be connected with the overcoming of resistance). So I would say that I intend to go to Toronto on October 27, but if the Philadelphia airport is closed down by bad weather that day, I do not know, and in fact I don't believe, that I will try to get there. If 'trying' is taken weakly (so that it might consist of nothing more than calling the airport for the bad news), then I think intending to go to Toronto on October 27 requires more than just believing one will try: the plans I have made, and the plans made by others, depend on the assumption that I will actually get there.

The importance of the belief condition, as I have formulated it, is brought out by some interesting examples which Thalberg presents in his discussion of trying-to-do. I shall not enter into the analysis of this concept beyond arguing that it must be kept clearly distinct from intending-to-do. Thalberg argues that one can try (attempt) to discover the Fountain of Youth, even though he does not believe that it exists – or, consequently, that he will find it. Granted: he can search for it, but it does not follow that he intends to find it. So here is no case in which we have intending without believing. Another example from Thalberg: to prove that his watch-crystal is shatter-proof, John bangs it with a sledge-hammer.[26] He tries to break it, but he does not believe he will break it. Thalberg concedes that "there is a sense in which we would *deny* that John intended to break the watch-crystal." But he claims that if John

pounded the watch vigorously with a sledge-hammer, he both attempted and intended, in some other sense, to break the crystal. For if the glass disintegrated, would it not be true to say that John broke it intentionally?

I think not. There is no such other sense. John pounded intentionally, but since he believed the watch would not break, he could only be surprised and disappointed if it did. In this case John had neither the belief nor the want required for intending to break the watch. Like a reckless skier who breaks his leg, John just took a regrettable risk.

A similar confusion of trying with intending, it seems to me, vitiates other attempts to show that intending does not require believing. Thus David. L. Perry asserts that "Simply having an intention is compatible with belief that one will or will not do what he intends,"[27] though he holds that it is 'irrational' to intend to do something you think you can't do, unless the situation is desperate. But his argument consists in an appeal to Anscombe's example of a man clinging to the edge of a precipice "with the conviction that he will be unable to hold" (as Perry puts it).[28] This is a good example of trying without confidence of success, but not of intending without belief, for though the man may intend to stay as long as he can, he surely believes that he will do this. Anscombe's expression, 'determined not to let go,' may be understood as describing a continuing state of intending to hold on for another few seconds (which surely includes a continuing state of belief that one *can* hold on that long).

Intendings, then, are datable states, which begin when a co-referring want-belief pair (that is, a want-to-do and a belief-that-one-will-do that refer to the same doing) comes into existence, and end either when one of the members of the pair ceases to exist or when the doing referred to is completed. Since wants and beliefs can be dispositions, they may be formed before they appear as yens or as conscious beliefs. Goldman has noted that one can pass gradually from knowing inductively that he will commit suicide to intending to commit suicide. "I begin to welcome the thought of suicide, to entertain the thought of committing suicide with pleasure and relief."[29] Here the belief comes first, and it is the arrival of the want that converts the belief into an intention. (Compare the statement of Eugene Ormandy in November, 1975, when rumors were rife that he was about to retire as conductor of the Philadelphia Orchestra: "Eugene Ormandy has no intention of retiring." Of course he knew that he would retire some day, but he did not yet want to.) Sometimes the want comes first, very often along with other wants, both supportive and conflicting, and then it may take a *decision* to initiate the intending.

I do not say there is no more to deciding than coming to believe in the presence of one or more wants — that is a question for another occasion. But the relation between deciding and intending needs to be reasonably clear here. Carl Ginet had written:

Yet the whole point of making up one's mind is to pass from uncertainty to a kind of knowledge about what one will do or try to do.[30]

For reasons already given, I agree with the first part of Goldman's response to Ginet:

Deciding to do *A* does not consist . . . in passing into a state of *knowing* that one will do (or try to do) *A*. Rather, it consists in passing into a state of *wanting*, or *intending*, to do *A*.[31]

Intending yes; and we can say that the decider is trying to organize diverse wants into a single main want. But deciding is (among other things) a coming-to-believe, and the necessity to decide only arises because there are already too many wants, which cannot all be satisfied.

Deciding may be said to be *deliberately forming an intention*, and one who intends-at-*t* to do *D* may be said to have-at-*t* the intention to do *D*. This nominative form has not yet been considered, and a few words about it are called for. What is an intention, then? In the light of all the discussion so far, it seems most sensible to say that an intention is simply a co-referring want-belief pair.[32] Thus I object to the way philosophers in a hurry sometimes write phrases like "the agent's desires, wishes, purposes, goals, intentions, etc." — as though intentions were something more than want-belief pairs.[33]

If we conceive of intentions in this way, there is a problem of understanding what is involved in saying, as we would often want to say, that a particular deed involves a plurality of intentions, and consequently (but that is another story) of motives. Corresponding to each intentional deed there is just one intention, the want-belief pair referring to that deed. But as we have seen — under the guidance of Goldman — a particular deed of one kind usually generates various deeds of other kinds. And each of these deeds of other kinds, if intentional, has its own intention. All these intentions are discriminable elements in the psychological conditions of the original deed, and will enter into our ultimate explanation of what was done. (Though I rejected the causal want-and-belief account of intending, I did not of course deny that intentions play essential roles in explanations of deeds.) But this is also another story.

We shall, finally, want to be able to speak of some intentions as playing a more central or decisive role in certain deeds, and sometimes of one intention as being the predominant one. Thus we may say of a particular painting that the painter intended to tell the story of St. Catherine dramatically and affectingly and that he intended to produce a beautiful visual design. And we may judge that the religious intention dominated the aesthetic one. Exactly how such statements are to be construed must be left an open question here; I only suggest that the want-belief analysis of intentions points the direction in which answers are to be sought.

4. ACTING

Though it has taken a fairly long path to arrive at a proposed definition of "action," I'm afraid suspense has long been dissipated. The comfort I substitute for an enjoyable climax is that this final step takes but a few words. Not that it doesn't have its own consequences, but that they are not to be pursued on this occasion. The account can first be present recursively in a series of stages:

(a)   An intentional deed is an action: John's playing the 'Meditation' from *Thais* on his violin.

(b)   A deed that is sortally generated by an intentional deed is an action: John's playing the 'Meditation' badly.

(c)   A deed that is causally generated by an intentional deed is an action: John's disturbing the neighbors.

(d)   A deed that is sortally generated by a deed causally generated by an intentional deed is an action: John's violating his lease (assuming that the lease prohibits neighbor-disturbing noises).

The alternative formulas used earlier in characterizing deeds are equally applicable to actions, once we have at hand the notion of an intentional deed. Anything Z does is an action of Z's if it is either an intentional deed of Z's or is a deed that Z does in or by or in/by or by/in doing an intentional deed. For example, John disturbs his neighbors *by* playing the violin, and violates his lease *in* disturbing neighbors. And John plays badly *in* playing, and disappoints his violin-teacher *by* playing badly. Of course (b), (c), and (d) in the list above are all nonintentional actions; an intentional action also causally generated by (a) might be

(e)   John's cheering himself up.

In view of the possibility, acknowledged in principle (13), that a deed may be partly intentional and partly not, we may want to adopt a rider to stipulation (a), even if common speech affords no confident guide to a decision on this point. Must a deed be wholly intentional to be counted as an action, or is it enough that (like the poisoning case above) it begin as an intentional deed? There is something to be said for setting up matters so that every distinct deed either is or is not an action. And in deciding whether a deed is to count as an action, its earliest segment, before its completion becomes ineluctable, has the greatest claim on our consideration. Thus it is the repentant poisoner's deed rather than the nephew's (in the example in which his deed becomes intentional at the end) that (in Hamlet's phrase) deserves the name of action. I therefore propose:

(a')   A deed that is initiated intentionally (i.e., that is initially intentional) is an action.

The class of actions marked out by my procedure thus turns out to correspond to the class of actions marked out by Donald Davidson:

A man is the agent of an act if what he does can be described under an aspect that makes it intentional . . . A person is the agent of an event if and only if there is a description of what he did that makes true a sentence that says he did it intentionally.[34]

But, for reasons given elsewhere,[35] I do not speak of alternative 'descriptions' of an action. My proposal does *not* seem to correspond with another way of characterizing actions that has occasionally been tried: that of every action it can be said that "the man who does it is able to [do it] intentionally — whether or not he actually does so in the particular case under consideration"[36] — or, in a variant version, that "the action which I in fact perform must be one which I could have intended."[37] History and daily experience reveal various reasons why these claims are not always true. For example, we can say that Richard Nixon (1) brought about the death of more than 20,000 American soldiers by continuing the Vietnam war after he was elected, (2) disgraced himself by making and preserving the White House tapes, (3) often mistook dissent for subversion and treason, and (4) provided many interesting examples of Alvin Goldman's 'act-trees.' I do not believe that he was capable of doing any of these things intentionally, or even of intending to do them.

The philosophical significance of the class of actions so marked out stems from their common trait: that somewhere in their ancestry (allowing this relation, as in formal logic, to be reflexive as well as transitive) there is an intentional action, to which some form of accountability might attach — so that the *question* of accountability arises, however the moral philosopher may answer it. It is a consequence of my account that actions are indeed (in the carefully-chosen words of A. I. Melden) those "cases in which what an individual does can be in principle and in the appropriate circumstances the subject of moral review."[38] In constrast to Melden, I think it is not true that every action actually falls under a rule or criterion of judgment,[39] but of every action it is in order to inquire whether it does or not.[40]

Temple University

NOTES

[1] *Enigmas of Agency: Studies in the Philosophy of Human Action*, London: Allen and Unwin, N.Y.: Humanities Press, 1972, ch. 2.
[2] Ibid., p. 46.
[3] Ibid., p. 47.

4 Ibid., p. 45.

5 *A Theory of Human Action*, Englewood Cliffs, N.J.: Prentice-Hall, 1970, ch. 2.

6 See 'Actions and Events: The Problem of Individuation', *American Philosophical Quarterly* 12 (1975), 263–76.

7 *Night of the Serpent* (*Dagar the Invincible*, no. 9), Poughkeepsie: Western Publishing Co., 1974; with thanks to Laura Beardsley for bringing this work to my attention.

8 Goldman, op. cit., ch. 4. Cf. William P. Alston, 'Dispositions and Occurrences', *Canadian Journal of Philosophy* 1 (1971), 125–54.

9 Goldman, op. cit., pp. 50ff.

10 Ibid., p. 105.

11 Richard B. Brandt and Jaegwon Kim, 'Wants as Explanations of Actions', *Journal of Philosophy* 60 (1963); in Norman S. Care and Charles Landesman, *Readings in the Theory of Action*, Bloomington: Indiana University Press, 1968, p. 201.

12 'On Intention', *Philosophical Review* 73 (1964), pp. 307–8.

13 Goldman, op. cit., p. 54.

14 Ibid., p. 61.

15 'The Descriptive Element in the Concept of Action', *Journal of Philosophy* 61 (1964), 616.

16 'The Structure of Intention', *Journal of Philosophy* 67 (1970), 644.

17 Cf. Annette C. Baier, 'Act and Intent', *Journal of Philosophy* 67 (1970), 649.

18 Op cit., p. 310.

19 Chisholm, 'Freedom and Action', in Keith Lehrer, ed., *Freedom and Determinism*, New York: Random House, 1966, p. 29; Berofsky, 'Purposive Action', *American Philosophical Quarterly* 7 (1970), p. 311.

20 See Kenny, 'Intention and Purpose in Law', in Robert S. Summers, ed., *Essays in Legal Philosophy*, Berkeley: University of California Press, 1968, pp. 149, 156; Hart, 'Intention and Punishment', *Oxford Review* 4 (1967), p. 5. Kenny's essay is interestingly discussed by Hans Oberdiek, 'Intention and Foresight in Criminal Law', *Mind* 81 (1972), 389–400, and Raymond Lyons, 'Intention and Foresight in Law', *Mind* 85 (1976), 84–89.

21 Stuart Hampshire and H. L. A. Hart, 'Decision, Intention and Certainty', *Mind* 67 (1958), 2.

22 Ibid., p. 5.

23 Ibid., p. 3.

24 Ibid., p. 11.

25 *Thought and Action*, New York: Viking Press, 1960, p. 102.

26 For these examples, see Thalberg, op. cit., pp. 101, 103–4.

27 'Prediction, Explanation and Freedom', *The Monist* 49 (1965), 238.

28 G. E. M. Anscombe, *Intention*, second edition, Ithaca: Cornell University Press, 1963, p. 94.

29 Goldman, op. cit., p. 194. Cf. Hampshire, op. cit., p. 101.

30 'Can the Will Be Caused?' *Philosophical Review* 71 (1962), 52.

31 Goldman, op. cit., p. 176.

32 This accords approximately with the definition from John Austin's *Lectures on Jurisprudence*, London: 1973, quoted by Chisholm ('The Structure of Intention', p. 645n): "Consequently a present intention to do a future act may be defined to be: 'A present *desire* of an object (either as an end or a means), coupled with a present *belief* that we shall do acts hereafter for the purpose of attaining the object'" (p. 451).

[33] 'Intention' is also used to mean 'what is intended', the deed or deed-type described by the infinitive of "His intention is − ." Intentions in this sense have been well discussed by, among others, Hector-Neri Castañeda, 'Intentions and Intending', *American Philosophical Quarterly* 9 (1972), 139–49.

[34] 'Agency', in Robert Binkley, Richard Bronaugh, and Ausonio Marras, eds., *Agent, Action, and Reason* (Toronto: University of Toronto Press, 1971) p. 7.

[35] See 'Actions and Events', note 6 above.

[36] James Bogen, 'Physical Determinism', in Care and Landesman, p. 131.

[37] D. W. Hamlyn, 'Causality and Human Behavior', *Proceedings of the Aristotelian Society*, Suppl. Vol. 38 (1964); in Care and Landesman, p. 60.

[38] 'Action', *Philosophical Review* 65 (1956); Care and Landesman, p. 27.

[39] Ibid., p. 43.

[40] I am particularly grateful to Ronald Hathaway Göran Hermerén, Joseph Margolis, Janice Moulton, and Gerald Vision, for beneficial comments.

HOLLY S. GOLDMAN

DOING THE BEST ONE CAN

I

Among the circumstances which must be counted as relevant to the moral status of a given action are the agent's own past actions: Smith ought not to exceed the speed limit not only because it is dangerous and illegal, but also because he promised his wife yesterday never to do so again. Do the agent's own future actions count among the relevant circumstances as well? Certainly future actions have some bearing on the moral status of current acts. Smith's making a check out to CARE has moral significance, not because writing a check is morally important *per se*, but rather because he then places the check in an envelope and mails it off. But there are different explanations as to why this is so. According to the view I defended in a previous paper, making out the check is morally significant because it would *actually be followed* by Smith's sending it off.[1] According to a contrary view, defended by several other philosophers, Smith's writing the check is morally significant because it would *enable* him to send it off.[2] These contrasting views can be represented by the following principles:

1. Whether or not S ought to do A depends on the sequence of subsequent acts S *would* perform if he performed A.

2. Whether or not S ought to do A depends on the best sequence of subsequent acts S *could* perform if he performed A.

On the first view, the future *acts* the agent would perform are counted as circumstances affecting the moral status of his current act. On the second view, only the agent's future *ability* to perform subsequent acts (whether or not he would perform them) counts as a circumstance affecting the status of his current act.

The difference between the two views can be seen in the following case. A graduate student asks Smith for comments on a paper he is planning to read at a job interview. If Smith accepts the task and comments on the paper, the student would make substantial improvements on it, have a highly successful interview, and receive an offer for a three-year position. If Smith accepts the task but fails to comment on the paper in time, the student will make no

A. I. Goldman and J. Kim (eds.), Values and Morals, 185–214. All Rights Reserved.
Copyright © 1978 by D. Reidel Publishing Company, Dordrecht, Holland.

revisions, have a dismal interview, and receive no job offer. If Smith does not accept the task, the student will elicit comments from another faculty member, make less helpful revisions in the paper, have a moderately success-ful interview, and receive a one-year job offer. Assuming a normal set of values, Principle 2 implies that Smith ought to accept the task of commenting on the paper, because doing so would enable him to perform a sequence of acts (reading the paper, making comments, discussing them with the student, etc.) which would have better results than any other scenario. But let us suppose that if Smith accepted the task, he would actually fail to comment on the paper on time — perhaps he would misunderstand what the deadline is, or perhaps he would become so bogged down in administrative work that he wouldn't get around to it. Then Principle 1, by contrast with Principle 2, instructs him *not* to accept the task, since the moderate revisions the student would make working with the other faculty member would be better than his making no revisions at all under Smith's inadequate stewardship. Principle 1's prescription to turn down the student's request seems to me the most reason-able advice in this situation: there is no point in recommending an act to an agent on the grounds that it would enable him to carry through some ideal course of action when he would actually bungle the affair and precipitate some disaster instead.

Despite its plausibility, Principle 1 now seems to me to require further examination. Let us approach the matter indirectly by turning our attention to a different, although related, issue. In determining the moral status of a current action, do the agent's own *simultaneous* acts count as circumstances which affect that status? Consider the following case: Jones is driving through a tunnel behind a slow-moving truck. It is illegal to change lanes in the tunnel, and Jones' doing so would disrupt traffic. Nevertheless she is going to change lanes — perhaps she doesn't realize it is illegal, or perhaps she is simply in a hurry. If she changes lanes without accelerating, traffic will be disrupted more severely than if she accelerates. If she accelerates without changing lanes, her car will collide with the back of a truck. Given that she is actually going to change lanes, it appears reasonable to say that she ought simul-taneously to accelerate. This case, and others like it, suggest the following principle:

3.   Whether or not S ought to do A depends on what act(s) S would perform at the same time as A, if he performed A.

Principle 3 is straightforwardly analogous to Principle 1, since both principles count what the agent *would* do, if he performed a given act, as a circumstance relevant to the moral assessment of that action. The intuition which supports Principle 1 can also be marshalled in support of Principle 3: whether act B would occur at the same time as A or later, if it is true that the agent would perform B if he were to do A, then it seems only rational to take B's occurrence into account in determining whether or not the agent ought to do A.

In fact it is difficult to see how only one of these two principles could be correct. Not only are they closely similar to each other, but whether a given action falls under one principle or the other depends on micro-second timing, a matter normally thought to be irrelevant within a moral context. For example, if Jones' act of accelerating were to begin just a split-second *before* her act of changing lanes, then the former act would be governed by Principle 1, rather than by Principle 3. In light of this it appears the two principles must stand or fall together, for otherwise a minute difference in the temporal relations — and *nothing* else — between two acts would make a critical, and seemingly inexplicable, difference to whether or not one of them counts as a circumstance relevant to the moral status of the other.

In this paper I will argue that both Principle 1 and Principle 3 are incorrect: that neithe⌐ governs our primary obligations in the way alleged. But I shall also argue that the most intuitive prescriptions stemming from Principle 1 can be preserved as primary obligations, even though the principle itself must be abandoned.[3]

II

Why is Jones' act of accelerating subject to moral assessment? Presumably because it is an act which she has the ability to perform, that is, one such that if she wanted to perform it, she would. One way of evaluating such an act is to apply a moral principle (such as act utilitarianism, a Rossian deontological system, Kant's Categorical Imperative, or so forth) directly to it — i.e., determine whether or not it would maximize happiness, or fulfill the most stringent duties incumbent upon the agent, or be in accord with a maxim which could be willed as a universal law. But if we directly assess the morality of Jones' act of accelerating in this fashion, then it is difficult to avoid counting her simultaneous act of changing lanes as one of the circumstances which affect its moral status. Few people will deny, for example, that the *consequences* of her accelerating are relevant to its moral status. But what consequences her accelerating would have is partly determined by events which would occur at the same time, such as the acts of other drivers and the simultaneous acts of Jones herself. Hence counting the consequences of Jones' accelerating as relevant to its moral status necessarily involves taking into account the fact that she would simultaneously change lanes, since those consequences would not occur if she did not change lanes.[4] And this amounts to allowing her changing lanes to count as morally relevant to her accelerating, in the same way that the activities of other drivers are so counted. The governing moral principle need not mention the agent's concurrent activities as the sort of feature which is *directly* relevant to the moral status of a given act (the way it might mention the value of the act's consequences), but nonetheless those activities help determine which of the explicitly mentioned features is present.

The value of an action's consequences is not the only feature which depends on the agent's simultaneous acts. Most people would view it as morally relevant that Jones' act of uttering "I never disobey the law" involves telling a lie. But her utterance only counts as telling a lie if it involves *asserting* that she never disobeys the law,[5] and what she asserts by her utterance depends in part on her simultaneous acts. For example, if she winked, rather than maintaining a straight face, while uttering the words, her utterance would have been ironic, and so involved asserting the truth that she frequently *disobeys* the law. Hence if we agree that her act of uttering "I never disobey the law" is wrong at least partly because it involves telling a lie, we must admit that her concurrent act of maintaining a straight face is, at least indirectly, relevant to its moral status.[6]

Since we can hardly give up the view that such features of an act as the value of its consequences, and whether or not it involves telling a lie, are relevant to its moral status, we seem forced to accept Principle 3. Nevertheless Principle 3 has extremely counterintuitive consequences, stemming from the fact that an agent has the ability to perform each one of his simultaneous acts. Jones has the ability to change lanes, as well as the ability to accelerate: if she wants to perform the former act, she will do so. Thus it, too, is a proper subject for moral evaluation. However, if we evaluate her act of changing lanes, we must accept Principle 3 in this context also, and view any acts Jones would perform simultaneously with it as circumstances affecting *its* moral status. Let us assume that whether or not Jones would change lanes, she would *not* accelerate — perhaps she under-estimates the speed required to make a smooth lane change, or perhaps she doesn't care how much she disrupts other traffic. In view of her not accelerating, it would be better for her not to change lanes. Thus, dual application of Principle 3 results in prescriptions for Jones to accelerate and not to change lanes. But Jones' fulfilling both these prescriptions (which involves colliding with the back of the truck) would be far less good, from the perspective of most moral principles, than performing another pair of acts which are also available to her, namely not accelerating and not changing lanes. Clearly there is something wrong with our normative theory as a whole if it results in prescriptions for acts which are less good in combination, according to the values embodied in that theory, than other acts which the agent could perform instead.[7]

The second difficulty with Principle 3 is seen more clearly if we look at another case. Suppose a dog runs out into the road in front of Jones' car. If Jones honks, the dog will leap back off the road; if she swerves, she will miss hitting the dog, although her passenger will suffer a minor cut on the head. However, Jones does neither of these — perhaps she doesn't notice the dog, or perhaps she isn't concerned for the welfare of animals. According to Principle 3, since she fails to honk, she ought at least to swerve. Also according to Principle 3, since she fails to swerve, she ought to honk. Thus Jones comes under two prescriptions, to honk and to swerve — but we can imagine that Jones is a poorly coordinated individual who *cannot* do both even if she wants to. Dual application of Principle 3 generates pragmatically incompatible prescriptions, ones which the agent cannot jointly fulfill. And no normative theory should place such unfulfillable requirements on an agent.[8]

We appear to be caught in a difficult dilemma. On the one hand, we must espouse Principle 3 in order to retain our belief that such features as an action's consequences are relevant to its moral status, for what those consequences would be depends on what concurrent acts the agent would perform. On the other hand, Principle 3 has two strongly objectionable features: in some cases it prescribes acts for the agent which are jointly worse than other acts he could perform, and in other cases it prescribes acts which are not jointly performable by the agent at all.

This dilemma appears harsh, but the way out is easily discovered. In addition to the kind of acts we have discussed so far, an agent also possesses the ability to perform 'conjunctive' acts. For example, in the original Jones case, in addition to such simple acts as accelerating or changing lanes, Jones can also accelerate-while-changing-lanes, accelerate-while-not-changing-lanes, not-accelerate-while-changing-lanes, or not-accelerate-while-not-changing-lanes. Each of these is an act, and she has the ability to perform each one in the sense that if she wants to perform it, she will do so. Since they are within her ability in precisely the same fashion that accelerating simpliciter is, or that changing lanes simpliciter is, they are just as legitimate candidates for moral evaluation as the original 'simple' acts are.[9]

The argument thus far has assumed that the governing moral principle (e.g., act-utilitarianism, the Categorical Imperative, etc.) is applied directly to simple acts such as accelerating. But it can be applied instead directly to *maximal conjunctive acts*, where a maximal conjunctive act is an act consisting of simultaneous conjuncts such that there is no additional act which the agent could perform at the same time.[10] If we apply our moral principle directly to maximal conjunctive acts, then Principle 3 simply drops out. There are no simultaneous acts of the same agent which *could* count as morally relevant, either directly or indirectly, to the status of the conjunctive act. If application of moral principles is restricted to maximal conjunctive acts, anyone wishing to persist in the defence of Principle 3 would have to reinterpret it as the claim that certain *internal* counterfactual characteristics of a conjunctive action are somehow relevant to its moral status. For example, it would have to be claimed that it is somehow relevant to the status of accelerating-while-changing-lanes that one component (changing lanes) would occur if the other component (accelerating) were to occur. But if our attention is focused securely on the moral status of the conjunctive act, rather than on its components taken in isolation, then this claim lacks any intrinsic plausibility. Nor are we forced to accept it in order to retain our views about the moral relevance of some *other* feature of the conjunctive act. For example, what consequences a conjunctive act would have does not depend on whether or not it possesses this counterfactual characteristic. What would happen if Jones accelerated-while-changing-lanes in no way turns on whether or not she *would* change lanes if she did accelerate. Thus if we apply our moral principles directly to maximal conjunctive acts, rather than to their simple components, we may simply reject Principle 3 and all its undesirable consequences. The acts prescribed (i.e., Jones' not-accelerating-while-not-changing-lanes) will be the best, according to the values of the governing moral principle, that the agent has the ability to perform. Nor will any pragmatically incompatible prescriptions be generated, for nothing (e.g., Jones' honking-while-swerving) counts as a maximal conjunctive act unless the agent has the ability to perform it, and the agent will only fall under one prescription for any given time. Or, if we wish to have prescriptions for simple acts as well as for maximal conjunctive acts, we may stipulate that such an act ought to be performed only if it is a component of a maximal conjunctive act which ought to be performed. The simple act is not required *itself* to satisfy the criteria of the governing moral principle. An agent will then fall under more than one prescription for a given time, but clearly those prescriptions will only be for acts which can jointly be performed.[11]

There remains a significant problem with this solution to our dilemma.

Although Principle 3 involves intolerable difficulties, nevertheless it has an undeniable intuitive appeal. We *do* reason the way it suggests on some occasions, both when we are ascertaining what to do ourselves, and when we are advising other agents about their actions.[12] To deprive ourselves entirely of this form of reasoning would be to deprive ourselves of a major instrument in the rational assessment of action. And denying the correctness of Principle 3 seems to do just that. I believe this problem must be handled by recognizing that there are (at least) two orders of obligation, primary obligations, which are not governed by Principle 3, and secondary obligations, which tell us what it would be best to do, subject to some constraint. One such secondary obligation tells us whether or not it would be best for the agent to perform act A, given the constraint that he would perform act B at the same time. An agent may satisfy both his primary and secondary obligations, or he may fail to satisfy his primary obligations but satisfy his secondary ones, or he may fail to satisfy either. In the original Jones case, she fails to satisfy her primary obligation in changing lanes, and she also fails to satisfy her secondary obligation in not accelerating. In this sense she would have done 'better' to accelerate, for then her only violation would have been of her primary obligation. Recognizing secondary obligations allows us to see the relevance of principle 3 without allowing it to govern primary obligations, as in effect I have argued it cannot and need not. An account needs to be given of the nature of secondary obligations and their relation to primary obligations, but I shall not attempt to do so here.[13]

III

In the last section we saw that Principle 3, which states that whether or not an agent ought to perform a given act depends on what act(s) he would perform at the same time, is unavoidable if we apply our moral principles directly to simple acts, and yet entails wholly unacceptable consequences for primary obligations. The dilemma is evaded by restricting the application of moral principles to maximal conjunctive acts, and the intuitive appeal of Principle 3 is accounted for by recognizing a species of secondary obligation where it may apply.

Let us now reconsider Principle 1, which states that whether or not an agent ought to perform a given action depends on the sequence of *subsequent* acts he would perform if he performed the act in question. Principle 1 possesses to an even stronger degree the intuitive attraction felt in Principle 3. Moreover, an argument parallel to that employed in the case of Principle 3 suggests that if we apply our moral principles directly to the maximal conjunctive acts recently recommended, we are forced to accept Principle 1 in order to preserve our views about what features of these acts may be counted as morally relevant. For example, most people would hold that the consequences of such acts are relevant to their moral status, and yet what those consequences would be depends on the acts the agent would perform subsequent to the act in question.[14] The moral status of Smith's accepting his student's request to comment on the paper surely depends in part on the consequences of that act. But the most significant of these consequences — what sort of job, if any, the student is offered — depends on whether or not Smith would comment on the paper after accepting the task. Thus if we apply our moral principles to maximal conjunctive acts, and count the consequences of such an act as relevant to its moral status, we must admit that the actions the agent would perform afterwards are also relevant. And this commits us to the truth of Principle 1.[15]

But would acceptance of Principle 1 involve us in difficulties parallel to those entailed by acceptance of Principle 3? These difficulties only arise because Principle 3 generates prescriptions for multiple simultaneous acts, acts which may be normatively unacceptable in combination, or else not jointly performable. If we restrict application of our moral principles to maximal conjunctive acts, there is no danger that Principle 1 will give rise to precisely these problems, for only one act can be prescribed for performance during any time period. However, several investigators, including myself, have urged that moral statements must be dated to indicate the time at which the obligation obtains, as well as the time at which the prescribed action would be performed.[16] Such a scheme makes possible a present obligation to perform an act in the non-immediate future, and this in turn makes it possible for a single agent to have several present obligations to perform acts which would occur at different times. And *this* opens the door for Principle 1 to prescribe multiple *nonsimultaneous* acts which may be normatively unacceptable in combination, or else not jointly performable.

In order to ascertain whether or not these problems actually affect Principle 1, let us first turn our attention to another issue. Since 'ought' implies 'can,' presumably an agent who ought now to perform a future act must have the *ability* to perform that act. But what is the relevant sense of 'ability' here? Clearly an agent's obligation at t_1 to perform act A at a later time t_n must be predicated on his having the ability *at* t_1 — not t_n — to perform A at t_n. For there are cases where we want to say that an agent has an earlier obligation to perform A, even though missteps between t_1 and t_n may render him unable at t_n itself to perform A. As an example, suppose Smith's class meets at nine a.m., but he is still asleep in bed at that time. We cannot say that he ought at nine a.m. to deliver his lecture to his class *at that time*, since he is then unable to. But we may want to say that he has an obligation at seven a.m., when his alarm clock wakes him, to deliver the lecture at nine, since he *then* has the ability to do so.

The following extremely natural account of an agent's present ability to perform a future act follows that suggested by numerous investigatiors.[17] It assumes we are already in possession of an analysis of the notion of an agent's having the ability at t_1 to perform an act at that same time.

I. An agent has the ability at t_1 to perform act A_n at t_n if and only if:

there is a sequence of acts such that the agent has the ability at t_1 to perform the first act in this sequence at t_1, and if he were to perform this act, then he would have the ability at a later time to perform the second act at that time, and if he were to perform the first two acts at their respective times, then he would have the ability at a still later time to perform the third act at that time, and so forth, until finally if he were to perform all the acts in the sequence at their respective times, then he would have the ability at t_n to perform act A_n at t_n.

The root idea behind this definition is that an agent's ability at t_1 to perform an act at t_n can be explicated in terms of a sequence of abilities he would have at the requisite times to then perform the necessary intervening acts. I have previously assumed that an agent's ability to perform an act should be explained in terms of what he would do if he wanted to. We can now interpret this to mean that an agent has the ability at t_1 to perform an act at t_1 just in case it is true that if he wanted at t_1 to perform it at t_1, he would do so. This analysis can be substituted for every occurrence of 'ability' in the analysans of Definition I. To see the implications of the resulting definition, let us represent the original Smith case (slightly expanded) in Figure 1:

Each of these acts is taken to be a maximal conjunctive act, although all the conjuncts obviously are not mentioned. For brevity I shall refer to each depicted act only in terms of its underlined conjunct. According to the interpretation of Definition I just given, Smith has the ability at t_1 to perform each of the possible acts depicted at t_2. For example, he has the ability

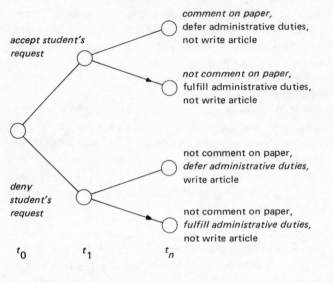

Figure 1

at t_1 to comment on the student's paper at t_2, because if he wanted at t_1 to accept the student's request, he would do so, and if he did so, then if he wanted at t_2 to comment on the paper at t_2, he would do so. The same is true for the other three acts as well.

But is Definition I the correct account of an agent's present ability to perform a future act? I would argue that in the context of moral theory it is not. A moral principle is an instrument for the theoretical evaluation of actions, but it has a practical function as well: it is a device which an agent can employ in order to guide his own activities.[18] Therefore the range of activities which a moral principle should assess, from the standpoint of time t_1, should be no wider than those activities which are available for guidance at t_1 itself — that is, those activities, of each of which it is true that the agent's desiring *at* t_1 to perform that activity would result in its performance. A prescription for any activity which is not so accessible to guidance would be pointless, because the agent could not make practical use of the prescription; he could not successfully choose to carry it out. For this reason we do not include among the alternatives to be assessed by a moral principle, actions which are logically possible but physically beyond the agent's capacities, e.g., we do not view swimming out to rescue a drowning person as an alternative for an agent who cannot swim. Similarly, I believe there is no point in prescribing at t_1 a future action to an agent unless the agent's wanting *at t_1 itself* to perform that action would actually be followed by its subsequent performance. If no present want of his could lead to performance of that action, then no present knowledge on his part that the action ought to be performed could lead to the obligation's being carried out. And in these circumstances, nothing is achieved by ascribing such an obligation to him.

In view of this, it appears that the correct account of an agent's present ability to perform a future action should strictly parallel the traditional account I have hitherto assumed of his present ability to perform a present action. Indeed, once the issue is called to our attention, it is hardly surprising that the same features which make a present act a candidate for moral evaluation should also be required of future acts. The following definition, then, is the one I shall adopt.

II.   An agent has the ability at t_1 to perform act A at later time t_n if and only if it is true that if the agent wanted at t_1 to perform A at t_n, he would do so.[19]

Of course, in the case of ability to perform a future action, the agent's present desire would not lead *directly* to his performing the action at the later time. A chain of events would intervene between the present desire and the future action, and a later desire of his would be the proximate (motivational) producer of the action itself. Nevertheless, insofar as his present desire would set this chain of events into motion, it *controls* whether or not he performs that later act. Naturally, not every present desire to perform a subsequent act would ultimately lead to its performance. For example, it may be true that even if Smith wanted at t_1 to comment on the student's paper at t_2, he would not do so. The desire to help the student might fade away by t_2, or competing desires (e.g., the desires to submit his report to the Budget Committee, and to grade a set of qualifying examinations) might come into existence or grow stronger under the stimulus of immediate pressures. If so, we must say that Smith does not have the ability at t_1 to comment on the student's paper at t_2 — even though it is true that, having accepted the student's request, if he wanted at t_2 to comment on the paper, he would do so. His ability at t_1 depends precisely on whether or not he *would have* the requisite desire in sufficient strength at t_2, and he might not. But he may not be in a position at t_1 to change this fact — nothing he can do or desire now may succeed in ensuring his possession of the necessary desire in the future. In such a case, it would be pointless to recommend to him now that he comment on the paper, since he cannot arrange to carry this recommendation out. (This does not negate the fact that, if he were to accept the student's request, there would be point in recommending *at* t_2 that he comment then on the paper, because at t_2 he *would* have the ability to perform this act. On the account of abilities I am arguing for, the extent of an agent's abilities may grow with time, rather than shrink.)

Armed with the appropriate definition of an agent's present ability to perform a future act, let us return to our examination of Principle 1. We were enquiring whether or not adoption of Principle 1 would lead to multiple simultaneous prescriptions to perform nonsimultaneous acts, acts which might be normatively unacceptable in combination, or else jointly unperformable. Let us look at the problem of incompatible prescriptions first. If Principle 1 is simply applied to acts which would occur at different times, and no attempt is made to coordinate these prescriptions, incompatibilities will arise. How this might occur can be seen from the following abstractly described case, in which it is assumed that the agent has the abilities at t_1 to perform all six acts depicted (Figure 2).

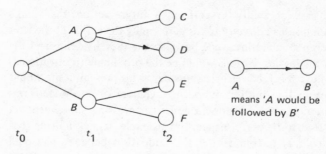

Figure 2

If we assume that A and B are intrinsically equivalent (according to the governing moral principle), but that B would be followed by a better sequence of subsequent acts than A, then Principle 1 implies that the agent ought at t_1 to perform B. But in addition, if we assume that of the four acts available for performance at t_2, C is best intrinsically and from the point of view of the sequence which would follow it, then Principle 1, when applied to future acts, implies that the agent ought at t_1 to perform C.[20] However, B and C are not jointly performable.

This form of diachronic incompatibility can be avoided by a technique which makes prescriptions for later acts dependent on the prescriptions for earlier acts. Thus we first prescribe the act to be performed immediately, then prescribe an act for the next moment only if it is possible for the agent to perform both it and the act first prescribed, then prescribe an act for the third moment only if it is possible for the agent to perform it together with the first two acts prescribed, and so forth. In order to formulate a version of Principle 1 which incorporates this technique, we need the technical notion of one act's being the *immediate successor* of another act, and also the notion of an agent's having the ability at one time to *jointly perform* acts at later times. The intuitive idea, when one act is an immediate successor of another act, is that the agent could not perform any act in between those two acts. I shall leave the formal definition of the term to a footnote.[21] The second notion can be defined as follows:

III.   An agent has the ability at t_1 to jointly perform maximal conjunctive acts A_i at t_i, A_j at t_j, . . . , A_n at t_n $(t_1 \leqslant t_i < t_j < t_n)$ if and only if it is true that if the agent wanted at t_1 to perform A_i at t_i, A_j at t_j, . . . , A_n at t_n, he would do so.

This definition of joint ability is the obvious extension of the correct definition for a single act given above. Employing these two notions, we can now state a recursive version of Principle 1 which avoids the sort of inconsistency just noted:

1*.   (A) Whether or not S ought at t_1 to perform A_1 at t_1 depends on:
           (i) S's having the ability at t_1 to perform A_1 at t_1, and
           (ii) the sequence of subsequent acts S would perform if he
              performed A_1 at t_1.
          (B) If S ought at t_1 to perform each of A_i, . . . , A_j at t_i, . . . , t_j,
              then whether or not he ought at t_1 to perform an immediate
              successor A_k to A_j depends on:
              (i) S's having the ability at t_1 to jointly perform A_i, . . . , A_j,
                 A_k at t_i, . . . , t_j, t_k, and
              (ii) the sequence of subsequent acts S would perform if he
                 performed A_k at t_k.
          (C) No other acts except those prescribed by applications of (A)
              and (B) ought at t_1 to be performed by S.

The notion of 'joint ability' employed in Clause (B) must be that stated in

Definition III above. Apart from that Principle 1* is a generalized version of the G* principle of obligation proposed in my previous paper.[22]

The use of the requirement of joint performability in Clause (B) of Principle 1* clearly avoids any problem with pragmatically incompatible prescriptions. To see how this is so, let us apply the principle to the Smith case as diagrammed on page 194. Assuming a normal set of values, Principle 1* implies that Smith ought at t_1 to deny the student's request, because that act would be followed by a better sequence of acts than his accepting the student's request. We may assume that the acts of deferring his administrative duties and fulfilling his administrative duties are each jointly performable with the initially prescribed act of not accepting the student's request. Since it is better to fulfill one's duties, and we may assume doing so would be followed by a better sequence of acts, Principle 1* instructs Smith at t_1 to fulfill his administrative duties at t_2. Thus Smith is instructed at t_1 to deny the request at t_1 and to fulfill his administrative dutes at t_2, acts which are jointly performable.

Since Smith's accepting the student's request would not in any case be followed by his commenting on the paper, and so would lead to the student's failing to receive a job offer, these recommendations should be appealing. We have found a version of Principle 1 which allows us to derive them while at the same time avoiding the problem of incompatible prescriptions which afflicted the analogous Principle 3. The explanation for this difference between the two principles lies in the fact that Principle 1*, unlike Principle 3, prescribes acts which would take place at different times. The chronological ordering of these acts can be taken advantage of in formulating the prescriptions, by making the prescription for any given act depend on the prescription for the immediately previous act, in such a way that incompatible prescriptions are avoided. There is no equally natural ordering obtaining among simultaneous acts which could be exploited to avoid incompatible prescriptions in the formulation of Principle 3.

However, Principle 3 is beset by another, equally damaging, problem, which Principle 1* does not escape. As we saw, when Principle 3 is applied to simple acts, it generates prescriptions for multiple simultaneous acts which may be worse, in combination, than other combinations of acts which the agent could also perform. Reflection shows that Principle 1* leads to a similar problem: it prescribes multiple nonsimultaneous acts which are worse, in combination, than other combinations of nonsimultaneous acts which the agent could perform instead. Let us see what sort of case would produce this result. Imagine in the Smith case, contrary to what we have previously assumed, that Smith has the abilities at t_1 to perform *each* of the following combinations of acts: accepting the student's request and commenting on the paper, accepting the request and not commenting on the paper, denying the request and fulfilling his administrative duties, and denying the request and deferring his administrative duties (we earlier assumed that the first of these combinations was *not* available to Smith). But imagine also that two previous assumptions continue to hold, namely that if Smith were to accept the request, then he would not comment on the paper, and that if he were to deny the request, then he would fulfill his administrative duties. Under all these assumptions, Principle 1* *still* implies that Smith ought at t_1 to deny the request at t_1 (since this act would be followed by the best sequence of acts), and that he ought at t_1 to fulfill his administrative duties at t_2. But these two acts in combination are less good, according to a normal set of values, than two other acts which he *also has the ability to perform jointly* — that is, accepting the student's request and commenting on the paper. Surely, if he *can* accept the request and comment on the paper, he ought to, for this would secure a three-year job offer for the student. If the situation so described is genuinely possible, then Principle 1* falls prey to a difficulty analogous to one of those afflicting Principle 3, and equally devastating.

But *is* the situation just described really possible? In particular, is it possible for both of the following to be true: (a) Smith has the ability at t_1 to jointly accept the student's request and comment on the paper, and (b) nevertheless if Smith were to accept the request, he would fail to comment on the paper? At first blush it certainly seems that they cannot both be true, since how *could* Smith have the ability to jointly accept the request and comment on the paper if, as a matter of fact, his accepting the request would inevitably be followed by his not commenting on the paper? I suspect that Howard Sobel, in his investigation of related problems, supposes that two such statements cannot both be possible, since he speaks of a sequence of acts which an agent can presently secure, and yet defines this in terms of the sequence the agent would perform if he were to perform the first action in that sequence.[23] I also suspect that such a belief implicitly underlay my previous defence of a principle similar to Principle 1*. Nevertheless (a) and (b) *are* both possible. To see this, let us ask why Smith's accepting the request would be followed by his failing to comment on the paper. So far we have assumed the reason for this is that Smith's desire at t_1 to comment on the paper would fade in strength by t_2, at least relative to competing desires. But there are other possible explanations. For example, it might be true that the reason he would fail to comment on the paper if he accepted the request is that he would *already have decided* by t_1 itself that is what he would do. Perhaps Smith would only accept the request because he wants to harm the student and knows that his falsely agreeing to comment on the student's paper would ruin the student's chances of finding a job. In this version of the case, it is true that his accepting the request would be followed by his failing to comment on the paper, but it does not follow that he does not have the ability now to both accept the request and comment on the paper. It may well be true that if he wanted now to perform these two acts (which regrettably he does not), then he would do so. The motivation with which Smith *would* perform the first of these two acts is simply irrelevant to the question of whether or not he would perform both acts if he now were to want to do so.[24] According to Definition III, only the answer to the latter question determines whether or not he presently has the ability to jointly perform the two acts.

Thus it may be true, both that Smith would fail to comment on the paper if he accepted the student's request, and also that he now has the ability to both accept the request and comment on the paper. This will happen in a case where Smith would only decide to accept the request if he had already decided not to comment on the paper. In such a case, as we have seen, Principle 1* prescribes two acts — denying the request and fulfilling his administrative duties — which are less good in combination than two other acts which Smith also has the ability to perform — accepting the request and commenting on the paper. We must conclude that Principle 1* is subject to a difficulty parallel to that which afflicted Principle 3. Indeed, its prescriptions for individual acts are not even intuitively attractive in such a case. It is not plausible to recommend, on the grounds that Smith has *already decided* not to comment on the paper, that he ought to deny the student's request to read it. In recommending an immediate act to an agent, we do not take into account the fact that he does not want to perform *it*. For similar reasons, our recommendation for an immediate act should not take into account the fact that he presently does not want to perform some desirable *future* act which is nevertheless within his power.

We are now in the following position. We have seen that if we apply our moral principles directly to maximal conjunctive acts, then we are forced to accept Principle 1 (or Principle 1*), because what the consequences of a given act are depends on what subsequent acts the agent performs, and we view those consequences as morally relevant. But we have also seen that when Principle 1 is applied to future acts, under the guise of Principle 1*, it gives rise to prescriptions for multiple nonsimultaneous acts which are less good in combination than other acts which the agent could perform instead. This is not acceptable in a normative theory.

When parallel problems were encountered with Principle 3, we discovered they could be avoided by simply stipulating that moral principles are to be directly applied only to maximal conjunctive acts, not to the simpler acts which are their components. A similar solution is available to us here. An agent has the ability, not only to perform maximal conjunctive acts, but also to perform sequences of such acts, or what might be called 'courses of action.' In fact Definition III, which gives an analysis of an agent's ability to jointly perform several acts, already implicitly provides us with a definition for an agent's ability to perform such sequences of acts. Let us say that X is a *maximal sequence* of acts for S at t_1 only if S has the ability at t_1 to perform X, and there is no other sequence which S has the ability at t_1 to perform which includes X as a proper part. That is to say, roughly speaking, the agent cannot perform any act in between the members of X, nor perform any acts after the last member of X. We may then stipulate that moral principles are to be applied directly only to maximal sequences of acts.[25] Thus we do not assess any individual act by reference to how much happiness it would produce, or whether or not it involves telling a lie, but rather assess whole sequences of acts in terms of their consequentialist or deontological properties.[26] If we wish to have prescriptions for individual acts, we may prescribe them only in view of their membership in sequences which are prescribed.

Under such a restriction, Principle 1 (and 1*) no longer have any bite. Since each maximal sequence includes as a final member the last act the agent would perform if he performed that sequence, there are no subsequent acts which could possibly be relevant to the moral status of the sequence. Anyone wishing to defend the spirit of Principle 1 further would have to claim that an *internal* counterfactual characteristic of such a sequence, namely the fact that if its earlier members were performed, its later members would be performed as well, is relevant to the moral status of the sequence. But once our moral sights are securely trained on sequences of actions, there is little to be said for this position. It has no inherent attraction, and it is not forced upon us by the fact that any obviously relevant characteristics of such a sequence, such as its consequences, depend on this internal characteristic. It is manifestly false, for example, that what consequences a given sequence would have depends on whether or not an earlier member of the sequence would actually be followed by the later members of the sequence. The consequences of a sequence are determined by asking what would happen if the

sequence *as a whole* were to be performed. Thus neither the intrinsic significance of this internal characteristic, nor any connection between it and other
morally relevant features of actions, impels us to accept this last-ditch
attempt to defend Principle 1. In restricting the direct application of our
moral principles to maximal sequences of actions, we have found a way of
constructing a normative theory which avoids the problems associated with
Principle 1 and Principle 1*.

However, Principle 1 (and 1*) are not merely sources of *trouble*. They also
give rise to prescriptions which in many cases we found intuitively correct. In
abandoning them, have we also abandoned the chance of making these prescriptions? The answer is that we have not. To see how this is so, let us make
the current suggestion slightly more precise, by formulating it in terms of the
following principle:

4. S ought at t_1 to perform maximal sequence X starting at t_1 if
          and only if S has the ability at t_1 to perform X, and X is better
          than any alternative maximal sequence starting from t_1 which S
          also has the ability at t_1 to perform.

The meaning of the technical terms employed in this principle should be
intuitively obvious enough to be left to a footnote.[27] The notion of 'ability'
used is that explained in Definition III.

Let us now apply this principle to the case of Smith, depicted in the
diagram on page 194. Let us first assume that Smith does *not* have the ability
at t_1 to perform the sequence of acts consisting of his accepting the student's
request and commenting on the paper.[28] In our original exposition of the
case (page 186), this inability was explained as arising from the fact that even
if Smith wanted at t_1 to accept the request and comment on the paper, this
desire would have faded by t_2 relative to his desire to fulfill his administrative
tasks, so that he would not have a sufficiently strong desire at t_2 itself to
comment on the paper, and so would not perform this act. His wanting at
t_1 to comment on the paper would not bring it about that he would comment. Under this assumption, the sequence consisting of accepting the task
and commenting on the paper is not available for moral assessment, since
he does not have the ability to perform it. There can be no objection to this,
since any such assessment might lead to a prescription to perform the
sequence, and this prescription would be pointless, since he could not successfully choose to carry it out. Thus our moral principle must evaluate the
remaining three sequences. On a normal set of values, the sequence consisting
of his denying the request and then fulfilling his administrative duties is the

best of the three, and so would be recommended by Principle 4. But notice that this sequence consists of the *very same acts* as those recommended by Principle 1* (see page 198). Thus although we are using a different moral principle, Smith's inabilities still make it the case that he ought to deny the request and fulfill his administrative duties, although this prescription assumes the form of a prescription to perform a certain sequence, rather than separate prescriptions for individual actions.

However, Principle 4 and Principle 1* do not deliver the same prescriptions in *every* case. Let us consider the alternative version of Smith's case, in which if he accepted the student's request, it would be because he had decided to harm the student by falsely promising to comment on his paper. In this version of the case, although it is true that Smith's accepting the request would be followed by his failing to comment on the paper, it is also true that he has the ability at t_1 to both accept the request and comment on the paper, because if he only wanted to at that time, the want would persist and lead him to comment on the paper at t_2. Under this assumption, the sequence consisting of his accepting the request and commenting on the paper *is* available for moral assessment. And this is as it should be, for after all, if the agent chose to perform this sequence, he would do so, and therefore there is point to prescribing it for him. Indeed, on a normal set of values, that is precisely what Principle 4 does. Thus Principle 4 instructs Smith to accept the request and comment on the paper, although Principle 1*, even in this version of the case, still instructs him to deny the request and to fulfill his administrative duties. In cases where the agent *could* perform a given sequence, but his *present* nefarious motivations would lead him not to perform it even if he performed an initial segment of it, Principle 4 and Principle 1* generate different prescriptions. As we saw above, it is precisely in these cases that the prescriptions generated by Principle 1* are counterintuitive, for they seem to offer the agent, as a justification for performing some otherwise objectionable immediate act, the excuse that he presently doesn't want to perform some desirable later act. One's present motivations can never be an acceptable justification of this sort. Thus to the extent to which the prescriptions generated by Principle 4 diverge from those generated by Principle 1*, it is precisely the least attractive prescriptions of 1* that are being abandoned.

In my previous paper, in which I defended a version of Principle 1* called the G* principles, I attempted to deal in another way with the counterintuitive prescriptions which these principles generate.[29] There I pointed out that decisions, as well as actions, are to some degree within our voluntary control, and therefore could be thought of as appropriate subjects for moral assessment in the same way that actions are. If this suggestion is pursued, and the G* principles applied to decisions as well as to actions, then it would seem that many of these objectionable prescriptions are avoided. For example, in the version of the Smith case where Smith desires to harm the student, we would derive prescriptions for him to *decide* that if he accepts the request, he will comment on the paper (for this decision would be followed by a desirable sequence of actions), and then to accept the request and comment on the paper (for each of these actions in turn would be followed by a desirable sequence of acts). Such prescriptions make sense, for we feel that he certainly oughtn't to have the evil motivation he does, and also think that the existence of this motivation should not provide him with an excuse to follow some undesirable course of action.

Clearly there are difficulties with working out the details of this suggestion. However, I believe that in at least some cases the prescriptions generated by this extended version of the G* principles are less satisfactory than those generated by Principle 4. For example, as I noted in the earlier paper, it is reasonable to suppose there is a point (perhaps very shortly before he actually begins acting) when Smith has made a decision which he can no longer change. Let us suppose his decision at this point is not to comment on the paper if he accepts the request (his spiteful frame of mind persists, despite our recommendation to the contrary). In this situation, since his accepting the request would be followed by a disastrous course of action, the G* principles recommend that he deny the request and fulfill his administrative duties. Principle 4, on the other hand, continues to recommend that Smith accept the request and comment on the paper. Thus the prescriptions generated by the two principles may differ. In such a case there is some inclination to suppose that the prescription generated by Principle G* is the correct one. For after all, if his accepting the request would be followed by a disastrous course of action, and there is nothing he can now do about the circumstance (namely his present motivation) which makes this true, how can it be rational to recommend that he accept the request? But it now seems to me that this temptation grows out of the implicit belief that if Smith can no longer change his mind, then he actually does not have the *ability* to both accept the request and comment on the paper. As we have seen before, this is false. According to the definition of ability I have argued for, he *does* have the ability to perform this sequence, even though he presently does not want to, and even though there is nothing he can do *now* to change that want.

Someone sufficiently tempted by Principle G*'s recommendation in this case might argue that it shows my definition of ability must be abandoned in favor of one which implies that Smith has the ability at t_1 to perform a sequence of actions only if he has the ability, also at t_1, to produce the desire to perform that sequence. By hypothesis, the argument could continue, Smith does not have both these abilities at t_1, so we cannot instruct him at t_1 to accept the request and comment on the paper. However, at some earlier time, say t_0, he does have both these abilities, and we can instruct him *then* to perform this sequence of acts. This would satisfy both our feeling that at some point this sequence ought to be recommended to him, and also our feeling that at t_1 itself it is too late to do this.

However, I believe that the proposed strategy would be a serious mistake. Consistent application of the strategy seems to require that we stipulate in addition that Smith has the ability at t_0 to produce the desire to perform a sequence of actions only if he has the ability, also at t_0, to produce the desire to produce the desire to perform that sequence of actions. For after all, Smith may *not* have the desire at t_0 to produce the desire to perform the sequence, and moreover it may not be possible for him to produce this second-order desire. Rehearsal of the reasoning above suggests that in such a case it would be no more legitimate to hold him responsible at t_0 for his failure to have the first-order desire than it was legitimate to hold him responsible at t_1 for failing to perform the sequence of acts in question. It is easy to see how this sort of reasoning will involve us in an infinite regress of required abilities. This in itself is fairly damning. Even worse, it appears that such an infinite series of requirements will only be satisfied (if it is satisfiable at all) by the act which the agent actually performs. But from the point of view of moral theory, it is disastrous to employ a notion of ability according to which the agent can only do what he does do. From this we can see that the recommendations of the expanded G* principles, where they diverge from those of Principle 4, can only be accepted if we found them on a notion of ability which is anathema within the context of moral theory. We may conclude that Principle 4 deals with cases such as the sinister version of the Smith case more successfully than the expanded version of the G* principles suggested in my earlier paper.

We have now seen that rejecting Principle 1* (or the G* principles) in favor of Principle 4 does not involve abandoning the intuitively attractive prescriptions derivable from 1*, since its recommendations and those of 4 are identical except in the special cases where the agent's present motivations would lead him to perform an undesirable act in the future. Nevertheless it must be said that we sometimes find it useful to be able to reason in the way suggested by Principle 1*, even in these cases. Smith might well say to himself

"I want to harm this student, so if I accept his request I will then fail to comment on the paper, in order to decrease his chance of receiving a job offer. It would be better for me to deny the request in the first place, than to allow that to happen." Someone advising Smith about what to do might reason the same way. To deprive ourselves of this form of reasoning entirely would be to deny a major instrument of rational decision-making. The same problem arose in the case of Principle 3, and I believe that we can follow the same line of thought in our solution. That is, we can recognize two orders of obligation, primary and secondary obligation. Primary obligation is governed properly by Principle 4. But secondary obligations, which tell us what to do relative to some constraint, may take account of what the agent's actual motivations are, since that is one possible constraint we may wish to work within. An agent does 'best' who satisfies both primary and secondary obligations, but does 'better' to satisfy at least his secondary obligations, if not his primary ones, than to violate both. Thus Smith, in the quotation above, is reasoning correctly concerning his secondary obligations, within the constraint of his present motivations. Principle 1* is irrelevant to primary obligations, but it finds a proper role within the sphere of secondary obligations. Once again, to fill out this account we need an explanation of the nature of these secondary obligations and their relation to primary ones.

In my previous paper, I introduced the notion of an 'ideal moral agent' – an agent who would do no wrong, whatever the circumstances.[30] There I pointed out that according to the G* principles (which parallel Principle 1*), what an ideal agent ought to do differs from what a normal agent ought to do in the same circumstances. When Definition III is employed in interpreting Principle 4, it, too, implies that ideal moral agents have different obligations than the rest of us do. To see this, imagine that in the Smith case as originally described Smith forms a strong commitment to comment on the student's paper, and agrees at t_1 to do so. In these circumstances, Principle 4 would instruct him at t_2 to comment on the paper. But as we have seen, Smith would not fulfill this obligation, since he would not maintain a strong enough desire at t_2 itself to ensure his commenting on the paper. Smith does not qualify as an ideal moral agent, since there is a possible circumstance, the one just described, in which he would do wrong. His failure in this circumstance reflects a defect of character, i.e., the disposition not to maintain a sufficiently strong desire to do that to which one has committed oneself. This same defect of character affects what his actual obligations at t_1 are, since it determines what his *abilities* at t_1 are. Since his commitment at t_1 to accept the request and comment on the paper would not be followed by his performing that course of action, it does not qualify as one of the alternatives he might be required to perform. Thus Smith's obligation in this case (to deny the request and fulfill his administrative duties) is different from the obligation (to accept the request and comment on the paper) that an ideal moral agent would have — an agent who, if he accepted the request, would carry through and comment on the paper.[31]

The obligations of the normal agent and those of the ideal agent differ because their moral characters, and therefore certain of their abilities, differ. It seems reasonable to hold that (in some senses) it ought to be the case that the normal agent has the same character as the ideal moral agent. But if he had the same character, he would have the same abilities and consequently the same obligations as the ideal agent, so we may conclude that it ought to be the case that the normal agent has the same obligations as an ideal agent would have in the same circumstances. An agent whose obligations diverge from those of an ideal agent is criticizable for having a defective character, even though he may satisfy all of his actual obligations.[32] This enables us to express our feeling that there is something wrong about Smith, in the case as originally described, even though he satisfies his obligation to deny the request and fulfill his administrative duties. The fact that *this* is his obligation shows us his character is defective, even if his actual actions are not.

The notion of what it ought to be the case that the agent ought to perform provides us with a third type of judgment to make in the kinds of cases under consideration, for we may now distinguish what it ought to be the case that the agent ought to perform, what he primarily ought to perform, and what he secondarily ought to perform, relative to the constraint of what his actual motivations are. This battery of judgments should be adequate to the complexity of our moral intuitions about these cases, even though the prescriptions forthcoming may coincide. For example, in the original version of the Smith case, what it ought to be the case that he ought to do (i.e., accept the request and comment on the paper) is distinct from what he primarily ought to do (i.e., deny the request and fulfill his administrative duties). But if we assume that he now wants to accept the request and comment on the paper, then what he ought primarily to do is identical with what he ought secondarily to do, relative to his present motivations (even given those motivations, the best thing for him to do is deny the request). But in the alternative version of the case, in which Smith maliciously desires to harm the student, what he primarily ought to do (i.e., accept the request and comment on the paper) is identical with what it ought to be the case that he ought to do (since an ideal agent would be obliged to accept the

request and comment on the paper). These obligations, however, are distinct
from what he secondarily ought to do, relative to his present motivations —
since he wants to harm the student, and would fail to comment on the paper
if he accepted the request, the best thing for him to do in the context of this
motivation is to deny the request and fulfill his administrative tasks.

The fact that two of these three kinds of judgments may converge in a
particular case may make it appear that we are really only dealing with two
distinct kinds of judgments, not three. It would be wrong to conclude this,
for all three judgments may diverge from each other in a case where the agent
has three or more alternative courses of action open to him.[33] The appearance
is misleading in any event, for even in the two cases just described, no two
kinds of judgment are coextensive with each other in *both* cases. And even
though the acts prescribed by two different kinds of judgments may be the
same, the functions of those prescriptions are distinct.

I V

We began with the question of whether or not an agent's own actions count
as part of the circumstances which are relevant to the moral status of any
given action of his. The view that they do count is articulated in two principles: Principle 1, which states that whether or not an agent ought to perform an action depends on the subsequent acts he would perform if he performed it, and Principle 3, which states that whether or not an agent ought
to perform an action depends on the simultaneous actions he would perform
if he performed the act in question. Both these principles have an undeniable
intuitive appeal. Moreover, it is possible to construct an argument for each of
them by showing that we can only reject the principle if we are willing to
abandon counting as morally relevant certain properties of an action which
are central in most moral theories. However, it is also possible to show that
each of these principles leads to wholly unacceptable results: in certain cases,
Principle 3 generates prescriptions for several acts which are jointly unperformable, or for acts which, taken in combination, are worse than others the
agent could perform instead, while Principle 1* (the tensed version of Principle 1) may generate prescriptions for several non-simultaneous acts which
are worse, in combination, than other acts which the agent could also perform. The dilemmas established by these arguments may be avoided by
parallel strategies — in the case of Principle 3, we must restrict the direct
application of moral principles to maximal conjunctive acts, rather than
allowing them to apply to the simpler conjuncts of these acts, and in the case

of Principle 1*, we must restrict the immediate application of moral principles to maximal sequences of acts, rather than allowing them to apply to the shorter-term components of these sequences. When these restrictions are employed, the two principles lose both their appeal and their force, and may be rejected. If we accept the correct account of 'ability', according to which an agent presently is able to perform a sequence of acts only if a present desire on his part to perform it would lead to its performance, then all the intuitively attractive prescriptions of Principle 1*, and none of the intuitively objectionable ones, may be preserved by adopting Principle 4, which instructs an agent to perform a sequence only if it is the best of those available to him.[34] The legitimacy of the form of reasoning sanctioned by Principles 1 and 3 is explained as belonging to our thinking about secondary obligations: those which obtain relative to some constraint. But for primary obligations, neither principle is correct, and we must conclude that the acts an agent would perform if he performed a given act are not to be counted as relevant circumstances in assessing the moral status of the given act.[35]

The University of Michigan

NOTES

[1] Holly S. Goldman, 'Dated Rightness and Moral Imperfection', *The Philosophical Review* 85 (October, 1977), 449–487.

[2] Lennart Aqvist, 'Improved Formulations of Act-Utilitarianism', *Nous* 3 (September, 1969), 299–323, and Fred Feldman, 'World Utilitarianism', in *Analysis and Metaphysics*, ed. Keith Lehrer (Dordrecht, Holland, 1975), pp. 255–271. This view may also be adopted by P. S. Greenspan in 'Conditional Oughts and Hypothetical Imperatives', *Journal of Philosophy* LXXII (1975), 259–276, and Richmond Thomason in an unpublished manuscript entitled 'Deontic Logic and the Role of Freedom in Moral Deliberation', read at the Pacific Division American Philosophical Association meetings in the spring of 1977.

[3] Throughout this paper, for stylistic reasons, I shall use the terms 'ought' and 'is obligated' interchangeably, although their logic is different. I mean always to investigate the *former*.

There are other principles analogous to Principle 3, e.g., the following:

4. Whether or not S ought to do A depends on what S would do if he didn't do A.
5. Whether or not S ought to do A depends on how S would do A.
6. Whether or not S ought now to perform A at a given future time depends on what acts S would perform between now and that future time if he were to perform A.

The rationale which tends to support each of these principles is the same as that which supports Principle 3, and the reasons for which I will eventually reject 3 would apply, with some alterations, to each of them.

⁴ This is true even if we take her future abilities into account as morally relevant in addition.

⁵ See Roderick M. Chisholm and Thomas D. Feehan, 'The Intent to Deceive', *The Journal of Philosophy* **LXXIV** (March, 1977), 148–153.

⁶ There is a possible, although unattractive, way of avoiding this problem. We could stipulate that an event only counts as a *consequence* of a given action if that action contributes causally to its occurrence, and no simultaneous act of the same agent contributes to its occurrence. Similarly we could stipulate that a deontic property, such as being a case of telling a lie, is morally relevant only if the fact that (what I shall later call) a simple action possesses that property in no way depends on other acts the same agent would perform at the same time. But adopting this strategy would involve asserting that many events and features of actions are simply irrelevant to the moral status of *any* action – events and features which we ordinarily take to be crucial in assessing what is obligatory.

⁷ One might attempt to evade this problem by claiming that the two obligations are merely *conditional* obligations, and moreover ones whose conditions are not the same, so that they cannot be conjoined to get the conclusion that Jones ought to accelerate and Jones ought to not change lanes. However, I am interested in examining their acceptability as *unconditional* obligations, with direct import for action, which are conjoinable at will.

⁸ Precisely how these difficulties must be characterized depends on the analysis of act-identity across possible worlds which one employs.

⁹ For a detailed account of this notion of conjunctive acts (which he terms 'compound' acts), and their relation to simple acts, see Alvin I. Goldman, *A Theory of Human Action*, Chapters I and II. In the text of this paper, when I refer to 'simple' acts, I have in mind what he refers to as 'act trees.' Thus conjunctive acts must be understood as compound act trees.

¹⁰ This definition is not precisely correct, but the issues involved are irrelevant to the main concerns of the paper.

¹¹ Specifying the conditions under which an individual act may be prescribed because of its membership in a prescribed maximal conjunctive act is somewhat complex. It appears possible for there to be a maximal conjunctive act, A&B&C, of which the following two conditions hold: (a) it is true that if the agent wanted to perform A&B&C, he would do so, and (b) if the agent wanted to perform A&B, he would *not* do so. This might arise if it were true that if the agent desired to perform A&B, he would also desire to perform −C, and his lack of coordination would prevent him from performing *any* of these acts under these circumstances. If such a case is possible, then either we must abandon the possibility of recommending individual acts, or segments of maximal conjunctive acts, on the grounds that they are components of maximal conjunctive acts, or else we must maintain that the problem of joint incompatibility of performance does not constitute a difficulty for prescriptions of individual acts under this scheme.

See Lars Bergstrom, 'On the Formulation and Application of Utilitarianism,' *Nous* **X** (May, 1976), 121–144, for a discussion of how to define the relevant alternatives in the context of utilitarianism, and references to the literature on the subject since his seminal book in 1966.

[12] P. S. Greenspan, both in her article 'Conditional Oughts and Hypothetical Imperatives', *Journal of Philosophy* **LXXII** (1975), and in her discussion, 'Oughts and Determinism: A Response to Goldman,' forthcoming in *The Philosophical Review*, seems to neglect the point that this form of reasoning is valid in personal decision-making, as well as in third-person judging and second-person advice-giving.

[13] Greenspan, in 'Conditional Oughts and Hypothetical Imperatives,' and in 'Oughts and Determinism: A Response to Goldman,' provides an account of secondary obligations as *merely* conditional obligations. The same strategy has been suggested by Fred Feldman in private correspondence. Until we have a more adequate account of the nature of conditional obligation, I cannot feel sure that this line of thought will prove satisfactory.

[14] If determinism is true, it might be more precise to say that the consequences of the earlier act depend, in part, on the occurrence of events simultaneous with that earlier act which also cause the performance of the agent's later acts.

[15] Once again, it would be possible to avoid this problem by stipulating that an event counts as a consequence of an earlier act only if no later acts of the same agent causally contribute to its occurrence. Thus only a small portion of events we would normally construe as consequences of the earlier act will be counted as such. I do not find this an attractive route out of the dilemma. See footnote 6 above.

[16] See, for example, Lennart Aqvist, *op. cit.*, pp. 315–323; Fred Feldman, 'World Utilitarianism,' Richmond Thomason, 'Deontic Logic as Founded on Tense Logic', unpublished manuscript, and Holly S. Goldman, 'Dated Rightness and Moral Imperfection', *op. cit.*, pp. 449–451.

[17] Cf. Roderick M. Chisholm, 'He Could Have Done Otherwise', in Myles Brand, ed., *The Nature of Human Action* (Glenview, Illinois: Scott, Foresman and Co., 1970), p. 300; Alvin I. Goldman, *op. cit.*, pp. 204–205; Holly S. Goldman, *op. cit.*, pp. 453–454; Lennart Aqvist, *op. cit.*, pp. 316–317; Fred Feldman, 'World Utilitarianism', and J. Howard Sobel, 'Utilitarianism and Past and Future Mistakes', *Nous* **X** (May, 1976), p. 198.

[18] For simplicity I shall speak as though standard moral principles were to be used in actual decision-making. In fact, many of the features of these principles make them unusable for this purpose (in particular, an agent rarely knows or believes that the conditions such a principle establishes for an action's being obligatory are satisfied, but at best has probabilistic views about this matter). Thus I believe we should distinguish principles of *objective* rightness from principles of *subjective* rightness. Only the latter are to be used in immediate decision-making, while most standard moral principles must be viewed as falling into the former class. In the passage in the text, then, I must be taken as discussing what notion of ability is appropriate within the context of principles of *objective* rightness, and it is not *obvious* that it must be one which is coherent within the context of actual decision-making and action-guidance. However, it seems to me that principles of objective rightness function primarily as ideals, relative to which we ascertain whether a particular principle of subjective rightness is correct, and hence that it makes sense to use the same notion of ability in both contexts.

[19] I owe to Allan Gibbard the suggestion that ability to perform a future act might be defined in this way.

[20] It is also possible to follow a scheme according to which C would only be compared with D, and E and F with each other. It, too, would lead to incompatible prescriptions.

[21] Act A_j is an *immediate successor* to act A_i, relative to t_1, if and only if:

(a)   the agent has the ability at t_1 to jointly perform A_i at t_i and A_j at t_j
             $(t_i < t_j)$, and
(b)   there is no act A_k such that:
             (i) $t_i < t_k < t_j$, and
             (ii) the agent has the ability at t_1 to jointly perform A_i at t_i, A_k at t_k, and
             A_j at t_j.

In the statement of Principle 1* in the text, I drop the relativization of this notion, for brevity.

[22] Holly S. Goldman, *op. cit.*, p. 473.

[23] Sobel, *op. cit.*, p. 199. Sobel actually uses the term 'life' rather than 'sequence of acts.'

[24] It is somewhat unclear whether, in assessing whether or not Smith would fail to comment on the paper if he accepted the request, we should take into account the motivations that he will *actually* have at t_1, or the motivations he would have at t_1 if he accepted the request. Either way we get the desired result.

[25] A number of philosophers have made this proposal, for varying reasons. See, for example, Aqvist, *op. cit.*, and Feldman, 'World Utilitarianism.'

[26] More needs to be said about how to assess the deontological characteristics of entire sequences of actions.

[27] A maximal sequence, X, *starts at* t_1 if and only if the first member of X would occur at t_1.

Two maximal sequences starting from t_1 are alternative sequences from t_1 for S if and only if S has the ability at t_1 to perform each of these sequences, and does not have the ability at t_1 to perform them jointly.

(The latter definition implies that two alternative sequences may partially overlap.)

[28] Notice that the sequences depicted in the diagram are not genuinely maximal sequences, since presumably Smith could perform acts subsequent to the last ones depicted. This is immaterial to the central argument.

[29] Holly S. Goldman, *op. cit.*, pp. 482–484.

[30] Holly S. Goldman, *op. cit.*, p. 485.

[31] In some cases the obligation of the normal (non-ideal) agent and that of the ideal agent will coincide. For example, as I point out below, in the second version of the Smith case, in which he presently desires to harm the student, his primary obligation is to accept the request and comment on the paper (since if only he wanted to perform this course of action, he would do so), and this is the obligation an ideal agent would have as well. Smith in this case is clearly not an ideal agent, since in the hypothetical circumstance that he accepted the request, then Principle 4 would instruct him at t_2 to comment on the paper, and he would fail to do so, thus doing wrong in at least one possible circumstance.

[32] This statement must be qualified to take account of the fact that an agent's obligations are a function of his knowledge as well as his character.

There is reason to suppose that the abilities of an ideal agent, according to Definition III, are identical with his abilities, according to the unstated definition for ability to perform a sequence of acts which is the natural extension of Definition I. Thus it makes no difference how we interpret ability when applying Principle 4 to ideal agents. We can say, then, that Principle 4, interpreted according to this new sense of 'ability,' expresses what it ought to be the case that a normal agent ought to do.

[33] An abstractly described case of this sort would be as in Figure 3:

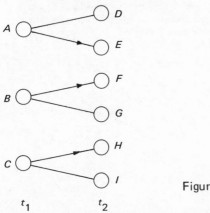

Figure 3

Let us assume that sequence A-and-D is the best of the six sequences described. Then it ought to be the case that the agent ought to perform A-and-D. But let us take it that no matter how much he wanted at t_1 to perform A-and-D, he would not perform D when the time came. On the other hand, if he wanted badly enough to perform B-and-G, he would do so, and let us take it that this is the second-best sequence. Then the agent ought primarily to perform B-and-G. However, he actually wants to perform E if A, F if B, and H if C. Of these three sequences, C-and-H is the best, so relative to his actual motivations, he ought secondarily to perform C-and-H. All three judgments diverge. (In this case, the ideal agent, although not the actual agent, has three alternative sequences of action open to him.)

[34] The definitions of ability I have argued for in this paper are probably only rough approximations of the definitions that will ultimately be found to be correct. For example, Definition II states than an agent has the ability now to perform a future act if and only if it is true that if he now wanted to perform that future act, he would do so. However, phrasing the definition in this way makes his ability depend on the *kind* of desire (with respect to strength and exact content) which he *would have*, if he were to want to perform that act. But it seems to me more plausible to make this ability depend on the strongest want, with the most appropriate content, that it would be possible for him to have, rather than the one he would have. I hope to explore this issue, and related ones, on another occasion. The answers to these questions may make a difference to how close a correspondence there is between the prescriptions generated by Principle 1* and those generated by Principle 4.

Of course there are familiar problems with the conditional analysis of 'ability' which I am here ignoring, since those problems would be common to (for example) both Definitions I and II, whereas I am interested in the contrast between them.

[35] The line of thought I have pursued in this paper was originally explored in my comment on Richard Thomason's paper, 'Deontic Logic and the Role of Freedom in Moral Deliberation', read at the Pacific Division American Philosophical Association meetings in the spring of 1977. I would like to thank John G. Bennett, Robert Cummins, Allan

Gibbard, Alvin Goldman, Louis Loeb, and David Lovelace for their helpful comments on the manuscript at various stages. In addition, I have profited from reading criticisms of my earlier paper communicated to me by Fred Feldman and P. S. Greenspan. The title of this paper comes from a phrase used by Feldman.

RODERICK FIRTH

ARE EPISTEMIC CONCEPTS REDUCIBLE TO ETHICAL CONCEPTS?

When discussing problems in theory of knowledge we often find ourselves using a terminology that is characteristically ethical. We may ask what it is that distinguishes a *good* hypothesis or explanation from a *bad* one. We may affirm or deny that mere simplicity can sometimes make one hypothesis *preferable* to another. We may say that we *ought* to trust our memories to the extent that they cohere with one another. We may decide that this or that kind of inference to theoretical entities is *permissible*. We may wonder if we could ever have the *right* to accept a theory if we knew of an equally plausible, but incompatible, alternative. And so forth. Facts of this kind suggest that epistemological questions are a species of ethical questions, and that epistemic concepts are reducible to ethical concepts to whatever extent this entails.

The issues at stake here do not include all the issues that might arise if we were to ask whether epistemology should be classified as a *normative* discipline. For even if epistemic concepts were in no respect reducible to ethical concepts, there might still be good reasons for classifying both ethics and epistemology as normative. Like logic and aesthetics they are both concerned with norms in the sense of 'standards'. Perhaps this is just a trivial similarity that fails to distinguish them from ontology or even chemistry. Perhaps it is not. But in any case the questions are different. To ask whether epistemic concepts are reducible to ethical concepts is not just to ask whether there is some important respect in which both ethics and epistemology can be described as normative. The questions are identical only if 'normative' and 'ethical' are used synonymously.

It is also important to keep in mind that we are here considering a question that is strictly conceptual. Some moral philosophers have attributed an important ethical status to certain states of affairs that can be identified only by using epistemic terms. They have said that the possession of (or search for) *knowledge* is intrinsically good, that we have a duty to develop our powers of *rational* thought, and so on. Whether such ethical doctrines are correct is not an issue here. For we can consistently accept such ethical doctrines while denying that epistemic concepts like knowledge and rationality are reducible to ethical concepts. If we held that knowledge is intrinsically

A. I. Goldman and J. Kim (eds.), Values and Morals, 215–229. All Rights Reserved.
Copyright © 1978 by D. Reidel Publishing Company, Dordrecht, Holland.

good we could even say that epistemology is an investigation of (part of) the intrinsically good. (On similar grounds an ethical hedonist might say that a study of the psychology of pleasure is an investigation of the intrinsically good.) But the question before us is logically independent of our ethical decisions about what kinds of things are good, what kinds of acts are right, and so forth. In one familiar terminology we could say that our question is independent of normative ethical issues. But it is also independent, in an important respect, of issues that are called, in contrast, metaethical. For philosophers who disagree radically about the analysis of ethical concepts can nevertheless use the same arguments for or against the reducibility of epistemic concepts to ethical concepts. Our question is a question about the analysis of *epistemic* concepts and is thus more aptly called metaepistemological than metaethical.

A full treatment of this metaepistemological question would require more space than is now available to me. I should have to begin by reviewing and classifying the wide variety of concepts that can appropriately be called epistemic. But we can learn a good deal about the general question if we concentrate our attention on one central concept that seems to be a good representative of epistemic concepts in general. For this purpose I have selected the epistemic concept that is sometimes expressed by adjectives like 'warranted' and 'justified' when these adjectives are used to modify the noun 'belief'.

There can be no doubt that this concept is a central concept in theory of knowledge. The ultimate task of a theory of knowledge is to answer the question 'What is knowledge?' But to do this it is first necessary to answer the question 'Under what conditions is a belief warranted?' This is not to assume that knowledge is constituted, as many philosophers have supposed, only of warranted beliefs. In fact there are reasons for denying this dogma. I assume only that in some cases, when confronted with a question of the form 'Does person S know that so and so?', a sufficient reason for a negative answer is that S's belief that so and so is not warranted. In some cases of this kind we might explain our answer by saying that the belief is true but that S just made a lucky guess. There certainly are such cases, and this is enough to show that we cannot give a complete account of the conditions of knowledge without first answering the question 'Under what conditions is a belief warranted?'. So let us consider whether this basic question in theory of knowledge is an ethical question. Does the term 'warranted' in this context express an ethical concept? If we can show that it does we shall probably be able to show that a great many other epistemic terms also express ethical concepts. Terms like 'rational', 'reasonable', 'valid', 'probably', 'certain', and 'evident', as they occur in some epistemological contexts, seem to be definable by reference to warrant.

What is the most promising line to follow if we hope to show that epistemic statements about warranted belief can be construed as ethical statements? At first thought it might seem that to attribute warrant to a belief is to make an epistemic assessment of a particular doxastic state, i.e., of a particular psychological state of believing. And it might seem, furthermore, that to make such an assessment is to make a favorable ethical appraisal of that very psychological state. This looks like a promising hypothesis because psychological states are of course suitable objects for ethical appraisal. We may say of someone that he ought to have felt sorrow rather than anger, that he ought not to have been embarrassed by the praise he received and so on. If the matter were as simple as this we could turn at once to the question: What *kind* of ethical appraisal? When we say that a state of believing is epistemically warranted, are we saying, perhaps, that someone has the *right* to be in that state, or that someone *ought* to be in that state?

Unfortunately for this hypothesis, the epistemic term 'warranted belief' is ambiguous in a way that deserves more attention than it ordinarily receives from philosophers. Although I have referred in the singular to *the* epistemic concept expressed by the term 'warranted' there are in fact two such concepts. For there is an important respect in which a belief may be warranted although we are subject to epistemic criticism for having that belief. We may be criticized on the ground that our doxastic state is not psychologically based on or derived from the relevant evidence in a rational way. We may not have taken account of enough of the relevant evidence. Or we may have made logical mistakes. Perhaps one mistake has compensated for another and has thereby yielded, fortuitously, the very conclusion that would have been reached by rational inference. In some of these cases we might be said to believe for the wrong reasons. Or perhaps we believe, at least in part, because we find the belief comforting. We may even believe, to take an extreme case, as a result of hypnotic suggestion, making it seem inappropriate, perhaps, to speak of our 'reasons' for believing. Yet in all these cases our belief might be justifiable by rational inference from our evidence. In all these cases there is some respect in which our belief is warranted and some respect in which it is not. Thus the term 'warranted belief' is ambiguous. There are two major epistemological questions, quite different from one another, that could be raised by asking 'Under what conditions is a belief warranted?'

To distinguish these two epistemic uses of the term 'warranted' we may adopt the traditional device for separating the 'logical content' of a belief from the psychological state of believing. We may distinguish *propositional* warrant from *doxastic* warrant. Let us suppose, for example, that Holmes knows at a certain time *t* that the coachman committed the murder. Holmes has studied the mud on the wheels of the carriage and from this and other evidence has reached a correct conclusion by rational inference. We may then employ the term 'warranted' to say two quite different things. We may say that the proposition 'The coachman did it' is warranted for Holmes at *t*. It is warranted *for* Holmes and not *for* Watson because it is warranted on the basis of evidence possessed only by Holmes. But we may also say that Holmes, because his conclusion is based rationally on the evidence, is warranted *in believing* that the coachman did it.

This distinction between propositional and doxastic warrant is dramatized if we now suppose that Holmes shows Watson the mud and gives him all the other relevant evidence he has, without telling him what conclusion he has drawn from it. In one important respect a change has occurred in Watson's epistemic condition. We may express this fact by saying that the proposition 'The coachman did it' is now warranted for Watson. It is warranted for Watson whether or not he believes that the coachman did it. But even if Watson does believe that the coachman did it, we cannot therefore conclude that Watson, like Holmes, is warranted *in believing* that the coachman did it. Believing a proposition *p* is a necessary condition for being warranted in believing *p*. But Watson's belief might not be based rationally on the evidence.

Thus we cannot construe all attributions of epistemic warrant as epistemic assessments of actual psychological states. Nor can we construe them all as assessments of the way actual psychological states are related to one another. For the proposition 'The coachman did it' may be warranted for Watson even though Watson does not believe the proposition. This is not to say, of course, that psychological states are irrelevant to propositional warrant. When Holmes shows Watson the mud on the carriage and provides him with other pertinent evidence, he adds to and changes some of Watson's psychological states. Watson subsequently believes, for example – something he had not noticed before – that the mud is reddish brown in color. Without raising the difficult problems posed by the concept of evidence, we may say loosely that Watson's 'evidential psychological states' have been changed. And it is just because of this change that the proposition 'The coachman did it' is now warranted for Watson. We might perhaps say, therefore, that this assessment of propositional warrant is a judgment about the evidential relationship between certain psychological states and the proposition 'The coachman did it.' With appropriate qualifications we might want to call this a 'logical' relationship.

This is enough to show that no single form of ethical analysis can be adequate to both of the epistemic concepts expressed by the term 'warranted'. For when we say of Holmes that, unlike Watson, he is warranted *in believing* that the coachman did it, we are obviously saying something about a causal relationship between one set of psychological states, viz., Holmes' evidential states, and another psychological state, viz., Holmes' belief that the coachman did it. We are attributing a particular belief to Holmes and we are making an epistemic judgment about the manner in which he arrived at his belief. We are judging, at least in part, that his conclusion was derived rationally from the evidence. Terms like 'caused', 'arrived at', and 'derived from', raise difficult philosophical problems. But it is enough for present purposes to agree that an assessment of doxastic warrant requires psychological information that is irrelevant to assessments of propositional warrant. We must know something about how Holmes' mind has worked if we are to know that he is warranted in believing that the coachman did it.

What has been said so far, however, does not show that assessments of epistemic warrant cannot be construed as ethical appraisals. It shows only that at least two different formulas would be required for the analysis of statements about epistemic warrant into ethical statements – one formula for propositional warrant and one for doxastic warrant. We might wonder, furthermore, whether there may not be some way of analyzing one kind of warrant in terms of the other. If we knew how to formulate such an analysis we could concentrate our attention on the more basic concept of warrant. If we knew how to reduce this more basic concept to ethical terms, we should know how to reduce the other as well. Is such a reduction possible?

We have observed that the epistemological question 'What is knowledge?' cannot be answered fully unless we first answer the question 'Under what conditions is a belief warranted?' But it is now clear that the latter question should be interpreted as a question about the conditions of doxastic warrant, not propositional warrant. To decide whether Watson knows that the coachman did it we must decide whether or not Watson is justified in believing that the coachman did it. Thus if Watson believes that the coachman did it we must decide whether his conclusion is based rationally on the evidence. To satisfy the conditions of knowledge it is not enough that the proposition believed be one that is warranted for Watson. Since doxastic warrant has this ultimate importance for theory of knowledge, it is tempting to suppose that we can analyze propositional warrant in terms of doxastic warrant.

But how could this be done? From the fact that a proposition p is warranted for a person S, together with the fact that S believes p, we cannot infer that S arrives at his doxastic state in a rational way. The two facts are compatible with the supposition that S believes p for the wrong reasons or even as a consequence of hypnotic suggestion. Thus we cannot hope to reduce propositional warrant to doxastic warrant by using a hypothetical statement in the subjunctive mood. We cannot say that 'p is warranted for S' is short for 'If S were to believe p then S would be warranted in believing p.' For if S were to believe p S might not do so rationally. And no elaboration of this formula is going to help. For in assessing doxastic warrant we must employ as a standard of rationality the very standard that we employ in assessing propositional warrant. There seem also to be other standards that must be satisfied in order for S to be warranted in believing p. But one standard, in any case, is the same. S cannot be warranted in believing p unless S arrives at his belief in a way that corresponds, in an appropriate way, to the evidential relationships in virtue of which p is warranted for S. For present purposes we can avoid the important philosophical problems raised by this talk of correspondence. It is enough for us to agree that we cannot know what it means to say that S arrives at his belief that p in a rational way unless we understand what it means to say that p is warranted for S.

This fact may encourage us to explore the alternative way of reducing one epistemic concept of warrant to the other. Perhaps when we say that S is warranted in believing p we may be saying (1) that p is warranted for S and (2) something else, something that does not presuppose any concept of warrant other than that of propositional warrant. Any analysis of this kind would have to be extremely complicated. It would take many pages even to describe the epistemological problems we should have to solve before such an analysis could be formulated. But with respect to the topic of this essay we can at least say this: To show that the two concepts of epistemic warrant can be analyzed in ethical terms, the unavoidable first step is to provide a satisfactory ethical analysis of propositional warrant. If we can do this we must next decide whether this ethical analysis can be transferred to doxastic warrant by way of some analysis of doxastic warrant into propositional warrant. If we decide that this cannot be done we may then attempt an independent ethical analysis of doxastic warrant — an analysis that does not presuppose the logical reducibility of one concept of warrant to the other. The rest of this essay will be devoted to discussion of the unavoidable first step in this series. There are good reasons for thinking that the entire enterprise is doomed to failure because propositional warrant cannot be analyzed in ethical terms.

In principle an ethical analysis of epistemic statements of the form 'p is warranted for S' might be either categorical or hypothetical. Suppose for example that someone proposed to interpret 'p is warranted for S' to mean that it would be good or fitting for S to believe p, or to mean that S has the duty (right, etc.) to behave in a way that will result in his believing p. Such analyses are categorical. They do not all involve the same ethical concept. But they all convert epistemic statements about propositional warrant into unqualified ethical appraisals of something or other – of doxastic states, of acts, of possible states of affairs, or perhaps of something else. Suppose, on the other hand, that these epistemic statements could be reduced to ethical statements of the form: 'If such and such conditions were to obtain then S would have the duty (right, etc.) to believe p (or to do such and such other thing).' In that case the epistemic assessment would be a qualified or restricted ethical appraisal. In saying that the proposition 'The coachman did it' is warranted for Watson, we should not be declaring categorically that Watson has the duty (right, etc.) to believe or do anything at all. But we could nevertheless be saying something of ethical significance about Watson, something that could not have been truthfully said of him before Holmes showed him the telltale mud on the carriage. For he would now have a conditional duty or right that he did not have previously. The if-clause in an analysis of this kind may or may not contain ethical terms; but any such non-categorical analysis can be classified as hypothetical.

It does not require much argument to show that no ethical analysis of propositional warrant will be satisfactory if it is categorical in form. The reason for this is simply that no epistemic fact is logically sufficient to settle a categorical ethical question. Categorical ethical questions remain 'open,' to use a familiar term, whatever assumptions we may make about epistemic warrant. Suppose for example that a person believes at a time t that (p) he has been completely cured of a dangerous illness. An epistemic question arises: we wonder whether p is warranted for S at t. It is obvious that we are not asking categorically whether it is good for S to believe that he has been cured – or whether it is desirable, fitting, right, virtuous, or praiseworthy for S to believe that he has been cured. We are not asking whether S ought to believe this or whether it is his duty or right to believe this. For to ask any of these questions is to raise issues that are irrelevant to our epistemic question. Has S made some commitments that impose on him a special obligation to avoid 'wishful thinking' about his own health? Would S be setting a bad example for someone else if he did not base his decision rationally on the evidence? What ethical weight should be given to the fact that S will be happier if he believes that he has been cured? These are important questions if we want to make a categorical ethical evaluation of S's believing that he has been cured. But they are irrelevant if we want to know only whether p is epistemically warranted for S.

A categorical ethical analysis of propositional warrant might be more subtle or more complex than any analysis just suggested. But the objection to analyses of this form is general enough to spare us the effort of exploring the whole range of possibilities. The argument is of course a dialectical one, one that assumes some degree of conceptual agreement. But it is as conclusive as any argument could be either for or against the reducibility of epistemic statements to categorical ethical statements. The truth of a categorical ethical statement may depend in some non-logical way on the truth of an epistemic statement. It could be maintained, for example, that the fact that a proposition is epistemically warranted for S always tends to *make* it a proposition that S ought to believe. More plausibly we could restrict this principle to cases in which S is choosing between two incompatible propositions. We could say, in one familiar terminology, that in such a case S has a *prima facie* duty to believe that proposition, if there is one, that is warranted for S. Someone might conceivably take a stronger position and argue that if a proposition is epistemically warranted for S in such a case, that fact is always *sufficient* to make it a proposition that S ought to believe. But whatever this 'ought-making' relationship may be, it is not the one required for conceptual reducibility. No epistemic fact is logically sufficient to settle a categorical ethical question.

The issues become more complicated when we ask whether assessments of propositional warrant can be construed not as categorical but as restricted or hypothetical ethical appraisals. Two possibilities should be distinguished: (1) The if-clause in a proposed ethical analysis may contain no ethical terms. Statements about propositional warrant are thus interpreted as statements about what it is good, right, fitting, etc. to believe, or about what someone ought to do, try to do, etc., under certain conditions describable in language that is 'ethically neutral.' They will presumably be conditions intended to discount certain factors that are supposed to be ought-making, obligation-making, good-making, etc. But the if-clause will be formulated without using terms like 'ought', 'obligation', and 'good'. Perhaps 'p is epistemically warranted for S' might be interpreted to mean that S ought to believe p if S's believing p would result in no less human happiness than S's failing to believe p. Perhaps the if-clause will refer to interests, to promises and agreements, to the development of rational powers, and so on. (2) The if-clause in a proposed analysis may contain ethical terms. Statements about propositional warrant may be interpreted, for example, as statements about what one ought to believe or do if one has such and such *duties*.

Hypothetical analyses of kind (1) are obviously open to the same objection that disposes so conclusively of proposed categorical analyses. However the hypothetical ethical statement is formulated, its truth can still be challenged by raising ethical issues that are irrelevant to the truth of the epistemic statement. The if-clause can discount some of the issues that would be relevant if the analysis were categorical. It can do this by stipulating that certain conditions, conditions that might be considered 'ought-making,' do not obtain. Thus in the example given above the if-clause rules out the argument that we ought sometimes to believe epistemically unwarranted propositions because believing them will increase human happiness. But in principle there is no limit to the factors that could be ethically relevant to the question whether we ought sometimes to believe unwarranted propositions. The fact that a proposition is epistemically warranted is not logically sufficient to determine the truth of any hypothetical ethical statement of type (1), even one that discounts, one by one, all the ethical arguments that anyone will ever use in favor of believing an epistemically unwarranted proposition.

Some hypothetical analyses of type (2), however, cannot be disposed of quite so easily. For by using ethical terms in the if-clause we are freed from the hopeless task of trying to discount, one by one, all the various ethical arguments that might be advanced in favor of believing an epistemically unwarranted proposition. We may be able, without circularity, to define some duties such that anyone who has just those duties ought to believe (has the right to believe, etc.) a proposition if it is epistemically warranted. And it may seem possible to do this in a way that protects our analysis fully from the 'open question' test. We may think that if *p* is warranted for *S* and the specified ethical conditions obtain, then it follows *logically* that *S* ought to believe *p*. If adequate conditions of this kind could be formulated, epistemic facts would be logically sufficient to settle certain ethical questions. From the fact that *p* is warranted for *S* we could indeed deduce that *S* ought to believe *p* under the conditions specified.

We must of course be careful to avoid the kind of circularity we have already discussed. If the conditions we define are to yield an analysis of propositional warrant, they must not be conditions describable only by presupposing the concept of propositional warrant. The conditions cannot refer, for example, to a duty to believe *rationally*. They cannot refer to a duty to *try one's best* to believe true propositions, if this entails trying rationally as opposed, say, to trying very hard by studying the entrails of sacrificial victims. Nor will it do to say that a statement of the form 'p is warranted for S' can be analysed roughly as follows: 'If S were choosing between p and *not-p*, and S's only duty were epistemic, then S ought to believe (or to react in some other specified way to) p.' For we have seen that the concept of propositional warrant, the concept we are attempting to analyze, is presupposed by the concept of doxastic warrant and hence by the concept of knowledge. And how could we identify what we call an epistemic duty without employing any of these concepts?

It should be observed, furthermore, that it is far from obvious that our epistemic duty is always to believe warranted propositions. The distinction between propositional and doxastic warrant suggests the possibility that we have duties with respect to each, duties that can conflict. Suppose that the proposition (p) 'The coachman did it' is warranted for Watson at t, but that Watson does not believe p at t. Suppose also that if Watson were to believe p at t he would not be warranted in believing it. He would reach his conclusion irrationally. Does Watson have a duty to believe p even though he would in fact do so irrationally? Or shall we say that his only epistemic duty with respect to believing any proposition is to believe it rationally? (This would mean, so to speak, that his only epistemic duty is doxastic and not propositional.) Or is this a case of conflicting *prima facie* duties? These and many similar questions would have to be answered before we should have an adequate theory of epistemic duty.

If the duties or obligations specified in the if-clause of our analysis must be defined without using epistemic terms, our only hope lies in making an appeal of some sort to a duty to believe propositions if and only if they are *true* — or, in short, a 'duty to truth.' To the extent that we are fully rational we consider a proposition to be true only if we consider it to be warranted. Does this fact provide us with a suitable ethical connection between believing a true proposition and believing a warranted proposition? Could we maintain, for example, that 'p is warranted for S at t' means that if S's only duty at t were to believe p if and only if p is true, then S ought to believe p at t^*. An analysis like this cannot be accused of circularity on the ground that the if-clause presupposes the concept of propositional warrant. If it is circular it is circular for another reason. It seems to me that the analysis has at least an initial plausibility, and some of the things I shall say about it are based on this assumption.

Let us begin by asking whether an analysis of this kind can survive the open question test. Is the truth of 'p is warranted for S' logically sufficient to guarantee the truth of the hypothetical statement that constitutes the proposed analysis? Or are there ethical issues that are relevant to the truth of the hypothetical statement but irrelevant to the truth of '*p* is warranted for *S*'? I shall consider just two examples of ethical issues that might seem to show that the analysis fails the open question test. It is important to see what form a defense of the analysis must take.

There are, first, the issues already discussed when we asked whether there are duties associated with doxastic warrant that can conflict with a duty to believe warranted propositions. It might be argued, for example, that if *p* is warranted for *S*, and if *S*'s only duty is to believe *p* if and only if *p* is true, what follows is not that *S* ought to believe *p* but that *S* ought to believe *p* rationally. *S* ought to believe *p* in such a way (or under such conditions) that *S* is warranted in believing *p*. Or it might be argued that there is at least an ethical issue here, an issue irrelevant to the truth of '*p* is warranted for *S*.' To this objection a natural reply, whether or not it is ultimately satisfactory, would be to say that it does not matter whether or not *S* believes *p* rationally. If *S*'s duty is just to believe *p* if and only if *p* is true, and *p* is warranted, what is required of *S* is just that he believe *p*. Believing *p* rationally may be a way to fulfill other duties, but it is not necessary in order to fulfill *S*'s duty to truth.

A second objection might run as follows: It is a mistake to say that under the conditions stipulated what *S* ought to do is to believe *p*. What *S* ought to do is to believe *p if and only if he thinks p is warranted*. For how could *S* be ethically required to believe *p* if he does not believe that *p* is warranted? This objection cannot be met simply by reminding us of the distinction often drawn between a 'subjective' and an 'objective' use of 'ought'. The proposal is not the trivial one that *S* ought (subjectively) to believe *p* if and only if *S* thinks he ought (objectively) to believe *p*. The proposal is that under the specified conditions *S* ought (objectively) to believe *p* if and only if he thinks *p* is warranted. What *S* may happen to think about the *ethical issues* is irrelevant. And again the natural reply, whatever its ultimate merit, is that it does not matter what *S* believes about the warrant of *p*. If *S*'s duty is to believe *p* if and only if *p* is true, and *p* is warranted, what is required of *S* is just that he believe *p*. That is all that is necessary to fulfill his duty to truth. Of course he cannot fulfill his duty to truth *intentionally* without making a judgment about the warrant of *p*. But that fact is irrelevant.

It is possible, then, to give some sort of reply to the charge that the proposed analysis fails to meet the open question test. But the reply is formulated in terms like 'required' and 'necessary', terms which suggest that to pass the open question test the analysis must be interpreted in a way that makes it circular. For what does it mean to say that if p is warranted and S believes p, S has done all that is *necessary* to fulfill his duty to believe p if and only if p is true? Why should we not say instead that if p is *true* and S believes p, S has done all that is necessary to fulfill his duty to believe p if and only if p is true? For if p is true surely S must believe p in order to fulfill his duty to truth. And if S does *that*, viz., believes p when p is true, why does it matter whether or not p is warranted? Are we perhaps tempted to think that what we have here is a causal connection, 'necessary' in virtue of laws of nature? If we could maintain that believing warranted propositions is a causally necessary condition for believing true propositions, we might be able to explain how a duty to truth becomes converted to a duty to warrant. We might appeal to the principle sometimes expressed by saying that a duty includes the necessary (causal) means. We might think that this is a logical principle derivable by analysis of the concept of duty. But whatever the theoretical status of this principle, and whatever its merits, it is irrelevant in the present context. It is an obvious fact that we do sometimes believe true propositions that are not warranted. Thus the 'necessary' connection, if there is one, between believing true propositions and believing warranted propositions, cannot be a causal connection.

This brings us to the heart of the difficulty faced by any proposed analysis of the kind we are considering, any analysis that presupposes that a duty (right, etc.) to believe warranted propositions can be derived from a duty to believe true propositions. To survive the 'open question' test the conclusion that S ought to believe p must follow logically from the conditions stated in the if-clause together with the assumption that p is warranted for S. But unless there is some concealed circularity, how could the connection be a logical one? It is of course possible for a warranted proposition to be false — false because, as we say, the evidence is misleading. Suppose then, that p is warranted but false and that S's only duty is to believe p if and only if p is true. From these premises it surely does not follow logically that S ought to believe p. Believing a false proposition, whether or not the proposition is warranted, can never be the way to fulfill one's duty to believe that proposition if and only if it is true, much less a logically necessary way to fulfill that duty.

Is there any respect at all, then, in which the duty to believe true propositions might be said to make it necessary for us to believe warranted propositions? Could we say, perhaps, that there is a necessary connection if, or to the extent that, we are *rational*? Do we unwittingly read some assumption about rationality into our analysis when we suppose that a duty to believe true propositions can impose on us a duty to believe warranted propositions? Do we in effect supply another if-clause so that the analysis, fully formulated, would be: 'If S were a perfectly rational person, and if S's only duty were to believe p if and only if p is true, S ought to believe p'? The analysis would of course be circular if some such if-clause were included in it. But we might at least have an explanation of its initial plausibility and of the kind of defense that comes to mind when we ask whether it can pass the 'open question' test.

Problems arise, however, when we try to define a perfectly rational person so that a duty to truth imposes on such a person a duty to believe warranted propositions. Although the term 'rational' is ambiguous, as our discussion of propositional and doxastic warrant has shown, for our present purpose we can define it by reference only to propositional warrant. Shall we say, then, that a perfectly rational being is a person who can believe propositions only if they are warranted? It would follow from this that a perfectly rational person *must* believe warranted propositions in order to believe true propositions. Such a person, unlike the rest of us, could never fulfill a duty to believe a proposition if and only if it is true by believing it if it is true but not warranted. Unfortunately, however, this is not enough to give us what we need. Rationality, so defined, restricts the ways in which a duty to truth can be fulfilled. But it still does not allow us to deduce a duty to believe a proposition if it is warranted from a duty to believe a proposition if and only if it is true. For suppose again that p is warranted but false. Can anyone, even a perfectly rational person, fulfill the duty to believe p if and only if p is true by believing p when p is false? We might say that the perfectly rational person who believes p when p is warranted but false has 'tried his best.' But in this case his best is not good enough. His very rationality, we might say, prevents him from fulfilling his duty to truth.

There is, I think, no other way to define rationality so that the additional if-clause allows us to deduce a duty to believe warranted propositions from a duty to truth. There is, that is to day, no ordinary use of the term 'rational' that can give us this result. If the analysis we are considering is circular, therefore, and if its initial plausibility is a consequence of its circularity, where is the hidden epistemic term? The answer, I think, lies in a certain familiar ambiguity of ethical terms, an ambiguity that moral philosophers have often recognized in one way or another. We may say that there is an 'epistemic use' of ethical terms, a use to be distinguished both from a subjective use and an objective use. The plausibility of the analysis lies in the fact that the word 'duty' in the if-clause ('S's only due is to believe p if and only if *p* is true') occurs in its objective use, but the word 'ought' in the consequent ('*S* ought to believe *p*') occurs in its epistemic use.

On reflection it is not surprising that ethical terms are ambiguous in this way and not surprising that the ambiguity should sometimes escape our notice. To the extent that we are morally motivated we want to do our objective duty (or what is objectively right, fitting, etc.). And if I am rational I shall believe that a particular act *x* is my objective duty only if the proposition '*x* is my objective duty' is epistemically warranted for me. So if I *want* to act rationally I shall want to know what act is my *epistemic* duty, *i.e.*, what act *x* is such that the proposition '*x* is my objective duty' is epistemically warranted for me. My epistemic duty may of course not be my objective duty. The evidence I have may be misleading. And it may not be my subjective duty (i.e., what I *think* to be my objective duty). But to the extent that I am rational it becomes, so to speak, the immediate object of my quest. When I ask 'What ought I to do?' I may be asking what I ought *epistemically* to do. And if I reply that I ought to do *x* I may mean that I ought *epistemically* to do *x*.

This is still not quite enough to explain the plausibility of the analysis we are considering. For if *p* is warranted for *S*, and if *S*'s only duty is to believe *p* if and only if *p* is true, we cannot deduce that *S* ought epistemically to believe *p*. We can only deduce, given our definition of the epistemic use of ethical terms, that *S* ought epistemically to believe *p* provided that the proposition 'My only objective duty is to believe *p* if and only if *p* is true' is warranted for him. If this ethical proposition is not warranted the fact that *p* is warranted will not yield the conclusion that *S* ought epistemically to believe *p*. But it is easy to read this additional premise into the analysis. One slightly indirect way to do this would be by assuming that *S knows* what his objective duty is. Thus the initial plausibility of the proposed analysis of '*p* is warranted for *S*' would be a result of the fact that we read it approximately as follows: 'If *S* knows that his only duty is to believe *p* if and only if *p* is true, *S* ought epistemically to believe *p*.' When read this way it presupposes at two points the concept of propositional warrant that it is supposed to analyze.

In all important respects this proposed analysis seems to be representative of analyses that attempt to derive a duty (right, etc.) to believe warranted propositions from a duty to truth. If an analysis of this kind is at all plausible, therefore, we shall probably discover that it employs ethical terms in their epistemic use, a use that presupposes the concept of propositional warrant. Thus there is good reason to think that epistemic concepts cannot be reduced to ethical concepts. Concepts of the two kinds may be similar in important respects. Perhaps they can be analyzed in somewhat analogous ways. But that is another matter.

Harvard University

NOTES

* An analysis of 'epistemic preferability,' of this general type though more complicated, is proposed by R.M. Chisholm in his *Person and Object*, Allen and Unwin, London, 1976, p. 176. My discussion of this type of analysis, in particular what I say about circularity, is intended to be general enough to apply to Chisholm's proposal.

KURT BAIER

MORAL REASONS AND REASONS TO BE MORAL*

From the thirties to the sixties the three moralists honored in this volume dominated ethical theory in this country. There are few areas on which none of them has left a lasting imprint. Where they disagree – and that is not infrequently – the controversy continues to be lively and illuminating.

In looking for a suitable topic on which all three have made contributions, and on which I have not merely adopted the view of one or the other of them (which conveniently narrows the field) I settled on the problem of the nature and scope of moral reasons. Stevenson's account[1] which denies validity to moral reasons is surely the most challenging and probably the most challenged. My views here are closer to those of Brandt[2] and closest to those of Frankena[3] as will be apparent to readers familiar with their work. But since in this paper I wish to develop further the theory of moral reasons they began, I shall arrange my discussion, not around their published work[4], but around an important problem which, though frequently tackled, has so far remained without a satisfactory solution. In the course of my investigation I hope to make clearer than this has been done before, the nature of moral and other practical reasons and with the help of the insights gained solve the problem. I also hope that my discussion will reveal the considerable debt all those who have written in this area owe to the celebrated Michigan Trio.

Since the appearance, in 1912, of Prichard's paper, 'Does Moral Philosophy Rest on a Mistake?'[5], many philosophers have regarded 'Why be moral?' as an illegitimate question. At first, this idea seemed to resolve a disturbing impasse which had arisen between those who saw no real conflict between duty and interest, and those who saw such a conflict but nevertheless insisted on the rationality of always doing one's duty even when that conflicted with one's interest. But the weaknesses of this idea soon became apparent. For if it is not legitimate to ask why one should be moral, then presumably there can *be* no reason to be moral. There can be nothing that is either an ingredient in, or can be brought about only by, being moral such that everyone has adequate reason to aim at it. But then, surely, morality is merely a predilection of 'moral' people, that is, of those who happen to *like* being moral for what it is. Virtue is truly its own reward, though only for those who go for that sort of thing. Following the precepts of morality

231

A. I. Goldman and J. Kim (eds.), Values and Morals, 231–256. All Rights Reserved.
Copyright © 1978 by D. Reidel Publishing Company, Dordrecht, Holland.

is like following the rules of chess or of etiquette: one does it because one likes to play chess or to be refined, and because one cannot do or be either, without following the relevant rules.[6] However, such a conception cannot make clear why we *should* feel guilty or ashamed if we do not thrill to the moral enterprise, or how we can in reason expect others to be moral who do not thrill to it. If we are rational, our attitude towards such people must be either, 'Well, too bad, you'll never know what you are missing' or 'You had better behave as if you did like it or else we shall make you regret it.' The former would imply that whether one is moral or immoral is solely one's own business, which seems to run counter to one of our deep convictions about morality. And the latter seems to imply that the social pressure in support of everyone's being moral is simply the brute imposition of the tastes of the dominant on the subject group.

To me, the Egoist position, that there can be no conflict between morality and self-interest, and the Prichardian position that there can be and frequently is such a conflict but that there is no sense to the question why one should be moral rather than selfish, seem deeply unsatisfactory. They draw their main support from the conviction that there can be no reason to be moral if and because duty and interest do not necessarily coincide. If this convinction could be shown to be false, the Egoist and Prichardian views would lose all appeal. In this paper I do three things: In section I, I elucidate one interpretation of 'Why be moral?', which I believe to be the central though not the only one in which that question makes perfectly good sense; in section II, I give an answer to this question which does not presuppose that duty and interest coincide; and in section III, I meet some objections and remove some common confusions and misunderstandings, which block acceptance of my answer to the question.

I

1.

Let us begin with the relatively unproblematic part of our question, namely, 'being moral'. We can deal briefly with one of its important senses, namely, 'being the opposite of *amoral*'. The amoralist is a person who does not participate in the moral enterprise. He does not play any of the various roles of what Butler called 'the institution of morality'. He not merely does not (like the immoral man) play the role of moral agent, i.e., the role of someone trying to conform his behavior to the requirements of morality, but he does not defend himself when others accuse him of wrongdoing, does not accuse others when they do wrong, nor pass judgment on them, nor attempt to change other people's moral convictions when he thinks they are mistaken: he simply ignores the whole moral enterprise. It is significant that no philosopher (as far as I know) has ever been troubled by the question why people should not be *a*moral. I believe the underlying reason is that everyone takes it to be in his own interest that other people should be moral and that, therefore, it is in his interest that he should play at least the subsidiary moral roles designed to keep others to the straight and narrow path of virtue. In any case, I shall not in this paper examine this particular interpretation of the question, although it is clearly an important sense and one not even prima facie open to the objection that it is illegitimate.

2.

The second, more commonly entertained sense of 'being moral' is 'being the opposite of immoral', i.e., of doing what one knows or has good reason to believe is wrong. One can grant that everyone has an interest in not being *a*moral without having to grant that the requirements of morality never conflict with the counsels of self-interest. And one may insist that on such occasions of conflict one does not have adequate reason to be moral, though one may well have adequate reason *to pretend* to be, in order not to lose the good will of one's neighbors on whom one depends. It is this second sense of 'being moral' with which I am concerned in this paper.

3.

More difficult is the interpretation of 'Why?' in 'Why be moral?' As Prichard rightly points out, this question "implies a state of unwillingness or indifference towards the action"[7], and so the question is naturally interpreted as a request to supply considerations in favor of this action, e.g., 'to keep our engagements [even] to our loss', or more generally, 'always to be moral even when it is not in our interest'.

4.

There are, however, two importantly different ways of interpreting such requests, which I shall call, 'motivation' and 'validation' requests, respectively.[8] A few preliminary remarks will make this distinction clearer.

5.

Some of a person's behavior, e.g., the contraction of the pupil, breathing, the knee jerk, and so on, is explicable without reference to what he takes to be the state of his environment. My interest in this paper is solely in behavior whose explanation involves such references to the agent's beliefs about the world around him. Consider, then, a set of people seeing, in their morning paper, an account of certain terrible happenings in a Nazi concentration camp during World War II. Some may quickly turn to other news items, others may read on avidly to the end, yet others may be moved to write something in their diaries, others to send letters to the local paper, and so on. The explanation of such behavior would need to make reference to the agent's attending to and interpreting certain supposed aspects of the world around him: that Jews and political opponents of the Nazis were tortured, starved, overworked, killed, and so on. We can call such facts 'motivating facts'. We can hope to discover general connections between such motivating facts and people's behavior. Thus, many people behave in characteristically angry or embarrassed ways when they attend to the (supposed) fact that they had made fools of themselves or had been laughed at behind their backs.

6.

An important subclass of such motivating facts is what we may call 'practical considerations,' that is, considerations to do certain specific things. They are those motivating facts which are, or involve, facts about the nature or consequences of *envisaged* behavior. If I believe that certain people have laughed at me behind my back, that may be for me a consideration to avoid them in future. Or if I believe that one eats well in a certain restaurant, this may be for me a consideration to go there the next time I eat out. What makes certain facts, e.g., that somebody laughed at one or that one eats well at Claridge's, considerations for one to do a certain specific thing, such as not to see that person again or to eat at Claridge's next time, is that doing these specific things, is a way of bringing about something one wants or preventing something one does not want: preventing being laughed at again by that person, and bringing it about that one is in a position to choose a good meal. What facts are such considerations may vary from person to person. The fact that someone laughed at him behind his back is not for everyone a consideration in favor of not seeing that person again. And, of course, even those for whom it is such a consideration may often not be actually moved to act in this way because this consideration is outbalanced by others which weigh more strongly with him.

7.

Practical considerations in this sense should be distinguished from practical reasons. Reasons for someone to do something are facts which *ought* to be considerations for him to do it, whether or not they actually are. Talk of reasons thus involves the ideal of rationality to which a rational agent (in the ability sense, see note 20) may or may not live up to. Suppose I have advertised a vacant position for a salesman in my business. Of the two applicants, one has blue eyes and blond hair, the other dark hair and a hook nose. Suppose also that these facts motivate me to choose the former rather than the latter. Such motivating facts may be practical considerations for me (as I have used the term) if I believe for instance that employing blue-eyed blonds and refusing employment to hook-nosed brunettes will have desired consequences. Suppose I also believe that all blue-eyed blonds are Aryans and all hook-nosed brunettes Semites, and suppose that the firm and I want to promote the interest of Aryans and to block that of Semites. Then these facts about these applicants will in all probability be considerations but they need not be *reasons* for me to act in this way. They may not be such even when I take them to be: thus, despite appearances both applicants may in fact be Aryans. And conversely, certain facts about these applicants, e.g., that the dark one speaks several languages and the other does not, may be reasons for me to appoint the dark one even though this fact does not weigh with me, i.e., is not *for me* a consideration to hire him. Again, there is the fact that the blond plays a good game of squash whereas the dark does not, which may be a consideration for me to appoint the blond, even though I believe that this fact is *not* a reason for me to do so: I believe, on the contrary, that this fact is irrelevant to the question of whom I should appoint. And again, this fact could well be a reason to appoint the blond even though I believe it is not.[9]

8.

When 'Why be moral?' is interpreted as a motivation request, the questioner wants to be told facts which would make the requirements of morality weigh with him, that is, would turn them into considerations for him to act accordingly. Suppose the fact that eating carbohydrates makes one fat is not for someone a consideration against eating carbohydrates. We can then probably turn this fact into a consideration for him if we tell him that he has a bad heart and that he is likely to have a heart attack soon if he does not lose weight. For presumably he will want to avoid having a heart attack soon. Similarly, if we can show to a merely prudent person, i.e., one for whom only the counsels of prudence are considerations, that his real interest is best promoted by following the precepts of morality, then we have 'reduced' the precepts of morality to the counsels of prudence and so have turned the precepts of morality into considerations for him.

'Being altruistic pays in the long run' or 'It is imprudent to be unpatriotic' purports to reduce considerations of altruism or patriotism ('Do this because it is altruistic or patriotic') to considerations of self-interest ('Do this because it pays or is prudent'). Such reductive claims can be supported by showing that considerations of one type are so related to considerations of another type, that if there is a consideration of the first type for doing something, there always is also a consideration of the other type for doing it.

Now, obviously, the appropriate direction of such a reduction must depend on the particular inclinations, tastes, aims, and principles of the questioner. A gambler or an artist may, for instance, ask 'Why should I be prudent?'. In such cases, 'It is immoral to be imprudent' or 'It would please mother' may be the appropriately directed reductions. They are appropriate, of course, if and only if morality and pleasing mother are already considerations for the questioner, i.e., already weigh with him.

Motivation requests of the form 'Why be X?', (e.g., patriotic, honest, prudent, moral) thus are properly raised only where *being X* is not already a consideration for the questioner. Suitable answers to such requests can therefore only be given by someone who knows what sorts of considerations already do weigh with the questioner and who knows of a reduction of the challenged considerations to others already weighing with the questioner. Motivation requests are thus typically made in contexts in which there is at least the appearance of conflict between following certain considerations which one does not yet accept and following those which one already accepts. An answer to such a request purports to show that in reality there is no such conflict because the considerations in question can be reduced to others the questioner already accepts.

It does seem plausible that 'Why be moral?' as a motivation request is illegitimate, or at best unlikely to receive a sound answer. Given the great variety of people's tastes, preferences, hopes and ideals, there are bound to be considerable individual differences in the considerations that weigh with them. It is therefore at best highly unlikely that there will always be suitable reductions of moral considerations, let alone that they will always be discoverable, and that they will be the same for everybody. Moreover, if, as many philosophers (including myself) believe, the moral order necessarily includes principles and precepts capable of coming into conflict with the counsels of self-interest, then the demand for a reduction of moral to prudential reasons is, from the nature of the case, incapable of being satisfied.

When it is a motivation request, 'Why be moral?' thus has a presupposition which is almost certainly false. For it presupposes that the requirements of morality can, for all of us, be turned, simply by an increase of suitable knowledge, into considerations for complying with them.[10]

9.

By contrast, when 'Why be moral?' is a validation request, it has no such presupposition. The agent may again be unwilling or indifferent towards an action required by morality, or he may be in doubt about the rationality of complying. In the typical case the agent believes, perhaps for good reasons, that in the situation in which he finds himself, the counsels of prudence and the requirements of morality conflict, and he wants to know which of these directives constitutes reasons for him (or anyone) to act accordingly; or if both are reasons, which of them is superior, which is the one he should in reason follow, and why? In such a case, the questioner acknowledges that there is no way of showing that the two apparently conflicting reasons do not really conflict, and that he must therefore set aside at least one of them. He wants to know which of these directives overrides which. As a validation request 'Why be moral?' implies either that everyone should or no one need always be moral, i.e., that either moral reasons always necessarily do or that they don't always necessarily override all other kinds of reason, and it asks for a demonstration and explanation of the answer.

10.

It may now, however, be objected that 'Why be moral?' is just as illegitimate when it is a validation request. We must examine three widely accepted objections of this type.

i) The first, Prichard's, is to the effect that the question expresses an illegitimate demand parallel to one made in epistemology. Prichard formulates it as follows:

Anyone who, stimulated by education, has come to feel the force of the various obligations in life, at some time or other comes to feel the irksomeness of carrying them out, and to recognize the sacrifice of interest involved; and, if thoughtful, he inevitably puts to himself the question: 'Is there really a reason why I should act in the ways in which hitherto I have thought I ought to act?'[11]

Prichard, then, argues, for reasons many (myself included) would consider insufficient, that one could never give a proof that what one had hitherto thought right really was right. Be that as it may, the impossibility of such a proof does not dispose of 'Why be moral?'. For in whatever way we can know what is right, whether by proof or by intuition, being moral will often be 'irksome' and involve 'sacrifice of interest', if our every-day intuitions and those of Prichard himself about the relation of morality and interest are correct. Prichard's and the classical moralists' formulation of their question, namely, 'What proof is there that we should follow our most firmly held moral convictions?' conceals the fact that it raises two rather different questions. One is Prichard's supposedly 'illegitimate' one, 'What proof is there that what we have always thought right really is right?'. The other is the question 'Why be moral when it is 'irksome'?'. The latter question is just as urgent (if not more so) if the first really is illegitimate and the requirements of morality are based merely on our intuitions. Thus, the mistake of the classical moralists was not that they asked a question which may (or may not) really be illegitimate. Their mistake was twofold: (i) that, like Prichard, they did not keep this possibly illegitimate question apart from 'Why be moral?' and (ii) their answer to 'Why be moral?' rested on an assumption which Prichard rightly rejects, namely, that requirements which are not in the individual's best interest cannot be sound moral requirements. They were driven to embrace this assumption because although, unlike Prichard, perceiving the importance of this question 'Why be moral?', they could construe it only as a motivation request by a merely prudent person.

ii) The second objection[12] begins with the premise that 'Why be moral?' as a validation request is asked when the questioner is confronted by conflicting prudential (or hedonic) reasons and moral ones. He wants reasons for being moral rather than prudent, i.e., for following the moral rather than the prudential reasons. There would therefore have to be, the argument continues, a third type of reasons, by references to which this sort of conflict could be settled. But, the argument concludes, there could not be such a third type of reasons, and if there were, it would be impossible to show that they were in a better position than either moral or prudential ones to serve as the supreme court of appeal when two types of reason conflicted. But if there can be no answer to 'Why be moral?', then the question must be illegitimate.

The answer to this objection is that 'Why be moral?' need not be a request for an additional type of practical reasons. Rather, it may be a request for an *elucidation* of the nature and content of prudential and moral reasons which would *explain why* what we call moral reasons always necessarily override prudential ones. This is not, of course, an easy thing to do, but the request to have it spelled out does not imply the existence of an impossible third type of practical reason, parallel to prudential and moral reasons, which could serve as a court of appeal.

iii) The third type of objection[13] says that 'Why be moral?' could not be such a request for an explanation of why moral reasons are necessarily overriding, for if they are to be necessarily so, they must be so by definition. But in that case, 'Why be moral?' unpacks into 'Why follow reasons which one always ought to follow?'. But this is as trivial a question as 'Why are circles circular?'.

Even if we accept this objection at face value, it is not very serious. For even if we grant that the question 'Why be moral?' is trivial, we could replace it by another non-trivial question, namely, 'Why call anything a *moral* reason?', i.e., a reason such that *by definition* it overrides all other kinds of reasons. Thus even granting the triviality of 'Why be moral?' would not get rid of the difficulties which made us raise that question in the first place.

In any case, we need not accept this objection at face value. From the fact that moral reasons are reasons which, *from their very nature*, override all other kinds of reasons, it does not follow that this is so, *by definition*. The difference can be brought out by an analogy. We can say that *smooth-cutting* carving knives are necessarily good ones, from the very definition of the terms involved, whereas *sharp* carving knives are from their very nature and necessarily good ones but not from the definition of the term involved.[14] Good carving knives are those which serve their purpose well. Their purpose is to cut meat smoothly. This much is implied by the meaning of the terms. But to show that a carving knife is the better the sharper it is, requires the establishment of a necessary factual (causal) connection between the sharpness and smooth-cuttingness of carving knives. The expression 'carving knife' is a partly functional one, in that it implies that the artefact referred to has the purpose of cutting meat smoothly. But it implies nothing about the smooth-cuttingness-*making* properties of carving knives. Hence the question, 'Why are smooth-cutting carving knives necessarily good ones?' is comparatively trivial, while 'Why are sharp carving knives necessarily good ones?' is not.

Now, the expression 'moral reasons' may be a partly functional expression like 'smooth-cutting carving knife'. It is then defined as 'reason which by definition overrides all others'. On that account 'Why be moral', (i.e., 'Why follow moral reasons when they conflict with other kinds?') may look relatively trivial. For it may be read as the request to spell out the functional definition. But it need not be read in this way, for even when 'moral reasons' is a partly functional expression, 'Why be moral?' need not, and normally would not be a request to spell out the functional definition. Rather, it may be a request to *spell out the moral-making properties* of such reasons and to show why the possession of such properties makes such reasons such as necessarily to override all other kinds.

In any case, 'moral reason' may also be used as an expression comparable to 'sharp carving knife', in which case 'Why be moral?' is analogous to 'Why are sharp carving knives necessarily good ones?', i.e., 'Why are reasons such as, 'you promised', 'it is a violation of someone's right', 'it would do him serious harm', etc., necessarily reasons overriding all other kinds?'. In that case, it is clearly not trivial at all.

II

11.

I now take it for granted that 'Why be moral?' often means, 'What is it about moral reasons that makes them necessarily overriding?' and that this question makes perfectly good sense, and is important. What is the answer?

The question breaks down into the following: (1) What makes something a practical reason? (2) What makes a practical reason a moral one? (3) What is it about moral reasons that makes them necessarily overriding? Obviously, a complete answer to 'Why be moral?' would involve an adequate theory of practical reasons and of morality, tasks far beyond the scope of this paper. However, I think I can formulate a set of intuitively plausible assumptions from which an answer to our question can be derived.

Concerning (1), I make assumptions of two kinds. The first kind concerns the nature of practical reasons and reasoning, the second is a single substantive assumption about what sorts of things are practical reasons.

I make four assumptions of the first kind: I have already mentioned one, namely,

(i) '*F* is a reason for *X* to do *A*' implies that if *X* were a perfectly rational person, a person conforming to the ideal of rationality, then *F* would *weigh with him* in favor of doing *A*.

(ii) The consequences concerning the satisfactoriness of the lives of those who believe that *F* is a reason for them to do *A* are relevant to the soundness of this belief.

(iii) The growth of practical knowledge (sound action-guides, as Frankena would say) requires a group's provisional acceptance of universal principles, the result of whose general employment provides a test for their soundness.

(iv) It must be possible for *everyone* always to be perfectly rational; or, in other words, no practical principles could be sound principles of practical reason which could be such only if they were not universally followed.

Assumption (i) tells us something about *the force of*, or what is *meant by saying that*, a certain fact is a reason for someone to do a certain thing. The other three assumptions state general constraints on substantive hypotheses about *the grounds* for claiming that a fact is such a reason. Now the only such substantive hypothesis I shall make is

(v) Facts showing that X's doing A would be in X's best interest, constitute reasons for X to do A.

12.

It is important to distinguish hypothesis (v) from the theory of reasons often called Rational Egoism which combines (v) with

(vi) *Only* facts showing that X's doing A would be in X's best interest constitute reasons for X to do A,

or

(vi') Facts showing that X's doing A would be in X's best interest are *the supreme reasons* for X to do A.

If Rational Egoism were sound, then either moral reasons could never conflict with the counsels of self-interest or moral reasons would necessarily be overriden by reasons of self-interest. Both of these corollaries run counter to our virtually axiomatic convictions about the nature of morality and moral reasons. It is, however, easy to see that self-interest is not the only or necessarily the supreme type of reason. As has been pointed out by those philosophers who claim that self-realization is man's highest aim, (T. H. Green, F. H. Bradley), it should be noted that, as a matter of psychological fact, many people, perhaps all, would find their lives more satisfying, fulfilling, or meaningful, if they cared for or loved not only themselves but also some other people and so were willing to promote the interests of these others, at times even at the expense of their own. A woman, herself poor and hungry, may send money and food to a soldier, not in the hope of reaping reciprocal benefits later, but simply because she loves him and wishes to give him pleasure and support, despite the fact that she can ill afford to part with what she is sending him. In being moral and at the same time acting contrary to her own interest, this woman nevertheless does not thereby make her own life poorer than it would be if she did not help him. On the contrary, she would forever despise herself if she had promoted her own interest in preference to that of her beloved.

It would seem, then, that always following what is in one's best interest might well make one's life less fulfilling and so less good than if one occasionally set aside one's best interest for the sake of others about whom one cared. I believe it would be generally conceded that facts showing that one's life would be more fulfilling if one did A rather than B, constitute reasons for doing A, that facts showing that it is in one's best interest to do B rather than A constitute reasons for doing B, and that reasons of self-fulfillment *override* reasons of self-interest when the two conflict. The main support one can give for this plausible belief is that self-interest as ordinarily understood is concerned mainly with one's well-being and one's position, both concerning protection against blows of fortune and opportunities and abilities to do things one considers worthwhile. The main reason why self-interest is basic to rationality, is thus simply that it is a *normally indispensable means* to a fulfilling life. But when promoting one's interest, i.e., improving one's position for making one's life more fulfilling actually makes it less fulfilling, then reasons of self-interest are overriden by reasons of self-fulfillment.

Reasons of self-fulfillment, whether self-interested or other-interested, are necessarily *self-anchored*, i.e., grounded in the satisfactoriness of *the agent's own* life. If I love my aunt, the fact that my visiting her in the hospital will please her, is a self-anchored other-interested reason for me to visit her in the hospital, and if I love her a lot, it may be a weightier reason than many of the self-anchored self-interested reasons I may also have for doing other things. But if I do not care for my aunt, I may have no self-anchored reason to visit her.

13.

The question now arises whether an adequate system of reasons could be built solely on the basis of such self-anchored reasons. Hobbes certainly and Bentham possibly thought so.[15] Hobbes believed that if everyone followed only reasons of self-interest, then in the absence of a coercive social order the resulting state of affairs would be necessarily undesirable. But he also believed that it was in everyone's interest to have such a coercive social order regulating interpersonal relations so as to make unnecessary and to prevent the settling of conflicts of interest by force or cunning. I accept this part of his argument. However, he also maintained that the existence of such an order so transforms the circumstances for those living under it that they have adequate reason to think that it is always in their best interest to satisfy the social requirements. In other words, he thought he could answer an egoist's motivation request why he should always obey the law. However, Hobbes' only argument for this conclusion seems to me specious. He argues, soundly enough, (in *Leviathan*, XV) that anyone violating the law can gain from his violation only by 'the errors of other men'. But then he goes on to say, what is surely false, that 'he could not foresee, nor reckon upon' such errors, and so he always acts contrary to reasons when he breaks the law. But plainly, in most societies if not all, it is not always impossible or even unlikely that a person should be able to tell with very great certainty, and with comparatively little risk to himself should he be mistaken, that he will not be caught. Thus, from the fact that Hobbes can demonstrate the universal need for a coercive social order which authoritatively settles conflicts of concerns, it does not follow that there is adequate self-anchored (let alone self-interested) reason for every member of such an order always to follow its coercive rules and requirements, nor of course that these requirements themselves constitute reasons for everyone to act accordingly.

There are important inherent weaknesses in this Hobbesian thesis. A community of rational egoists who suspect each other of being rational egoists, have adequate reason both to break the social rules when doing so is to their advantage and to ensure that others will never be in that position. They will therefore want to ensure, by stringent policies of 'law and order', that crime does not pay *other people*. At the same time they will attempt, perhaps by bribes, threats, and other methods, to bend the law to their own advantage. Again, their egoistic officials, whose task it is to ensure that the rules are enforced, will try to enrich themselves by bending the law, for a consideration. Given the unequal abilities of different people to promote their interest, such a social order will tend towards an increasingly unjust absolutism. But as the society moves in that direction, it will be more and more in the interest of more and more people to try and break the law, even at greater risk. Such societies will, to the extent that their members are 'rational' in Hobbes' sense, tend to be unstable, with periodic revolutions and many of the drawbacks of the state of nature.

And what is true for a society of Rational Egoists, is true also, though perhaps to a lesser extent, for a society of Rational Self-fulfillers, even if all of them love some of their fellows. For the difference between a society of Rational Egoists and Rational Self-fulfillers will be no greater than that, to put it roughly, between a society made up of egoistic individuals and one made up of small altruistic communities or common interest groups, e.g., families, clubs, parties, lobbies and the like, which feel about such other groups much as an egoistic individual feels about other such individuals.

It should by now be clear what is unsatisfactory about an order which recognizes only self-anchored reasons: it cannot recognize as overriding reasons any directives (principles, rules, precepts) designed to adjudicate interpersonal conflicts of self-anchored reasons. To the extent that they approximate perfect rationality, the members of such an order will therefore endeavor to modify their compulsory social order, its laws, customs, and conventions, in a direction counseled by their self-anchored reasons. And they can never be satisfied with any settlement these rules provide, because they can always envisage rules that would favor them more. Such persons will necessarily regard the social order as no more than a row of hurdles in the race for self-fulfillment or, in the worst case, self-aggrandisement. Their aim must always be to remove such hurdles from their own path and place them in the path of others with conflicting aims. Such an ideal of reason merely duplicates the miserable 'cops and robbers' business of the actual world.

It seems, then, that a theory of reason which admits only self-anchored reasons, even if they are not narrowly self-interested ones, cannot cope with the difficulties first outlined by Hobbes. For to the extent that such people approximate to perfect rationality, they must go counter to and eventually undermine the very order they need, to alleviate the worst features of the state of nature. But surely if a group of 'perfectly rational people' (that is, people who are always motivated only by what, according to that theory, are the best reasons) lead a life that is worse than a group of people who are less perfectly rational, then such a theory of reasons cannot be sound. Thus, if my assumptions (i)–(iv) are sound, then these considerations amount to a refutation of any theory of reasons such as Rational Egoism and Rational Self-fulfillment, which admits only self-anchored reasons.

14.

The problem, then, is this. On the one hand, Hobbes is mistaken in thinking that there is a necessary coincidence between self-anchored reasons and the requirements of the coercive social order whose continued existence must be supported by every member who accepts self-anchored reasons. On the other hand, the recognition of self-anchored reasons as supreme makes the coercive social order unstable, which is undesirable from every member's self-anchored point of view. The instability could, however, be avoided if the requirements of the social order were themselves regarded by its members as reasons to act accordingly and as reasons overriding self-anchored reasons. Our problem could thus be solved if we abandoned Rational Egoism, that is, gave up (vi) or (vi′) and replaced it by Rational Conventionalism, i.e.,

(vii) The requirements of the coercive social order are to be regarded by the members of that order as reasons for acting accordingly and, where they come into conflict with self-anchored reasons, as overriding them.

But how could (vii) be sound? The fact that if these requirements *were* regarded as such reasons in that social order, then life would be better for all its members than if they were not so regarded, looks like a good reason for accepting (vii), but it clearly is not a sufficient one. A slave in a slave society would surely not *rightly* regard the coercive rules concerning slavery as reasons to act as they require of him. He would surely act in accordance with reason if he tried to escape. But why is this so? Exactly why is it a mistake to move from the fact that life would be more fulfilling for everyone living under such an order if its requirements were so regarded than if they were not, to the conclusion that the requirements of any such coercive social order constitute reasons to act accordingly?

It seems that if this inference is to be acceptable, at least two further conditions must be satisfied. The first is *the condition of generality*. It may not be desirable, from a given person's self-anchored point of view, to regard the requirements of the coercive social order as overriding reasons unless these requirements are generally so regarded. The desirable benefits of their being so regarded accrue to everyone only if they are generally so regarded. This does not mean that literally everybody must so regard them, but that their being so regarded is part of the society's culture, passed on from one generation to the next and insisted on as the *correct* way of looking upon these requirements. This condition of generality is, however, satisfied in most societies, though the positivist doctrine of the separation of law and morality tends to undermine it.

As the slavery example makes clear, however, there must also be a second condition *concerning the content* of these social requirements. It suggests that the second condition demands that the social requirements be not merely for the good of everyone (by comparison with the state of nature) but for the good of everyone *alike* (by comparison with other possible social orders). For if the condition is met then no possible change of the social order would be an improvement from the point of view of reason. By this I mean a point of view which requires the social order to be such that everyone has the best possible self-anchored reason everyone (not anyone) can possibly have for wanting the requirements of the actual coercive social order under which he lives generally recognized in that order as constituting reasons overriding all others.

To sum up: I raised the question of when the social requirements of the coercive social order must be regarded as reasons to comply with them, which override the individuals' own self-anchored reasons. We saw that not only did every member of the society have some self-anchored reason to want to live under some coercive social order but also some self-anchored reason to have its requirements generally regarded as reasons overriding the individuals' own self-anchored reasons. Therefore, the refusal *ever* to recognize these requirements as such reasons is contrary to reason. However, accepting such requirements as such reasons quite irrespective of content is also contrary to reason. Not because the existence of a social order may not be for the good of all its members, for it may well be the case that almost all social orders, including slave societies, provide conditions of life which are superior, even for the slaves, to those prevailing in a state of nature. Nor because some social requirements fail to provide the weightiest possible self-anchored reasons for complying with them, for that is true whatever the social requirements: even in the most privilege-ridden class societies legislation could benefit the privileged still more. The reason is, rather, that only social requirements which are just, that is, for the good of everyone alike, provide *adequate* self-anchored reasons for *everyone* to accept the social requirements of over-riding reasons. Social justice is the ideal limit point at which anyone's reasons for refusing to recognize the social requirements as overriding reasons give out, for it is the point at which everyone has the weightiest possible self-anchored reason which everyone can have for recognizing these requirements as overriding reasons. But then they must be adequate reasons for so recog-nizing them, since there could not possibly be better reasons everyone could have. That they are adequate does not of course mean that they ensure the non-occurrence of sacrifices, that is, of courses of action less beneficial or more harmful than would be alternatives supported by the weightiest available self-anchored reasons. To demand this of adequacy at this point is to forget that one has already granted the need for a coercive social order adjudicating conflicts of self-anchored concerns, i.e., authoritative directives conflicting with and overriding some self-anchored reasons.

If my argument so far has been sound, it shows two things: that there is a need for a 'two-tier' theory of practical reasons, including reasons which over-ride self-anchored reasons, and that being for the good of everyone alike (social justice), is the substantive criterion which the requirements of a social order must satisfy in order to constitute reasons overriding self-anchored reasons.

15.

Our main question 'Why be moral?' could now be answered quite easily if the society-related overriding reasons I discussed in the previous sections were moral reasons. For then we could say that one should be moral because moral reasons from their nature are overriding reasons and because it would be contrary to reason not to follow the reasons which override all others. But are these society-related reasons really moral reasons?

I cannot, of course, deny that only an adequate theory of the whole of morality could satisfactorily lay this doubt to rest. In its absence we must be satisfied with something not quite so effective. What I can show is that the overriding reasons I spoke of in the previous sections, have the most important characteristics we normally attribute to moral reasons. What is more, on my account, these characteristics, which on most accounts are mutually incompatible, can be seen to be in complete harmony if we suppose that moral reasons are these reasons (or a subclass of them). The characteristics I have in mind are the following:

(i)   They are necessarily reasons for all members of the relevant order but not necessarily for others.

(ii)   They are universalizable in the strongest sense of the word.

(iii)   They are suitably related to self-fulfillment without actually being reasons of self-fulfillment.

(iv)   They override self-interested and, more generally, self-anchored reasons.

(v)   They are not hypothetical but categorical, in the sense that they are reasons not only for those who have certain specific ends, as are for instance the rules of etiquette.

(vi)   They rightly have the peculiar 'binding force' implied by moral obligatoriness and wrongness, a binding force whose nature is expressed in our conviction that it is not solely the moral agent's business whether or not he follows moral reasons. And that conviction is given effect in our moral practice of scrutinizing the behavior of others from the moral point of view and condemning them if they fail to live up to any moral requirements. The nature of the reasons I have just sketched explains why such reasons have the binding force our intuition ascribes to moral but not, for instance, to self-interested reasons: since they are from their nature directives designed to adjudicate conflicts of self-anchored concerns, every such directive necessarily runs counter to some concern based on a self-anchored reason and promotes some other concern similarly based. Wherever such a reason applies, therefore, somebody will have self-anchored reasons, and so probably be tempted, to act counter to it, and any such violation will run counter to a concern legitimated by such an overriding reason, and so someone will have self-anchored reasons to ensure that such violations do not occur. And since the order is ex hypothesi just, everyone will have the best possible self-anchored reason *everyone* can have to ensure that such violations do not occur.

This completely explains why conformity or nonconformity with such reasons cannot be solely the business of the agent.[16]

III

The kind of view I have presented here has met with a great many objections and, no doubt on account of my confused presentation of it in the past, many misunderstandings. I here select a few which I have encountered repeatedly and which would, therefore, seem to be cogent to many. Their discussion may help to make clearer what I intend to assert. Of course, the list cannot pretend to be exhaustive.

16.

It may for instance be objected that while reason does indeed require of us that we publicly advocate acting morally, it would be a mistake to infer from this that it is contrary to reason to act immorally.[17] Now it has of course to be admitted that having reasons for acknowledging something in public is quite different from having reasons for acknowledging it in one's mind. The weaker but brighter school boys may have excellent reasons for publicly acknowledging the superiority of the stupid bully who demands their public recognition of his superiority, but they have no reason to acknowledge it in their minds. One might think that similarly one has excellent reasons for publicly acknowledging the superiority (overridingness) of moral reasons but not for doing so in the privacy of one's mind. But this would be a mistake. The bully contributes nothing to the well-being of the boys: they would be better off if he did not exist. The public recognition of his superiority benefits them only under the undesirable and remediable condition of his existence. By contrast, there is nothing similarly undesirable and remediable in the case of moral reasons. As long as it remains true that life in society is better than life in solitude, the presence and cooperation of other people is an indispensable condition of that better life, even for those who do not love their fellows or their company. It is certainly not something undesirable which the rational man would wish to be without. Hence if the cooperation is best achieved by a general recognition that the just requirements of the social order constitute reasons overriding self-anchored ones, then these requirements really deserve to be so regarded and treated. Thus, if the Rational Egoist thinks it a mistake to recognize the overridingness of moral reasons not only in public but also in private, then it is he who is making the mistake. If he thinks that moral reasons ought to be recognized and treated as overriding, but then fails to treat them thus, then he acts contrary to what he himself rightly believes reason requires, and so acts contrary to reason.

It may be thought that the Rational Egoist can avoid this conclusion by adopting a half-way house between believing and not believing that moral reasons ought to be recognized as overriding: that is, by believing that others ought but that oneself ought not so to recognize them. However, such a position could not be consistently adopted by a Rational Egoist who advocates a certain theory of reasons, namely, the theory that self-interested (or at least self-anchored) reasons are the only reasons or the supreme ones. He is therefore committed to axiom (iv), that it must be possible for everyone always to be perfectly rational.[18] But then it is clear that in adopting such a half-way house position, the Rational Egoist would be involved in a self-contradiction, if he distinguished in this way between 'one' (himself) and 'others'. For this would commit him to the view that it is true of *everybody* that *he* should not acknowledge the overridingness of moral reasons, but that *everybody other than him* should; in other words, that everybody should not and that everybody should!

This is often overlooked because Rational Egoism, a theory of reasons, is not kept apart from egoism in the everyday sense. For, of course, an ordinary egoist is not committed to axiom (iv), since he is not advancing a theory of reasons. He simply assumes, with some show of plausibility, that as things are not all others will be egoists. He is happy to be an egoist in a world of many non-egoists.

17.

A closely related objection is that, whatever an answer such as mine may show, it does not show that being immoral is necessarily contrary to reason — for being immoral, far from being necessarily irrational, is often perfectly rational. Thus, Plamenatz[19] argues that a person "would not act irrationally were he to break the [moral] rule whenever, to the best of his information and taking the future into account as far as he reasonably could, he stood to gain by doing so." This is plausible because irrationality as we ordinarily understand it is running counter to reason in a particularly flagrant way, as when there is every reason or a particularly strong reason in favor of one course and no reason at all or only a very weak reason in favor of the other while yet the agent follows that other course. Plamenatz's prudent but immoral man does not act irrationally, for he has excellent reasons for doing what he does, and I am not of course arguing that he is acting irrationally. I am merely arguing that he is acting contrary to reason though not in the particularly flagrant way involved in irrationality.

However, many writers who argue that immorality is not necessarily irrational intend to make the stronger claim that it is also not necessarily contrary to reason.[20] This stronger claim is concealed from their readers, and sometimes from themselves also, by the fact that they do not distinguish between irrationality and the less flagrant ways of acting contrary to reason.

My response to this objection is therefore this. The objection rests on a misunderstanding if it assumes that my answer implies that immorality is necessarily irrational (in the strong everyday sense). And it is entirely baseless if it infers from the uncontroversial premiss that immorality is not necessarily irrational, that it is therefore not necessarily contrary to reason.

18.

Another frequently raised objection is to the effect that answers such as mine overlook an ambiguity of the question 'Why be moral?'.[21] They can deal with the less important (collective) sense, namely, 'Why should we all (everybody) be moral?', but not with the more important (distributive) sense, 'Why should I (one) be moral?'.

It is true that I have no answer — and I believe there can be no answer — to 'Why should I be moral *irrespective of what others do*?' or 'Why should I be moral *when no one else is*?' For, as I mentioned before, if the generality condition is not satisfied, then even a set of just requirements adjudicating conflicts of self-anchored concerns does not constitute overriding reasons. And if the generality condition is satisfied, then one should indeed be moral but (since the generality condition *is* satisfied) it will no longer be a case of being moral when no one else is, or irrespective of what others do.

However, someone might want to speak of a merely potential morality when he has found a set of just requirements adjudicating between conflicting self-anchored concerns but when the generality condition is not satisfied. One could say that such a potential morality becomes actual when the generality condition becomes satisfied. 'Why be moral?' might perhaps be read as referring to such a merely potential morality. It would then mean, 'Why should one follow the precepts of a certain potential morality?'. In such a case my answer would have to be that *there is no adequate* reason why.[22]

However, 'being moral' could be interpreted in yet a different way. As Howard Warrender has pointed out, following Hobbes, persons in a state of nature (e.g., states in the international arena) are in such a poor condition and the gains of establishing mutual trust and the recognition of an interpersonally (internationally) valid order are so great that *any* move in that direction, even at some risk to the party making it, would be in accordance with reason.[23] Perhaps we can say, following Hobbes, that in such a state of nature what morality requires is not conformity to a specific set of adjudicating requirements (Hobbes' laws of nature) but rather conformity to canons designed to bring about an effective coercive social order. In that case, the answer to 'Why should I (one) be moral?' is that the present condition is so bad and the gains are so great that everyone has adequate self-anchored reasons to take minimal risks in doing what offers the best hope of realizing these gains.

Finally, the reason I gave why one should be moral applies also when our question is asked in what is perhaps its most common sense, namely, 'Why should I be moral rather than make an exception in my favor *when other people are treating moral reasons as overriding*?'. For when the social requirements are just and the generality condition is satisfied then there is no adequate reason not to recognize them as overriding reasons.

Perhaps some writers overlook this because they fail to distinguish the present interpretation of the question (which implies that the generality condition is satisfied) from a previous interpretation (which implies its non-satisfaction). The previous question asked how the perfectly rational person would behave in a world without a moral order, while the present one asks how he would behave under a functioning and just moral order. If one overlooks that difference one is likely to infer, from the fact that there is no answer to why one should be moral under the conditions implied by the previous question, that there also is no answer to it under the very different conditions implied by the present question.

There is another reason why some philosophers may have been impressed by the present objection, namely, their failure to distinguish between motivation and validation requests. For if one thinks that 'Why should I (one) be moral?' must be a motivation request by a merely prudent person, then of course there cannot be a satisfactory answer if it is true, as I and many others believe, that prudence and morality can come into conflict. For in that case there will be occasions on which one ought, prudentially speaking, to be immoral.

19.

I want, finally, to present an objection[24] whose substance I concede. The objection begins by claiming, quite correctly, that I have so interpreted 'Why be moral?' that it means 'Why comply with the requirements of a perfectly just coercive social order when these requirements are generally recognized

as overriding reasons?' However, the objection continues, no existing moralities are perfectly just. But then, the objection concludes, the answer is
practically useless since it does not tell us whether there is adequate reason to
follow our own morality.

When I say I concede the substance of this objection, I mean only that
from the fact that there is adequate reason for following a perfect morality,
even though this will often mean going against what is supported by the best
self-anchored or even self-interested reasons, we cannot infer from this that
everybody has adequate reason to follow the morality of his group or his
own modifications of it. I do not concede that, for this reason, my demonstration is practically useless. To show that it need not be, I offer, tentatively,
a general principle which, if sound, would point the way towards working out
a method for ascertaining whether one has adequate reason to acknowledge a
given morality as overriding one's self-anchored reasons. The principle I mean
is essentially that of methodological conservatism:[25] the burden of proof lies
with the innovator. The defense of this principle is simply the fact that the
main reason why a Hobbesian absolutism or conventialism is mistaken is that
we can often tell that, and in what respects, a given social order is unjust; and
the extent to which such views are mistaken is precisely the extent to which
we can tell. Where we are unable to show that the adjudicating requirements
of the existing social order are unjust, we have no adequate reason to refuse
to recognize them as overriding reasons. Applied to our case, this would mean
that a given and obviously imperfect moral order should be treated as if it
were perfect, unless one has adequate reason not to. Every morality should
contain principles for determining what are such adequate reasons and for
spelling out what a person should do in such cases. Of course, these principles
will, themselves, be open to rational criticism. Now, in some cases, such
principles will require one to express one's disagreement with the prevailing
morality and at the same time, in one's practice, to depart from it in the
direction of improvement. A slave-owner who comes to believe that slavery
is morally wrong should perhaps not only speak out against slavery but also
release his slaves. In other cases, all that is required or even permissible
according to such principles may be speaking out against the practice while
still conforming to it. Thus, a factory owner who thinks it wrong to pollute
the environment should perhaps merely speak out against the practice, support
legislation against it, and so on, but not actually install the costly equipment,
if *unilateral compliance* with the ideal rule were to be economically ruinous
to him. And in the case of international disarmament, it would perhaps be
not merely foolish but morally wrong for a government to disarm unilaterally

if that invited some other country to use its military preponderance to start a war.[26]

If this conservative principle is sound, then it enables us to get from the overridingness of *perfect* recognized moral reasons to the status of our own imperfect recognized moral reasons with a commitment to the status quo. Such a conservative principle does not even exclude the possibility that in certain circumstances it may be morally permissible, perhaps required, to organize a revolution. Of course, these last remarks do no more than hint at how one could argue from ideal moral reasons to imperfect ones: to *show* how it is done in the case of our own or any particular morality would take more than another long paper.

University of Pittsburgh

NOTES

[*] Completion of this paper, begun some time ago, was made possible by a NEH Independent Study Fellowship F77-4 held from Jan. 1 to June 30, 1977.

[1] C. L. Stevenson, *Ethics and Language*. Yale University Press, New Haven, 1944, pp. 30/31, 113, 114–115, 133–135, 152 n. 2. I have discussed some aspects of Stevenson's treatment in 'Fact, Value, and Norm in Stevenson's Ethics', *Nous*, 1, 2, May, 1967.

[2] R. B. Brandt, *Ethical Theory*. Prentice-Hall, Inc., Englewood Cliffs, 1959. Esp. chapter 10. See also his 'Toward a Credible Form of Utilitarianism' in Hector-Neri Castañeda and George Nakhnikian, *Morality and the Language of Conduct*. Wayne State University Press, Detroit, 1959, and his 'Some Merits of One Form of Rule Utilitarianism', in the *University of Colorado Studies Series in Philosophy, No. 3*; also, Richard Brandt, 'Rationality, Egoism, and Morality', *The Journal of Philosophy*, LXIX, 20, Nov. 9, 1972.

[3] William K. Frankena, 'Obligation and Motivation in Recent Moral Philosophy' in A. I. Melden, *Essays in Moral Philosophy*. University of Washington Press, Seattle, 1958. See also his 'Recent Conceptions of Morality' in Hector-Neri Castañeda and George Nakhnikian, *Morality and the Language of Conduct*. Wayne State University Press, Detroit, 1963, and his 'McIntyre on defining Morality' and 'The Concept of Morality' both reprinted in G. Wallace and A. D. M. Walker, ed., *The Definition of Morality*. Methuen & Co., Ltd., London, 1970.

[4] For their views are too well known for me simply to summarize them and I am too much in sympathy with them to wish to attack them.

[5] *Mind*, XXI, 81, Jan., 1912, reprinted in H. A. Prichard, *Moral Obligation*. Oxford University Press, Oxford, 1968, pp. 1–17.

[6] Cf. Philippa Foot's recent paper, 'Morality as a System of Hypothetical Imperatives', *Philosophical Review*, July, 1972, in which such a conception of morality as an autotelic activity is defended. Cf. also Frankena's paper critical of Foot, entitled 'The Philosopher's Attack on Morality', *Philosophy*, 46, 190, 345–356 and Foot's rejoinder, 'A Reply to Professor Frankena', *Philosophy*, 50, 194, 455–459.

[7] Op. cit., p. 3.

[8] My distinction between motivation and validation requests is similar to the distinction, which Frankena (in 'Obligation and Motivation in Recent Moral Philosophy', pp. 40–81) takes over from Hutcheson, between 'exciting reasons' and 'justifying reasons'. However, there are also minor differences. In the first place, while for Frankena 'Why should I . . . ?' as a request for a justifying reason is a request 'for an ethical justification of the action proposed' (p. 44), for me a validation request is a request for a reason, whether moral or non-moral. In the second place, while for Frankena 'Why should I . . .?' as a request for an exciting reason is a request 'for a motive for doing it' (Ibid.), for me a motivation request is a request for anything that would motivate the questioner to do it. This need not be a motive; it may for instance be a consideration or a proof that two types of considerations necessarily coincide. In the third place, I reject the view entertained by Frankena that 'a motive is one kind of reason for acting' (Ibid.). But these differences are at least in part merely verbal, if not entirely so.

[9] There are thus important similarities and differences between calling something a consideration and calling it a reason for someone to do something. In both cases something is asserted about a suitable relationship between four things, two of which are common to considerations and reasons, two different. The two common things are: (1): Something, F, is the case. (2): F is evidence that N's doing A will produce S. The two things in respect of which considerations and reasons differ are: (3C): N finds S desirable. (3R): S is desirable. (4C): If N believes (1) and (2) and if (3C), then he is motivated to do A. (I shall star all belief propositions. Thus (4C) becomes: If (1^*), (2^*) and (3C), then N is motivated to do A.) (4R): If (1^*), (2^*), and (3^*), [i.e., if N believes (1), (2), and (3R)], then he is motivated to do A.

Now to assert (5): that F is a consideration for N to do A, is to assert (3C), (4C), and (2^*), but not (1^*). (1^*) is, however, implied when we claim that F was a consideration for N in (actually) doing A, i.e., that when N did A, F actually weighed with him; or to put it differently, that (1^*) [N's believing F], was part of the explanation of his doing A. And, of course, (5) does not imply the truth of either (1), or (2), or (3R). [We should note that (3C): that N finds S desirable, is not the same as $(3R^*)$: that N believes (3R).]. By contrast, to assert (6): that F is a reason for N to do A, is to assert merely (2) and (3R). It does not imply (7), (1^*), (2^*), $(3R^*)$, or (4R). It should be noted that (6) is logically independent of (6^*): that N believes (6). I here leave open the question, long a hotly debated issue between so-called Internalists and Externalists, of whether (4R) is true. For the distinction between Internalism and Externalism, see William K. Frankena, 'Obligation and Motivation in Recent Moral Philosophy', pp. 40ff.

[10] Cf., e.g., David P. Gauthier, Morality and Advantage, in David P. Gauthier, ed., Morality and Rational Self-Interest. Prentice-Hall, Englewood Cliffs, 1970, p. 175. John Hospers, Human Conduct. Harcourt, Brace & World Inc., New York, 1961, pp. 193–195.

[11] Prichard, op. cit., p. 1.

[12] Cf., John Hospers, Human Conduct. Harcourt, Brace, World Inc., New York, 1961, pp. 194 f. J. C. Thornton, 'Can the Moral Point of View be Justified?', Australasian Journal of Philosophy, XLII (1964): reprinted in Kenneth Pahel and Marvin Schiller, eds., Readings in Contemporary Ethical Theory. Prentice-Hall, Englewood Cliffs, N.J., 1970, esp. p. 445 f. and 451; see also D. H. Monro, Empiricism and Ethics. Cambridge University Press, 1967, pp. 101 ff.

[13] Kai Nielsen, 'Is 'Why should I be moral?' an Absurdity?', *Australasian Journal of Philosophy*, **XXXVI** (1958), 25–32.

[14] Here I am indebted to G. H. von Wright, *The Varieties of Goodness*. Humanities Press, New York, 1962, pp. 24–27, though he may disagree with the use I make of his distinctions.

[15] For an interpretation of Bentham which bases the principle of utility on a system of individual self-anchored reasons, see David Lyons, *In the Interest of the Governed*. Clarendon Press, Oxford, 1973.

[16] I have discussed this point more fully in my paper 'Moral Obligation', *APQ*, 3, July, 1966.

[17] For such a view, see for instance, Bernard Gert, *The Moral Rules*. Harper & Row, New York, 1966, 1967, 1970, p. 205. "The confusion involves the relationship between what reason publicly requires and what reason requires. 'Reason publicly requires acting morally' simply means that all rational men publicly advocate acting morally. 'Reason requires acting morally' means that it is irrational to act immorally. . . . If one does not clearly distinguish between what reason requires and what reason publicly requires, then he may conclude that it is irrational to act immorally. It seems likely that Kant was involved in this confusion."

Or John Plamenatz, *Democracy and Illusion*. Longman, London, 1973, p. 26. "The dishonest man, no less than the honest one, needs to make use of social rules, especially those general rules whose breach evokes the strongest feelings of resentment and disapproval, the moral rules. . . . He would fail of his purpose if he invoked the rule in such a way as to suggest that he himself was not bound by it. He would act irrationally were he to claim for himself an exemption which he would not, if challenged, show to be in the general interest, or justify by appealing to some principle accepted by the person he was trying to influence. But he would not act irrationally were he to break the rule whenever, to the best of his information and taking the future into account as far as he reasonably could, he stood to gain by doing so."

[18] See above, p. 240.

[19] Op. cit., p. 26; see also Gert, op. cit., chapter 10.

[20] Thus Kai Nielsen asks "Why is he (or is he) irrational or mistaken if he follows his egoistic policy?" ('Why Should I be Moral?', K. Pahel and M. Schiller, eds., *Readings in Contemporary Ethical Theory*, Prentice-Hall, Inc., Englewood Cliffs, 1970, p. 458; cf., also p. 466.) and it is plain that by 'irrationality' he means *any* sin against reason. I believe this is true also of Gert and Plamenatz, but I have not found any passage which would by itself, demonstrate this. It is, however, fairly clear in G. J. Warnock's *The Object of Morality*. Methuen & Co., Ltd., London, 1971. He there appears to think that contrariety to reason and irrationality are much the same. Thus, thinking the worse what is in fact the better alternative and so presumably the one supported by weightier reasons, he regards as not contrary to reason but at most as "contrary to good sense" (p. 162). He does so because of his account of rationality and irrationality: "To be *irrational*, I take it, is to fail, or refuse, or be unable to *recognize* a reason." (p. 162, see also p. 163). However, we should distinguish at least three or possibly four senses of 'rational', only one of which, namely, (ii) has the opposite 'irrational'. (i) Something close to Warnock's 'ability sense': possessing the minimal ability to recognize *and use* reasons. Every normal adult is a rational being in this sense. Idiots are not rational beings, but neither are they irrational, for to be an irrational man, one must be a rational being.

Now babies and puppies lack rationality in the ability sense. However, while babies are rational in the capacity (the possible fourth) sense, i.e., prerational in the ability sense, puppies are not – they are, however, non-rational beings and not irrational ones, as they would be by Warnock's definition. (ii) The 'low evaluative sense': Actually exercising the ability to recognize and use reasons to a minimal standard of acceptability. Those falling below that standard are irrational. I have tried to define that standard. (iii) Perfect rationality: Exercising this ability flawlessly. Falling short of that standard is not necessarily flawed enough to amount to irrationality, but it is necessarily contrary to reason.

[21] David Gauthier, 'Morality and Advantage', in David Gauthier, ed., *Morality and Rational Self-Interest.* Prentice-Hall, Inc., Englewood Cliffs, 1970, p. 175. Hector Monro, 'Critical Notice', *Australasian Journal of Philosophy,* **XXXVII**, May, 1959, 77 ff. Kai Nielsen, 'Why should I be moral?' Pahel and Schiller, op. cit., p. 460–469. J. C. Thornton, 'Can the Moral Point of View be Justified?', reprinted in Pahel & Schiller, op. cit., pp. 446 f.

[22] To be accurate, we would have to distinguish between the 'general' and the 'particular' senses of 'what others are doing'. If the generality condition is satisfied, then the question of what others are doing (being moral or not being moral) is by implication settled, though only in the 'general sense'. That is to say, since the adjudicating social requirements are generally recognized as overriding reasons, *many people* will treat them as overriding reasons, and those who do not will be criticized and subjected to suitable sanctions. But it is still possible that in a particular case, what the relevant others (say, one's contractual partners or the particular judge dealing with the contract) will do remains an open question. I call this the 'particular sense' of 'what others are doing'. In light of this distinction, what I have argued is that the reason why one should be moral applies even if it is an open question what others will do, in the particular sense, as long as the generality condition is satisfied and the question of what others are doing in the general sense is therefore settled (i.e., others are moral). But, I argued, that reason does not apply when the generality condition is not satisfied and when it is therefore an open question what others are doing, in the general sense.

[23] Howard Warrender, *The Moral and Political Philosophy of Thomas Hobbes.* The Clarendon Press, Oxford, 1957, pp. 53–56.

[24] This objection was raised by Annette Baier.

[25] See e.g., Lawrence Sklar, 'Methodological Conservatism', *The Philosophical Review,* **LXXXIV**, 3, July, 1975, pp. 374–400.

[26] See above, footnote 23.

WARREN S. QUINN

MORAL AND OTHER REALISMS:
SOME INITIAL DIFFICULTIES

Some very similar problems and disputes arise in ethics, aesthetics, and the philosophy of perception. One of the most basic of these parallel controversies concerns the connection between certain *features* we attribute to objects and certain mental *responses* that somehow or other provide a basis for these attributions.[1] Three examples of such feature-response pairs drawn from ethics, aesthetics, and philosophy of perception respectively are (a) moral goodness and moral approval, (b) funniness and amusement, and (c) something's being red and its looking red. What makes these and many other examples controversial is the fact that one kind of philosopher (the *realist*) finds it plausible to claim first that whether an object possesses one or another of these features is independent of and prior to the question whether it provokes the correlative response and second that the response itself is a genuinely cognitive state of mind in some way directed to the feature as part of its object.[2] While another kind of philosopher (the *mentalist*) finds it plausible to deny both these claims and to assert instead that the response has conceptual priority over the feature and that what the realist takes in the response as cognitive of the feature is really some noncognitive attitude, disposition, sensation, or act of will. In other words, the realist regards the response as a response *to* the feature while the mentalist sees the feature as some sort of construction *out of* the response. In considering the dispute it will be convenient to have a way of generalizing over all feature-response pairs that tend to generate this kind of controversy; thus I shall take the liberty of speaking of *C*-pairs ('*C*' for '*C*ontroversial') and, in the context of discussing such pairs, *C*-features and *C*-responses.

For the realist, a true occurrence of the *C*-response necessarily involves the *thought* or tendency to think that the object responded to has the *C*-feature, perhaps as that thought is embedded in a perception of the thing as having the feature.[3] Implicit in this, of course, is the idea that the feature is objectively present in its objects and therefore that ascriptions of it are objectively true or false. Also implicit is the claim that the concept of the *C*-feature is *prior* to that of the *C*-response. The mentalist, reversing the order

257

A. I. Goldman and J. Kim (eds.), Values and Morals, 257–273. All Rights Reserved.
Copyright © 1978 by D. Reidel Publishing Company, Dordrecht, Holland.

of things, analyzes the feature into the response and strips the response of any cognitive function vis-à-vis the feature. Of course a mentalist may allow or even insist that the C-response involves any number of genuine cognitions of *other* features of the object if only because some thoughts about the object will be needed to get it in focus as an object of response. A mentalist about color (e.g. a secondary quality theorist like Locke) must admit that in paradigm cases of color experience color sensations are 'superimposed' on genuine perceptions of an object's shape qualities.[4] And in ethics, mentalists typically grant thought a more or less prominent role in the composition or formation of ethical attitudes and decisions.[5] The issue between the mentalist and realist is thus not whether the C-state is cognitive, but whether it is cognitive *of the C-feature*.

Both realism and mentalism come in importantly different varieties. A realist may hold that the C-response is logically separable into some pure cognition of the C-feature on the one hand and some noncognitive concomitant state on the other. But another form of realism denies that it is in this way possible to distill a purely noncognitive component out of the C-response. Furthermore, a realist may or may not hold that a given C-response is, for human beings at least, *the* central epistemic mental state regarding the C-feature, i.e. may or may not hold that it is only because we or someone we depend on is capable of experiencing the C-response that we are able to ascribe the C-feature.[6] When the C-response is intrinsically motivational or affective (as it seems to be in the two examples from ethics and aesthetics) a realist who regards it as both homogeneously cognitive and epistemically central must take the motivation or affect to be in some sense *internal* to ascriptions of the C-feature.[7]

Mentalism also embraces a wide variety of viewpoints. Some mentalists regard C-feature ascriptions as objectively true or false. This means that although they suppose that there are genuine beliefs and/or perceptions directed toward the C-feature, they deny that the C-response is itself among them. For them, the C-response enters the picture at a pre-epistemic stage, serving to constitute the essence rather than the recognition of the C-feature. This may be explained in a number of different ways. Some mentalists define the feature as a disposition to produce the response; others hold that to say that a thing has the feature is to say that the response is a reasonable or appropriate reaction to it.[8] Still others, of course, deny the externality of the C-feature altogether and with it the idea that there is *any* genuine cognition that takes it as an object. In modern ethical theory this position is held by the emotivists and prescriptivists, who claim that the feature term functions to express, evoke or prescribe the response. Note that a mentalist of this last variety may nevertheless hold that occurrences of the C-response and corresponding C-feature speech acts can be rationally justified or unjustified even though they are neither true nor false.[9]

The noncognitive as a classification of theories of meaning is to be distinguished from the noncognitive as a category of mental state.[10] It is this latter sense of the cognitive-noncognitive distinction that directly concerns us here because it is this sense that generates the distinction between realism and mentalism. With its roots reaching back as far as Plato and Aristotle's division of the psyche into rational and nonrational components, the distinction is meant to capture our natural inclination to draw a line between appetite, feeling and sensation on the one hand and belief, judgment, perception and acquaintance on the other. Hume formulates his version of the distinction with typical ingenuous vigor. Some actions of the mind viz. judgments and opinions, having reference to truth and reason, are thereby capable of 'agreement or disagreement either to the *real* relations of ideas or to *real* existence and matter fact.' But . . . 'our passions, volitions, and actions are not susceptible of any such agreement or disagreement; being original facts and realities, compleat in themselves . . .'[11] It is not my intention here to examine critically or choose between any of the historically important formulations of the distinction between cognitive and noncognitive mental states but simply to note that it is hard to see how philosophy could do without such a distinction and to see how far we can go by appealing to our intuitive sense of it in formulating and attempting to resolve the dispute between realists and mentalists.

The dispute appears to be a real one, clouded no doubt by various confusions but not wholly generated by them. This impression of genuineness is supported by our familiarity with some response-feature pairs that seem to admit only of a mentalist interpretation and others that seem to admit only a realist. Among the former are a) wanting and something's being wanted, b) pain and painfulness and c) fear and fearfulness. Of course these three mentalist paradigms differ in many respects. Wanting and fear take what is wanted and what is fearful as objects, while pain takes no object at all.[12] And while it is natural to think that wanting requires no particular thought about its object (although some would deny this), fear seems to require the thought (however self-consciously irrational) that its object is dangerous. But despite such differences, each response is naturally taken to be conceptually prior to its paired feature. What is wanted is what someone wants. What is painful is what causes or is disposed to cause pain. And the fearful either marks the category of things that tend to arouse fear or the things that are its appropriate objects. Perhaps even some occurrences of the expression 'fearful' fit an emotivist interpretation as linguistically suited to express or arouse fear. On the other hand, realist paradigms are even more abundant. Most of us regard the concept of something's looking square as dependent on the prior concept of squareness. The same could be said for being taller than and looking taller than, being a person and seeming to be a person, being a drum and sounding like a drum, etc. A mentalist interpretation of these concept pairs could be warranted only on the assumption of wholesale phenomenalism.

Of course it is one thing for an issue to be genuine (or even partly genuine) and another for it to be easily solved. In the following I will investigate what seem to me to be three promising ways in which one might hope to settle or at least alleviate the controversy. The first attempts to turn interpersonal agreement or disagreement into a criterion by which one may rule out at least some forms of realism or mentalism. The second is a sceptical argument against the realist that appeals to the contingency of the way we map C-features onto the world. And the third is an argument designed to play against the mentalist's alleged inability to provide suitable differentiating accounts of the C-response. The net result will be negative − that is I will try to show that each criterion or argument proves in the end either irrelevant or incomplete in ways that are far from easily remedied, and in the conclusion I will indulge in a brief reflection on why in general this should be so.

I

When facing issues having to do with objectivity and subjectivity, it is customary to look for help from some criterion of interpersonal agreement and disagreement.[13] So it seems natural to wonder whether if it were the case that we agreed or disagreed with each other in our C-responses to things, we could as a result rule out certain forms of mentalism or realism. To this end we might try to make something of the common hunch that knowledge and intelligence determine one's *beliefs* far more than they determine one's *attitudes*, *choices*, or *sensations*. Perhaps some maximal list of cognitive advantages − pieces of knowledge, mental abilities, intellectual virtues, etc. − could be found that would uniquely determine our C-responses were it the case that these responses really were cognitive of the C-feature but would leave them undetermined were this not the case. Of course the list could not contain any item that begged the question against some variety of mentalism or realism that was being tested. So it should not, on pain of offending a mentalist who offers a noncognitivist account of the C-feature, contain such advantages as *knowledge* of which things have the C-feature or *sensitivity* to the C-feature, etc. But let us suppose for the sake of argument that we have some such non-question begging, maximally complete list.

The first question to be asked is whether universal agreement in C-responses (the fact that all would respond and fail to respond to exactly the same things) among the qualified responders who satisfy our list would rule out any form of mentalism. It would certainly not seem to threaten any variety that held that C-feature judgments are empirically true or false; such theories might even *define* the C-feature in terms of the uniform C-responses of qualified responders.[14] But it might seem plausible to think that at least some forms of agreement among qualified responders would be incompatible with subjectivist varieties of mentalism that allow for relativism among responders at large. Just how plausible this is would depend, I think, on the kind of agreement we had in mind, and especially the modality attached to it. That all qualified responders *in fact* agree in their C-responses should give the subjectivist little cause for alarm, since the agreement could result from common conditioning in contingent noncognitive attitudes. And even that all qualified persons should of *psychological necessity* agree in their C-responses seems at least theoretically compatible with any reasonable form of subjectivism. Thus it seems the only interesting possibility that agreement could be used against the subjectivist depends on whether *logically* or *metaphysically necessary* agreement would be incompatible with his theory.

In facing this question one is likely to confuse two different issues. It is true that many contemporary subjectivists, say the noncognitivists in ethics or aesthetics, regard their position as incompatible with this sort of agreement. But this is because they see themselves as belonging to an empiricist tradition going back to Hume according to which all motivations, attitudes, passions, feelings, sensations and choices can, even in fully rational and informed agents, be no more than contingently related to their objects. This dogma, however, does not appear in other philosophical traditions. For example, both Plato and Aristotle can be interpreted to hold that there are motivations that every rational person must have; and in this respect at least they have been followed — although in quite different ways — by Kant and Sidgwick.[15] The relevance of this to the present issue lies in the fact that it seems possible to combine an acceptance of some such necessary connection between cognitive excellence and agreement in response (although not perhaps in a form acceptable to any of these authors) with the doubt that this connection entails that the responses are themselves cognitively assessible as true or false or even as justified or unjustified. It might be useful to consider the converse: whether one would, for example, think that *any* valid argument to the conclusion that all morally perfect agents agree in thinking logically about certain matters, e.g. consequences, would by itself establish that it is morally good to think logically about consequences. It would seem that whether an argument that establishes a necessary connection between some set of excellences and a certain pattern of response guarantees that such responses are assessible in terms of the excellences depends on the specific nature of its premises.

But if agreement cannot by itself be used against the mentalist, perhaps disagreement among the qualified responders can be used against some form of realism. A realist who holds that the *C*-response is some separable combination of pure cognitive state and noncognitive response may perhaps attribute some sorts of disagreement to the disturbing presence of the latter element. And even a realist who holds that the *C*-response is thoroughly cognitive may nevertheless regard it as a very specialized variety of cognition whose vagaries would not rule out an interpersonally consistent assignment of *C*-features via some other cognitive route. But it might seem plausible to suppose that disagreement among the qualified responders is incompatible with a realism according to which the *C*-response is not only cognitive through and through but is for us the basic epistemic state by which we recognise the *C*-feature. The idea is that the knowledge and other advantages included in our list ought to be sufficient to eliminate any possibility of uncorrectable error in identifying objects as having or lacking the *C*-feature. And this rests on the assumption that every instantiation of an intrinsic characteristic is entailed by or inductively implied by some fact that can be *independently known*.

. But on reflection this assumption seems highly suspect. Such logical integration of knowledge may be an ideal of natural science, but natural science may not exhaust all knowledge. The idea of aesthetic facts that are not entailed or implied by any facts that could be known independently has been energetically defended.[16] At the very least, therefore, we need some additional reasoning to show that the assumption is compelling. Until it is brought forward the realist may be allowed simply to suppose, for example, that some qualified responders are better able to discriminate the *C*-feature than others, and to explain any disagreement arising among them in this way.

But the issue of the impact of disagreement on realism is not quite as simple as this. To see why, we must turn our attention from the qualified responders to the linguistic community at large. Unless we can find certain relevant patterns of linguistic agreement there we will, given realism, find ourselves unable to justify the very supposition that the community possesses the concept of the C-feature. In order to be justified in supposing that a community possesses a concept we generally have to be in a position to pick our parts of its language — perhaps a term — as expressing the concept. But given a realistic view of the C-feature, we could justifiably suppose a term to play this role only if it were commonly applied to objects that we could understand either to have or to seem to have the C-feature. The possibility of a realist's ascribing the C-feature concept to a linguistic community therefore seems to presuppose the presence of certain patterns of prediction there, and these patterns seem tantamount to some form of interpersonal agreement — even if limited to some few paradigm cases.

But those mentalists who espouse a relativistic account of the C-feature in terms of the C-response may be able to do without such agreement. For they regard talk about the C-feature as reducible to talk about, or other kinds of expression of, the speaker's C-responses. And presumably we could identify that sort of talk, if it exists, if we were able to identify the concept of the C-response. But on some mentalist conceptions we should be able to do this simply by finding members of the community applying certain purely non-cognitive behavioral or phenomenological criteria to themselves and others. A mentalist need not assert this, of course. He may conceive the C-response on the model of fear, i.e. as necessarily including certain specific judgments about its objects. Or he may simply hold that the C-response, while not tied to any specific thoughts about its object must be subject to certain orderly causal explanations which would imply certain regularities in the objects that provoke the response. If his conception of the C-response were of either of these types, then the mentalist would probably be just as dependent on some pattern of agreement in C-feature ascriptions as the realist. But a mentalist need not regard the C-response as thus restricted to certain objects. He may think that we can find it in a community just in case we can find a common recognition of certain noncognitive phenomenological or behavioral patterns. And once we have found the concept of the C-response we need find no further patterns of classification in order to find the concept of the C-feature (should it be present). Thus it would appear that the absence of certain forms of agreement in the community at large would count against realism but be compatible with certain forms of mentalism.

This appearance is deceptive. It is perhaps true that if we *assume* that the speakers in a community in which no uniform pattern of C-feature predication emerges have the concept of the C-feature then this fact could only be explained by mentalism. But this does not show that the absence of the relevant forms of agreement is tolerable under mentalism but not realism. For there is the prior question whether the assumption is legitimate, i.e. whether the concept of the C-feature should be assigned to a linguistic community whose classifications of independent objects are in the relevant sort of disarray. The realist will insist that no reason has as yet been put forward to show that it could be assigned in such a case. And so far as I can see, that is correct. So we have still failed to produce a possible condition of disagreement that would settle the dispute in the mentalist's favor.

II

The mentalist has not yet had his full say about the question of agreement. Even if he admits the force of the preceding observations he may well suspect that we have been missing the point of what is really relevant in the matter of agreement and disagreement. Instead of dwelling on the implications of the possibility that we either agree or disagree in our ascriptions of the C-feature, we should consider just how contingent any possible pattern of our C-feature ascriptions would be.[17] It is not the disagreement present in a possible situation that argues against realism, it is rather the fact that whatever agreement is present might easily have taken some other form — that instead of finding *these* things funny we might have found *those* things funny instead, that instead of *these* things (apples and roses) looking red *those* things (grass and avocados, or for that matter, grass and bananas) might have, etc.

We must be extremely careful in formulating any objection to realism based on such alleged contingencies. As we have seen, what makes a mentalist a mentalist is his opinion that there is enough in the nature of the C-response to enable us to identify it for what it is independently of first finding in it any *thought* about the C-feature. And we have also seen that this is exactly what the realist finds implausible. It is important to remember that it is precisely here that the dispute lies when trying to fashion a non-question begging argument against realism. It will not do for the mentalist simply to insist on the contingency of the connection between our C-responses and their objects if what underlies his claim is nothing more than the controversial assumption with which the realist disagrees. If he wants to merit our attention he must argue to the contingency from premises that the realist can grant.

The following is an attempt to fashion such an argument. To begin, suppose we grant the realist's assumption that a C-response is cognitive in the sense that it essentially contains some genuine thought of its object as having the C-feature. Now whatever else we think about C-features, it seems pretty clear that a C-feature is never an *identifying* feature of an object it characterizes — it is not one of these features one would *need* to know about in order to settle possible problems of distinguishing one object from another or problems of deciding what are or are not an object's proper parts.[18] Size, shape and location serve to identify material bodies. Color, as ordinarily conceived, and not redefined by a physicist, is theoretically dispensable. Time and agent are among the identifying features of action, moral goodness is not. One story or joke may be distinguished from another by its content or by the precise words that make it up. Its funniness or unfunniness doesn't make it the story that it is. (There is strong reason to insist on these last two points, since we have to know exactly what an action or story is in order to know whether it is morally good or funny.)

The idea that C-features are supervenient, and therefore gratuitous from the point of view of strict identification, is not granted by some realists; for them the mentalist's argument is aborted here.[19] But some important realists would grant and even embrace the point, so we may continue the argument as addressed to them. Drawing the distinction between identifying and non-identifying features leads to some important (if rather difficult to formulate) implications concerning the possibility of error. So long as we are not concerned to mark a thing off precisely, we may make some mistakes about its identifying features without jeopardizing our claim to be acquainted with it. But even so, the more frequent or substantial our mistakes about a thing's identifying features become, the more our claim to be experiencing that thing as an element of an independent reality is threatened. If I sincerely report to see an ordinary watermelon that I am holding in one hand as smaller than an ordinary grape that I am holding in the other, you may well suspect that I am undergoing some strange hallucination and reporting on the content of it rather than on the real objects in my hands. And you will be confirmed in this if my other alleged perceptions of their identifying features are equally eccentric.[20]

But the case is different with non-identifying features. Even if we grant the realist's assumption that these features are objective qualities or relations inhering in independent objects, experience *of* those objects does not by itself require a unique assignment of the features. This is shown by the fact that we may radically disagree about such assignments without even a suspicion arising that we are not disputing about the very same reality. We may be ever so color-blind, morally blind or perverse, an insensitive or even moronic in our sense of humor without losing hold of the world.[21] It follows from this that even if we agree in mapping C-features onto the world in such and such a way, we might *in experiencing the very same objective world* have mapped the features quite differently even though the objects mapped remain the same in all intrinsic aspects.

Radical, systematic error as to which things have a given C-feature is not incompatible with a correct identification of the things in question, whereas such error in the case of identifying features is. Identifying features are thus proof against radical misplacement in a way that C-features are not. This means that even if we suppose that the C-response essentially contains the thought of the object as having the C-feature, it could nevertheless have been evoked by objects quite other than those which in fact now evoke it. We do not have to deny the realist's basic claim in order to assert that had the laws of psychology been different, the things that now arouse a sense of moral approval or a feeling of amusement might not have and the things that do not now have even the slightest tendency to arouse these responses might. And all this might have occurred without supposing any alteration in the intrinsic natures of the objects themselves. Of course, if the realist assumes that here in the actual world we locate the C-features with a fair degree of accuracy, then he would have to say that in the possibility under consideration we would be systematically deluded. We would think things morally good, funny, or red that do not even come close to having these features. And what is more nightmarish, these illusions might be as internally and interpersonally consistent as our present patterns of response. We would and should have just as much reason to be confident in our judgments as we now have. So realism with respect to C-features not only entails the possibility of complete, undetectable illusion, but gives us no greater chance than that afforded by cosmic luck that we are not here and now in its grip. The old-fashioned scepticism cries out for the old-fashioned phenomenalist remedy. Rather than tolerate these dreadful notions of undetectable illusion and cosmic luck, we should adopt the mentalist interpretation of the C-responses with its more sensible and modest way of explaining their contingency.

The argument is, in its way, impressive and seems to present considerations with which the realist must come to terms. It depends on the assumption that where C-features are concerned, we can credit a thought (type) as being the thought of a thing that it has the C-feature without worrying about the character of the things at which the thought is typically aimed. The mentalist is not prepared to grant this with regard to identifying features for the simple reason that mistakes about them tend to draw a veil between the thinker and the alleged objects of his thought. A thought about a thing's identifying features has a certain double life: it enables us to be acquainted with the thing and at the same time to take in its character. Any flaw in the latter is at least a potential flaw in the former. The obstacle to the radical misplacement of identifying features is thus a *reference* problem — a problem of seeing a thought *as a thought about this or that thing*. And the mentalist has argued, persuasively, that there is no correspondingly serious reference problem raised by the radical misplacement of *C*-features.

But the reference problem is not the only problem with respect to the identification of thoughts. This can be seen by setting *de dicto* (or internally quantified) thoughts alongside the *de re* (or externally quantified) thoughts we have been hitherto exclusively examining. Since the reference problem is the problem of our right to credit someone with a *de re* thought about a particular object (e.g. the thought *of that object* that one perceives it to be square), it does not speak directly to the question of how we can credit someone with a *de dicto* thought (e.g. the thought that we perceive some object to be square). But surely there are limits to what we can accept here as well. A *de dicto* thought (type) could not plausibly be interpreted as the specific thought that *p* if that interpretation made all or most occurrences of the thought inexplicably false. We could not reasonably credit a thought (in a given community) as the thought that one is seeing something square if the thought never occurs in people when they are in fact seeing such a shape. And that we cannot credit this does not simply seem due to an inability to get into the heads of these people to see if the totally inappropriate thought really is there; for even if we could get into their heads (whatever that would be like) we would still have the problem of identifying what we found there. The mentalist's mistake lies in supposing that anything, whether a mental event or a bit of language, can be identified as being or expressing a specific thought — whether *de re* or *de dicto* — independently of determining its role in its subject's interactions with the public world.[22] Surely there is a truth problem, as well as a reference problem, in identifying thoughts of any type.

The implications of this for thoughts about *C*-features are immediate. The mentalist has argued that there can be no objection arising from the reference problem to one's identifying a type of thought as the thought of a thing that it has the *C*-feature. But this is just to say that there is no problem in attributing these thoughts, *supposing that we can find them*, to the unlikeliest things. Well and good. But can we find them? It is one thing to ask whether a thought that we have interpreted in a certain way can, so interpreted, be understood as a thought about these objects, and quite another to ask whether it was reasonable of us to have interpreted it that way in the first place. The mentalist's argument was directed to the first question and not to the second. It is preposterous to think that *any* thought – even about non-identifying features – could be interpreted without con-' cern for the truth problem. A realist therefore is entitled to reject as senseless the hypothesis that in a given possible setting some thought (type) is functioning as the thought of a thing that it is morally good, funny, or red if that interpretation does not make the thought true or plausible often enough, and so he need not – given his insistence that the thought is essential to the C-response – be frightened by the possibility of our C-responses running riot. Thus it seems that the contingency has not been successfully argued from the realist's assumption that the C-response contains a thought about the C-feature.

III

From the discussion so far, it might seem that realism is merely a reactive (not to say reactionary) position. But realists have offensive strategies, one of the most important and interesting of which I should now like to consider. The argument I have in mind begins by granting provisionally the mentalist's claim that the C-response is noncognitive – some species of mere feeling, affect sensation, etc. But which species? The feeling of moral approval is not just any pro-attitude; it is different presumably from something we might call aesthetic approval. Amusement is not just any form of affect; it differs from fear, excitement, delight, etc. And even if we grant that something's looking red to one involves some species of mere sensation not to be confused with genuine perception, that kind of sensation must be different from the kind involved in something's looking blue to one. But this need to *differentiate* the C-state leads the mentalist into a fatal trap. For he will find that he cannot differentiate the C-state except by referring in one way or another to the C-feature. This difficulty is most familiar in the case of mentalist accounts of the colors. It seems impossible to imagine how one could even begin to provide a conceptually necessary differentiating feature for a color sensation without mentioning the color of which it was the sensation. What makes the sensation of red different from the sensation of blue is that it is the sensation of *red*. Any other feature that would serve to demarcate the species of sensation, e.g. that it was correlated with a certain brain state, would seem to be a conceptually contingent feature of the state and thus would not provide the kind of differentia that explicates the concept of the color.

This type of argument has also been brought to bear on mentalist accounts of moral approval. The realist objects that some instances of approval cannot count as moral. But how can moral approval be distinguished from other types? The realist then goes on to argue in one way or another that we can do so only by reference to some judgment that is inextricably involved in the approval — some judgment ascribing moral features to things.[23] Moral approval can thus be differentiated only by reference to the feature or range of features that on the mentalist view it is supposed to explicate. From this the realist draws the inference that moral goodness (or some other moral feature) has the prior status.

The key premise in all such arguments is the assertion that in order to differentiate the C-response, reference must occur sooner or later, directly or indirectly, to the C-feature. The trick for the mentalist is to cast doubt on this premise without thereby denying its natural appeal. One way of doing this is the familiar maneuver which asserts the feature term to be ambiguous, meaning one thing when it names the C-feature (when it stands for a feature of independent objects) and meaning another when it occurs in the differentiating account of the C-response. In the former use it is to be given some complex, perhaps dispositional or emotivist, explication in terms of the latter use where it is to be understood phenomenologically or behaviorally.[24] The differentiation of the C-response does not therefore really involve reference to the C-feature but only involves the use of the ambiguous C-feature term. Because the ambiguity (like ambiguities in general) may be masked, the key premise will seem to bear the realist's interpretation.

Since I am not strongly attracted to this reply, I mention it only to mark it off from another perhaps less familiar response to the realist's argument. This consists in the employment of two maneuvers. The first concerns the realist's challenge to differentiate the C-response from other responses in its genus. The maneuver is to reject the demand as illegitimate. It is not proper to argue from the fact that one thing is different from other coordinate items belonging to some common more general type to the conclusion that there is some concept which can be employed to differentiate the thing as a species of the type. A simple look at colors in the way that many realists conceive them should be enough to convince us of this. Red is certainly a color, and it is certainly different from other colors such as blue; but it is far from clear that it can be differentiated from these other colors in the way the realist demands a differentiation of the C-response. If conceptual analysis is formally analogous to definition of terms (and it is usually taken to be in at least the following respect) then some of our concepts will be incapable of analysis.

And there is no reason why some of these unanalyzable concepts should not cluster together into families under some parental concept (which may itself be unanalyzable). (Note that in adopting this intuitionist strategy, the mentalist should not feel bound to adopt any of the typical intuitionist's other ideas. In particular he need not feel committed to the view that every unanalyzable concept is *simple*, if that insinuates not only that analysis cannot be completed but also that it cannot, as it were, get started. There is nothing in the fact that e.g. amusement is, in principle, not completely formulable that prevents us from listing any number of interesting conceptual truths about it — such as that it is a pleasant affective state disposed to express itself behaviorally and directed toward a perceived or contemplated object. What makes a concept unanalyzable is not the lack of formula but the conceptual space left beside it for a *distinct* concept that shares the formula.) The push to differentiate these family members from one another will be understandable, but unless resisted will inevitably lead to some form of circularity. That circularity in fact occurs, the mentalist will conclude, just at the point where we are forced to refer to the *C*-feature in trying to explicate the *C*-response. For the *C*-feature itself should be analyzed into the *C*-response and not vice versa.

Here the realist is likely to object that this reply could be accepted only on condition that it didn't seem as intuitively correct as it in fact does to differentiate the *C*-response by reference to the *C*-feature. One is not forced to make the differentiation, one is *drawn* to make it. The harder we focus on the *C*-response itself, the surer we become that it is a transparent phenomenon, one that appears to present some unique quality or relation to us. The more we reflect on the nature of amusement, for example, the more we are driven to see it as the *discernment* (or apparent discernment) of the funny. Amusement does not present itself to us as some opaque sensation like pain; nor can it even remotely be captured by any reference to behavior. There is more to amusement than laughter, which is also characteristically associated with various forms of hysteria. Amusement is marked off as what it is by the fact that it feels like the cognition of something about a thing. And the same, or something similar, can be said about the other *C*-responses.

Perhaps this line will not make sense to some mentalists — not strike them as answering to anything in their own reflective experience of the *C*-response. But I am certain that it will seem to do so for some, even if they regard my formulation as crude. Even these sympathetic mentalists, however, have a provocative and not contemptible reply (the second maneuver) reminiscent of moves originally designed to meet Moore's naturalistic fallacy. Let it be

granted that the phenomenology of the C-response is as the realist says —
that there is an important way in which moral approval, amusement, and
something's looking red feel as if they fall on a different side of the cognitive
divide from appetite, fear and pain. But while far from irrelevant, this consideration does not settle the question of analysis. That the C-feature should
or should not be analyzed into the C-response — indeed that any concept
should or should not be construed as posterior to some other — need
not be one of those transparently obvious truths that immediately recommends itself to any possessor of the conceptual scheme. Like all theoretical questions, it is a matter of finding a systematic organization of the scheme
that satisfies various desiderata — only one of which is conformity to pre-
theoretical phenomenological intuition.[25] Whether the mentalist's construction of the scheme has other advantages that compensate, such as
giving us a less cumbersome account of the apparent relativity of C-feature
judgments and a less magical account of their internalist aspects, is a matter
for painstaking evaluation about which men of theoretical good will may
disagree. But what should be admitted by all is that introspective intuition
does not settle the matter by itself, and thus that the way in which we were
drawn to the differentiating account proposed by the realist does not really
force our hand.

IV

The preceding discussion was obviously far too selective and incomplete
to warrant sweeping conclusions. But it may be taken as illustrative, I
think of the vastness of the problem. The instincts that separate the mentalist from the realist involve or at least touch on the most basic matters
of which philosophy treats: the nature of objectivity, conceptual analysis,
essentialism, private languages, and so on. That is to say we should have
been forced to face these and many other basic problems of epistemology,
metaphysics and philosophy of mind in pushing our discussions beyond
the points at which I relaxed my efforts. In no case does this appear more
forcefully than in the closing remarks of the last section. The realist we
were considering there regarded what we might call the *phenomenological
cognitivity* of the C-response as *the* salient aspect of the case, something
that must either be explained away or yielded to. While the mentalist, para-
doxically enough, was ready to treat these introspective mental data more
casually, feeling that they may be made to yield to a theory defensible
on other grounds. Here, quite obviously, we are confronted by unsettling

questions of philosophical methodology – questions for which the special disciplines of ethics, aesthetics and theory of perception may not adequately equip us.

University of California, Los Angeles

NOTES

[1] I mean 'feature' to be given a neutral reading according to which, e.g., even a non-cognitivist could call moral goodness a 'feature' of things. Note that R. Brandt in *Ethical Theory* (Englewood Cliffs: Prentice Hall, 1959), p. 265, correlates ethical features and responses by means of the following principle: " ... a 'corresponding' attitude is the attitude someone justifiably has if some ethical statement is properly asserted by him." But for present purposes (mainly to avoid begging questions in setting up the problem) I prefer to leave the principles of correlation undefined.

[2] Some recent writers in ethics (e.g. S.W. Blackburn in 'Moral Realism', J. Casey, ed., *Morality and Moral Reasoning* (London: Methuen, 1971), pp. 101–124) use a weaker sense of 'realist' to mark off theories holding that feature-ascribing sentences are true or false in virtue of their correspondence or noncorrespondence with extra-linguistic fact. But my stronger sense of 'realist' also implies that the feature is mind-independent in the manner indicated. All naturalistic theories that count as nonrealist in my scheme count as realist in Blackburn's.

[3] See Sidgwick, *The Methods of Ethics*, Seventh Edition, (London: Macmillan, 1907), p. 27 for a classic statement of the realist view of moral feeling. See also Philippa Foot's arguments in 'Moral Beliefs', *Proceedings of the Aristotelian Society*, 59 (1958–59), that moral attitudes are *internally related* to their objects.

[4] For Locke's account of the distinction between primary and secondary qualities see *Essay Concerning Human Understanding* Book II, Chapters viii, 9–26 and xxiii, 9–11; and Book IV, Chapter iii, 11–13 and 28.

[5] Stevenson in 'The Emotive Conception of Ethics and Its Cognitive Implications', *Facts and Values* (New Haven: Yale University Press, 1963), esp. p. 67, finds an essential role for thought in the formation of ethical attitudes. Frankena, a noncognitivist of a different sort, suggests that ethical assertions imply the thought that others will under certain conditions share the relevant attitude. See *Ethics*, Second Edition (Englewood Cliffs: Prentice Hall, 1973), p. 108.

[6] John McDowell drew my attention to David Wiggins' use of the 'perspective' metaphor to express a related point. The possession of a range of affective, motivational or sensory responses creates the perspective without which certain features could not be descried. See the 'Philosophical Lecture: Truth, Invention and the Meaning of Life', forthcoming in the *Proceedings of the British Academy*, 1976.

[7] See Frankena, 'Obligation and Motivation in Recent Moral Philosophy' in A.I. Melden, ed., *Essays in Moral Philosophy* (Seattle: University of Washington Press, 1958), pp. 40–81.

[8] R. Firth's Ideal Observer theory is a prominent example of the former view that

could be modified to fit the latter as well. See 'Ethical Absolutism and the Ideal Observer', *Philosophy and Phenomenological Research*, **XII** (1952), pp. 317–345.

[9] Both Brandt (*Ethical Theory*, p. 267) and Frankena (*Ethics*, pp. 110–113) endorse this qualification.

[10] For Stevenson, the former clearly derives from the latter. See *Ethics and Language* (New Haven: Yale University Press, 1944), Chapter 3. esp. sections 6–7.

[11] *A Treatise of Human Nature*, ed. L.A. Selby-Bigge (Oxford: Clarendon Press, 1888), p. 458. See also pp. 413–418.

[12] But see G. Pitcher 'Pain Perception', *The Philosophical Review*, **LXXIX** (July 1970), pp. 368–393.

[13] For a recent discussion of issues related to this criterion, see C. Wellman, 'Ethical Disagreement and Objective Truth', *American Philosophical Quarterly*, **12** (July, 1975), 211–221.

[14] As Firth does in the Ideal Observer Theory.

[15] Some relevant passages: Plato, *Meno*, 77b–78b, *Gorgias*, 468c, *Protagoras*, 352a–355d; Aristotle, *Nicomachean Ethics* VII, iii, esp. 1147b; Kant, *Groundwork of the Metaphysics of Morals*, p. 460 (Royal Prussian Academy Edition), and *Critique of Practical Reason* Ch. III; Sidgwick, *The Methods of Ethics*, p. 34.

[16] By F. Sibley, for example, in "Aesthetic Concepts," *The Philosophical Review*, **LXVIII** (1959), 421–450.

[17] See Jonathan Bennett's defense of the distinction between primary and secondary qualities in *Locke, Berkeley, Hume: Central Themes* (Oxford: Clarendon Press, 1971) Ch. IV, esp. section 20.

[18] This is perhaps part of what Moore meant by his odd claim that intrinsic goodness is *not* an intrinsic property of a thing that possesses it. See 'The Conception of Intrinsic Value' in *Philosphical Studies* (London: Routledge and Kegan Paul, 1922), esp. pp. 272–273.

[19] I am thinking of realists who accept a *reduction* of C-features to the properties on which others would say they supervene – e.g. a deontologist who identifies moral rightness with the disjunctive property of falling under one or another of such and such rules or a color theorist who identifies the colors with various physical properties.

[20] Cf. Bennett, op. cit., p. 98.

[21] The realist may point out here that a hold on reality is more than a hold on the objects of that reality. For if these eccentricities go far enough we will in fact regard a person as mad.

[22] Cf. Wittgenstein's claim in *Philosophical Investigations* II, xi p. 217, that even "if God had looked into our minds he would not have been able to see there whom we were speaking of" and the immediately preceding remarks. See also Part I, sections 452–453.

[23] W. Alston provides an interesting example of this line of argument – as addressed to emotivists – in 'Moral Attitudes and Moral Judgments,' *Nous* **II** (Feb. 1968), 1–23.

[24] Firth puts this forward as a live possibility for both color and moral terms in 'Ethical Absolutism and the Ideal Observer,' p. 324.

[25] The realist might try to appropriate S. Kripke's comments – intended for a quite different dispute – on the force of intuitive content. See 'Naming and Necessity,' G. Harman and D. Davidson eds., *Semantics of Natural Language* (Dordrecht-Holland, 1972), pp. 265–266.

WILLIAM P. ALSTON

META-ETHICS AND META-EPISTEMOLOGY

Recent epistemology has been heavily concerned with the conceptual and methodological foundations of the subject – in particular with the concepts of knowledge, certainty, basic knowledge, justification, and so on. In other words to a considerable extent it has been taken up with meta-epistemology, in contrast with substantive epistemology, in contrast with questions about what we know, how we know it, and how various parts of our knowledge are interrelated. Just as with ethics, meta-inquiries have been pursued throughout the history of the subject (see, e.g., the discussions of the concept of knowledge in Plato's *Theaetetus* and in Book IV of Locke's *Essay*), but also as in ethics, meta concerns have been more prominent in twentieth century Anglo-American philosophy than ever before.

However meta-epistemology has not yet attained the pitch of self-consciousness displayed by recent meta-ethics. Writers on epistemology, unlike their ethical brethren, rarely signal the shifting of gears between meta and substantive. Nor do most of them seem to be aware of the range of alternatives in meta-epistemology and their interrelations or of the ways in which decisions in meta-epistemology do and do not narrow one's options in substantive epistemology. The time is ripe for an advance to a new level of self-consciousness in this regard. We need to take a hard look at the problems of meta-epistemology, their possible solutions, and their relations to the problems of substantive epistemology.

This paper is designed to make a contribution to that enterprise. I take as my point of departure the fact that all these matters have been, if anything, over-discussed in recent meta-ethics. Here the territory has been extensively mapped, the problems catalogued, the alternative positions delineated and interrelated, the connections with substantive ethics explored. The idea suggests itself that we might take all this as an initial model and try to do something of the same sort for meta-epistemology. In this paper I shall exploit only the grosser features of the meta-epistemological terrain, leaving the finer grain for future exploration.

A. I. Goldman and J. Kim (eds.), Values and Morals, 275–297. All Rights Reserved.
Copyright © 1978 by D. Reidel Publishing Company, Dordrecht, Holland.

I

According to a fairly young, but very well entrenched, tradition, the major divide in meta-ethics is between Cognitivism and Non-Cognitivism, with the former divided in turn into Intuitionism and Naturalism, thus yielding the familiar trichotomy of textbook and classroom. The major division can be formulated in terms of whether ethical judgments (statements, sentences, propositions) are susceptible of objective truth values — Cognitivism affirming and Non-Cognitivism denying this. Within Cognitivism, the Naturalist holds that ethical terms (concepts, statements) can be defined, explicated, or analyzed in 'factual' terms, that they, at bottom *are* factual terms, and that ethical questions are, at bottom, questions of fact, perhaps of an especially complicated sort. The Intuitionist, on the other hand, maintains that ethical concepts are *sui generis*, that they are of a distinctively and irreducibly normative or evaluative sort, not to be reduced to matters of fact, however complex.[1]

In looking for meta-epistemological analogues of these distinctions we will concentrate on the two forms of Cognitivism. To be sure, despite the paradoxicality of the phrase 'non-cognitivist theory of *knowledge*', suggestions along this line have not been absent from the literature. The best known is John Austin's 'performative' theory, the basic idea of which is that when I say 'I know that *p*' I am not 'describing' some condition I am in, but rather giving others my *authority* for saying that *p*[2]. However non-cognitivism is much less prevalent here than in meta-ethics. Most epistemologists, past and present, have taken it that attributions of knowledge have definite truth values (subject to qualifications concerning vagueness and indeterminacy of concepts along with most of the rest of factual discourse). I shall go along with this trend and restrict consideration to cognitivist theories.

The most obvious analogue to meta-ethical intuitionism is the form of Justified True Belief (JTB) conception of knowledge that is set out with exemplary explicitness by R. M. Chisholm.[3] On this view the fact that *S* knows that *p* is thought of as consisting of at least three component facts, viz.,:

(1)   It is the case that *p* (it is true that *p*)
(2)   *S* believes that *p*
(3)   *S* is justified in believing that *p*.[4]

To these is sometimes added a fourth condition to take care of Gettier-type counter-examples. The similarity with Intuitionism is based on the third condition. 'Justified' is naturally construed as an evaluative term. To say that someone is justified in believing that p is to say that in believing that p he is proceeding as he *ought*, that he has every *right* to suppose that p, that it is *reasonable* of him to do so, that he is conducting himself in an *acceptable* manner. Furthermore this dimension of evaluation is a distinctively epistemic one. What counts towards S's knowing that p is not that he is morally, prudentially, or legally justified in believing that p, but rather that his belief that p satisfies some specifically epistemic standards, standards that have to do with a kind of excellence that is appropriate to the quest for knowledge. One way of putting it would be this. Being epistemically justified in believing that p is the kind of state that an ideal epistemic subject, one whose overriding concern in cognition is to believe that p *iff* p is true, would take as a sufficient ground for a positive attitude toward S's belief.

Thus on the JTB conception the concept of knowledge is, in part, an evaluative concept. Now if we hold, as Chisholm does, that this evaluative concept is indefinable in factual terms, we will be taking the position that the concept of knowledge is *sui generis* for just the same reason that Intuitionists in meta-ethics take ethical terms to be *sui generis*, viz., by reason of essentially involving an irreducibly evaluative or normative component. Admittedly, most philosophers who construe knowledge in JTB terms have not explicitly confronted the basic questions about the concept of justification; Chisholm is exceptional in this respect. Nevertheless I think that we may take Chisholm to be following out the tendencies inherent in this way of thinking about knowledge, and take his meta-epistemology as paradigmatic for JTB theorists.

The most obvious meta-epistemological analogue to meta-ethical naturalism is found in the various causal and reliability theories propounded by, e.g., A. I. Goldman,[5] D. M. Armstrong,[6] and F. Dretske.[7] This kind of view is best presented as a different answer to the same question answered by JTB in terms of justification, viz., what makes a true belief that p into knowledge that p? This second answer is either in terms of some kind of causal or nomological relation between the belief that p and the fact that p, or in terms of the belief's being produced by a reliable belief-producing mechanism, one that can be relied on to produce true beliefs either all or most of the time (in most kinds of situations or at least in most kinds of situations we are likely to encounter, or at least in situations like this one). Whichever way we do it, there is a clear sense in which, on this conception, what makes a true belief into knowledge is a state of affairs of a sort that is by no means confined to the subject matter of epistemology. Causal relations obtain between inorganic things that are quite incapable of knowledge. And although a reliable belief-producing mechanism can be possessed only by beings capable of belief, still the general notion of a mechanism's output being a reliable indication of some external state of affairs is one that applies to such humble non-knowers as thermometers. Thus on this sort of account knowledge that *p* is a special case of facts of a sort that are by no means unique to the epistemic realm. This view is like meta-ethical naturalism, both in that it takes the concepts in question to be factual in character, and because it supposes these concepts to be made up of concepts that are not at all peculiar to the body of discourse in question.

However there are other meta-epistemological views of a cognitivist sort that do not fit so neatly into this dichotomy. The possibility of recalcitrant cases follows from the fact that JTB theories and causal-reliability theories differ in two respects: (a) the former but not the latter take the concept of knowledge to be, in part, irreducibly evaluative; (b) the former but not the latter take epistemic concepts to include elements that are peculiar to epistemology, not composable out of pieces that are found elsewhere. This suggests the possibility of views that differ from JTB in one of these respects and from causal-reliability in the other. I know of no view that combines the claim that knowledge involves an irreducibly evaluative element with the denial that epistemic concepts are *sui generis*, but the opposite combination is quite prominent in the history of the subject, in the form of what we may call the Intuitive conception of knowledge. According to this view "Knowledge is something ultimate and not further analysable. It is simply the situation in which some entity or some fact is directly present to consciousness"[8]. This view of knowledge is found throughout the history of philosophy. There is a particularly clear exposition in Locke's *Essay* (IV, i, 1) where knowledge is defined as the perception of the agreement and disagreement of ideas.

On this view the concept of knowledge is *sui generis*. The concept of something being *directly present to consciousness* or *given* to consciousness, of our being *directly aware* of it, is supposed not to be analysable or explainable in terms of simpler concepts, though it is held that we can point to familiar examples of it, e.g., our awareness of sense-data and of facts about sense-data. However what makes the concept *sui generis* is not the presence of some irreducibly evaluative component. The presence of *x* to consciousness will presumably be a clear case of something factual as opposed to evaluative.

How is the Intuitive conception to be classified? If we take the defining characteristic of the epistemological analogue of Naturalism to be the claim that epistemic concepts are purely factual, it will be a form of Naturalism. Whereas if we take the defining characteristic to be the claim that epistemic concepts are (at least in part) *sui generis*, then it will be a form of Intuition-ism. We can, of course, set things up in either of these ways, or set up a third category; it is simply a question of what classification highlights the most important features. For reasons to be brought out in the course of this paper I feel that the most fundamental division in meta-epistemology con-cerns the reducibility or irreducibility of epistemic concepts. Therefore I shall adopt the second alternative of those mentioned. The analogue to Intuitionism will be the view that epistemic concepts are *sui generis*, in whole or part; the JTB and Intuitive conceptions will be alternative forms of this position. Since this position differs trom meta-ethical intuitionism in not necessarily holding that irreducibly *evaluative* or *normative* concepts are involved, I shall choose a different term. And since the position, as we shall see, stresses the self-containedness, the independence of epistemology I shall call it the Autonomy position, or, at the cost of a very ugly neologism, Autonomism. The opposite position, that epistemic concepts can be analyzed into components that are not distinctively epistemic, I shall correspondingly call the Heteronomy position, or Heteronomism.[9]

Since the Intuitive conception is presently out of favor, I shall focus on the JTB version of Autonomism in the ensuing discussion. So long as we are restricting ourselves to the opposition between the JTB view and causal-reliability views, we may as well avail ourselves of the familiar meta-ethical terms, Intuitionism and Naturalism. I shall take R. M. Chisholm as my para-digmatic intuitionist and D. M. Armstrong as my paradigmatic naturalist. These thinkers not only present fully developed theories of the kind specified, but they are also much more self-conscious methodologically than most of their colleagues.

II

It will help in understanding our basic meta-epistemological distinction it we see how it crosscuts some more familiar divides in epistemology. First con-sider the opposition between foundationalist and coherence theorists. The interrelations are complicated by the fact that theories of these latter types are conceived in quite different ways. Thus we may have a coherence meta-epistemology, i.e., a view according to which knowledge that p is to be *defined* in terms of the involvement of one's belief that p in a coherent system of beliefs. In that case, depending on how 'coherence' is defined, this will be a particular form of an autonomist or a heteronomist meta-epistemology. It would be more unusual for a foundationalist to state his position as an account of the meaning of 'S knows that p'. It is commonly presented as a substantive position in epistemology more specifically as a position about the conditions under which a belief is justified; and it is opposed to a coherence position on the same issue. It may be possible to formulate analogues of foundationalist and coherence epistemologies for a causal or reliability conception of knowledge, but the job remains to be done. I hope that even this quick glance at the issue will suffice to show that the Autonomy-Heteronomy divide by no means coincides with the foundationalist-coherence divide. Just to extract the most easily made point from the foregoing, a coherence theorist might either be a Heteronomist who takes knowledge to be definable in terms of certain kinds of logical relations between propositions, or he may be an Autonomist who holds the substantive normative view that what it takes for a belief to be justified is that it participate in a certain kind of system with other beliefs.

Another crosscutting issue is whether knowledge requires certainty. In order to formulate the issue with sufficient generality, let us use the term 'epistemization' for whatever transforms a true belief that p into knowledge that p. Thus for the JTB conception one's belief is epistemized *iff* it is (adequately) justified, whereas for Armstrong what epistemizes a belief is the fact that, in the circumstances, one's belief that p is empirically sufficient for its being the case that p[10]. Now 'certainty' is a term that ranges widely over this conceptual territory[11], and we will not have time to explore all the varieties. Suffice it for the present to consider impossibility of mistake (infallibility), and even here let us not pause to ask just what sort of *impossibility* is in question. The points I want to make are, first, that some epistemologists take knowledge that p to require an epistemization strong enough to rule out the possibility that one's belief that p is in error, while others are willing to settle for a weaker epistemization, one that merely renders p highly probable; and, second, that both infallibilists and fallibilists are found on both sides of our divide. Among Heteronomists, Armstrong[12] and Dretske[13] are 'infallibilists', requiring epistemization to render mistake (empirically or causally) impossible; while Goldman[14] is a fallibilist. On the Autonomist side, Chisholm in company with most contemporary JTB theorists, sets things up so that it is possible for a false proposition to be evident for S[15], while Panayot Butchvarov requires of 'justification sufficient for knowledge'[16] that it rule out the possibility of error.

III

Now I want to explore the consequences of each position on our basic divide for some central issues in epistemology and meta-epistemology. At the outset it will be well to remind ourselves that the main thrust of meta-ethics has always been toward the methodology of substantive ethics. The detailed investigations of the meanings of ethical terms, so prominent in this century, have not been undertaken out of an intrinsic interest in the semantics of this segment of language, but rather for the light this throws on the status of ethical judgments: how they are properly evaluated, defended, attacked; what sorts of considerations may be relevantly brought to bear on them; how we settle ethical questions and disagreements. Presumably the same is true of meta-epistemology. Let's see what happens if we try to apply to epistemology the main methodological implications that have been typically drawn from naturalism and intuitionism in meta-ethics.

A naturalist analysis of ethical terms will exhibit ethical statements as factual statements, the truth or falsity of which can, in principle, be determined by empirical investigation.[17] If 'right' is defined as 'conducive to the survival of the species', then it is a matter for (very complex) empirical investigation to determine whether a given action is the right thing to do. The naturalist definition lays out the lines along which we are to determine whether the term applies in a given instance. If, on the other hand, 'right', 'justified' or 'know' is a term for an unanalysable non-natural quality, status, or act, as the intuitionist maintains, we are provided no such lead. The analysis does not tell us what to look for to determine whether the term applies in a particular case. That is the price we pay for irreducibility. Of course, once we have established one or more ethical principles *they* will tell us something of the conditions under which an act is right or a state of affairs good. But how do we establish those initial principles? How do we get started on the enterprise of determining the conditions of application for ethical terms? The intuitionist's position leaves him no alternative to claiming that we have an immediate apprehension of the truth of certain ethical statements – either singular or general. Either we have a 'moral sense' that enables us to spot rightness or goodness in the particular case; or we have a capacity to recognize the self-evidence of certain general ethical principles; or both. Since these apprehensions are immediate we do not need to have previously ascertained that the terms apply under certain conditions. Having exercised our intuition in particular cases or with general principles, or both, we are thereby given a basis for building up the body of ethical knowledge.

We may sum this up by saying that for the naturalist all ethical questions, including the most fundamental ones, are to be settled like any other empirical, factual questions, by the usual methods of empirical investigation — observation, experiment, induction, and the testing of hypotheses. Whereas for the intuitionist ethical investigation is built on the intuitive unmediated apprehensions of ethical truths.

Similar conclusions follow from the analogous meta-epistemological positions. According to the Heteronomist whether *S* knows that *p* is a question of whether *S*'s belief that *p* stands in the right kind of causal or nomological relation to the fact that *p*, or alternatively, whether *S*'s belief that *p* was produced by a reliable belief-producing mechanism. Thus the question is properly investigated by whatever procedures are suitable for settling questions about nomological relations and/or the reliability of input-output mechanisms; and this at least includes the standard empirical procedures of observation, experiment, induction, and the testing of hypotheses. Because of the relatively undeveloped self-consciousness of meta-epistemology, noted at the outset, this point is not prominent in the literature, but we do find it popping out at certain points.[18]

If, on the other hand, the concept of knowledge contains an irreducibly evaluative component, we can hardly expect to get any handle on determining who knows what without having some immediate knowledge either of particular instances of this evaluative status, or of general principles specifying the conditions under which it obtains. Chisholm, our paradigmatic intuitionist, is, as I have suggested, much more clearly aware of the problems of meta-epistemology than his colleagues, and his presentation of this point in *Theory of Knowledge* is admirably explicit.

We presuppose, first, that there *is* something that we know and we adopt the working hypothesis that *what* we know is pretty much that which, on reflection, we think we know. This may seem the wrong place to start. But where else *could* we start? . . .

We presuppose, second, that the things we know are justified for us in the following sense: *we* can know what it is, on any occasion, that constitutes our grounds, or reason, or evidence for thinking that we know . . .

And we presuppose, third, that if we do thus have grounds or reasons for the things we think we know, then there are valid general principles of evidence — principles stating the general conditions under which we may be said to have grounds or reasons for what we believe . . .

In order to formulate, or make explicit, our rules of evidence, we will do well to proceed as we do in logic, when formulating the rules of inference, or in moral philosophy, when formulating rules of action. We suppose that we have at our disposal certain instances which the rules should countenance or permit and other instances which the rules should reject or forbid; and we suppose that by investigating these instances we can formulate criteria which any instance must satisfy if it is to be rejected or forbidden. To obtain the instances we need if we are to formulate rules of evidence, we may proceed in the following way.

We consider certain things that we know to be true, or think we know to be true, or certain things which, upon reflection, we would be willing to call *evident*. With respect to each of these, we then try to formulate a reasonable answer to the question, 'What justification do you have for thinking you know this thing to be true?' or 'What justification do you have for counting this thing to be evident?' . . . (pp. 16-17)[19]

Here and elsewhere in the book Chisholm emphasizes the point that we have to *begin* with the assumption that we know certain things and that certain propositions are evident. ('Where else *could* we start?') It is not that we are to *establish* propositions to the effect that we know certain things, on the basis of other things we know, by empirical investigation or otherwise. Rather we must have knowledge of our knowledges and justifications at the outset of our epistemological inquiry.

It is clear from this passage that Chisholm's position is analogous to the *moral-sense* form of intuitionism rather than to the *self-evident first principles* forms. He proposes to start with immediate knowledge of particular instances of knowledge or evidence and then determine what general principles will cover those cases.

IV

It is against this background that we can understand the insistence of Autonomists on the accessibility to a subject of his own epistemic conditions. It is a striking fact that JTB theorists, as well as partisans of the Intuitive conception, almost universally take some form of what we may call the High Accessibility position, the position that epistemic states are, in one way or another, readily accessible to their possessor. The most extreme form of this thesis is that knowledge that *p* entails, implies, or otherwise necessarily carries with it knowledge that one knows that *p*. However this extreme position has been widely recognized of late to run into serious difficulties, particularly over the fact that it seems quite possible to know that *p* without having the concept of knowledge, and so without satisfying the most elementary requirements for knowing that one knows that *p*. Chisholm takes a more modest position. More or less following Prichard, an eminent 20th century Intuitive theorist, he holds that:

If S considers the proposition that he knows that p, and if he does know that p, then he knows that he knows that p.[20]

In other words, if one knows that p he can come to realize that he knows that p just by considering the matter, just by turning his attention to the question. (He could not, of course 'consider the matter' unless he had the concept of knowledge.) One doesn't need any other knowledge or justified belief as grounds or reasons for the higher level belief than he knows that p. The lower level epistemic fact that makes the higher level belief true is all that is needed, provided the person will open himself to it and has the conceptual equipment needed for 'grasping' it. Thus a normal adult human being is capable of an unlimited amount of *immediate* knowledge of his own knowledge, limited only by the knowledge that is there to be known.

We may take the Heteronomist to hold the same principle for other epistemic conditions, like being justified. This principle is clearly designed to guarantee the Heteronomist the basis of particular cases he needs to get his investigation started. If the epistemic states of a reflective individual are all available to him on demand, the epistemologist will have no dearth of data to use in testing epistemic principles. These considerations enable one to understand the fact that intuitionists regularly embrace High Accessibility principles, despite the fact that the arguments with which they support these principles are, in my judgment, totally lacking in cogency. If one is convinced that there is nowhere else to start, then he will find the means to convince himself of the required assumptions that one can ascertain his own particular knowings and justifications just by considering the matter.

In view of the centrality of High Accessibility for the intuitionist's scheme, it is of interest to determine what position the naturalist does, or should, take on the issue. We would have an ideally clear cut opposition if we could represent the Naturalist as constrained by his meta-epistemology to deny Chisholm's principle, to hold that mere reflection is (always or sometimes) insufficient for one to ascertain his epistemic condition. And, indeed, one may be tempted to suppose that this is the way the land lies. For, it would seem, knowledge, as construed by the Naturalist, is just not the sort of thing one could ascertain in this way. For Armstrong and for Dretske to know that p is, roughly, to have a belief that p in such circumstances that one would not have had that belief in those circumstances unless it were the case that p. How on earth could one be expected to know that such a counter-factual is true just by turning one's attention to the issue? Surely to know that requires that I have reasons or evidence that I would not automatically acquire just by raising the question. On Goldman's version of Naturalism one knows that p only if one's belief that p was produced by a belief producing mechanism that can be relied on to (always or usually) produce true beliefs (at least in certain kinds of circumstances). Again, for me to know that what produced my belief has this feature it seems that I would have to know a lot about my psychology and perhaps other things as well. On either version I need general knowledge about the way things go in the world. And surely I cannot acquire all that just by turning my attention to the issue.

But this would be a superficial reading of the situation. It is not inconceivable, on Naturalist principles, that knowledge of knowledge should be available for the asking. The Naturalist concept of knowledge does not itself put any particular restrictions on the objects of *immediate* knowledge, on what one can know apart from evidence in the shape of other things one knows. On Naturalist principles, one can know that p not on the basis of evidence (non-inferentially) if one possesses a belief forming mechanism that reliably produces beliefs that p from inputs that do not include other knowledge one has. The question of whether one possesses such a mechanism for a certain type of belief, e.g., beliefs about one's own knowledge, is a question of psychological fact; we cannot expect it to be resolved just by the definition of knowledge. Thus the Naturalist meta-epistemology leaves open the *possibility* of Chisholmian knowledge of knowledge.[21]

However the very considerations that show the Heteronomist not to be constrained by his position to deny Chisholm's principle, can also show us a more abstract respect in which the Heteronomist *is* necessarily in opposition to the Autonomist on the accessibility issue. For what the above considerations show is that, for the Heteronomist, it is a question of empirical fact as the conditions under which one has knowledge of knowledge, or, indeed, any other knowledge. But clearly that is not the case for Chisholm, and in this again he is typical of Autonomists. Chisholm does not purport to be performing an induction from a number of cases in which he has *discovered* reflection to possess this efficacy. Nor is his principle offered as an empirical hypothesis, to be evaluated in terms of how well it explains the empirical facts. Rather he attempts to derive the principle from his system of epistemic principles (which are themselves not construed as empirical hypotheses) and definitions of epistemic terms.[22] Thus he takes high accessibility to be required by basic epistemological principles. It is a question of (epistemological) principle, not a question of fact. Whereas for the Heteronomist it is *not* required by the fundamental principles of his epistemology; it is up for grabs in terms of detailed empirical investigations.

It is possible for A to know that p without knowing that he knows it . . . , and even for A to know that p and disbelieve that he knows it. (Armstrong, *op. cit.*, p. 212)

One qualifies for knowledge when one has conclusive reasons for believing; one need not, in addition, know that one has conclusive grounds. (Dretske, *op. cit.*, p. 17)

The possibility of which Armstrong speaks should not be interpreted as mere logical possibility; Chisholm might well agree with the statement on that reading. Rather he is saying that the basic principles of epistemology leave open this possibility; the epistemology doesn't rule it out.

Since the opposition between Autonomist and Heteronomist on the accessibility issue is going to play a large role in the sequel, it is important to get clear as to its exact nature. To repeat, the opposition is not over whether in fact one can have immediate knowledge of all one's knowledge, but over whether this is guaranteed by basic epistemological principles. Let's use the term 'Accessibility in Principle' for what is affirmed by the Auton-omist and denied by the Heteronomist.

Though it is clear to me that the meta-epistemological positions we are considering do constrain their proponents to take differing positions on accessibility, it may be that the analysis of knowledge does not constitute the deepest roots of those positions. It is certainly a striking fact that the main tradition in epistemology since Descartes, which has been strongly Autonomist, has also been preoccupied with answering skepticism, with vindicating our claims to knowledge (or some of them) in the face of skeptical doubts. It has, I believe, been widely felt that we will have a chance of meeting the skeptical challenge only if our knowledge and other epistemic conditions are immediately available to us. For otherwise we would have to depend on other knowledge to show that we know anything, and so the enterprise would bog down in circularity. Now it seems clear to me that the immediate accessibility of ones own epistemic states does in fact give one no advantage whatsoever in meeting the demand of the skeptic, *if* that requires *showing* that one knows something. For to *show* this, in the relevant sense of constructing a discursive argument for it, requires that one use certain premises that one is presupposing one knows to be true. If one were not making that presupposition one could hardly be claiming to establish the conclusion by exhibiting its relation to the premises. And this means that any attempt to *show* that one knows something is going to be infected with circularity, however much immediate knowledge one in fact has. But this point has *not* been appreciated in the tradition; the classical epistemologists from Descartes on have supposed that our capacity for immediate apprehension of our own knowings is what enables us to meet the skeptical challenge. And perhaps it does in a sense – not by way of enabling me to construct an argument that establishes the thesis that I know something, but by way of satisfying *myself* that I do. In any event, it is not implausible to suppose that this overriding aim of stilling skeptical doubts has given an impetus *both* to Autonomist meta-epistemology *and* to an Accessibility in Principle thesis, perhaps to each of these coordinately, perhaps to one through the other, perhaps in all these ways. Obviously this matter needs much more exploration; in this paper I am just throwing it out as a suggestion.

This suggestion is reinforced by what we find on the other side of the fence. Heteronomists have been markedly unconcerned with meeting skepticism. They typically start from the assumption that knowledge is a 'natural fact', one of the distinctive achievements of human beings and other animals; they suppose that knowledge simply confronts them as one of the things in the world to be studied, and understood. They feel no need to show that there is such a thing before investigating it. Hence they are without this motive for embracing an Accessibility in Principle thesis.

The difference over accessibility is going to have crucial implications for the Cartesian programme. Suppose we set out to build up knowledge from scratch, starting from whatever propositions can be known with certainty, apart from any support from other assumed knowledge. Let us further suppose, with Descartes, that no propositions about the physical world fall in that class. Now clearly, assuming there are such propositions we have to be able to identify them as such at the outset of our construction if we are going to get it off the ground. The bearing of the contrast just sketched is clear. Autonomism carries a guarantee that this will be possible while Heteronomism does not. For the Autonomist, if I do know that *p* with certainty at this moment, that itself can be known by me just for the asking. And so whatever isolated certainties I possess can be reliably identified by me as such, provided I persist in my reflection. But Heteronomism provides no such guarantee. Heteronomism doesn't rule out the possibility, but neither does it affirm it. It is no wonder that autonomist meta-epistemology and the Cartesian programme have always had close affinities for each other.

V

So far our discussion of intuitionist and naturalist 'methodology' has focused on the epistemological status of particular epistemic propositions, propositions attributing knowledge or justification to a particular subject at a particular

time vis-a-vis a particular proposition. Now let's turn to the implications of
our two meta-epistemological positions for the more general enterprise of
constructing a systematic epistemological theory — establishing general
principles that lay down the conditions under which propositions of a general
sort are known, evident, justified, or what have you.

We have already sketched Chisholm's typically intuitionist position on
this matter. Armed with an unlimited quantity of data in the form of particular pieces of knowledge and evidence from his own cognitive experience, the
epistemologist proceeds to formulate general principles that will certify the
cases of knowledge and rule out the cases of non-knowledge.

Now in the light of the point made earlier, that it is consistent with
Naturalism to hold that one does have immediate access to all or some of
one's own knowledge, it is clear that it does not follow from the general
principles of Naturalism that the epistemologist cannot proceed as Chisholm
recommends. If in fact we do have sufficient immediate access to our own
epistemic states, then, whatever the correct account of epistemic concepts,
we *can* use Chisholm's methodology. But even if we are so endowed there is
still a basic methodological difference between intuitionist and naturalist on
the conduct of epistemology. For the latter, but not for the former, there
will be a more fundamental, a theoretically more satisfying way of doing the
job. Let's concentrate on the form of Naturalism according to which a true
believe that p is a case of knowledge that p when it was produced by a
reliable mechanism. Clearly on that construal of knowledge, even if I do have
some immediate knowledge of my own epistemic states, the preferred way of
developing a systematic epistemology would be to build on (or build up) an
adequate psychological theory of belief-forming mechanisms, and then
determine which of these are reliable under what conditions. This would be
the preferred method for two closely interrelated reasons.

First, it investigates the matter in terms of what knowledge *is*, in terms of
the real character of what is being investigated, whereas in Chisholm's inductive approach that is bypassed. And because it proceeds by way of what is
(according to the meta-epistemology being assumed) the real nature of the
subject-matter, it does not have to limit itself to listing the conditions under
which a given epistemic status is in fact forthcoming; it can aspire to *explaining*
why one or another set of conditions is required for the attainment of that
status. According to this meta-epistemology the reason why one's belief that
p, for a certain type of p, is epistemized by one set of conditions rather than
another, is that it is under those conditions that the belief is produced by a
reliable mechanism. And by carrying through the enterprise in the way

specified, this connection would be brought to light. The second reason is this. Principles arrived at in this explanatorily fundamental way are more likely to hold up over the entire spread of possible cases than principles arrived at by a mere induction from a sample of positive and negative cases. For the particular sample with which we work may be biased in ways that do not reflect the nature and operation of the underlying mechanisms that are responsible for the outcome.

These points are worth an illustration. One of Chisholm's epistemic principles is the following:

For any subject S, if S believes, without ground for doubt, that he is perceiving something to be F, then it is beyond reasonable doubt for S that he perceives something to be F. (*Op. cit.*, p. 76)

Chisholm's defense of this principle will be that it lays down as little as possible in the way of requirements to fit actual cases of justified perceptual beliefs, as revealed by our immediate knowledge of our own epistemic states. But from the standpoint of the 'reliable mechanism' theory, if such beliefs are actually beyond reasonable doubt this is because the conditions of human perception are such that most such perceptual beliefs are formed by a reliable mechanism. Thus even if Chisholm's principle is in fact correct, we have not seen why it is correct until we have brought out the pertinent facts concerning the cognitive mechanisms that are responsible for perceptual belief formation. And, second, until we have an adequate account of those mechanisms and the conditions of their efficient operation, we will not be able to specify the limits within which the principles hold, or specify what environmental conditions are responsible for the fact that it does fit the general run of cases that actually do occur. Let's spell out this last point a bit further. If anything is clear from the millenia of discussions of perception, it is that for any perceptual mechanism that yields reliable outputs under normal conditions it is easy to imagine, and possible to institute, conditions under which that reliability will diminish. Our visual apparatus no doubts works very well in the ordinary run of things, but it is easily fooled by cleverly constructed imitations, not to mention more sophisticated neuro-physiological possibilities of deception. If it is true that every perceptual belief concerning which the perceived *has* no doubts deserves to be called 'beyond reasonable doubt', this is undoubtedly, in part, because our perceptual mechanisms are quite reliable in the environments in which they are usually called upon to operate. But unless our epistemic principles are based on an adequate theory of those mechanisms and their operations we will not be able to specify those environing conditions on which Chisholm's principle depends for its acceptability. We will be blindly reflecting our destiny, rather than delineating it.

Thus we may say that for Naturalism the ideal for epistemological theory will be the development of a fundamental psychological theory of belief-producing mechanisms, and an account of the conditions under which they are reliable — all this to be achieved by the usual methods of empirical science. Whereas, as Chisholm makes explicit, the intuitionist has no other recourse than to look for principles that fit his initial intuitive epistemic data.

This means that, for the Heteronomist, whatever temporary expedients he might adopt, epistemology is not the exclusive province of the philosopher. The philosopher has the analytical job of explicating the basic concepts, laying out conceptual alternatives, and exhibiting logical relationships; but then it is up to psychology to give us the theory of cognitive mechanisms on which epistemic principles will be built. The philosopher can't do it all in his armchair. Whereas the autonomist methodology, as expounded by Chisholm, is nicely calculated to insure that possibility. The relevant data are available to one who never leaves his armchair except to acquire some common sense knowledge. There is a close analogy in all this to be the intuitionism-naturalism opposition in meta-ethics.

It follows that epistemology, in its ideal realization, will occupy very different places in the organization of human inquiry, for our own two positions. To put it shortly, for the Autonomist epistemology comes earlier. Heteronomist epistemology, done properly, must come rather late. For it presupposes considerable development of scientific knowledge and methodology in general, and of psychological theory in particular. It cannot be done any earlier than any other specialized branch of psychological theory; and psychology, for whatever reasons, is not an early bloomer among the sciences. Whereas for the Autonomist, epistemology, at least those parts that have to do with commonsense knowledge, could in principle be done before any development of scientific theory. It is *autonomous*, not dependent on other developed branches of knowledge. To be sure, even for the Autonomist it could not be our very first cognitive achievement. The presence of a truth condition for knowledge ensures that one cannot know that he knows that *p* without at least simultaneously knowing that *p*. And pieces of knowledge like the former are required by the Autonomist as bases for the systematic development of the discipline. But to develop epistemology the Autonomist requires nothing more than the possession of various individual pieces of lower level knowledge. He doesn't need other bodies of theory.

VI

Let's now look at the implications of our two positions for the distinction of mediate and immediate knowledge and for what is required for knowledge of each type.

The distinction between mediate (indirect) and immediate (direct) knowledge is generally made within the JTB conception. Knowledge is mediate when the justification involved is mediate, and immediate when the justification involved is immediate. The most fundamental way of distinguishing between mediate and immediate justification, and the way most neutral between different substantive positions, is the following.

> S is mediately justified in believing that $p = df$. What justifies S in believing that p is the fact that this belief stands in the appropriate relations to some other justified beliefs of S.

> S is immediately justified in believing that $p = df$. What justifies S in believing that S is something other than this belief standing in appropriate relations to other justified beliefs of S.

In more familiar, though less careful terms, S is mediately justified in believing that p when he has adequate evidence, grounds, or reasons for believing that p (in the form of other things he knows or is justified in believing), whereas he is immediately justified in believing that p when he is justified by something other than that.

A Heteronomist cannot, of course, make the distinction in just those terms, but we can use the wider concept of 'epistemizing' introduced earlier to give a more general statement of the distinction between mediate and immediate knowledge, one that is applicable to any conception of knowledge that recognizes that knowledge that p entails belief that p. We begin by defining mediate and immediate epistemization in exactly the say way as that in which mediate and immediate justification were defined on the preceeding page.

> S's belief that p is mediately epistemized $=_{df}$. What epistemizes S's belief that p is the fact that this belief stands in an appropriate relation to other epistemized beliefs of S. S's belief that p is immediately epistemized $=_{df}$. What epistemizes S's belief that p is something other than its standing in an appropriate relation to some other epistemized beliefs of S.

Then, as before, mediate knowledge is knowledge that involves mediate epistemization, and immediate knowledge is knowledge that involves immediate epistemization.

Even though this conception of immediacy is purely negative with respect to what does the epistemizing, it is, given certain plausible assumptions, quite important to determine what kinds of propositions can be immediately known in this sense. For if the regress argument is cogent, we can mediately know that p only if p can be connected by the right kind of inferential links to propositions all of which are known immediately. Hence, what we can know immediately puts limitations on what can be known in any way.

So let's consider the question of what can be recognized on our two positions to immediately epistemize a belief, and what sorts of beliefs might acquire this status on the two positions. The first question has a definite clear-cut answer for the Heteronomist but not the the Autonomist. On the 'reliable mechanism' version of Naturalism S's belief that p is epistemized *iff* it was produced by a reliable belief-producing mechanism. The epistemizing will be immediate *iff* the reliability of that mechanism does not essentially depend on any input from other epistemized beliefs of S. In other words, the epistemization is immediate *iff* it does not require that p has been inferred (or otherwise generated) from premises that are themselves epistemized for S. Now of course it is a further question (the second question above) as to just what kinds of beliefs *can* be epistemized in this way. Presumably beliefs about one's own current conscious experiences are so epistemized; and it is not at all implausible to think of perceptual beliefs about the physical environment (or some of them) as being produced by a reliable perceptual mechanism that does not depend on input from other beliefs that are antecedently epistemized.[24] Thus on Naturalism we have good prospects for a fairly extensive variety of immediately known propositions, ranging over singular propositions about objects as well as propositions about the believer's current experience, and possibly over quite different matters as well. This gives the Heteronomist hope of being able to avoid the notorious blind alleys encountered in the attempt to derive all one's knowledge from propositions about one's current experience.

The situation is cloudier for the Intuitionist. There is always liable to be persistent controversy over the conditions of application of irreducibly evaluative terms. Thus on the first question, we find one or another Autonomist holding that S's belief that p is immediately justified *if and only if*, (a) S is immediately aware of the fact that p (or, alternatively, of the object the proposition that p is 'about'),[25] (b) it is true that p and p belongs to a certain select class of propositions,[26] (c) p belongs to a certain select class of propositions (the belief is 'self-justified' or 'self-warranted').[27] However on one point Autonomist theorists are in agreement — a belief cannot be immediately justified just by the fact that it was non-inferentially produced by a reliable mechanism. Chisholm puts this point succinctly.

But aren't we overlooking the most obvious type of epistemic justification? Thus one might object; 'The best justification we could have for a given proposition would be the fact that it comes from a *reliable source*. What could be more reasonable than accepting the deliverances of such a source — whether the source be an authority, or a computer, or a sense organ, or some kind of psychological faculty, or science itself?' The answer is, of course, that it is reasonable to put one's faith in a source which is such that one *knows* it to be reliable or one has good *ground* or *reason* or *evidence* for thinking it to be reliable. (*Op. cit.*, p. 63)

Note that Chisholm not only rejects this suggestion but regards it as *obviously* mistaken; he seems to think that one only needs to have its defects called to one's attention to recognize them as such. This indicates that his rejection must have fairly deep roots in his system; and we do not have to look far for those roots. Since the Autonomist is committed to holding that any epistemic status is readily recognizable on reflection, he cannot admit that a belief can be epistemized by a fact that might obtain without being readily available to the believer. And the modes put forward by Heteronomists clearly do not meet that condition. I can't ascertain that my belief was produced by a reliable mechanism just by considering the question.

Thus in the sphere of immediate justification Autonomists restrict themselves to epistemizers that (they believe) are readily available to the believer. It is plausible to suppose that p's being 'presented' to my consciousness is something I can ascertain just by considering the matter. Likewise if what immediately justifies a belief is just that it is of a certain sort, e.g., a belief about the believer's current thoughts, then, provided I have the concept of that belief-type, it seems that I can hardly fail to be aware that it is of that type, if the question is raised. It may be doubted that these matters are as easily accessible as Autonomists suppose.[28] But at any rate, the plausibilities are such as to enable us to understand why Autonomists have restricted the sphere of the immediately known in the way they have, and therefore why they have persistently placed themselves in the suicidal position of trying to derive all one's knowledge from propositions about one's current experience.

Now let's take a brief look at what it takes for mediate epistemization. The standard JTB line (at least among theorists who discuss this issue in its full generality) is that in order for S to be mediately justified in believing that p, not only must he in fact know or be justified in believing certain propositions that are so related to p as to constitute adequate reasons for accepting p; and not only must he come to believe, and/or continue to believe, that p because he has those reasons. In addition he must know or be justified in believing *that* those other propositions constitute adequate grounds for accepting p.[29] The reason for this extra requirement is essentially the same as the reason for rejecting *de facto* reliability as an immediate justifier. If epistemic statuses are readily available to reflection, we cannot allow an epistemic status to depend on some fact outside the subject's epistemic field, unless that fact could not hold without being knowable on reflection. Since not all relations between propositions, especially inductive relations, meet this latter condition, we can allow a belief to be justified by its bearing the right relations to other justified beliefs, only on condition that the subject realize that these relations obtain.[30]

Just as the demand for readily accessible higher level knowledge leads to a sharp restriction in the class of immediately justified beliefs, so this requirement will narrowly restrict the class of mediately justified beliefs. It seems that we are quite often in the position of having sufficient grounds for a belief but without realizing (or being able to realize on reflection) that our grounds are sufficient. Perhaps we cannot even consciously recall our grounds or give them an adequate formulation, so as to consider whether they are adequate. This is the case with most of what most people have learned about science, history, geography, and so on. And even where we can formulate our grounds, we may have no firm opinions as to whether they are sufficient, much less know (or have justification for supposing) that they are sufficient. The Autonomist will naturally be led to deny such cases the title of knowledge.

The Heteronomist, by contrast, is not motivated, *by his general epistemological orientation*, to impose any such requirements on mediate knowledge.[31] So long as the true belief that p arose from the knowledge that q, and so long as the mechanism by which it arose is sufficiently selective so that (with proper qualifications) it produces a belief output from a knowledge input only when the latter constitutes adequate grounds for the former, the reliability theorist can, in good conscience, allow that S knows that p, without adding the extra requirement that S must have the higher-level knowledge *that* the input constitutes adequate grounds for the output. Dretske argues this, for perceptual knowledge, in *Seeing and Knowing*, Ch. III, sec. 4, and for knowledge in general, in 'Conclusive Reasons', pp. 16–19.

VII

I hope that this paper has demonstrated the value of a self-conscious consideration of meta-epistemology, in contrast to and in relation with, substantive epistemology. Further explorations along this line, using more refined distinctions than the relatively crude ones with which we have been operating, should yield a greater harvest of insights into the basic issues of epistemology.

University of Illinois at Urbana-Champaign

NOTES

[1] Needless to say, this quick characterization glosses over many complexities and subleties, which will have to be ignored in this paper.

[2] 'Other Minds', *Proc. Arist. Soc. Supplement*, **XX** (1946). Reprinted in *Philosophical Papers* (New York: Oxford U. Press, 1946). See also A. J. Ayer's suggestion in *The Problem of Knowledge* (London: Macmillan & Co. Ltd., 1956), to the effect that whether we will judge that a person knows that *p* under certain conditions is a matter of 'attitudes' that cannot be proved to be correct or mistaken. (p. 32). This sounds very much like Ayer's emotivist position in meta-ethics.

[3] See especially the second edition of his *Theory of Knowledge* (Englewood Cliffs, N. J.: Prentice-Hall, Inc., 1977).

[4] Not all epistemologists who present this kind of analysis use the term 'justified'. 'Warranted' is quite common, and Chisholm has a generous budget of terms for various degrees of positive epistemic status — 'some presumption in its favor', 'acceptable', 'reasonable', 'evident', 'certain'.

[5] 'A Causal Theory of Knowing', *Journ. Philos.* **LXIV**, 12 (June 22, 1967): 357–372; 'Discrimination and Perceptual Knowledge', *Journ. Philos.* **LXXIII**, 20 (Nov, 18, 1976): 771–791.

[6] *Belief, Truth, and Knowledge* (New York: Cambridge University Press, 1973), Pt. III.

[7] *Seeing and Knowing* (London: Routledge & Kegan Paul, 1969), Ch. 2; 'Conclusive Reasons', *Austral. Journ. Philos.*, 49, 1 (May, 1971), 1–22.

[8] H. H. Price, 'Some Considerations About Belief', *Proc. Arist. Soc.*, 35 (1934–35), 229.

[9] Admittedly this scheme oversimplifies some complicated historical relationships. As I read the situation, the JTB view developed out of the Intuitive view in the following way. The pure 'Intuitive' view, as found, e.g., in Locke, was felt to be too confining in several respects. First, and most obviously, it does not easily accommodate knowledge gained by inference (particularly complicated inference) from pieces of intuitive knowledge. Second, it restricts knowing to the condition one is in at the moment when a fact is presented to ones consciousness; it does not allow for knowledge as a more or less permanent possession. To remedy these deficiencies philosophers (1) allowed knowledge to include not only intuitive knowledge but also what is arrived at by acceptable inferences from that; and, (2) often implicity, treated knowledge obtained in either of these

ways to be 'possessed' for a period of time. A good place to see a 'snapshot' of this stage of development is Chapters XI and XII of Russell's *Problems of Philosophy*. But then it became evident that we no longer have a unified concept of propositional knowledge. What is common to intuitive knowledge and that gained by inferences therefrom? An answer that suggested itself is that in both cases one's belief or judgment is 'reasonable' or 'justified', has sufficient 'evidence' or 'grounds'. This move involved two important steps. First these concepts had previously been attached to beliefs that fall short of knowledge: a belief can be more or less reasonable, have stronger or weaker grounds or reasons; but knowledge is something quite different from all that; it stands outside that field of comparison altogether. In taking knowledge itself to be true justified belief, the earlier separation was broken down; now one envisaged a degree of justification strong enough to make the true belief count as knowledge. Second, these notions, previously restricted to beliefs that receive their justification from other justified beliefs, were extended to cover beliefs not so justified. We now recognize 'immediate' as well as 'mediate' justification. With these moves the full-blown JTB conception of knowledge is born.

[10] Though the 'epistemization' jargon gives us a *linqua franca* for justificationists and causal-reliabilists it is still not completely general; it leaves out the intuitive conception, which doesn't construe knowledge as involving belief at all.

[11] For a chronicle of some of its wanderings see R. Firth, 'The Anatomy of Certainty', *Phil. Rev.*, 76 (1967), 3–27.

[12] *Op. cit.*, Ch. 13, sec. 1.

[13] 'Conclusive Reasons', esp. section 1.

[14] See his analysis of non-inferential perceptual knowledge on pp. 785–786 of 'Discrimination and Perceptual Knowledge'. The fallibilism stems from the fact that the knower is required to be capable of ruling out only 'relevant' alternatives. In some 'irrelevant' state of affairs he might form a false non-inferential perceptual belief that *p*. Thus the conditions of belief formation do not strictly rule out the falsity of the belief.

[15] *Op. cit.*, p. 103.

[16] See his *The Concept of Knowledge* (Evanston, I11.: Northwestern University Press, 1970), Pt. I., sec. 4.

[17] For simplicity of exposition I am leaving out of account what some writers call 'metaphysical' and 'theological' naturalism, in which ethical terms are defined in terms of non-empirical metaphysical or theological facts, such as the will of God.

[18] See, e.g., Armstrong, *op. cit.*, p. 191, and Goldman, 'Epistemology and Epistemics' (unpublished), pp. 23–25.

[19] After my buildup this passage may seem a bit disappointing, in that Chisholm speaks of 'presupposing' or 'adopting as a working hypothesis' or 'supposing', rather than taking a more extreme intuitionist line that we have *immediate knowledge* that we know various things and are justified in various beliefs. But it is not clear that Chisholm is not wholly in earnest in this cautious talk of 'working hypotheses'. As we shall see in a moment, he lays down a principle to the effect that whenever anyone knows anything, he can, just by reflecting on that fact, come to know that he knows.

[20] *Op. cit.*, p. 116. See also Butchvarov, *op. cit.*, p. 28–29, and K. Lehrer, *Knowledge* (Oxford: Clarendon Press, 1974), pp. 228–232. For Prichard's view see his *Knowledge and Perception* (Oxford: Clarendon Press, 1950), p. 86.

[21] I owe my appreciation of this point to Lawrence Davis and Robert Gordon. Of course,

it seems highly implausible that, given the Heteronomist conception of knowledge, *all* one's knowledge should be so readily accessible, even if common everyday knowledge is. One might well have a highly reliable mechanism for generating scientific explanations without realizing how reliable it is. But I shall suppress this consideration, in the interest of preserving the clean lines of the opposition.

²² See also Butchvarov, *op. cit.*, pp. 28–29, and Lehrer, *op. cit.*, pp. 228–232.

²³ I cannot take time to align this brief note with what actually goes on in the *Meditations*. What I am talking of under this title is an enterprise often associated with the name of Descartes and which has become prominent largely because of Descartes' influence.

²⁴ For suggestions along this line see Armstrong, *op. cit.*, p. 163, and Goldman, 'Discrimination and Perceptual Knowledge.'

²⁵ C. I. Lewis, *An Analysis of Knowledge and Valuation* (La Salle, Ill.: Open Court Pub. Co., 1946), Ch. VII. Bertrand Russell, *Problems of Philosophy* (London: Williams & Norgate, 1912), p. 77: G. E. Moore, *Some Main Problems of Philosophy* (London: George Allen & Unwin, Ltd., 1953), Ch. II.

²⁶ R. M. Chisholm, *op. cit.*, Ch. 2.

²⁷ Panayot Butchvarov, *The Concept of Knowledge* (Evanston Ill: Northwestern University Press, 1970), Pt. I, sec. 6: W.P. Alston, *op. cit.*

²⁸ In claiming that one can realize that his belief is justified when it is, the Autonomist is committed to the easy accessibility not only of the presence of what justifies the belief but also of the fact that it is sufficient to justify it. And one may doubt that the latter is so easily accessible. Can I come to know that all beliefs of a certain type are justified by being of that type, just by raising the question? Can persistent controversies in epistemology be settled that easily? Is it that the opponents of the self-justification position, or of Chisholm's truth-justification position, have never reflected on the matter?

²⁹ See, e.g., two articles reprinted in M.D. Roth & L. Galis, eds., *Knowing* (New York: Random House, 1970): Keith Lehrer, 'Knowledge, Truth, and Evidence', p. 57; and Brian Skyrms, 'The Explication of 'X Knows That p' ', p. 91, fn.5.

³⁰ Chisholm is a notable exception to this trend in JTB theory. For example, his principle (G) on p. 82 of *Theory of Knowledge* reads:

If the conjunction of all those propositions *e*, such that *e* is acceptable for *S* at *t* tends to confirm *h*, then *h* has some presumption in its favor for *S* at *t*.

He does not also require that *S* know that the conjunction of those propositions tends to confirm *h*. It would seem that this principle does not sort well with Chisholm's position that when a proposition has a certain epistemic status for me I can know that it does just by considering the matter. Is there any guarantee that I can realize that the above relationship holds when it does hold. Considering that one term of the relationship is *all the propositions that are acceptable to me at t* I may well be at a loss to determine whether the relation does hold.

³¹ Just as we find Chisholm deviating from the natural Autonomist line, so we find Armstrong arguing for the necessity of the subject's knowing that the evidence really is adequate evidence. (*op. cit.*, pp. 151, 199). In Ch. 14, Armstrong finds himself enmeshed in considerable difficulties because of this requirement.

RICHARD WASSERSTROM

SOME PROBLEMS IN THE DEFINITION AND JUSTIFICATION OF PUNISHMENT

I

Punishment, whatever else may be true of it, involves the intentional infliction of unpleasantness or pain upon human beings by other human beings. For this reason most persons believe, and I think correctly, that punishment is a problem that must be confronted by all human beings concerned to be moral. It is a problem in the sense that because pain is intentionally imposed a justification is required before we are entitled to regard punishment as morally acceptable.

One approach to the problem of punishment advocates the abolition of punishment as a distinctive mode of action and its replacement by something variously called a system of treatment, reform or rehabilitation. According to this view, the problem of punishment is solved by seeing first that rehabilitation, or treatment, is different from punishment and second that it is preferable to it.[1]

A second approach thinks that a system of punishment is justifiable, and wholly so on utilitarian, or consequentialist, grounds. On this view punishment is justifiable because there are classes of cases in which a greater amount of unpleasantness would be produced in a society by its absence than by its presence. On this view punishment is that form of social control which rationally uses the intentional infliction of pain on persons as a way to induce other persons to behave in ways which will keep that unpleasantness from being visited upon them.[2] In this sense, a utilitarian theory of punishment is forward-looking, focusing as it does upon the social consequences that attend the presence or absence of punishment.

And a third approach, retributivism, agrees with the second in its insistence that a system of punishment can be justifiable. But it sees punishment as essentially connected with the wrongdoing of the person punished, and it sees the justifiability of punishment as residing in the appropriateness, or justice, of punishment as a response to this wrongdoing. Backward-looking considerations constitute the primary justification for a retributivist theory of punishment.

Many recent philosophical discussions of punishment, in an attempt to bring order and understanding to conflicting discussions of punishment,

A. I. Goldman and J. Kim (eds.), Values and Morals, 299–315. All Rights Reserved.
Copyright © 1978 by D. Reidel Publishing Company, Dordrecht, Holland.

proceed in the following way. First, seeing the need to distinguish punishment from treatment, as well as from other things with which punishment might be confused, they often begin by offering a description, if not an analysis, of the features of the standard case of punishment. In this way they hope to make it possible both to identify what punishment is and to distinguish cases of punishment from all of those other cases in which an unpleasantness is imposed by some person upon another person, and which are not cases of punishment. And second, many of those that are utilitarian in approach, offer what they take to be a way out of the apparent conflict between retributive and utilitarian theories. The reconciliation, they claim, is attainable once it is realized that there are two different questions, or issues, that may be being addressed. One question is concerned with whether a particular case of punishment is justifiable. The other question is concerned with whether the practice or institution of punishment is itself justifiable. Retributivism, it is claimed, is most plausibly construed as dealing with the former question; utilitarian justifications of punishment, it is claimed, are most plausibly construed as dealing with the latter question.

In the paper I endeavor to do two things. First, I argue that the attempts by the utilitarians to reconcile utilitarian and retributive justifications do not succeed. They do not succeed both because the account they offer of what punishment is is more problematic than they suppose and because the proposed 'two-level' justification of punishment does not work. In this respect, I want to show that conceptually there is more to be said for retributivism than some of the recent literature suggests. Second, I argue that the attempts by the retributivists to give arguments for the justifiability of punishment are not wholly satisfactory. Here, I want to show that the case for what I call a strong retributivist theory of punishment has yet to be made out. Thus, there are continuing problems in providing a theory that both adequately describes and justifies punishment.

II

Many of the most influential recent philosophical discussions of punishment, which seek to show that whatever good sense there may be to retributivism is readily assimilated into a consequentialist account, begin by providing a characterization of what punishment is in terms of the standard case of punishment. The aim of such characterizations is to provide an account that is strong enough to distinguish punishment from other things with which it might be confused while at the same time to provide an account that is weak enough to avoid the retributivist claim that punishment is in some important respect essentially linked with wrongdoing. Typical is H.L.A. Hart's characterization of punishment which he acknowledges to be similar to those provided by philosophers such as Baier, Flew, and Benn.

...[I] shall define the standard or central case of 'punishment' in terms of five elements:

(i) It must involve pain or other consequences normally considered unpleasant.

(ii) It must be for an offence against legal rules.

(iii) It must be of an actual or supposed offender for his offence.

(iv) It must be intentionally administered by human beings other than the offender.

(v) It must be imposed and administered by an authority constituted by a legal system against which the offence is committed.[3]

Hart then relegates to the position of 'substandard' or 'secondary' cases those which involve:

(a) Punishment for breaches of legal rules imposed or administered otherwise than by officials (decentralized sanctions).

(b) Punishments for breaches of nonlegal rules or orders (punishments in a family or school).

(c) Vicarious or collective punishment of some members of a social group for actions done by others without the former's authorization, encouragement, control, or permission.

(d) Punishment of persons (otherwise than under (c)) who neither are in fact nor supposed to be offenders.[4]

There is no question but that it is instructive, if not essential, to give a characterization of punishment, and to do so in terms of the standard case of punishment. One important reason for doing so is that there are many things that a legal system does or authorizes that may be done to persons that involve pain or other consequences normally considered unpleasant. Among those that any characterization of punishment would want to be able to distinguish (as not cases of punishment at all) are: being drafted into the army, being quarantined if one has an infectious disease, being incarcerated pursuant to a scheme of preventive detention, being required to pay damages to the person injured by your negligence, being involuntarily committed to an institution because one is insane, being required to pay damages to the person injured by your breach of contract, and being deported as an alien present within the country without permission. Another part of the analytic challenge is to provide an account of punishment which is both strong enough to distinguish it from those other intentionally imposed unpleasantnesses that are clearly not punishments and weak enough to include cases of unjustified as well as justified punishments. And still a third part of the task is to provide an account of punishment which is non-narrowly circular. The problem is that when all this is done punishment comes out to be conceptually more closely connected with wrongdoing than these utilitarian accounts appear either willing to acknowledge or able to accommodate comfortably.

The difficulty with a definition such as Hart's is that it seems, on the surface at least, to be circular — and in a way that is serious because the circularity is so abrupt. The circularity occurs in part because the idea of punishment invoked by Hart depends so heavily upon the concept of an offense, which concept is utilized to some degree in (ii), (iii), (iv), and (v) of his account. It is the notion of an offense in these characterizations of punishment which carries the primary burden of differentiating punishment from these other unpleasantnesses.

But what is an offense? Well, we might say, it is a crime. But what is a crime? One answer might be: a crime is a legal violation that the law deals with via punishment rather than other possible modes of response. The circularity is sufficiently direct that this way of proceeding is unsatisfactory. We cannot give meaning to the standard case of punishment through introduction of the concept of an offense, and also have it be the case that an offense can be understood only through the concept of a crime, which concept itself can be understood only through the invocation of the concept of punishment.

There are two possible ways out. On the one hand, we can try to give a definition or a characterization of the idea of crime which does not directly involve the concept of punishment. And, on the other hand, we can try to give meaning to the concept of an offense in a way that does not involve the concept of crime.

Consider the latter possibility first. Suppose we were to characterize an offense not as a crime but rather as any violation of the law. Here we would have a noncircular account of punishment which depended only on understanding the idea of a violation of the law. But is that idea sufficiently clear, or sufficiently strong to do the job required of it? What constitutes a violation of the law? Is it a violation of the law to breach one's legal obligation, e.g., by intentionally breaching a contract? Is it a violation of the law to operate one's car negligently thereby injuring someone? Is it a violation of the law to be in the country without a permit? If the answer to any of these questions is yes, then 'violation' cannot be substituted for 'offense' because even though paying damages for breach of contract is an unpleasantness, it is not a punishment; nor is paying damages for negligence a punishment; nor is deportation (at least obviously). If the answer is that these things are not violations of the law, while robbery, rape, and murder are, then the question is how are they distinguishable. What will not do is to say that things such as breach of contract are not violations because they do not involve the punishment of persons for these kinds of behaviors. For this response is circular because it, too, uses the idea of punishment to explain the idea of a violation.

As I have indicated, the other approach is to treat 'crime' and 'offense' as roughly synonymous and to attempt to give a characterization of the idea of crime that does not so directly or exclusively depend on the idea of punishment. The most plausible candidate seems to me to be some more generic idea of wrongdoing. One thing to be said in favor of building the idea of wrongdoing directly into the account of punishment or indirectly into it through the concept of criminality is that it seems to belong there. That is to say, most cases that we would identify as the core cases of criminality in a society do involve behavior that is regarded as seriously wrong by the society wholly apart from the illegality of the behavior. Typically, it is behavior that, viewed just as conduct, is thought seriously harmful or dangerous Typically, too, it is behavior that, viewed in terms of the actor's culpability, was seriously culpable, i.e., it involved either the intentional or knowing infliction of injury on another.[5] Thus, the core idea of criminality does appear to involve this idea of moral wrongdoing — coupled, perhaps, with the added idea that it is wrongdoing of the sort that is appropriately publicly condemned or denounced.[6] And for this reason it does seem to be both less circular and more illuminating to construct an account of punishment which utilizes this idea of criminality (or just serious, denounceable wrongdoing in the nonlegal context) instead of one which takes the undefined notion of an offense as central.

But even this approach is not without its difficulties. And the most serious one, I think, is that many activities can be and are crimes even though they do not involve wrongdoing — or to put what I take to be a similar point somewhat differently — even though they do not involve something that we can properly call seriously blameworthy behavior on the part of the actor. Thus, in our own society, it is a crime, for example, to possess various weapons, to use drugs of various sorts, and to engage in various consensual sexual behaviors. The point is not that there is disagreement over whether these things are morally wrong, over whether the lawmakers all believe (although perhaps mistakenly) that they are morally wrong and, hence, over whether they should be criminal. Rather, the point is that it looks as though it is both conceptually and empirically possible to have behavior that is clearly and unmistakably understood and recognized as criminal, and that is thought by no one within the society to be 'intrinsically' immoral.

Now, one way to deal with this problem is to show that there is a perfectly plausible sense in which the law can and should make behavior wrongful even though it is not 'intrinsically' immoral. Thus, someone might plausibly claim that while it is not 'intrinsically' wrong, or even dangerous, to drive on the left rather than the right side of the road, it is important to drive on only one side or the other, and it is, therefore, dangerous and wrong to drive on the 'wrong' side of the road, whatever side that may be in any given society. This modification works very well for a number of cases but less well for others, e.g., the prohibition of drug use on paternalistic grounds.

Another way to deal with this problem is to make the wrongdoing, what might be termed, 'second order' rather than 'primary' wrongdoing. On this view what would be a necessary characteristic of any crime would be the fact either that the behavior itself was thought wrong, or that the behavior was thought wrong in virtue of its being an intentional (or otherwise culpable) violation of a law. One problem with this approach is that it reintroduces the circularity, previously discussed, latent in the idea of a violation of the law. That is to say, we would still require some independent account of the idea of a violation of the law that did not explicate that idea through recourse to the concept of punishment. And a second problem is that it would have to be explained why it is always immoral intentionally to disobey the law. I do not think that such an explanation can easily be produced.[7]

I do not think that the definitional problems are wholly solvable in any neat and simple way. But I do think it correct that the core cases of criminality do involve the idea of serious, culpable wrongdoing, even though there may be some things that are unmistakably illegal and yet are not seriously, culpably wrong; nor would they be even at most prima facie wrong or culpable were it not for the contingent fact that they happened to be crimes in a particular legal system.

But this is surely enough to make the retributivist's point that punishment is more centrally connected with wrongdoing than is often supposed, and that it is, therefore, more plausible than might have been thought both to locate a justification for punishment within a context of the already occurred fact of wrongdoing and to connect punishment conceptually with a response to that wrongdoing. What all of this shows is that the typical, utilitarian accounts of punishment are either too weak to distinguish punishment from other intentionally imposed unpleasantnesses or circular in an unilluminating way. What all of this shows is that some features of the retributivist thesis are built into the concept of punishment; namely those that see punishment as necessarily linked with the idea of a response to wrongdoing on the part of the person punished. What all of this does not show, of course, is whether it is ever justifiable to punish anyone, and if it is on what grounds. It remains, that is, an open question whether there are any sound arguments, retributivist or otherwise, which justify punishing persons. It is to the various retributivist arguments that I turn in the remainder of this paper.

III

One way to defend a very weak version of retributivism is to adopt the position of Hart, Benn and others which is that utilitarian and retributivist theories are not in conflict because they are asking two different questions. Thus Benn puts the case this way. Utilitarianism, he says, has

.. the merit, as an approach to the justification of punishment, that it provides a clear procedure for determining whether the institution is acceptable in general terms. This he retributivist approach cannot do because it denies the relevance of weighing advantages and disadvantages, which is what we ultimately must do in moral criticism of rules and institutions. Consequently, a retributivist justification of punishment as an institution usually turns out to be denial of the necessity for justification, a veiled reference to the beneficial results of punishment (a utilitarianism in disguise), or an appeal to religious authority.

When it is a question of justifying a particular case of punishment, however, the retributivist is in a far stronger position. There would be no point in having a general rule if on every occasion that it had to be applied one had to consider whether the advantages in this particular case warranted acting in accordance with it. Moreover, the point of punishment as deterrent would be quite lost were there no general expectation, based on the general operation of the rule, that guilty men would be punished. Assuming, then, that a penal system can be justified in utilitarian terms, any offense is at least prima facie an occasion for a penalty. Equally, without an offense there is no question of penalty. The retributivist contention that punishment is justified if, and only if, it is deserved is really applicable, therefore, to the justification of particular instances of punishment, the institution as such being taken for granted.[8]

This surely will not, and ought not, satisfy any genuine retributivist. On a view such as Benn's virtually all of the interesting questions concerning whether it is right to punish people, and if so why, are the utilitarian questions. Retributivism is reduced to a special instance of the general case for having a system follow and apply its own rules whatever they may happen to be. This is a general view of doubtful plausibility,[9] but even if it were plausible as a defense of rule-applying behavior, it misses most, if not all, of the point. What the retributivist can show fairly persuasively I believe, is that any consequentialist justification of this form is just not very convincing.

To begin with, it does not explain why we should attach the importance that we do to the state of mind of the offender. Thus, in 'Legal Responsibility and Excuses,'[10] H.L.A. Hart says that the principle that is involved is

... that it is unfair and unjust to punish those who have not 'voluntarily' broken the law ... And again, that [w]hat we need to escape confusion here is a distinction between two sets of questions. The first is a general question about the moral value of the laws: Will enforcing them produce more good than evil? If it does, then it is morally permissible to enforce them by punishing those who have broken them, unless in any particular case there is some 'excuse.'[11]

The last sentence is the crucial one. Why is it morally permissible to punish persons just as long as there is not some excusing condition present in the case of the otherwise guilty person? In 'Legal Responsibility and Excuses' Hart does explain to some degree why it should be worse if persons were punished even when the excusing condition were present. But he does not ever really provide a reason why it *is* appropriate to punish in the presence of guilt and the absence of any of the excusing conditions. The retributivist can claim that that is one of the crucial questions, and that if there is an answer it has got to have a good deal to do with the wrongdoing of the actor and the deservedness of the punishment. The deterrence of others cannot be an adequate answer because that would make the punishment of the guilty (in the absence of excusing conditions) unjustifiable whenever it was the case that no increase in deterrence would result from the punishment of this individual or individuals engaged in this type of behavior. And the deterrence of others cannot be an adequate answer, in addition, because it leaves unanswered the question of why it is not unjust to punish the guilty in the absence of excusing conditions, as well as those for whom the excusing conditions obtain.[12]

The point can be put somewhat differently. What is missing is a very satisfactory explanation of why it is so important to punish only the guilty. An account such as Benn's or Hart's, a retributivist could argue, does not very fully even capture the force of the wrongfully punished person's complaint that a special, serious injustice was done to him or her because he or she was not guilty of any wrongdoing. If the overall system was fair, if the person was not intentionally convicted falsely, and if the consequences were on the whole good in terms of general deterrence, it is hard to see why the complaint should be thought such a serious one. But it is. And any utilitarian account that could be constructed does not seem able to account easily for the perceived gravity of that wrong.

In addition, the retributivist can continue to proceed in a negative way by elaborating on the observation that there are some important facts that need explaining and that justifications founded on the consequences cannot explain; namely, that there are cases in which punishment seems appropriate and in which appeals to the aim of deterrence appear to be thoroughly beside the point.

The retributivist might say something like this. Consider the following thought-experiment. Suppose that somehow Hitler had been found alive and well in Argentina, say, five years after the end of World War II. The Nazi apparatus had been fully dismantled, the East and West German governments were fully viable, and the Nazi ideology was quite unpopular. Isn't it clear that if Hitler had been found it would have been right, perhaps even important, to punish him? Yet, surely the case even for the permissibility of punishing him could not have rested very plausibly on the ground that punishment was appropriate or required in order to convince future Hitlers that they would be punished were they to do what he had done. More to the point, even if punishment in order to achieve deterrence made some sense, would we not also want to say that any appeal to the consequences just does not get to the heart of what would be involved in punishing persons such as Hitler?

Now, of course, the retributivist might add, if you regard these as marginal cases for punishment, then you can simply reject them as confusing border-line cases. But if you feel that these are central cases, then rejection of retributivism as a justification for punishment is less easy.

I think the retributivist is right in calling attention to the fact that there are these cases and that they are central rather than marginal cases just in the sense that they are clear cases of potentially appropriate punishment. If anyone deserved to be punished for his or her wrongdoing — one might be tempted to say — it was persons such as the Nazi leaders. And if that is so, then any adequate theory of punishment must provide a convincing justification for punishment in instances like these. Since justifications focused upon deterrence (or rehabilitation for that matter) cannot do so, this at least counts as a mark against them both.

All of this, in a way, relates back to the discussion in Part II, above. The relationship between blame and punishment is both more important and more intimate than alternative theories appear to allow. While it would doubtless be too strong a view to propose that punishment *is* simply a harsher form of blame, it is not at all implausible to observe that the standard case of punishment is reserved for those cases in which at least blame is appropriate and in which mere blame is insufficient. Insufficient, however, not in the sense that blaming would not deter while punishment would, but rather insufficient in the sense that blaming would not do justice to the seriousness of the wrong. Thus, if punishment in the standard case is a more extreme version of blame, and if blame cannot be justified on consequentialist grounds, then this, too, casts doubt upon the justification of punishment by appeal to the consequences.

At the very least, it is much harder to develop a convincing consequentialist rationale for blaming than for punishment. We can and do blame others silently, to ourselves. We can and do decide that those long since dead are properly to blame for things they did while alive; or that someone long considered blameworthy is, in fact, not blameworthy at all. These activities are clear cases of blaming. They play important roles in the lives of many persons. We can, of course, if pressed, construct a consequentialist account that takes these activities into account and justifies them on consequentialist grounds. But the arguments do not ring true. The theory can always be saved, but at a price. We do not always, or even typically, blame in order to deter or to reform — or even publicly to denounce.

Any adequate theory of blame would, I think, have to acknowledge this, and either account for all the important cases or urge that all of the non-conforming cases be extinguished from the repertoire of acceptable human behaviors. Hence, given the intimacy of the connection between blame and punishment and the implausibility of consequentialist theories of blame, consequentialist defenses of punishment are rendered suspect.

There are, in addition, what might be regarded as affirmative arguments for a weak kind of retributivism. Thus one easy way to defend retributivism is to construe it merely as a theory that is worth considering because of the importance that it places on the concept of a person. It can be understood in this light as a point of view which seeks to limit, for instance, things that can be done to human beings by other human beings — say, in the guise of treatment. In other words, it can in its most modest form be construed as establishing necessary conditions for the intentional infliction of any unpleasantness including punishment. As has been indicated, Hart gives one rationale in 'Legal Responsibility and Excuses,' and Herbert Morris gives a somewhat different one in his piece, 'Persons and Punishment.'[13] It is important, of course, and worth doing, but it is too weak a thesis for my purpose. For so construed, all of these types of weak retributivism leave wholly unanswered the question of for what reason it is ever justifiable to punish persons.

Another argument, often thought of as retributivist, is both 'forward-looking' and different from the typical utilitarian justifications for punishment.

It is that punishment can function as a social mechanism by which an offender can achieve expiation for his or her wrongdoing. As such, punishment can play an essential and humanizing role in the maintenance of society. Submission to punishment can be a means by which an offender retains his or her membership in society despite the serious transgression. So we speak of punishment as involving the 'paying' of one's 'debt' to society, and, equally importantly, we speak of an offender's right to renewed acceptance in the society once his or her punishment has terminated and the 'debt' to society has been paid by the offender.

The reason why it, too, is a justification for only a very weak version of retributivism is that it is an argument only for the rightness of punishing those who desire expiation, or perhaps for those who desire to live in a system in which expiation for wrongdoing is attainable. But it is not an adequate justification for punishing those who desire neither expiation nor a system in which achieving expiation through such a mechanism is possible. If retributivism is to be genuinely interesting and persuasive it ought to be a strong enough theory to be able to explain how and why it is right to punish those who do wrong irrespective of the wrongdoer's desires and interests. There are several such arguments that have been given for a strong version of retributivism. The problem with them, however, is that none of them is wholly satisfactory.

One argument goes something like this. As many even nonretributivists acknowledge, e.g., Hart, it is unjust to punish those who are in fact innocent. Indeed, as has been suggested, all of us would recognize the claim of any innocent person (no matter how fair the procedure by which he or she was found guilty and punished) that an injustice of some sort had occurred. But if we can understand so readily and clearly that it is unjust to punish the innocent, that can only be because it is also the case that it is just to punish the guilty. To understand that the innocent do not deserve punishment is also necessarily to understand that the guilty do deserve it. That justice requires the punishment of the guilty is but a different aspect of the widely accepted idea that justice forbids the punishment of the innocent.

This argument does not work. Even if it is a fairly straightforward move from 'It is unjust to punish the innocent,' to 'It is not unjust to punish the guilty,' and even if the connection between the two is one of entailment, there is an important difference in meaning between 'It is not unjust to punish the guilty' and 'It is just to punish the guilty.' And there is an even more important difference in meaning between 'It is just to punish the guilty' and 'Justice requires the punishment of the guilty.' There is a special injustice in punishing the innocent such that *that* injustice is not present when the guilty are punished. In this sense, at least, it is true that it is not unjust to punish the guilty. Furthermore, it may even be the case that if anyone is to be punished, justice requires that it be the guilty, rather than the innocent. But none of this gets any strong version of retributivism where it wants to go: to the claim that justice itself requires, and hence justifies, that there be the punishment of the guilty. If we are to be convinced of that truth about justice and punishment, then other arguments must be forthcoming.

The two that seem to me to be worth taking the most seriously are both advanced by Morris in 'Persons and Punishment.' The first argument involves the fairness of imposing those burdens that the criminal law imposes on us all. The second concerns the unfairness of letting the criminal keep the benefits he or she has unfairly appropriated through violating the law.

The first argument goes like this:

It is only reasonable that those who voluntarily comply with the rules be provided some assurance that they will not be assuming burdens which others are unprepared to assume. Their disposition to comply voluntarily will diminish as they learn that others are with impunity renouncing burdens they are assuming.[14]

There are, I take it, two related points here. One is that the system will not work well, if at all, unless the guilty are punished. Not because the threat needs to be made credible to those who have not yet broken the law, but who otherwise might.[15] But because those who have not broken the law will have no reason to continue to be law abiding (indeed, it will soon become extremely imprudent for them to continue to be law abiding) unless they can count on reasonably successful efforts being made to keep down the amount of dangerous crime.[16]

The other point to be extracted from the quotation above is more overtly retributivist. It is this. One way to understand the criminal law is to see it as a system of prohibitions which directs us all not to act in those various ways that it is wrong to act, although we are all inclined to do so. To act in accordance with the criminal law is, therefore, to take on a kind of burden — the burden that is connected with voluntarily restraining ourself from doing many things that we would like to do. And this burden is only fairly assumed by anyone if it is equally assumed by everyone. Or, to put it another way, it is not fair that the criminal in committing the crime has thrown off the burden assumed by the rest. Punishment is fair — is required by justice — because it is the way to most nearly replace the missing burden where it properly belonged.

The other affirmative retributive argument is so closely related to this one that they can most profitably be discussed together.

... [I] t is just to punish those who have violated the rules and caused the unfair distribution of benefits and burdens. A person who violates the rules has something others have – the benefits of the system – but by renouncing what others have assumed, the burdens of self-restraint, he has acquired an unfair advantage. Matters are not even until this advantage is in some way erased. Another way of putting it is that he owes something to others, for he has something that does not rightfully belong to him. Justice – that is, punishing such individuals – restores the equilibrium of benefits and burdens by taking from the individual what he owes, that is, exacting the debt.[17]

Justice, in other words, requires that the guilty be punished because of two, interrelated facts: burdens have been unfairly assumed vis-à-vis the criminal by the law-abiding citizens and benefits have been unfairly appropriated by the criminal. The wrongdoer has obtained a benefit to which he or she is not entitled by not restraining himself or herself from acting on inclination and desire in the way in which the rest of us did. Thus, in punishing the offender we take away that benefit and thereby restore the social equilibrium which existed before the offense.

There are, I believe, at least two problems with this way of thinking about the justifiability of punishment. In the first place, it is not always plausible to think of criminal and law-abiding behavior in terms of benefits and burdens. Sometimes it is, but sometimes it is not. The basic scheme seems to fit reasonably well cases like that of tax evasion. Paying taxes is a burden. No one is naturally inclined or disposed to pay them. If everyone else does pay their taxes and I do not, I do benefit unfairly – and in two ways. I get to keep more of my income than the rest, and I also get the 'public' benefits that are bought by the tax monies, e.g., the security provided by an army or a fire department. In addition, the taxpayers are unfairly burdened – also in two ways. They bear a burden that they ought reasonably be required to bear only if everyone bears it. And the burden is, perhaps, greater than it otherwise would have been, because of my evasion.

There are, I believe, problems with this way of analyzing the injustice of tax evasion.[18] But even if there are none, the more central question is whether most cases of serious criminality are fundamentally analogous. There appear to be some important respects in which they are not. Consider, for example, rape instead of tax evasion. If someone, who is inclined to rape a woman, fails to restrain that inclination and commits a rape, it is hard to see how he has been unfairly benefited in respect to others. For suppose, as seems reasonably likely, they lack the inclination to rape anyone – irrespective so to speak, of what the law does or does not prohibit. Because they are not, therefore, burdened at all by the criminalization of rape, it is difficult to understand in what respect they have been unfairly burdened; nor, is it easy to see the manner in which the rapist has unfairly benefited himself, *as against those who abstain from rape.* Of course rape is wrong. Of course rape is a case of the rapist treating the victim very wrongly. But rape, torture, murder — many of the worst things one person can possibly do to another — do not neatly fit the model of the misallocation of benefits and burdens described by Morris and constituting the background justification for the punishment of the guilty.

There are at least two ways to try to produce a better fit. The first is to make explicit and defend a view of human nature that would make the claim of burden more plausible. That is to say, if it is the case that all humans are strongly and naturally inclined to do most if not all of the things that the criminal law properly forbids, and if it is the case that they do work long and hard to restrain themselves from doing those things they are inclined to do, then the criminal has thrown aside the burden that the rest of us continue to bear. This is certainly a possible theory of human nature, but not obviously a correct one.[19] Hence an argument such as the above is at best incomplete in the absence of a vindication of the theory of human nature upon which it depends. What is surely instructive is the respect in which a consideration of an argument such as Morris' does reveal the degree to which some if not all theories of punishment and crime do depend upon theories of human nature.

The second way to try to make these cases fit better would be, I think, to retreat to a kind of second-order set of benefits and burdens. It is not, on this view, the inclination to do what a particular law prohibits that is involved. Instead, it is the inclination in each individual to do some of the things prohibited by the criminal law that underlies the analysis in terms of benefits and burdens. I restrain myself from doing those wrong things I am inclined to do and it is only fair that you restrain yourself from doing those wrong things you are inclined to do. You benefit from my law abidingness and I benefit from yours. A theory of human nature still underlies the argument, but it is a somewhat more benign or optimistic one.

But even if the underlying theory of human nature were correct, this approach would assimilate the additional cases only by paying a high price. For much of the force of the original claim is dissipated once this retreat is made. What began as a powerful appeal to a direct and obvious sense in which committing a particular crime burdened unfairly those who did not commit that crime and benefited unfairly those who did, has been altered to become a far more abstract, more controversial appeal to the general benefits and burdens of law abidingness.

A second general objection concerns the relevance of an analysis such as Morris' (even if it is correct in terms of benefits and burdens) to punishment. For it remains hard to understand precisely how it is that punishing the wrongdoer constitutes taking the wrongfully appropriate benefit away from him or her. Where the benefit is a tangible good still in existence, e.g., the payroll from the bank robbery, we do, of course, take it away from the bank robber and return it to the bank. But that is not even punishment; that is restitution. That seems to restore the social equilibrium in respect to the thing wrongfully appropriated. Compensation or restitution to the victim by the wrongdoer, not his or her punishment, appears to be the natural and direct way to restore the balance.

Perhaps, though, the argument is that punishment can be seen as preventing the wrongdoer from enjoying the fruits of his or her wrongdoing. Perhaps in some sense, punishment is appropriately inflicted to restore the equilibrium when, for example, we cannot find the stolen payroll and we know it has not yet been spent or enjoyed by the robber. But in many, if not most, cases the 'removal' of the benefit through punishment will be as metaphorical and indirect as the resulting restoration of the social equilibrium through punishment.

How, for instance, does punishment for rape take the unfairly appropriated benefit away from the rapist? How does it even keep him from enjoying the benefits of his wrongdoing? To speak of punishment for rape as restoring the social equilibrium does not seem thereby to explain why it is that the punishment of the rapist is justified. It seems no more or less illuminating than to speak of punishment for rape as deserved because of the seriousness of the wrong. It is to return, perhaps, to the fairly plausible intuition with which retributivism begins — that serious crime, seriously culpable behavior, deserves to be punished — but it is not to give a clear or convincing reason for moving beyond that intuition.

Thus, we do not, I believe, yet have in retributivism a set of moral arguments sufficiently sound, unambiguous, and persuasive upon which to rest the justifiability of punishment. For this reason it is, I think, still an open question whether it is right to punish persons, if so, under what circumstances, and in virtue of what arguments.

University of California, Los Angeles

BIBLIOGRAPHY OF WILLIAM K. FRANKENA

1. 'The Naturalistic Fallacy', *Mind* 48 (1939) 464–477. Reprinted in several anthologies.
2. 'Obligation and Value in the Ethics of G. E. Moore', *The Philosophy of G. E. Moore*, P. A. Schilpp (ed.), Open Court Publishing Co., LaSalle, Illinois, 1942, pp. 91–110.
3. 'Our Belief in Reason', *Papers of the Michigan Academy of Science, Arts and Letters* 19, 1943, 571–586.
4. 'Ewing's Case Against Naturalistic Theories of Value', *Philosophical Review* 57, (1948) 481–492.
5. Review of A. C. Ewing, *The Definition of Good; Philosophical Review* 57, (1948) 605–607.
6. Review of Ray Lepley (ed.), *Value: A Cooperative Enquiry; Philosophy and Phenomenological Research* 10, (1949) 99–101.
7. Review of Stephen C. Pepper, *A Digest of Purposive Values; Philosophy and Phenomenological Research* 10, (1949) 130–132.
8. 'Arguments for Non-Naturalism About Intrinsic Value', *Philosophical Studies* 1, (1950) 56–60.
9. 'Obligation and Ability', *Philosophical Analysis*, Max Black (ed.), Cornell University Press, Ithaca, New York, 1950, pp. 157–175.
10. Review of A. N. Prior, *Logic and the Basis of Ethics; Philosophical Review* 59, 1950, 554–556.
11. 'Moral Philosophy at Mid-Century', *Philosophical Review* 60, (1951) 44–55. Reprinted in Rosalind Ekman (ed.), *Readings in the Problems of Ethics*.
12. 'The Concept of Universal Human Rights', *Science, Language and Human Rights*. Volume I, Symposia, Eastern Division, American Philosophical Association, 1952, pp. 189–207.
13. Review of E. W. Hall, *What is Value?; Philosophy and Phenomenological Research* 14, (1953) 253–258.
14. 'Sellars' Theory of Valuation', *Philosophy and Phenomenological Research* 15, (1954) 65–81.
15. 'Hutchesons's Moral Sense Theory', *Journal of the History of Ideas* 16, (1955) 356–375.
16. 'Natural and Inalienable Rights', *Philosophical Review* 64, (1955) 212–232.
17. 'Towards a Philosophy of the Philosophy of Education', *Harvard Educational Review* 26, (1956) 94–98.
18. 'Ethical Naturalism Renovated', *Review of Metaphysics* 10, (1957) 457–473.
19. 'Moral Philosophy in America', *Encyclopedia of Morals*, Vergilius Ferm (ed.), Philosophical Library, Inc., New York, 1957, pp. 348–360.
20. 'Henry Sidgwick', *Encyclopedia of Morals*, Vergilius Ferm (ed.), Philosophical Library, Inc., New York, 1957, pp. 534–544.
21. 'Sir (William) David Ross', *Encyclopedia of Morals*, Vergilius Ferm (ed.), Philosophical Library, Inc., New York, 1957, pp. 504–511.

A. I. Goldman and J. Kim (eds.), Values and Morals, 317–321. All Rights Reserved.
Copyright © 1978 by D. Reidel Publishing Company, Dordrecht, Holland.

22. Preface to D. H. Parker, *The Philosophy of Value*, University of Michigan Press, Ann Arbor, 1957.
23. Review of C. I. Lewis, *The Ground and Nature of the Right; Philosophical Review* 66, (1957) 398–402.
24. 'Ethics, 1949–1955', *Philosophy in the Mid-Century: A Survey*, III, R. Klibansky (ed.), Nuova Italia, Florence, 1958, pp. 42–77.
25. 'MacIntyre on Defining Morality', *Philosophy* 33, (1958) 158–162.
26. 'Obligation and Motivation in Recent Moral Philosophy', *Essays in Moral Philosophy*, A. I. Melden (ed.), University of Washington Press, Seattle, 1958 pp. 40–81.
27. 'A Point of View for the Future', *Religion and the State University*, E. A. Walter (ed.), University of Michigan Press, Ann Arbor, 1958, pp. 295–309.
28. 'Some Aspects of Language and 'Cognitive' and 'Non-Cognitive', *Language, Thought and Culture*, Paul Henle (ed.), University of Michigan Press, Ann Arbor, 1958, pp. 121–172.
29. 'Toward a Philosophy of Moral Education', *Harvard Education Review* 28, (1958) 300–313. Reprinted in several anthologies.
30. 'Broad's Analysis of Ethical Terms', *The Philosophy of C. D. Broad*, P. A. Schilpp (ed.), Tudor Publishing Co., New York, 1959, pp. 537–562.
31. 'The Teaching of Religion: Some Guiding Principles', *Religious Education* 54, (1959) 108–109.
32. Review of C. A. Baylis, *Ethics; Harvard Educational Review* 29, (1959) 251–253.
33. 'Ethics in an Age of Science', *The Association of Princeton Alumni, Report of the Eighth Conference*, 1960, pp. 91–104.
34. Foreward in Jonathan Edwards, *On the Nature of True Virtue*, University of Michigan Press, Ann Arbor, 1960. Ann Arbor Paperbacks.
35. 'Is the Philosophy of Education Intellectually Responsible?', *Proceedings of the Philosophy of Education Society* 17, (1961) 36–45.
36. 'Public Education and the Good Life', *Harvard Educational Review* 30, (1961) 413–426. Reprinted in several anthologies.
37. 'The Concept of Social Justice', *Social Justice*, R. B. Brandt (ed.), Prentice-Hall, Inc., Englewood Cliffs, New Jersey, 1962, pp. 1–29.
38. Review of Carl Wellman, *The Language of Ethics; Journal of Philosophy* 59, (1962) 293–296.
39. *Ethics*, Prentice-Hall, Inc., Englewood Cliffs, New Jersey, 1963.
40. 'Lewis' Imperatives of Right', *Philosophical Studies* 14, (1963) 25–28.
41. 'Recent Conceptions of Morality', *Morality and the Language of Conduct*, H. N. Castaneda and G. Nakhnikian (eds.), Wayne State University Press, Detroit, 1963, pp. 1–24.
42. 'Decisionism and Separatism in Social Philosophy', *Nomos VII: Rational Decision*, C. J. Friedrich (ed.), Atherton Press, New York, 1964 pp. 18–25.
43. 'Ethical Theory', *Philosophy*, R. Schlatter (ed.). Humanities Scholarship in America: The Princeton Studies, Prentice-Hall, Inc., Englewood Cliffs, New Jersey, 1964, pp. 345–463.
44. 'C. I. Lewis on the Ground and Nature of the Right', *Journal of Philosophy* 61, (1964) 489–496.
45. 'Love and Principle in Christian Ethics', *Faith and Philosophy*, Alvin Plantinga (ed.), William B. Eerdmans Publishing Co., Grand Rapids, Michigan, 1964, pp. 203–225.

46. 'On Defining and Defending Natural Law', *Law and Philosophy*, Sidney Hook (ed.), New York University Press, New York, 1964, pp. 200–209.
47. 'La philosophie moral contemporaine aux Etats-Unis', *Les Etudes Philosophiques* 2, (1964) 233–243.
48. 'Three Comments on Lewis's Views on the Right and the Good', *Journal of Philosophy* 61, (1964) 567–570.
49. (Editor), *Philosophy of Education*, Macmillan, New York, 1965.
50. *Three Historical Philosophies of Education*, Scott, Foresman, Chicago, 1965.
51. 'The Concept of Morality', *Journal of Philosophy* 63, (1966) 688–696. Reprinted in K. Pahel and M. Schiller (eds.), *Readings in Contemporary Ethical Theory*.
52. 'A Model for Analyzing a Philosophy of Education', *High School Journal* 2, (1966) 8–13.
53. 'On Saying the Ethical Thing', *Proceedings and Addresses of the American Philosophical Association* 39, (1966) 21–42.
54. 'Philosophical Enquiry', *The Changing American School*, John I. Goodlad (ed.), 1966, pp. 243–265 (Chapter X). The 65th Yearbook of the National Society for the Study of Education, Part II. University of Chicago Press, Chicago.
55. *Some Beliefs About Justice*. The Lindley Lecture, University of Kansas, delivered March 2, 1966.
56. 'G. H. von Wright on the Theory of Morals, Legislation and Value', *Ethics* 76, (1966) 131–136.
57. 'J. D. Wild on Responsibility', *Philosophy and Phenomenological Research* 27, (1966) 90–96.
58. 'Reply to Professor Wild', *Philosophy and Phenomenological Research* 27, (1966) 103.
59. 'The Concept of Morality', *University of Colorado Studies in Philosophy*, No. 3, 1967, pp. 1–22. Reprinted in G. Wallace and A. Walker (eds.), *The Definition of Morality*. This is an earlier version of 'The Concept of Morality', *Journal of Philosophy* 63, 1966.
60. 'Frondizi on the Foundations of Moral Norms', *Proceedings of the Seventh Inter-American Congress of Philosophy*, Laval University Press, 1967, pp. 13–19.
61. 'Value and Valuation', *The Encyclopedia of Philosophy*, Paul Edwards (ed.), 8, 1967, pp. 229–232. Macmillan and Free Press, New York.
62. 'Educational Values and Goals: Some Dispositions To Be Fostered', *Monist* 52, (1968) 1–10.
63. 'Freedom: Responsibility and Decision', *Proceedings of the XIVth International Congress of Philosophy* 1, 1968, pp. 143–154.
64. 'Two Notes on Representation', *Nomos X: Representation*, Roland Pennock (ed.), Atherton Press, New York, 1968, pp. 49–51.
65. 'War and the New Morality', *Reformed Journal* 18, (1968) 20–21.
66. (Editor and Introduction with Arnold S. Kaufman), Jonathan Edwards, *Freedom of the Will*. Library of Liberal Arts, Bobbs-Merrill Co., Inc., Indianapolis and New York, 1969.
67. 'Ought and Is Once More', *Man and World* 2, (1969) 515–533.
68. 'Educating for the Good Life', *Perspectives in Education, Religion and the Arts*, H. E. Kiefer and M. K. Munitz (eds.), University of New York Press, Albany, New York, 1970, pp. 17–42.

69. 'A Model for Analyzing a Philosophy of Education', *Readings in the Philosophy of Education: A Study of the Curriculum*, J. R. Martin (ed.), Allyn and Bacon, Boston, 1970, pp. 15–22.
70. 'Prichard and the Ethics of Virtue', *Monist* 54, (1970) 1–17.
71. 'The Principles and Categories of Morality', *Contemporary American Philosophy, Second Series*. J. E. Smith (ed.), Allen and Unwin, London, 1970, pp. 93–106.
72. 'Moral Education', *The Encyclopedia of Education*, 6, L. C. Deighton (ed.), Macmillan and Free Press, New York, 1971, pp. 394–398.
73. 'Philosophy of Education', *The Encyclopedia of Education*, 7, L. C. Deighton (ed.), Macmillan and Free Press, New York, 1971, pp. 101–104.
74. 'The Concept of Education Today', *Educational Judgments*, J. F. Doyle (ed.), Routledge and Kegan Paul, London, 1973, pp. 19–32.
75. 'Education', *Dictionary of the History of Ideas*, 2, P. P. Wiener (ed.), Charles Scribner's Sons, New York, 1973, pp. 71–85.
76. *Ethics*, Second Edition, Prentice-Hall, Inc., Englewood Cliffs, New Jersey, 1973.
77. 'The Ethics of Love Conceived as an Ethics of Virtue', *Journal of Religious Ethics* 1, (1973) 21–36.
78. 'Is Morality Logically Dependent on Religion?', *Religion and Morality*, Gene Outka and John P. Reeder (eds.), Anchor Books, Garden City, New York, 1973, pp. 195–317.
79. 'On Defining Moral Judgments, Principles, and Codes', *Etycka* 11, (1973) 45–56. [In Polish.]
80. 'The Principles of Morality', *Skepticism and Moral Principles*, C. L. Carter (ed.), New University Press, Evanston, Illinois, 1973, pp. 43–76.
81. 'Under What Net?', *Philosophy* 48, (1973) 319–326.
82. (Editor, with John T. Granrose), *Introductory Readings in Ethics*, Prentice-Hall, Inc., Englewood Cliffs, New Jersey, 1974.
83. 'The Philosopher's Attack on Morality', *Philosophy* 49, (1974) 345–356.
84. 'Sidgwick and the Dualism of Practical Reason', *Monist* 58, (1974) 449–467.
85. 'Spinoza's 'New Morality': Notes on Book IV', *Spinoza: Essays and Interpretation*, Eugene Freeman and Maurice Mandelbaum (eds.), Open Court Press, La Salle, Illinois, 1975, pp. 85–100.
86. 'Conversations with Carney and Hauerwas', *Journal of Religious Ethics* 3, (1975) 45–62. Also includes complete bibliography of Frankena's writings.
87. 'The Philosophy of Vocation', *Thought* 51, (1976) 393–408.
88. 'Concluding More or Less Philosophical Postscript', *Perspectives on Morality: Essays by William K. Frankena*, K. E. Goodpaster (ed.), University of Notre Dame Press, 1976, pp. 208–217.
89. 'The Ethics of Respect for Life', Thalheimer Lecture, Johns Hopkins University, 1975. Published in *Respect for Life*, Stephen Barker (ed.), the Johns Hopkins University Press, Baltimore, 1977, pp. 24–62.
90. 'Moral Philosophy and World Hunger', *World Hunger and Moral Obligation*, W. Aiken and H. La Follette (eds.), Prentice-Hall, Englewood Cliffs, New Jersey, 1977, pp. 66–84.

Forthcoming:
91. 'Spinoza on the Knowledge of Good and Evil', to appear in *Philosophia*.

92. 'Moral Authority, Moral Autonomy, and Moral Education', to appear in *Moral Education and Community Control*, Mark Sheldon (ed.).
93. 'McCormick and the Traditional Distinction', to appear in *Essays on Ambiguity in Moral Choice*, Paul Ramsey (ed.), Loyola Press.
94. 'G. H. von Wright on the Nature of Morality', to appear in *The Philosophy of G. H. von Wright*, Paul Schilpp (ed.).
95. *Three Questions About Morality*, The Carus Lectures for 1974, to be published by Open Court.
96. 'Is Morality a Purely Personal Matter?', to appear in *Midwest Studies in Philosophy*.
97. 'Ethics and the Environment', to appear in *Ethics, The Environment and the Future*, K. Sayre and K. E. Goodpaster (eds.).
98. 'Philosophy and Moral Standards', to appear in *Philosophy: The American Way*, P. Caws (ed.).
99. 'Methods of Ethics, 1977', to be published in the Proceedings of the Leonard Nelson Symposium for 1977.

BIBLIOGRAPHY OF CHARLES L. STEVENSON

1. 'The Emotive Meaning of Ethical Terms', *Mind* **46**, (1937) 14–31.
2. 'Ethical Judgments and Avoidability', *Mind* **47**, (1938) 45–57.
3. 'Persuasive Definitions', *Mind* **47**, (1938) 331–350.
4. 'Moore's Arguments against Certain Forms of Ethical Naturalism', in *The Philosophy of G.E. Moore*, P.A. Schilpp (ed.) Northwestern University Press, 1942.
5. Review of Adler, *A Dialectic of Morals*, *Journal of Philosophy* **39**, (1942) 48–51.
6. Review of Lanz, *In Quest of Morals*, *Journal of Philosophy* **39**, (1942),
7. Review of Leys, *Ethics and Social Policy*, *Journal of Philosophy* **39**, (1942) 165–166.
8. Review of Maritain, *Art and Poetry*, *Journal of Philosophy* **39**, (1942) 722–723.
9. Review of Shoemaker, *Aesthetic Experience*, *Journal of Philosophy* **40**, (1943) 586–587.
10. *Ethics and Language*, Yale University Press, 1944.
11. Review of Muller, *Science and Criticism*, *Journal of Philosophy* **41**, (1944) 21–23.
12. Review of Nelson, *Structure of Normative Ethics*, *Journal of Philosophy* **41**, (1944) 248–250.
13. Review of Heyl, *New Bearings in Aesthetics*, *Journal of Philosophy* **41**, (1944) 360–362.
14. Review of Lepley, *Verifiability of Value*, *Journal of Philosophy* **41**, (1944) 385–388.
15. Review of Eby, *Quest for Moral Law*, *Journal of Philosophy* **41**, (1944) 529.
16. Review of Frank, *Fate and Freedom*, *Journal of Philosophy* **42**, (1945) 722–723.
17. Review of Nahm, *Aesthetic Experience*, *International Journal of Ethics* **61**, (1946) 231–232.
18. Review of Hospers, *Meaning and Truth in the Arts*, *Philosophical Review* **56**, (1947) 434–438.
19. 'Some Relations between Philosophy and the Study of Language', *Analysis* **9**, (1947) 1–16.
20. Review of Parker, *Principles of Aesthetics*, *Journal of Philosophy* **45**, (1948) 245.
21. 'Meaning: Descriptive and Emotive', *Philosophical Review* **57**, (1948) 127–144.
22. 'The Nature of Ethical Disagreement', *Readings in Philosophical Analysis*, H. Feigl and W. Sellars (eds.) Appleton Century, 1949, pp. 587–593.
23. 'Interpretation and Evaluation in Aesthetics', *Essays in Philosophical Analysis*, Max Black (ed.) Cornell University Press, 1949.
24. 'The Emotive Conception of Ethics and its Cognitive Implications', *Philosophical Review* **59**, (1950) 291–304.
25. 'Brandt's Questions about Emotive Ethics', *Philosophical Review* **59**, (1950) 528–534.
26. 'The Scientist's Role and the Aims of Education', *Harvard Educational Review*, Fall, (1954) 231–238.

A. I. Goldman and J. Kim (eds.), Values and Morals, 323–324. All Rights Reserved
Copyright © 1978 by D. Reidel Publishing Company, Dordrecht, Holland.

27. Review of Nowell-Smith, *Ethics*, *Mind*, July 1955.
28. Comments on a paper by Brandt. *The Language of Value*, edited by Ray Lepley, Columbia University Press, 1957, pp. 317–323.
29. 'On 'What is a Poem?'" *Philosophical Review*, July 1957, 329–362.
30. 'On the 'Analysis' of a Work of Art', *Philosophical Review*, January, 1958, 33–51.
31. 'Symbolism in the Non-Representational Arts', and 'Symbolism in the Representational Arts'. Both are chapters in *Language, Thought and Culture*, edited by Paul Henle. The University of Michigan Press, 1958.
32. 'On the Reasons that can be Given for the Interpretation of a Poem', in *Philosophy Looks at the Arts*, edited by Joseph Margolis, Scribners, 1962, pp. 121–139.
33. 'Reflections on John Dewey's Ethics', *Proceedings of Aristotelian Society*, 1961–62, pp. 25–44.
34. 'Relativism and Nonrelativism in the Theory of Value', *Proceedings of the American Philosophical Association*, 1961–62.
35. *Facts and Values*, Yale University Press, 1963. A collection of earlier articles, but Essay XI (pp. 186–232), entitled 'Retrospective Comments' was new.
36. Review of Aiken, *Reason and Conduct*, *Journal of Philosophy*, 1964.
37. 'Éthique et Science', *Les Études Philosophiques*, April–June, 1964, pp. 245–254.
38. 'Ethical Fallibility', in *Ethics and Society*, edited by Richard T. DeGeorge, Anchor Books, 1966, pp. 197–217. Delivered previously as Whitehead lecture at Harvard.
39. 'If-iculties', *Philosophy of Science*, March 1970. Reprinted with a few changes in *Logic and Art: Essays in Honor of Nelson Goodman*, edited by Rudner and Scheffler, Bobbs Merrill, 1972. In Goodman volume, pp. 279–309.
40. 'The Rhythm of English Verse', *Journal of Aesthetics and Art Criticism*, Spring 1970, 327–344.
41. 'Richards on the Theory of Value', in *I.A. Richards: Essays in his Honor*, edited by Brower, Vendler, and Hollander. Oxford University Press, 1973, pp. 119–134.
42. Review of Isenberg, *Aesthetics and the Theory of Criticism*, *Journal of Philosophy*, (1974) 821–832.
43. Introduction to Vol. V of the *Middle Works of John Dewey*, Southern Illinois University Press, 1978.
44. Review of D.W. Harding, *Words into Rhythm*, scheduled to appear in *Journal of Aesthetics and Art Criticism*.

BIBLIOGRAPHY OF RICHARD B. BRANDT

1. 'On the Possibility of Reference to Inferred Entities', *Journal of Philosophy*, **35**, (1938) 393–405.
2. 'An Emotional Theory of the Judgment of Moral Worth', *Ethics*, **52**, (1941) 41–79.
3. *The Philosophy of Schleiermacher*, viii and 350, Harper and Brothers, New York, 1941.
4. 'The Significance of Differences of Ethical Opinion for Ethical Rationalism', *Philosophy and Phenomenological Research* **4**, (1944) 469–494.
5. 'Moral Valuation', *Ethics* **56**, (1946) 106–121.
6. 'The Emotive Theory of Ethics', *Philosophical Review* **59**, (1950) 305–318.
7. 'Stevenson's Defense of the Emotive Theory', *Philosophical Review* **59**, (1950) 535–540.
8. 'A Criterion of Necessity', *Review of Metaphysics* **6**, (1952) 125–126.
9. 'The Status of Empirical Assertion Theories in Ethics', *Mind* **61**, (1952) 458–479.
10. 'Thinking and Experience', *Review of Metaphysics* **7**, (1954) 632–643.
11. 'Knowledge and Certainty', *Review of Metaphysics* **7**, (1954) 682–684.
12. 'The Definition of an 'Ideal Observer' Theory in Ethics', *Philosophy and Phenomenological Research* **15**, (1954) 407–413.
13. 'Comments on Professor Firth's Reply', *Philosophy and Phenomenological Research* **15**, (1954) 422–423.
14. *Hopi Ethics: A Theoretical Analysis*, viii and 386, University of Chicago Press, 1954.
15. 'A Puzzle in Lewis' Theory of Memory', *Philosophical Studies* **5**, (1954) 88–95.
16. 'The Epistemological Status of Memory Beliefs', *Philosophical Review* **64**, (1955) 78–95.
17. 'Philip Blair Rice on Ethical Theory', *Philosophy and Phenomenological Research* **17**, (1957) 404–411.
18. 'The Languages of Realism and Nominalism', *Philosophy and Phenomenological Research* **17**, (1957) 516–535.
19. 'Some Puzzles for Attitude Theories of Value', in R. Lepley (ed.) *The Language of Value*, Columbia University Press, 1957, pp. 153–177; and 'Response to Stevenson's Comments', *ibid.*, pp. 323–325.
20. 'Blameworthiness and Obligation', in A. I. Melden (ed.) *Essays in Moral Philosophy*, University of Washington Press, 1958, pp. 3–39.
21. Articles on 'Duty' and 'Ethics' in *Encyclopedia Americana*.
22. 'Determinism and the Justifiability of Moral Blame', in Sidney Hood (ed.) *Determinism and Freedom*, New York University Press, 1958, pp. 137–143.
23. *Ethical Theory*, vii and 528, Prentice-Hall, Englewood Cliffs, New Jersey, 1959.
24. 'The Conditions of Criminal Responsibility', *Nomos* **3**, (1960) 106–115.
25. 'Doubts About the Identity Theory', in Sidney Hook (ed.) *Dimensions of Mind*, New York University Press, 1960, pp. 57–67.

A. I. Goldman and J. Kim (eds.), Values and Morals, 325–327. All Rights Reserved.
Copyright © 1978 by D. Reidel Publishing Company, Dordrecht, Holland.

26. *Value and Obligation: Systematic Readings in Ethics*, vi and 707, Harcourt Brace, 1961.
27. Editor, *Social Justice*, vi and 169, Prentice-Hall, Englewood Cliffs, New Jersey, 1962.
28. 'Toward a Credible Form of Utilitarianism', in H. Castaneda and G. Nakhnikian (eds.), *Morality and the Language of Conduct*, Wayne State University Press, 1963, pp. 107–143.
29. 'Personality Traits as Causal Explanations in Biography', in S. Hook (ed.), *Philosophy and History*, New York University Press, New York, 1963, pp. 192–204.
30. *Moral Philosophy and the Analysis of Language*, The Lindley Lecture, published in the Department of Philosophy, University of Kansas, 1963, pp. 1–24.
31. – with Jaegwon Kim, 'Wants as Explanations of Actions', *Journal of Philosophy*, LX, (1963) 425–435.
32. 'The Concepts of Obligation and Duty', *Mind* LXXIII, (1964) 374–393.
33. 'Utility and the Obligation to Obey the Law', in Sidney Hook (ed.) *Law and Philosophy*, New York University Press, New York, 1964.
34. 'Epistemic Priority and Coherence', *Journal of Philosophy*, LXI, (1964) pp. 557–559.
35. 'Critique of MacIntyre's Starting-Point', in John Hick (ed.), *Faith and the Philosophers*, St. Martin's Press, Inc., New York, 1964, pp. 150–153.
36. – with Ernest Nagel, editors, *Meaning and Knowledge: Systematic Readings in Epistemology*, Harcourt, Brace and World, New York, xiv and 668, 1964.
37. 'The Concept of Welfare', in S. R. Krupp (ed.), *The Structure of Economic Science: Essays on Methodology*, Prentice-Hall, Inc., Englewood Cliffs, New Jersey, 1966, pp. 257–276.
38. – with W. P. Alston, *The Problems of Philosophy: Introductory Readings*, Allyn and Bacon, Boston, 1966, 704 pp.
39. 'Personal Values and the Justification of Institutions', in Sidney Hook (ed.) *Human Values and Economic Policy*, New York University Press, New York, 1967, pp. 22–40.
40. – with Jaegwon Kim, 'The Logic of the Identity Theory', *Journal of Philosophy* LXIV, (1967) 515–537.
41. 'Some Merits of One Form of Rule-utilitarianism', *University of Colorado Studies in Philosophy*, 1967 pp. 39–65.
42. Articles in the *Encyclopedia of Philosophy* (ed., Paul Edwards), New York, Macmillan and Free Press, 8 vols.; on Hedonism, Ethical Relativism; Emotive Theory of Ethics; Epistemology and Ethics, The Parallel Between.
43. 'A Utilitarian Theory of Excuses', *Philosophical Review* 78, (1969) 337–361.
44. 'Traits of Character: A Conceptual Analysis', *American Philosophical Quarterly* 7, (1970) 23–37.
45. 'Rational Desires', *Proceedings and Addresses, The American Philosophical Association* (Presidential Address, Western Division), XLIII, (1970) 43–64.
46. 'Comment on MacCallum', *Inquiry* 14, (1971) 314–317.
47. 'Comment on Kaufman', *Inquiry* 14, (1971) 207–212.
48. 'Utilitarianism and the Rules of War', *Philosophy and Public Affairs*, 2, (1972) 145–165.
49. 'The Morality of Abortion', *The Monist*, 56, 4 (1972) 503–526.
50. 'Rationality, Egoism, and Morality', *The Journal of Philosophy* 69, (1972) 681–697.

51. 'Should the Choice of a Moral System be Impartial?', *Etyka* (Warsaw), **XI**, (1973) 57–85.
52. 'The Morality of Abortion', revised version, in R. L. Perkins (ed.), *Abortion: Pro and Con*, Schenkman Publishing Corp., Cambridge, Massachusetts, 1974, pp. 151–172.
53. 'A Moral Principle About Killing', in Marvin Kohl (ed.), *Beneficient Euthanasia*, Prometheus Books, 1975.
54. 'The Morality and Rationality of Suicide', in S. Perlin (ed.), *A Handbook for the Study of Suicide*, Oxford Press, 1975, pp. 61–76. Reprinted in enlarged and revised form in Edwin Schneidman (ed.), *Suicidology: Contemporary Developments*, Grune and Stratton, New York, 1975, pp. 378–399.
55. 'The Psychology of Benevolence and Its Implications for Philosophy', *Journal of Philosophy* 78, (1976) 429–453.

Forthcoming:
56. *A Theory of the Good and the Right*, Oxford University Press.
57. 'The Concept of Rationality in Ethical and Political Theory', to be published in *Nomos* volume, edited by J. R. Pennock and John Chapman.
58. 'Philosophy and Planning for the Future', in J. Grunfeld (ed.).
59. 'Defective Newborns and the Morality of Termination', in Marvin Kohl (ed.).

INDEX OF NAMES

PHILOSOPHICAL STUDIES SERIES
IN PHILOSOPHY